Understanding Dennis Robertson

For my family

Understanding Dennis Robertson

The Man and His Work

Gordon Fletcher

Lecturer in Economics, The University of Liverpool, UK

Edward Elgar

Cheltenham, UK • Northampton, MA, USA

Published by
Edward Elgar Publishing Limited
Glensanda House
Montpellier Parade
Cheltenham
Glos GL50 1UA
UK

Edward Elgar Publishing, Inc.
136 West Street
Suite 202
Northampton
Massachusetts 01060
USA

HB
103
. R63
F55
2000

A catalogue record for this book
is available from the British Library

Library of Congress Cataloguing in Publication Data

Fletcher, Gordon A., 1942
    Understanding Dennis Robertson : the man and his work / Gordon Fletcher.
    Includes bibliographical references.
        1. Robertson, Dennis Holme, Sir, 1890-1963. 2. Economists-Great
    Britain-Biography. I. Title.
    HB103.R63 F55 2000
    330'.092-dc21   00-023573

ISBN 1 84064 343 9

Printed and bound in Great Britain by MPG Books Ltd, Bodmin, Cornwall

Contents

Acknowledgements

I have incurred many debts in writing this book and gratefully record my thanks to the following individuals and institutions.

I

Dr Geoffrey Harcourt of Jesus College, Cambridge for his kindness and encouragement, and for valuable suggestions for improvement of the text; Professor Mark Blaug of the University of Amsterdam for his generous and encouraging appraisal of my draft submission to Edward Elgar Publishing; Professor Victoria Chick of University College, London and Professor John R. Presley of Loughborough University for their helpful comments on an earlier version. My colleagues at Liverpool: Dr David Hojman, who kindly undertook to read the entire manuscript and whose comments and advice helped materially to improve my first draft; Dr Arthur Thomas, the late Professor Brian Hillier and Dr Robert Wynn for their help in arranging Departmental finance for research visits and the preparation of the manuscript. The Royal Economic Society, for grants from the Society's Small Budget Scheme to finance three research visits to Cambridge.

II

Mr Jonathan Smith, Manuscript Cataloguer, of the Wren Library, Trinity College, Cambridge, for his unfailing help in arranging visits to consult the Robertson Papers, for answering queries arising therefrom and for his congenial company; Ms Jacqueline Cox and Dr Rosalind Moad, of the Modern Archive Centre, King's College, Cambridge for help with visits to consult the Keynes Papers, the Rylands Papers and other material and for answering my queries; Mrs Aude Fitzsimons, Assistant Librarian, of the Pepys Library, Magdalene College, Cambridge, for making arrangements for me to consult A.C. Benson's Diary; Dr Alan Kucia and Ms Carolyn Lye of the Churchill Archives Centre, Churchill College, Cambridge, for help in connection with my visits to consult the Hawtrey Papers.

III

Apart from the principal manuscript collections, I have also benefited from information supplied (both photocopied material and correspondence) by a range of other institutions, as follows: BBC Written Archives Centre (Mr James Codd); Cambridgeshire County Record Office (Ms Sue Neville, Archivist); Eton College (Mrs P. Hatfield, College Archivist); Imperial War Museum: Department of Printed Books (Mrs Sarah Patterson); Jesus College, Cambridge (Dr E.F. Mills, College Archivist); Liverpool Daily Post and Echo Ltd (Mr Colin Hunt, Head of Library Services); Liverpool Record Office (Ms Gina Kehoe); Magdalene College, Cambridge (Dr R. Luckett, Pepys Librarian); Marshall Library, Cambridge University (Ms Alex Saunders, Archivist); Trinity College, Cambridge (Mrs Selene Webb, Chapel Secretary); University Library, Cambridge (Mr David J. Hall, Deputy Librarian; Kathleen Cann, Department of Manuscripts and University Archives); Whittlesford Society, Whittlesford, Cambridgeshire (Mr Ian L. Wright and Mr Tony Carter).

IV

The following were kind enough to grant me an interview and/or to enter into correspondence: the late Professor H.J. Blumenthal (University of Liverpool) for help with Robertson's quotations from the classical Greek and with the philosophy of Heraclitus; Mr Nicholas Byam Shaw (Chairman, Macmillan Limited) for correspondence in connection with his uncle Glen Byam Shaw (1904–1986, actor and director); Dr J.R.G. Bradfield CBE (Fellow of Trinity College, Cambridge and Chairman, New Towns Commission) for his personal recollections of Dennis Robertson as a colleague at Trinity; Dr G.C. Harcourt AO (Emeritus Reader in the History of Economic Theory, University of Cambridge and Fellow of Jesus College, Cambridge) and Professor Robin Marris (late of the University of Cambridge) for their reminiscences of Robertson in his later years at Cambridge; the late Dr George 'Dadie' Rylands CH (Fellow of King's College, Cambridge) for kindly offering me an interview, for his hospitality, for his readiness to answer my questions and for subsequent correspondence; Professor David Vines (Balliol College, Oxford).

V

For permission to quote from the various collections I have consulted I wish to thank: Ms Judy M.R. Brown (Dennis Robertson's papers deposited at Trinity, King's and Churchill Colleges, Cambridge); the Master and Fellows of Trinity College, Cambridge (the Robertson Papers); the Provost and

Scholars of King's College, Cambridge (the Keynes Papers; the Rylands Papers); the Master and Fellows of Magdalene College, Cambridge (A.C. Benson's Diary); the Master, Fellows and Scholars of Churchill College, Cambridge (the Hawtrey Papers).

VI

For permission to quote from published works I am grateful to: Constable & Co. Ltd (Hudson, Derek, 1976, *Lewis Carroll: An Illustrated Biography*); The Haileybury Society (Thomas, Imogen, 1987, *Haileybury 1806-1987*); King's College, Cambridge (Wilkinson, L.P., 1980, *A Century of King's 1873-1972*; Wilkinson, L.P., 1981, *Kingsmen of a Century 1873-1972*); The London School of Economics and Political Science (Robertson, D.H., 1948 (1915) *A Study of Industrial Fluctuation*); James Nisbet & Co. Ltd (Robertson, D.H., 1922 and subsequent editions, *Money*; Robertson, D.H., 1923, *The Control of Industry*). Macmillan Limited and the Royal Economic Society (*The Collected Writings of John Maynard Keynes*). Every effort has been made to trace all the copyright holders but if any have been inadvertently overlooked the publishers will be pleased to make the necessary arrangements at the first opportunity.

VII

For her skill in processing successive drafts of a substantial manuscript I owe a debt of gratitude to Marie Williams. I am also grateful to Paula Ferrington, who prepared the final version, and to Viv Moss, Anne Turner and Sheila Hastings, each of whom typed portions of an earlier draft. Dymphna Evans and her colleagues at Edward Elgar Publishing Ltd, have been both helpful and efficient and have seen the book safely through the press. Finally, research and writing have been done during a period increasingly crowded with teaching, administration and other academic commitments and I wish to reserve a special thank-you to my family for their support and encouragement throughout.

While I am pleased to acknowledge the help of all of the above, the usual disclaimer applies: for the final version, the views expressed and the errors that remain I alone am responsible.

GORDON FLETCHER
University of Liverpool
11 August 2000

Abbreviations

Note: This list is arranged in relative order of frequency of use.

Robertson Papers: Trinity College, Cambridge	RPTC
A.C. Benson, Diaries: Magdalene College, Cambridge	BDMC
Keynes Papers: King's College, Cambridge	KPKC
Rylands Papers: King's College, Cambridge	RPKC
Hawtrey Papers: Churchill College, Cambridge	HPCC
Cambridge County Record Office	CCRO
Liverpool Daily Post and Echo Ltd	LDPE
Liverpool Record Office	LRO

D.H. Robertson: a brief chronology

1890	Born 23 May at Lowestoft, Suffolk.
1891	Moves to Whittlesford, Cambridgeshire.
1902	King's Scholar at Eton College.
1908	Captain of the School. Plays part of the White Queen in Lewis Carroll's *Alice Through the Looking Glass* [sic]. Beginning of career on the amateur stage.
1908	Major scholarship, Trinity College, Cambridge.
1910	First class honours, Part I, Classical Tripos.
1912	First class honours, Part II, Economics Tripos.
1914	First World War: commissioned into 11th Battalion, London Regiment. Fellow of Trinity.
1915	*A Study of Industrial Fluctuation* published.
1917	First Battle of Gaza: awarded MC.
1919	Return to Trinity. Years of collaboration with J.M. Keynes ensue.
1922	*Money* published.
1923	*The Control of Industry* published.
1926	*Banking Policy and the Price Level* published.
1926–7	Asian tour: eight months.
1930	Reader in Economics, Cambridge University. Gives evidence to Macmillan Committee.
1932	Fellow of the British Academy.
1933–4	Indian Statistical Survey, with A.L. Bowley.
1936	Keynes's *General Theory* published. Open professional breach with Keynes.
1939	(January) Professor of Money and Banking, London School of Economics.
1939	(September) Second World War: Adviser, HM Treasury.
1944	Professor of Political Economy, Cambridge University. Awarded CMG.
1944–6	Member, Royal Commission on Equal Pay.
1948–50	President, Royal Economic Society.
1953	Knighthood.
1957	Retires from Cambridge Chair.
1957–8	Member of (Cohen) Council on Prices, Productivity and Incomes ('Three Wise Men').

1957–9   *Lectures on Economic Principles* published.
1962   Gives evidence to Canadian Royal Commission on Banking and Finance.
1963   Dies 21 April in Cambridge.

... perhaps we shall find the land of lost content, but I hardly think it likely.

(Dennis Robertson to George 'Dadie' Rylands,
31 August 1923, RPKC)

Introduction

I

Sir Dennis Holme Robertson (1890–1963) was one of the most highly regarded British economists of his time; in the eyes of many he was also one of the best loved. Robertson spent the bulk of his professional life at Cambridge, as a fellow of Trinity College and as holder of a succession of University appointments, including the Chair of Political Economy. He published prolifically, gave evidence to expert inquiries, served on official committees and was much sought after as a lecturer and book reviewer. He made contributions in several areas of economics but chiefly to the study of the relationship between short-run cycles and long-run trends in national economic activity. His work on the interlinking of real and monetary factors in the determination of the trade cycle was of seminal importance.

Robertson received abundant public recognition for his achievements: fellow of the British Academy from 1932, Companion of the Order of St Michael and St George (CMG) 1944, fellow of Eton College 1948, President of the Royal Economic Society 1948–50, knighthood 1953. Honorary degrees were conferred by universities at home (London, Manchester, Durham and Sheffield) and abroad (Harvard, Columbia, Amsterdam and Louvain). It was a measure of his reputation internationally that he was singled out to be honoured by Harvard University on the occasion of its Tercentenary celebrations in 1936. On his seventieth birthday he received a letter of congratulations and tribute from his 'American friends' – including some of the world's most prominent economists – and signed *inter alia* by: A.W. Marget, Fritz Machlup, Jacob Viner, William Fellner, Gottfried Haberler, Milton Friedman, F.A. Hayek, Tibor Scitovsky, James Duesenberry, Edward H. Chamberlin and John Williams (23 May 1960, in C18/182 RPTC).

II

At the same time, he was, as J.R. Hicks once noted, a 'most unusual kind of economist, with a dimension to him that went far outside economics, expressed in a style that was peculiarly his own' (Hicks, 1966, p. 9). Hicks did not elaborate and Robertson has remained in many ways the mystery-man of modern macroeconomics, chiefly known through a few central ideas connected with the attack on the Keynesian Revolution and for his practice of decorating his texts with quotations from Lewis Carroll's *Alice* books.

In the chapters that follow we shall, in effect, explore the ways in which Robertson was an economist of a 'most unusual' kind, attempt to account for the 'dimension that went far outside economics' and make clear the reasons for his affecting 'a style that was peculiarly his own'.

What emerges provides a fascinating insight into the role of the temperamental forces that lie behind and shape what appear to be purely intellectual ideas and controversies. In this most interesting of stories we glimpse the hidden human face of what is all too often regarded as the bloodless discipline, the dismal science.

We shall find that Robertsonian economics is indelibly stamped with the impression of Robertson the man and that by explaining the man we shall explain his economics. This is particularly so with respect to the way in which his theory developed, or failed to develop, and to its particular characteristics, which have often been described by commentators but never explained. It also brings to light profound and hitherto unsuspected facets of his thought and reveals his ultimate concerns. Above all, in the context of previous interest in Robertson, it accounts for his professional breach with J.M. Keynes, the broken relationship that resulted from a dispute generally regarded as inexplicable, wasteful and ultimately futile.

III

Robertson provides a rewarding subject, worthy of enquiry in his own right, as the following chapters will show. Traditionally, however, interest in Robertson has arisen from his position *vis-à-vis* John Maynard Keynes and in particular as Keynes's principal critic following the publication of *The General Theory of Employment, Interest and Money* in 1936. In the scheme of what follows, the Keynesian Revolution plays an integral part, though as a culminating episode, rather than as the principal focus in its own right.

Robertson's opposition to Keynes was to have unfortunate consequences, not least for Robertson himself, for it brought in its train alienation, unhappiness and an end to fruitful, creative partnership. From a professional perspective the triumph of Keynesian economics was to put Robertsonian economics into a shade from which it ever after struggled to emerge, its claimed delights denied to all but a few aficionados.

On the other hand, until the rise of monetarism the most telling criticism of the Keynesian Revolution centred on the work of Robertson. Of Keynes's other critics of the period, F.A. Hayek in effect absented himself from the arena and vanished into an obscurity that lasted until his recall in the 1970s to lead the Austrian revival; while A.C. Pigou, Alvin Hansen and Lionel Robbins initially opposed the position Keynes took in the *General Theory* but all, sooner or later, recanted. Robertson, however, remained obdurate.

In subsequent years his work has continued to provide an important rallying-point for opponents of Keynesianism. And though in this role it has never possessed the *réclame* of Milton Friedman's 'Counterrevolution' or Hayek's Austrian critique, it has been cherished as a source of strength and inspiration for those who have believed with Robertson that Keynes, in his contribution to the development of economic thought, had gone a revolution too far and that he had,

> marred by distortions and exaggerations of various kinds, a fruitful body of doctrine which had been moulded over several decades by many hands. (Robertson, 1963a, p. 326)

IV

Also, in more recent years, there has been a resurgence of interest in Robertsonian economics itself, together with an attempt to ensure that Robertson is accorded due recognition for his contributions. Robertson's work has been brought into increased prominence by the attentions of a loyal and growing band of supporters who believe it has suffered undue neglect. One of the most assiduous in this respect was the late Sir Stanley Dennison, who in a collection of Robertsonian essays published shortly before his (Dennison's) death wrote:

> in most British universities few students read a word of Robertson or are informed by their teachers of his contributions, which in turn reflects their own limitations. Instead they are mostly fed on the latest dogmas of debased neo-Keynesianism and mathematical growth models. (Dennison in Presley ed., 1992, p. viii; see also Danes, 1979, p. 12)

The concept of a 'neglected' economist is a difficult one to pin down, and in the present study we throw light on the phenomenon to which Dennison alludes by way of (a) an explanation for the inaccessible nature of some of Robertson's writings and (b) an account of the way in which Robertson came to be underestimated as an economist, despite his achievements.

V

The resurgence of interest has also seen an attempt to promote Robertson and Robertsonian economics at the expense of Keynes and Keynesian economics

- with particular reference to the theoretical rationale for macroeconomic policy - and so settle the Robertson–Keynes controversy in Robertson's favour. In addition to the reprinting of essays and addresses that warn against the dangers of governments attempting to do too much (Dennison and Presley eds, 1992), there is also the practice of seeking to establish Robertson as a precursor of modern theoretical developments, often combined with implicit or explicit criticism of the corresponding Keynesian approach. Of particular relevance here is the promotion of the buffer-stock theory of the demand for money, which Robertson's work is seen to prefigure (Mizen and Presley, 1994), together with the questioning of the adequacy of Keynes's liquidity preference theory (Goodhart, 1989, pp. 106–20). This last may, therefore, be seen as a further blow against one side in the dispute that blossomed in Cambridge in the 1930s and 1940s between members of the factions that formed around Robertson and Keynes and which continued in stylised form in the ensuing decades as the liquidity preference versus loanable funds debate.

On the other hand, there has been an attempt to appraise the nature and validity of Robertson's criticisms of Keynes and to discover the true sources of differences between them (Fletcher 1987, 1989a, 1989b, 1996). The present work can be seen to extend that line of enquiry by looking much more closely at the relationship between Robertson the man and Robertsonian economics.

VI

The developments outlined above provide the Keynesian context within which much of the renewed interest in Robertsonian economics must inevitably be seen. Even in cases in which the issues do not relate directly to the post-1936 controversy, a Keynesian dimension is detectable. In death as in life, Keynes's long shadow lies over Robertson.

As a case in point we might mention the recent article by Costabile which 'belongs to a "tradition" proposing to rediscover Robertson's contributions and to reappraise them'. Costabile believes Robertson has much to offer Keynesians and Post-Keynesians, once they come to evaluate him less as a critic of Keynes and more in his proper role as precursor of the Post-Keynesian approach to the theory of growth and cycles (Costabile in Arestis, Palma and Sawyer eds, 1997, p. 310).

In addition to her own estimate of Robertson's contribution, which is based on a reading of *Banking Policy and the Price Level* (Robertson, 1926) and subsequent, derivative, works, Costabile usefully draws attention to other contributions on Robertson and to other matters at issue. One of these concerns the question of whether Robertson's analysis was essentially long-run or short-run in nature – a question on which there is a variety of opinion (see Costabile's Notes and References, 1997, pp. 322 n.13, 323, 324).

We shall find that the short-period, long-period question does play a significant part but strictly in the context of our overall theme, so that the short period is defined as that which is relevant to the dimension of biography. Here Robertson is seen as a precursor of Keynes but also as one who modified his position in the light of circumstances as time went on.

VII

Work on Robertson includes more positive, non-Keynes-tinted elements. There has been, for example, a convincing attempt to establish Robertson as a pioneer of the real business cycle theory developed in the USA in recent years (see Goodhart in Presley ed., 1992, pp. 8–34; also Goodhart and Presley, 1994) and with it his credentials as a classical economist (see again the birthday letter, quoted earlier, from US economists in the classical tradition; see also the correspondence between Lord Harris and Jean Bromley of October 1977 in G17/1–7 RPTC). We might also mention Boianovsky and Presley, 'Dennis Robertson and the Natural Rate of Unemployment Hypothesis' (1998).

Finally, we should notice that prospects for future work on Robertson will be greatly enhanced by the publication of the forthcoming edition of his professional correspondence (see Mizen, Moggridge and Presley, 1997, for an indication of the scope of the work). Not only will interest in Robertson be stimulated but it will be possible to make a more accurate assessment of the importance of this 'neglected' economist.

VIII

It is against the background, outlined above, of a quickening of interest in Robertson over recent years that we embark on a re-examination of Robertson's life and work and the relationship between them. Using biographical and literary evidence, it will be argued that Robertson's temperament and outlook on life had a profound influence on his approach to economics and on the course of development of his economic ideas. It was this relationship above all else that conditioned Robertson's response to the Keynesian Revolution, the most significant event of his life.

We shall appeal to three kinds of evidence as follows: biographical (an examination of the formative influences at work in Robertson's life); literary (the clues furnished by the literary references scattered liberally throughout the work of one widely regarded as a 'literary economist'); economic (a fresh reading of Robertson's principal professional writings and in particular his two monographs, *A Study of Industrial Fluctuation* (1915) and *Banking Policy and the Price Level* (1926)).

In each case we shall use original, unpublished material set within the context, where appropriate, of a critical review of extant published accounts.

IX

The plan of the book and the subject matter of the individual chapters is indicated in the Contents. It will be helpful, however, to be aware of the broad grouping of chapters to reflect particular themes within the whole. There are five main parts – reflecting the three types of material drawn upon, biographical, literary and economic (the last in two parts), together with the episode of the Keynesian Revolution.

Part I (Chapters 1–6) first explains the nature of biography and justifies the use of biographical information in the study of an economist, before going on to outline the main theme of the whole work. Three further chapters examine the first three decades, the formative years of Robertson's life, dealing in turn with his home background, his time at school and university and his war service. The final chapter covers the 1920s, the period that saw the end of the positive, creative phase of Robertson's life and career.

Part II (Chapters 7–12) explores at length the notion of Robertson as a literary economist and suggests possible implications of this for the way in which he was perceived as an economist. The incidence of literary quotations and allusions in his work is surveyed and commented upon. Finally, the significance of the most important literary reference – the *Alice* books – for the interpretation of Robertson's life and work is made plain.

Part III (Chapters 13–17) deals with Robertson's economics as represented by the *Study* (1915). Five chapters examine the text afresh and interpret it in the context of Robertson's life-view. New light is thrown on the significance of his ethical question regarding the 'most desirable distribution of the community's income through time' (Robertson, 1915, p. 253). This in turn leads to an important new conclusion on Robertson's attitude towards the short period and how this changed over time.

Part IV (Chapters 18–22) deals with Robertson's economics as represented by *Banking Policy and the Price Level* (1926) (hereafter, *BPPL*) and subsequent, derivative, publications. Again, five chapters examine the texts afresh and interpret their significance in the context of the Robertson life-view. *BPPL* provides a theoretical basis for the management of the short period, as a means of reconciling ethical and economic considerations in a growing economy. As compared to the parent work (the *Study*), however, *BPPL* includes consideration of both real and monetary variables and the seminal nature of Robertson's thinking at this time is emphasised by the parallels which can be drawn with aspects of later Keynesian theorising.

Above all, *BPPL* provides evidence of the conflict between Robertson's desire to pursue new insights and his need to retain firm links with his intellectual origins in Cambridge (micro)economics. The interpretation of Robertson's position on this point, together with the threat posed by the new economics of the *General Theory*, is carried out through the medium of Lewis Carroll's *Alice* books as an exercise in 'nonsense'.

This part contains the crux of the argument of the whole work. Robertson's economics is seen to reflect his approach to life and death in the context of the theory of evolution and the conflict between progressive and regressive elements in his personality.

Part V (Chapters 23–28) deals with Robertson's reaction to the Keynesian Revolution. A contrast is drawn between two kinds of economics: equilibrium or classical economics, which is the economics of Robertson; and historical economics, interpreted as economics relevant to the dimension of biography, which is the economics of Keynes. The approach adopted will determine whether money is to be regarded as important or unimportant in the theoretical scheme.

The principal features of Keynes's new theory are outlined together with Robertson's criticisms, which in turn provide important insights into his own thinking. It is shown that Robertson and later writers sympathetic to his viewpoint emphasise the strategic importance of liquidity preference as a theory of interest in Keynes's scheme. This in Robertsonian eyes both: (a) exalted money to the extent that it posed a threat to the classical ordering of real and monetary variables and so to the theoretical heartland of Cambridge economics; (b) released real variables for service in Keynesian schemes of national economic management. The implications of giving pivotal importance to the liquidity preference theory in the development of Keynes's thought is that by doing so his entire case can be made to rest upon its validity. To discredit liquidity preference is thus to discredit Keynes and promote Robertson.

We examine the whole question of the relative ranking of real and monetary variables and of the dispositions of investment, saving, money and the rate of interest in Robertson's and Keynes's thought. The conclusions reached provide no support for the Robertsonian line of argument. All hinges on the comparative sequence of development of Robertson's and Keynes's theories and in the latter case it is argued that liquidity preference appeared at a comparatively late stage as Keynes's theory moved forward from *A Treatise on Money* (the *Treatise*, 1930) to *The General Theory* (1936) and that it cannot be the linchpin of Keynes's position.

In contrast to the Robertsonian perception of Keynes's new departures, it is argued that the true differentia lies in Robertson's failure to take account of the fallacy of composition, which formed an essential element in Keynes's scheme of model-building. As a consequence, though the Keynesian Revolution did subvert Robertson's economics, it was not for the reason he supposed. Instead, it was because of the creation of a new (macro)economics based on the fallacy of composition. This is in turn derived from a recognition of the organic nature of the real-world economy: a recognition that Robertson did not and, indeed, could not concede.

PART I

Robertson the Man

1. Writing the life: received and unreceived opinions

I

The introduction of the details of an economist's life into an otherwise technical discussion can often be justified on the grounds that they will add colour and interest. There is always the idea that readers will enjoy what Samuel Brittan once referred to as 'a good wallow' (Brittan, 1977, p. 41). Brittan was, however, thinking of Keynes, whose life was inherently interesting, and it remains true that, as with people in general, interesting economists are more interesting than uninteresting ones.

What is more contentious is the question of how relevant such details are to an understanding of the economist's work. The extent, that is, to which they enable the reader to grasp the meaning and significance of the professional writings and of the events of the professional career. The whole issue of the place of biography in a profession in which it has, with notable exceptions, largely been disdained or ignored, has been examined by Donald Moggridge in his major biography of Keynes (Moggridge, 1992, pp. xviff). In paraphrase, Moggridge argues as follows.

First, economic analysis does not take place in a vacuum but within a particular historical (social, political, religious) context. We might gloss this to mean that it is the product of a real economist in a real place at a real time, so that reference to the *particular* may be relevant for interpetation of analysis that is intended to have general application.

Second, the occasion for a biography will usually be the celebration of a subject's achievement. If achievement involves, say, a contribution to economic theory, that contribution will take the form, first, of an intuitive vision, followed by formalisation in the individual economist's distinctive style. Though the profession may subsequently homogenise or develop the contribution, at this initial stage it will depend more on the peculiarities of the individual than on the regularities of the group.

Moggridge argues that by repeatedly observing the process of creation the biographer may be able to help the analyst and historian of thought towards a better understanding of the work – for in the event of dispute it is to interpretation of the meaning of the original text that we must ultimately turn.

11

These claims for biography are, therefore, relatively modest, seeing it in some sense as the handmaid of other specialisms. But there is, perhaps, more to it than this, and for present purposes two aspects of biography dealt with by Moggridge are particularly relevant and must be stressed. The first is that individual contributions to economic analysis are acts of artistic creation and are marked by the peculiarity of style (the personality) of their creators. We shall see that, in the case of Robertson, style provides a most important clue to the proper understanding of the life and work. The second is that biography involves both the selection of material from the evidence available and its recasting in a form which is truly representative of the life and work of the subject. On this basis, we might add, the finished biography will be more than W.H. Auden's 'shilling life' which will 'give you all the facts' ('Who's Who' in Auden, 1966, p. 78). It will itself be a work of art: the creation of the individual biographer.

We shall take this to mean that the selection and arrangement of material will have to be in accordance with some overall view or 'vision' of the subject that the biographer forms on the basis of his consideration of the available evidence. This overall view will be expressed in terms of a motif or theme which will enable the biographer to provide explanations not available by other means – and, in particular, the narrowly 'scientific'. For example, it could be used to reveal linkages between matters that might otherwise appear unrelated or incidental.

Biography, therefore, is a point of view: an argument rather than a record. The argument is constructed on the basis of an objective consideration of the available evidence and is testable by reference to it. It remains, nevertheless, a more or less enduring point of view rather than a recital of fact.

Support for this standpoint is provided by the poet and biographer Andrew Motion, who in a review in *The Times* accused the writer of a life of Siegfried Sassoon of 'deluging us with detail' so that the result of her 'most assiduous effort' and 'tremendous diligence' is to place 'an almost insupportable load on her subject'. Motion argues that, by contrast, 'art is in a vital sense produced against the grain of everyday events, in a kind of secret time that does not show up in diaries and calendars' (Motion, 1998).

In this, biography has much in common with history, which also is concerned with the reconstruction and explanation of (past) events on the basis of the traces left behind, together with the view formed by the historian as to how they should be interpreted. Indeed, biography is properly seen as a branch of history and shares those 'habits of mind' suggested by G.R. Elton in *The Practice of History* (1967) as criteria delineating the field of the historian: a concern with events and with change rather than with states; and a concern with the particular rather than with generalisation. Furthermore, in history –

as, therefore, in biography – there is always an objective truth to be uncovered: that is, the events did take place. However,

> Because a period or a person is many-faceted or complex, to present its history is to seek to present the essence or reality buried within the detail: the 'essence' being the explanation. There may indeed be several. (Elton, 1967)

Thus, the recovery of that objective reality, to a greater or lesser extent, comes from consideration of the available evidence: 'the consideration being the individual historian's contribution'.

And the parallel continues in biography's other link – that with literature – in that it uses those tools of enquiry specified by Elton for the practice of history: 'imagination controlled by learning and scholarship, learning and scholarship rendered meaningful by imagination' (Elton, 1967, p. 87).

Biography is also naturally related to economics in being concerned with what Alfred Marshall, on the first page of the *Principles*, referred to as 'mankind in the ordinary business of life' (Marshall, 1890, p. 1). At bottom, each individual man or woman is occupied in getting and spending, moving from an irrevocable past into an unknown future, making decisions under uncertainty and influenced by endowment, volition, calculation, accident, chance and coincidence, all in a social context.

On the other hand, biography is unique in that *individual* lives are finite: the story must end. But for this reason also the parallel continues. Just as individuals caught in the web of a transitory life have sought comfort in the other-worldly, beyond the reach of time, decay and death; so have economists sought to avoid the multifarious untidiness of the real world by constructing artificial worlds of pure theory, from which time and uncertainty are excluded. These ideal worlds are logical and technically ingenious in their construction but are nevertheless flawed by reason of the premises from which they begin and so may be criticised as a basis on which to derive conclusions about the real world.

The contrast between these two worlds: the one of reality, in which all is shifting and uncertain; the other a desired world of unreality in which all is permanent and reassuring, therefore, has parallels in biography and economics, in as much as they treat of the ultimate concerns of man – whilst he is 'engaged in the ordinary business of life'. The notion has considerable explanatory power and will play an important part in the argument below.

II

There is, of course, a caveat in all this that springs from the nature of biography itself. Because the finished work will reflect the input of the individual biographer, through the stages of selection, arrangement, recasting and overall explanatory motif, a circumspect reading is not out of place. One reason is that fashions in biography change (see, for example, the splendid brief accounts by Gittings, 1978; and by Shelston, 1977). The nineteenth-century notion of biography as a pious memorial to a worthy public figure – at whatever cost in terms of distortion – gave way in May 1918, with the publication of Lytton Strachey's *Eminent Victorians*, to a new style which combined literary elegance with a more critical (cynical?) concern to get behind the public image to the all-too human figure inside. The advent of Freud initiated a search for symbols as clues for analysis of the personality. More recently has come acceptance of the idea that every detail must be revealed, no matter how intimate, or trivial; while the rise of 'Political Correctness' has led to the adoption of overtly partisan 'perspectives' and the rewriting of history to humour or flatter fashionable groups.

On a more individual level, biographies written by those who have been closely involved with the subject, whether personally or professionally, may serve equally to catch facets of a life before the colours fade; but also to distort, either through lack of the necessary detachment or, worse, through an attempt to pass on to posterity an image that the author in some sense deems appropriate. Again, we shall point to examples of this phenomenon in connection with Robertson.

Finally, while idiosyncrasy in the selection of material leading to distortion may in the nature of the medium be thought a problem particularly of 'brief lives', it is also to be found in full-length studies.

A prime example of a biography that suffered from many of the above shortcomings is, of course, Roy Harrod's 'authorised' biography of Keynes (Harrod, 1951). Later studies have revealed the extent to which Harrod was selective and to which he suppressed evidence concerning Keynes's private life and in particular his homosexual exploits, in an attempt to preserve what he regarded as the proper image of a great economist and public figure (see, for example, Hession, 1984: Moggridge, 1992; Skidelsky, 1983, 1992). He also, having just witnessed the collapse of British power following the disastrous war of 1939–45, used the biography to celebrate the life and work of an admired and respected friend in the context of a eulogistic valediction to a vanished order, national and international.

In Harrod's defence, however, it must be said that he wrote according to the fashions, inhibitions and mores of his period and that he produced within a remarkably short time a flawed but nevertheless impressive work of art. In reply to Skidelsky's judgement that Harrod was a 'great economist but not a great biographer' (Skidelsky, 1992, p. 696), one is tempted to retort that, had the world been worldly enough and he had had time, Harrod's coyness would have been a crime! As it was he was only partly culpable.

III

There is as yet no full-length biography of Dennis Robertson, though he is of sufficient interest and importance to justify one. What follows does not pretend to supply the deficiency. It is, rather, a study in interpretation with the more limited objective of exploring the all-important relationship between Robertson the man and Robertsonian economics, and of demonstrating the significance of this relationship for an understanding of Robertson's response to the Keynesian Revolution.

Having made that proviso, however, the study does make considerable use of biographical and literary evidence to explain that Robertson's economics was but a particular manifestation of the nature of the whole man. To that extent, therefore, it relies for its justification on the kind of arguments outlined above.

In place of the absent full-length biography, the main published sources of information on Robertson's life consist of a handful of much briefer whole-life assessments in the form of obituaries, dictionary entries and biographical essays. Leaving aside for the time being items which are devoted largely to exposition or assessment of Robertson's work, the most important contributions are those by Austin Robinson (1963), J.R.M. Butler (1963), Stanley Dennison (1992b) and J.R. Hicks (1966). To this list we should also add those by Paul Samuelson and Sir Frank Lee (both 1963).

Taken together, these provide a valuable account of the major events of Robertson's life and, to some extent, insights into the nature of the man. Nevertheless, the 'circumspect reading' referred to earlier is not inappropriate and reveals that even in such a company of distinguished contemporaries perspectives are essentially individual and variable.

IV

From a composite reading of the published accounts and at the risk of some oversimplification, it is possible to construct what we might refer to as received opinion on Robertson. This is that Robertson's life falls into two parts divided by the Keynesian Revolution, the event that marks the watershed between happiness and growth; unhappiness and decline. The accepted sequence runs as follows.

An idyllic childhood in Victorian England as the son of a country clergyman and former headmaster, from whom he learns his love of the classics, leads to a brilliant and prize-strewn career as King's Scholar at Eton. Continuing in the 'great tradition' (Lee, 1963), Robertson enjoys even greater success as a classical scholar at Trinity College, Cambridge. Under the promptings of a well-developed social conscience Robertson abandons classics for economics, at which he again excels. Research on the trade cycle follows, bringing both a fellowship at Trinity and publication of a classic work of applied economics.

At the outbreak of war in 1914, Robertson's inherited sense of duty overcomes a commitment to pacifism and he serves in the army, winning both the Military Cross and the respect of his men.

On returning to Cambridge he throws himself into academic work and becomes widely known for his prowess as a writer and lecturer. His career as an amateur actor, begun at school and continued at Cambridge, now comes into full flower. Most of all he enters into an extremely fertile period of collaboration with Keynes which results in a number of significant publications on both sides:

> separate publications, but a series that belongs together. Robertson *Money* (1922); Keynes, *Tract on Monetary Reform* (1924 [sic]); Keynes, *Economic Consequences of Mr Churchill* (1925); Robertson, *Banking Policy and the Price Level* (1926); Robertson, the new *Money* (1928) with his important lecture, 'Theories of Banking Policy' (also 1928); Keynes, *Treatise on Money* (1930). (Hicks ed., 1966, pp. 13-14)

The second part of Robertson's life stands in marked contrast to the first. Increasing dissatisfaction with Keynes's new line of thought in the 1930s culminates in his failure to endorse the Keynesian Revolution. This brings strained relations with Keynes and persecution by the newly converted Keynesians at Cambridge. The pressure is such that Robertson is driven to leave Cambridge for the London School of Economics (LSE). Under the exigencies of war he again works with Keynes and there is at least partial reconciliation. He is appointed Professor of Political Economy at Cambridge in succession to Pigou but his homecoming is marred by the resumption of hostilities by the Keynesians, under whose influence his life is increasingly sad and lonely. Ever sensitive, he finds solace in books and music, in the many honours he receives from home and abroad, and in the company of his brilliant young pupils, by whom he is remembered as a much-loved and revered teacher.

Though he produces no work of the originality of earlier years, he sustains his reputation with published volumes of papers and lectures written in his inimitable, highly literate and witty style. He postpones his retirement for two years, as was his right, to the age of sixty-seven but lives on in Trinity to the end. Afterwards his work is ignored in favour of Keynesian economics and the mathematical growth-models against which he had warned.

As a sequence of cause and effect, this account of events is plausible and satisfyingly neat. Precocious youth of the most socially acceptable kind ripens into fulfilled and happy maturity only to be blighted by a disagreement over economic theory. It is nevertheless oversimple, even on the basis of the published accounts, and is achieved only by smoothing out some awkward jags and protrusions. Nevertheless, it does contain the essence of the story and we are justified in referring to it as 'received opinion'. The qualifications are quickly dealt with as follows.

Samuelson, for example, suggested that, 'perhaps the friction between the two men [Robertson and Keynes] was quite independent of scholarship: one really does not want to know, except as personal information illuminates scholarly issues' (Samuelson, 1963, p. 520). Well, we shall see that personal information *does* illuminate scholarly issues in this case. On the other hand, though the published accounts are in agreement in arguing that the 'friction' was *not* 'independent of scholarship', Samuelson did have an inkling of the real nature of the problem – of the underlying disagreement. The explanation is, as we shall see, that the differences of theory between Robertson and Keynes had their origins in the very different temperaments of the two men. Everything else is built upon that.

Finally, we might notice that, though the differences brought collaboration to an end, warm personal regard continued. The real 'friction' lay between Robertson and Keynes's disciples – the Keynesian neophytes. It was a later incident that was seriously to injure relations between Robertson and Keynes and to leave Robertson with a permanent scar.

The other inconsistency that we should notice is the weight given by Sir Frank Lee to the experience of war as a factor destructive of Robertson's sense of well-being. Also, although he mentions the Keynesian Revolution, it is Keynes himself to which he directs attention. That is, war and the Keynes phenomenon are adventitious factors that desolated an ideal existence:

> a fellowship at Trinity, teaching in the steps of Marshall; amateur dramatics; laughter and the love of friends. Three things broke across that *life of content* in Cambridge cloisters (those cloisters sacred as Lytton Strachey said, to poetry and to common sense): two wars and the genius of Keynes. The wars left Dennis Robertson with a sense of tragic waste and loss which never really left him. The genius of Keynes – so much more brilliant, worldly, intellectually reckless – meant an apparent eclipse, after an initial springtime of hopeful partnership, and an unhappy series of disputes, not so much with Keynes himself (who deep down always held Robertson in high regard) as with the young Turks around him.   (Lee, 1963, p. 312; emphasis added)

Lee's account usefully brings together many of the *symptoms* of Robertson's condition but is less successful in identifying causes – even for so brief a notice. Nevertheless, his assessment will provide a useful stalking-horse for the new assessment that follows.

The main problem with his explanation is that of chronology. For example,

Robertson was elected to his fellowship in October 1914 when he was already in the army and immediately left Cambridge for five years while involved in the first of his two wars (and the only one in which he was on active service). Only afterwards did he begin 'teaching in the steps of Marshall'. What effect the experience of war had on him it is difficult to tell but it was only one of several influences to which he was subject in his early adult life and there is evidence to suggest that it may even have had a beneficial effect, as we shall see. Indeed, the 1920s that followed were to be the years of the 'initial springtime' of hope.

It is much more likely that the long, dreary years from 1939 to 1945 would have had a depressing influence on his spirit but even here life was enlivened by visits to the USA for negotiations over war finance and by his return to Cambridge in 1944 well before the end of hostilities. In any case, even before the war began, the episode with the Keynesian Revolution had had its effect and Robertson had been persuaded to abandon his life in Cambridge. After the war, it was to his trouble with Keynes that Robertson constantly referred in his writings, not to the experience of war.

The related point, that it was the 'genius of Keynes' rather than the Keynesian Revolution itself, that destroyed Robertson's content, has validity in as much as it captures the idea of the pervasiveness of Keynes's influence in Cambridge so that one must either be with him or against him. The shrewd ones were with him but kept a little back shop of their own work so as to retain a separate identity. Robertson suffered by the extraordinary coincidence of there being in Cambridge at the same time as himself an economist working on the same problems but who was even more brilliant than the wholly exceptional Robertson. For Robertson there could be no escape.

On the other hand, of course, that same 'genius' also contributed to the 'initial springtime of hopeful partnership'. It was only when Keynes changed direction and achieved his revolutionary breakthrough that matters were brought to a head.

In short, Lee's chronology of cause and effect does not work. The wars are either too early or too late. The genius of Keynes is inspirational and promotional before it overwhelms. Nevertheless, Lee had, by including this latter element, grasped an important truth; and while the Keynesian Revolution remains central to our scheme of explanation, the 'genius' of Keynes will be seen to assume importance as a phenomenon in its own right.

V

Having dealt with some qualifications to our account, we return to received opinion, which is itself too simple to explain events. That Robertson's life after 1936 was often unhappy and lonely is generally agreed. Also, although he produced a large body of high-quality work in this period, the tone is typically critical and negative. The confidence and originality of the earlier years are absent. The theoretical treatise that would have stood against the excesses of Keynesianism – so eagerly called for by Robertson's admirers – never materialised (see, for example, Danes, 1987, pp. 208–10; and Datta, 1953, pp. 695–8 in D7/6 RPTC).

Sir Frank Lee sees Robertson's malaise as being *caused* by his unhappiness and this in turn as being due to Robertson's persecution at Cambridge. Is it really possible that such a profound change could flow from a disagreement on points of economic theory – even given the fervour of the converts? The reasonable expectation would be that there is more to it than that and raises the question of whether the Keynesian Revolution was perhaps the *occasion* that brought long-standing problems to a crisis, rather than a cause in itself?

In an attempt to find out, attention will naturally focus on the earlier years, before the break, in order to see whether they provide such a marked contrast to the later period. In other words, what we require is some indication of the real extent of that idyllic 'life of content in Cambridge cloisters'.

In reality, for most of Robertson's life there, Cambridge was, to use the famous line of his Trinity contemporary A.E. Housman, a 'land of lost content' (Housman, 1896, XL), in the sense that content was always potential and denied rather than actual and realised. Robertson's life is a record of his vain attempt to achieve the content which ever eluded him. The reason for his failure lay within himself. The emptiness, tragic waste and loss, unhappiness and so on, which are seen as stemming from the experience of war or the disputes following the Keynesian Revolution, were *always* there during his time at Cambridge.

From his undergraduate days, Robertson, for a number of reasons, felt ill at ease with himself: he disliked the self he was. Because of this and despite his enormous natural advantages, he experienced a sense of hopelessness that was to have a profound influence on his approach to life and work. His career charts his attempts to find that configuration of circumstances in which he could find a happier self. That is, he sought a persona in which the various elements in his make-up would assume the harmonious pattern that would deliver the life of content he felt was his due.

The parallel in his academic work was that he sought to find that configuration of key economic variables that would make possible the short-term management of a growing monetary economy. Here the influence of temperamental factors led him to attempt to reconcile old wisdom with new insights and set him on a collision course with Keynes.

In other words, Robertson's life was one of attempted *escape*, from the unhappy to the happy, from the unsatisfactory to the satisfactory, from discontent to content. But because the problem lay within himself, the attempts were doomed to failure. Escape is the motif or theme that runs through the various episodes of Robertson's life and provides the link between apparently disparate or unrelated elements. Most important, it is by adopting this viewpoint that we shall be able to get the Keynesian Revolution in true perspective and it is to a consideration of that question that we now turn.

In one sense at least the Keynesian Revolution *did* provide the watershed between happiness and unhappiness in Robertson's life; but only in the partial sense that it marked the division between the happy *public* Robertson and the unhappy *public* Robertson. There was, however, a far more significant, longitudinal, divide – a fault line – that ran between the (intially happy and successful) *public* Robertson and the perennially unhappy and emotionally desolate *private* Robertson. The Keynesian Revolution was the point at which the two selves converged and Robertson abandoned any hope of escaping into a happier life. Thereafter, what his niece Jean Bromley referred to as his 'tragic vision' reigned unchallenged (Bromley to Harris, November 1977, G17/4 RPTC).

VI

For his public self, Robertson chose throughout to utilise his exceptional intellectual gifts in the service of economics as his main life's work. It is widely accepted that his thought shows great consistency of content and inspiration, from *A Study of Industrial Fluctuation* of 1915 to his Memorandum for the Canadian Royal Commission on Banking and Finance of 1962. In addition, it is clear that Robertson's theoretical position, in his main field of interest of fluctuations and money, was fully developed by the late 1920s, after which he became primarily a critic and reviewer (though he did, in the 1930s, spell out a dynamic period-analysis of saving, based on the concept of the Robertsonian 'day' and recast his theory in Wicksellian, interest rate, terms following initiatives by Keynes and Hayek). This, taken together with other evidence, which we shall consider in due course, suggests that by that time he had perfected a scheme of thought, evolved from that which had gone before but which did not fundamentally challenge it. It was, therefore, inherently limited, being constrained by the basic assumptions of that from which it sprang.

By the late 1920s Robertson had said what he had to say, so that the timing of his creative phase gives emphasis to the biography during the period to, say, 1928.

Robertson's intellectual work (the public Robertson) was constrained by the emotional forces that encompassed his world-view and tragic vision (the private Robertson). These forces influenced the extent to which he was able to develop his economic theory. They also caused him to write his most important book in a private language. *Banking Policy and the Price Level* (1926) was private, both in the sense of being 'unreadable': that is, dense and concise; and in employing a formidable array of Robertsonian neologisms, which formed a *chevaux de frise* in defence of his theoretical redoubt.

As noted earlier, Robertson's approach to his public life was constrained by his drive to find a persona in which he would find happiness and so *escape* the self he didn't like – taking into account his intellectual and artistic endowments. His task was complicated by the fact that he carried within him a deeply ingrained sense of duty, and this struggled for possession of his public self with a similarly deep-seated yearning for fulfilment as an artist and free spirit. As his colleague at Trinity A.E. Housman *almost* wrote:

> And through his reins in ice and fire
> Duty contended with desire.
> (see Housman, 1896, XXX)

At Cambridge the conflict was personified by the choice of Trinity, which to Robertson represented duty and the inescapable forces of destiny; and King's, which stood for art and love and remained a never-never land for which he ever pined. In reality, however, the duteous Robertson was the only possible Robertson, both because duty was so deeply rooted in his nature and because the desired self was insufficiently endowed to sustain a career.

At the outset, an ideal compromise had seemed possible, as economics, which was useful, relevant and intellectually satisfying, both served the duteous self *and* formed, along with the rejection of the classics, part of Robertson's escape from his beginnings. The demands of the artistic self could then be satisfied, in parallel, on a spare-time basis, through the writing of poetry and, more importantly, the continuation of his career as an amateur actor.

The fly in the ointment was that Robertson found economics aesthetically arid and he sought to leaven the lump by employing an overtly literary approach to economics which in actuality meant giving full rein to his natural talent for precise, elegant writing, decorating his texts with literary quotations and allusions and lacing them with wit. The effect was to produce a style that was utterly distinctive but also to earn him the reputation for doing economics 'lightly'. This effect was compounded because Robertson's literary approach acted partly as compensation for his inability to make extensive use of mathematics – a lack he felt increasingly as the years went by.

Robertson's ideal compromise was not to endure. Though his outstanding natural talent enabled him early to reach prominence as an economist – and in due course to be recognised as a great economist – the dismal science turned increasingly scientific and, therefore, for Robertson, increasingly dismal. What had begun as escape became confinement.

At the same time, by contrast, his desired self achieved success as an actor, with universal critical acclaim for his performances in classical, Shakespearean and lighter roles. Robertson decided to press his advantage and abandon Cambridge and academic life for a professional career on the stage – only to fail.

VII

Robertson was left with economics and with Cambridge. Initially, his collaboration with Keynes had proved mutually stimulating, but as the 1920s wore on Robertson found the strain of working with Keynes increasingly hard to bear. The publication of *Banking Policy and the Price Level* (1926) sounded the first trumpet-call of rebellion which signalled the beginning of a phase of intellectual wariness that culminated in an open breach a decade later.

The Keynesian Revolution, when it came, precipitated for Robertson a crisis that was both public and private, for it marked the failure of economics as the ideal compromise that would reconcile the demands of escape and duty. He who had the intellectual capacity and the professional interests to become the leading expert on matters that immediately affected the prosperity of the major industrial nations was eclipsed by one who was even greater, and who was seen to succeed (his economics supplanted orthodoxy) where Robertson must by definition be seen to fail. The attendant hostility from the Keynesians was merely salt in a very deep wound. It was the fact itself that accounts for Robertson's pain and unhappiness in the succeeding years. The 'sense of tragic waste and loss which never really left him' stemmed from the realisation that things would now never come right.

The Keynesian Revolution laid bare the fact that Robertson's intellectual self, as expressed in his approach to the relationship between the key variables of his principal economic theory (saving, investment, money and the rate of interest), was constrained by his emotional self. This in turn required security rooted in the past and in myth and the imperative of unchanging fundamental relations between significant factors in his life. This was so as much in his attempt to have complete control over the relationships with and possession of those with whom he was emotionally involved, as in maintaining in their familiar and proper stations the key variables of his economic theory.

A secure past, emotional control and familiar, unchanging economic relations were the essentials of Robertson's survival. By disturbing and overturning fundamental economic relationships, the Keynesian Revolution posed a threat not only to Robertsonian economics but also to Robertson's emotional security and, therefore, to his very being. As it was, the strains imposed by the conflicts in Robertson's life gave rise to psychological problems, from which he perennially suffered, and these were intensified by the challenges posed by the Keynesian Revolution.

Though the open break with Keynes that followed the publication of the *General Theory* in 1936 seemed to promise final emancipation (escape) from 'collaboration', Robertson again found himself bound in the Keynesian toils, because of the need to defend his own theoretical position and with it his own emotional integrity.

VIII

Along the Robertson fault line, intellectual success ran on with emotional desolation. This much was clear even during his years of glittering success as an undergraduate. The cataclysm of war seems to have brought relief – as it often does – but by the 1920s Robertson's feelings were governed by what, in the heyday of Freudianism, used to be called an inferiority complex. He believed himself to be old, unattractive and of a sexual orientation which the world was not ready to accept. Worst of all, in some ways, he had no natural facility for mathematics, a medium that already seemed likely to shape the future of economics.

For clues to explain his actual behaviour, we have his own words which speak of Calvinism, excessive conservatism, ossification, indecision and so on, but there are also important literary pointers. In particular, Robertson's characteristic use of quotations from Lewis Carroll's *Alice* books provides important insights into the nature of his life-view. We shall argue that the frame-poems of these books, which do so much to illuminate the meaning of the texts, find parallel in the frame-materials of Robertson's economics works, which similarly provide guidance as to the interpretation of the works themselves.

Support for the view advanced here will be provided by reference to a variety of other literary sources: to the parts played by Robertson with such feeling on the amateur stage; to the poetry he wrote (which is often explicit); and finally to the literary references used by Keynes in his criticism of Robertson's inability to follow him in new lines of thought.

We shall find that, while neither Keynes nor Robertson entertained any hope of a life after death in Heaven, and believed, therefore, that the earthly life must be lived for itself, their responses were completely different. While one was fiercely activist: informing, campaigning, organising and reforming in the face of the great indifference of nature; the other was dominated by feelings of hopelessness, had no faith in the possibility of real improvement –

only amelioration on a modest scale – and increasingly devoted himself to warning against the folly of trying to do too much.

While Keynes was sufficiently sure of himself to risk the consequences of overturning established ₊economic theory, Robertson's 'evolutionism' in economics had its counterpart and foundation in his emotional need for security and certainty. Thus while Keynes looked forward, Robertson looked back – to a reassuring, sunny past which, if it did not exist in reality, must exist at least in myth.

Hence the apparent paradox – the conflict – in Robertson's life, between, on the one hand, a struggle to escape the self he did not like and, on the other, his need to retain a reference back. For if the happy self cannot be realised in the present then it must for sanity's sake exist in the past, as nostalgia for a happy childhood, real or imagined. This explains the need for *Alice*.

Robertson's temperamental regressiveness, his nostalgic yearning for lost content, found expression in his reverence for the *Alice* books and in an 'evolutionary' approach to the development of economic theory. These were but two manifestations of the same underlying problem. And just as Robertson failed in his bid to escape into a new persona, in which the various facets of his uncomfortable self could assume their true and harmonious dispositions, so he failed in his economic theory to escape from his classical roots to find the new and harmonious disposition of key variables which could have brought agreement with Keynes.

Failure was assured because the underlying problem lay with Robertson himself – the self from which he could not escape. Robertson's temperamentally determined 'evolutionism' (though it is more properly seen as the ability to make only constrained advance) absolutely precluded the break with the past that would have allowed him to see the significance of Keynes's new formulations.

As the ideas outlined above are developed and given substance in the chapters that follow, we shall confirm that it is from the evidence of his life and literariness that the link between the economics and the man is to be traced.

2. Public self and private self

If we are to understand Dennis Robertson the economist, we must seek to understand Dennis Robertson the man; to assess the work of the intellectual, public Robertson, we must be aware of the constraints imposed by the more diffuse and largely unrecognised influence of the private Robertson.

It is a relationship that has been hinted at in the writings of some of the more perceptive observers in the economics profession (in particular see Danes, 1979, pp. 96ff) and at least sensed by those who knew Robertson personally and have felt that, in coming to a full appreciation, reference should be made to temperament as well as to intellect. Jean Bromley, Robertson's niece, wrote to J.R. Hicks to say that his draft obituary of her uncle, written for the British Academy, was

> a first rate piece of intellectual history . . . So I don't mind that the private uncle I knew is not greatly present in what you have written; he is invoked in your first paragraph, and you warn readers to keep this in mind.   (19 September 1964, G11/ 6 RPTC)

Dennis Proctor, a 'close personal friend' of Robertson, was not so forbearing, saying that Hicks 'flatters himself if he thinks he has adequately compounded his utter failure to *evoke* Denis' [sic] personality by his two opening paragraphs' (Proctor to Bromley, 8 January 1968, G11/10, 11 RPTC).

An indication of what Mrs Bromley believed the private Robertson to be, usefully juxtaposed with the other elements in his makeup, is provided by the response she made to a request from the Institute of Economic Affairs for 'a photograph of Sir Dennis Robertson to add to our gallery of distinguished classical economists in our boardroom' (Harris to Bromley, 31 October 1977, G17 RPTC). She assured the writer Ralph (Lord) Harris that Robertson

> would have been utterly in sympathy with the aims and achievements of the IEA [and] would have felt honoured to have his photograph hung in your gallery of classical economists.   (November 1977, G17/4 RPTC)

The image of Robertson as an eminent economist, conservative in his views and having his roots firmly planted in classical soil, is a familiar one.

However, in choosing a photograph to send (and taking into account those already chosen for use elsewhere), Mrs Bromley selected one taken by a New York studio in 1962 and which, though not a 'good likeness', evidently displayed what she took to be the two characteristic features of Robertson's makeup, namely, 'the domed forehead and his tragic vision'.

Clearly the 'domed forehead' is symbolic of the intellectual, public Robertson, while the 'tragic vision' is expressive of the darker temperamental forces of the private self. The private self constrained the public self; temperament checked the advance of intellect. Robertson's 'tragic vision' was the life-view that determined his characteristic approach to economics, with developments in theory subject always to the restraining hand of older authorities and older certainties.

That this was an accurate reading of Robertson's outlook – that his world was indeed stalked by the spectre of tragedy – was confirmed by his friend and colleague at Trinity, J.R.M. Butler who, in the memoir he wrote for the College, thought it necessary to mention that Robertson had a 'profound sense of the harshness of human destiny' (Butler, 1963, pp. 41–2). If for 'human destiny' we read 'universal human condition' and Robertson's sense of being particularly ill-equipped to come to terms with it, we have the basis for an explanation of why Robertson's vision should have been tragic.

II

In the chapters that follow we shall explore this theme and so come to understand what was a most important and pervasive influence in his life. We shall proceed by seeking to answer the following questions:

1. How did Robertson come to acquire a sense of ultimate futility and hence his tragic vision?
2. How did his vision influence and interact with the events of his life?
3. How in particular did his vision shape his approach to economics and his reaction to the seismic conceptual shift in economic theory presented by Keynes's change of direction in the 1930s?

As the first part of this process we must concern ourselves with the making of Dennis Robertson, with an examination of the main formative influences in his life: family circumstances, school, university, war service, the professional career. How far are we justified in accepting the composite – received view of Robertson as the conventional, though outstandingly talented product of Sir Frank Lee's 'great tradition'? How accurate, in fact, is Samuelson's neat and striking, though typically slightly deprecating, encapsulation?

If being English were a quantity instead of a quality, Robertson would merit a high cardinal score. First he was the son of a clergyman-headmaster . . . Robertson proceeded to Eton and apparently belonged to that happy few of public school men who were both (1) literate enough to record memories and (2) possessed of pleasant memories to record. He went up to Trinity and remained in Cambridge virtually all his life. . . . The man who in his bath first said, 'Eureka: there does exist something I shall call the Establishment', might well have been thinking of Dennis Robertson when inspiration struck. (Samuelson, 1963, pp. 518–19)

There is, of course, much here that is recognisably the case but, as with all caricatures, the effect is achieved by emphasising some features at the expense of others. To obtain a fuller picture and therefore a truer one, we shall find it necessary in our consideration of the evidence to make a distinction between the outer form and the inner reality; between the public Robertson and the private Robertson.

3. Home and Eton

I

Dennis Holme Robertson was born on 23 May 1890, the youngest of the six children – he had three brothers and two sisters – of the Reverend James Robertson and his wife Constance Elizabeth Wilson. He was of mixed Scots and English ancestry and born into the established middle class. Hicks, in his 'Memoir', caught the point well enough and put the emphasis on the family's links with the world of education:

> He came by birth as well as by education, from the world of the English public school. The Robertsons were of Scottish origin, but his ancestors (on both sides) had for generations been clergymen and schoolmasters, at various schools and in several parts of England.   (Hicks ed., 1966, p.10)

It is an assessment confirmed by Robertson himself in a strongly auto-biographical fragment of a novel he left among his papers. Note how here, however, there is more emphasis on the family's links with the church:

> a family belonging to what is known as the British Professional Class. There would have been lean Scotch parsons and stout English parsons . . . the majority would probably be yeomen and parsons and clerks.   (Robertson, 'The Curse of Electra', 1908, in D9/9 RPTC)

There is also an interesting and unexpected Liverpool connection on his mother's side. Dennis Robertson's great-grandfather, Samuel Holme, was Mayor of Liverpool in 1852 and at the time that Robertson was appointed to succeed A.C Pigou as Professor of Political Economy at Cambridge in 1944 the local press was quick to point to the origin of Robertson's second forename – Holme (22 February 1944, LDPE).

The Holmeses were a local family, with roots in Everton, and Samuel himself was born 'within gun-shot' of Liverpool Town Hall (Shimmin, 1866, p. 29, LRO). They developed an extensive building and contracting business and undertook railway construction and public works, including a share in the building of Harvey Lonsdale Elmes's neo-classical masterpiece, St George's Hall.

As an interesting parallel with our argument in respect of Dennis Robertson himself, we might note here the comment made about Samuel Holme in the nineteenth century:

> It has been a matter of surprise to many that a gentleman possessing so much perception and who has always been a man of progress, should have continued so steadily attached to a political party which has almost become fossilised; and that one who has been foremost in the race of mechanical science should yet attach himself to the megatheriums [pre-historic sloth-like animals] of extinct Toryism . . . His mind is essentially Conservative.   (Shimmin, 1866, p. 29)

We shall observe the same curious conjunction of progress and reaction in Robertson's approach to economics.

For their part, at least one branch of the Robertson clan regarded themselves as 'a Liverpool family' during the years of Robertson's maturity and made a distinctive contribution to the city's life through several generations (see Bromley to Editor, *Liverpool Daily Post*, 27 January 1965 and attached *curriculum vitae* in A10/3 RPTC). This later association with the city arose through Dennis's eldest brother Ainslie, who, after graduating with first-class honours in classics from Trinity College, Cambridge, obtained a situation in Liverpool in 1903, the year of his father's death, and stayed for forty-one years.

Ainslie had a genuine interest in the classics and retained lifelong membership of the Classical Association. But he was no retiring scholar. He entered into a career in business, first with the Booth Line Steamship Co. Ltd (in which he held a management position during the 1914–18 war) and then as a partner with a firm of fruit brokers (he was President of the Liverpool Fruit Brokers' Association in 1926). Subsequently he was the proprietor of a small business, The Hurricane Smock Co. Ltd. In addition he was tireless in his efforts on behalf of a variety of charitable organisations on Merseyside and played an important part in the Philharmonic Society's project to rebuild the Philharmonic Hall after the fire of 1933. Finally, he served as a special constable during the First World War and remained a keen cricketer. Overall, in his willingness to make common cause with local people and to serve on committees, he was the opposite of Dennis (cuttings relating to A.J. Robertson, LDPE).

II

Dennis himself was born at Lowestoft in Suffolk in a year that was a critical one for the family. His father had recently been compelled to resign as Master (that is head-master) of Haileybury, the major public school and former East India [Company] College, following an incident which, it was felt, he had failed to handle with a sufficient degree of tact.

Appointed in 1884 at the age of forty-eight, Robertson's previous record had greatly impressed the school's Council. After school at Cheltenham College, Robertson senior read classics at Jesus College, Cambridge (where he is recorded as having been born in Dundee though his county is given as Berwickshire) and was bracketed Second Classic in the University lists for 1858. For twenty years from 1859 he held a fellowship in classics at the College but vacated it under University rules on his marriage to Constance Wilson in 1879 (Mills to Fletcher, 21 December 1994).

Thereafter, he was assistant master at Rugby School and then at Harrow, where he was, apparently, 'remembered for his energy and wit' (Thomas, 1987, p. 69). He was also a keen Alpine mountaineer and something of a poet (a collection of his occasional verse was published by Ainslie in 1904: see Robertson ed., *Arachnia*, Macmillan, 1904) and continued to compose verse and doggerel in a manner that was taken up by Ainslie and which became characteristic of Dennis himself. Perhaps most striking of all, he presented his testimonials in the form of a printed booklet, eighty pages long.

The Reverend James Robertson was described by his successor, Canon Lyttelton, as 'a man of brilliant brainpower and likeable under a somewhat rough exterior'; and by one of his pupils as 'gruff in manner and rather sarcastic'. The historian of Haileybury comments: 'It was this brusque side to his essentially kind character which was to be his undoing at Haileybury' (Thomas, 1987, p.70).

His Mastership was marked by significant contributions, such as the building of the Bradby Hall complex, the establishment of the Haileybury College Rifle Volunteer Corps and the encouragement of musical activity in the school (Constance was a gifted musician). But there were problems. The school continued to be 'plagued by illness' and in December 1889 the Council met to discuss: 'the depressed condition of Haileybury College'. This they attributed to two causes, namely:

> The effect produced on the Public by the prevalence of Diphtheria in the School for two or three successive Terms more than a year ago [and] The Hutt trial and the Articles and Comments thereon in the Press of a prejudicial character to the School. (Thomas, 1987, p. 80)

The Hutt trial was a national sensation in its day and dominated the headlines (it is seen by some as the inspiration for Terence Rattigan's play *The Winslow Boy*). It was far more than the 'mistake in administration the blame for which [Robertson] had insisted on taking upon himself', which is Hicks's account of the matter (Hicks ed., 1966, p. 10); or Dennison's description as 'a lawsuit brought by a parent (who received a farthing damages), even though he had been involved only indirectly' (Dennison, 1992b, p. 16). Robertson played a crucial role and was perceived by the College to mishandle the matter

– largely on account of his temperament. It brought him down and transformed his life and, with it, that of his family.

The case concerned a boy who was expelled for stealing. The evidence against him was circumstantial and involved an element of entrapment. Robertson as Master dealt intemperately both with the boy and especially so with the parent, who sued the School. The School view is that:

> Robertson made an unfavourable impression in this case, and that . . . The name of Haileybury had suffered . . . Robertson knew who should take the rap and he tendered his resignation, which was accepted by the Council. (Thomas, 1987, p. 82)

There were expressions of support and the school put on record its appreciation of one 'who served the College with complete devotion of heart and mind'. His portrait was painted; Mrs Robertson received similar encomiums. But it was the end. Robertson resigned and, after an uncomfortable period of waiting whilst a suitable living in the gift of Jesus College was found for him, he spent the following twelve years until his death in 1903 as vicar of Whittlesford near Cambridge.

III

It was during this uncomfortable transition period in the spring of 1890 that Dennis Robertson was born, in the accommodation the family had rented in Lowestoft. Here the atmosphere was charged with the shock of the past – Jean Bromley referred to the Haileybury episode as a 'debacle' (letter to Hicks, 2 November 1976, G16/2 RPTC); uncertainty about the future; and the general unpleasantness of the present, caused by the behaviour of the landladies. Twenty-five years later Dennis wrote to his mother expressing gratitude 'for all you went through there' (from Egypt, 19 January 1916, A4/3/4-5 RPTC). It was overwhelmingly a time of change with (note the dating): Robertson conceived in the old life (in the summer of 1889); born in the turmoil of the transition (the school's Council met in the December of 1889, the Robertsons left directly afterwards in January and Dennis was born in May: see Wise to Bromley, 27 January 1965, G11/22 RPTC); and growing up in the radically reduced circumstances of the new life (from 1891).

Hence it would be wrong to paint too rosy a picture of Robertson's beginnings. There were, it is true, many advantages. Whittlesford had woods and fields enough to satisfy the need for adventure and provide ample opportunity for botany and for ornithology. His father was always in work and eminently qualified to give the child an excellent educational grounding. The family was numerous enough to provide society and support. Still, the sense of 'waste and loss' must have hung heavy in the air. Hicks's description of the Reverend James as having 'spent his last years as a country parson . . . with ample time to devote himself to the education of his children' (Hicks ed., 1966, p. 10) could be a euphemism for underemployment and fretting. It completely disguises the fact that this brilliant and ambitious man, with his printed booklet of testimonials, ended his professional career in full flight (he was only fifty-four) and then remained for the next twelve years in a quiet country backwater, a big fish in a small pond: a financially constrained grandee.

It was a twilight period that gave Dennis what John Vaizey later referred to as 'the sad family history of genteel poverty, the minor parsonical snobbery', and left him with 'a desperate fear of poverty' (Vaizey, 1977, pp. 12, 17). On the other hand there is no reason to believe that Robertson senior was other than conscientious, hardworking and successful as a parish priest or that he did not fill his time usefully and to effect.

It is unfortunate that the period of his incumbency should be so poorly documented: it is the one the Whittlesford Society 'know least about' (Wright to Fletcher, 17 April 1998) and similarly the Cambridgeshire County Record Office are able to 'throw little light on [the] Reverend Robertson's activities during his time at Whittlesford' (Neville to Fletcher, 12 May 1998). It is known that he would have been *ex officio*, as vicar, Chairman of Governors of the local Church of England Primary School (Wright to Fletcher, 17 April 1998), but the volume of manager's minutes which survives 'was very patchily kept and there are no references to Robertson save in his capacity as Treasurer' (Neville to Fletcher, 12 May 1998). Similarly, he would, again *ex officio*, have been Trustee of Swallow's Charity, a sixteenth-century foundation for the relief of need among Whittlesford residents, but the minute books for the relevant period are unfortunately lost (Wright to Fletcher, 17 April 1998).

One interesting sidelight is that the *Victoria County History of Cambridgeshire* records that a girls' boarding school was kept between about 1892 and 1904 at The Grove, Whittlesford (Wright to Fletcher, 17 April 1998). Given the dates, could this possibly have been an enterprise of Constance's, set up as a means of supplementing the family budget?

There are, to be sure, tributes both in stone and in the press to mark his passing and, despite inevitable doubts as to their value as historical documents, we may safely give them due weight here. On the south side of the chancel arch of the flint and clunch-built church of St Mary and St Andrew, Whittlesford, parts of which date from the eleventh century and which numbers among its former lay-rectors Roger Ascham, tutor and Latin secretary to Elizabeth I, is a prominent marble tablet. It records that it was placed there by his parishioners, and in addition to the usual pieties and a brief *curriculum vitae*, contains a tribute cast in suitably comprehensive terms:

> A Scholar   A Teacher   A Preacher
> . Whose word was with power .
> A Father and Friend in Home and
> School and Parish. Steadfast and
> Tender and True. A Servant of Christ

As at Haileybury so at Whittlesford, the Reverend James's helpmeet is duly honoured. Outside, on the south wall of the chancel, a slate tablet is dedicated to the memory of Constance, 'His helper in this parish 1891–1903'. Her 'rare kindness and gaiety and music' are remembered but so also, and equally prominently, is her role as mother. Furthermore, as the dedication includes 'her two daughters: Who followed the way of both parents: In lives of devoted service to others' and the second of these, Gerda, died only in 1951, long after the incumbency ended, hands other than those of the parishioners of 1891–1904 must have been involved: namely, those of the family.

This does not of course mean that the epithets are any the less apt or well-deserved but in confirmation and as a final word we might turn to the report of James's funeral in the local press which contains the following considered assessment:

> Here he spent the last twelve years of his life, engaged on his parish duties, on the preparation of his four sons for the public schools, on intercourse with Cambridge friends, and correspondence with others – often accompanied with verses or problems . . . Mr Robertson's loss will be sorely felt at Whittlesford, where he had worked in the friendliest spirit towards all and shown a fine example of playing a public part. Unswerving sincerity and honesty had marked all his dealings throughout life; and it is on this characteristic, and on his chivalry and largeness of heart, that his friends chiefly dwell. (*Cambridge Chronicle and University Journal*, 30 October 1903, CCRO)

IV

'Preparation of his . . . sons for the public schools' meant that the boys would not attend a preparatory school as was the normal practice but remain at home to be taught (cheaply) by their father until they were old enough to take the examination for direct entry into a major school. One of the sons to be so prepared was his youngest, Dennis, and at this juncture it will help to pay attention to the nature of the 'preparation', for use later on (in Chapter 4, below).

The point to be made concerns the position of classics in Robertson's early and later education. In the account given in the memoir in the *Trinity Review* for 1957, the year Robertson retired:

> Instead of going to a preparatory school [Robertson] was grounded in Latin and Greek by his father so successfully that he gained the second scholarship in classics at Eton.   (p. 23 in Gl1/5 RPTC)

However, the scholarship to Eton was not in classics *per se* and Robertson was careful to delete the words 'in classics' when he filed the article away.

This misconception (see also Skidelsky, 1992, pp. 272-3, who seems to follow the same line) is symptomatic of a wider view that sees Robertson as the essential classicist who public-spiritedly forsakes his beloved ancient texts for the less sympathetic realms of economics. H.G. Johnson, who was a colleague in the economics faculty at Cambridge after the Second World War, has explicitly suggested that the classics were where his heart really lay (in Johnson and Johnson, 1978, p. 136). Others, both fellow economists and members of his family, have stressed his love and high regard for his classical studies (see, for example, Robbins, 1971, p. 221; and Great Aunt Elize H. Holme to Robertson, 24 June 1909, Al/9/1 RPTC).

It is this view that endorses the appropriateness of Robertson's early education:

> Until Dennis went to Eton in 1902 . . . his father was his only teacher. Not much of a preparation for the world; for the making of a classical scholar, a flying start. (Hicks ed., 1966, p. 10)

And, to the extent that Robertson shone as a classicist at school, won a major scholarship in classics to Trinity College, Cambridge, and was placed in the first division of the first class in Part I of the Classical Tripos, such a view is entirely justified. But after that he ceased to be a classicist, and in the next chapter we shall argue that he gave it up as soon as he decently could. Despite his undoubted prowess in the subject one wonders whether that was indeed where his heart really lay.

Up until 1910, at the end of his second year at Cambridge, Robertson's education was constrained by circumstances from which he thenceforth sought to free himself. Consider first that the Reverend James was himself a classical scholar, as undergraduate, don and schoolmaster. Consider also that the study of the classics was becoming a family tradition, for Ainslie, ten years Robertson's senior had won a major scholarship in classics to Trinity College, Cambridge, and had duly graduated with first class honours. Consider, third, that the recognised educational pathways at that time forced boys to be either classicists or mathematicians – and that Dennis was to demonstrate ever after his lack of sympathy for maths. Consider, finally, that in any case Dennis would have been ill-equipped to resist the promptings of the brilliant but 'brusque' former headmaster and frustrated pedagogue – in the way that Alfred Marshall resisted his father's attempts to force-feed him with Hebrew rather than allow him to study mathematics (see Keynes in Pigou ed., 1925, p. 3).

The answer to the question of where his heart really did lie is bound up with the distinction between the desired self and the duteous self and will become apparent as we proceed. For the moment, however, two straws in the wind will point us in the right direction. They are comments in letters, the first sent to Dennis's parents by a master at Eton and the second sent to Dennis by Great Aunt Elize, whom we met above.

Alington to Robertson, 1902–4 (A2/4/1 RPTC):

> I really think that his work sits as lightly on him as one could wish [only criticism Latin verbs – 'a little disappointing']. His English verse calls for no such criticism: he has a great facility in metre and a refreshing flow of ideas.

Holme to Robertson, 24 June 1909 (A1/9/1 RPTC):

> It is a great pleasure that you are such a master of our beautiful English tongue – *over and above the Latin and Greek that you love so well.*   (Emphasis added)

Robertson was indeed to prove himself a master in the use of English, and though his verse, temperamentally constrained, is earth-bound and plodding, he possesses the true poet's precision and aptness in the use of words. This facility, as in the case of Lewis Carroll, with whom we shall draw a close parallel below (Chapters 10 and 11), endows much of his prose with a poetic quality.

English, however, was not really an option. For many years it was not considered a subject worthy of serious study in its own right. At Cambridge it could only be read as a component of the Medieval and Modern Languages Tripos until after the First World War (see Heath, 1994, pp. 20–1). Even for those whose heart or genius lay in English, progression from major public school to Cambridge meant grinding through the Classical Tripos until the debt to formal education had been paid. Only then could private desires be indulged.

V

According to Stanley Dennison, Robertson's later pupil, colleague, friend and confidant, 'Whittlesford provided a very happy childhood' (in Dennison and

Presley eds, 1992, p.16) and letters to Dennis from members of the family and from servants indicate that this was indeed the case (see especially the letters from Constance of 25 March 1905, A1/1/42 RPTC; and from Fanny Andrews, cook, of 22 May 1905, Al/7/1 RPTC). It is true that there is a reference in a verse-letter in capitals from James which refers to crying (24 June 1894, A1/1/24 RPTC) and a letter from Constance on his tenth birthday urging him to accept God's help and expressing the conviction that he is 'in calmer waters in all ways [now]' (22 May 1900, A1/1 RPTC). Dennis has endorsed this in capital letters in pencil 'NO'. In the main, however, it was with the growth of awareness that the shadows were to lengthen perceptibly. But this is a matter for a later section and for the moment we might usefully seek a perspective on Dennis's outlook on the world through the medium of his early verse.

The evidence of the handful of Robertson's surviving childhood poems, preserved by his own hand, indicates a marked preference for death subjects, though at this stage of his life it is death relieved by the certainty of the immortality of the soul – as befits a child of the vicarage.

Robertson wrote poetry from an early age and continued to do so throughout his life. His first poem, 'Mr G--------'s Aunts' was written at the age of six, according to his father, who copied it out 'exactly' later. It tells an amusing tale of two old aunts robbed by burglars. Thereafter the majority take death as their subject and we find examples written 'in memoriam' of pets/domestic animals that have died: 'Darby Fatty Penny' and 'Marial Felis' (both written at the age of ten and a half) and 'Dido' (at age 14); or, in the case of 'The Guinea's Solitude' (no date), a poem about a fictional old hen living bereft in a barn, longing for death ('For I of life do tire / And I believe and hope that I shall soon expire'). There is also a poem written in French (at age nine and a half): 'Les Jeunes Rouge-Gorges Morts', the first verse of which begins: 'Les voilà, ils sont mort et froid'; and the second verse begins: 'Les voilà, ils sont froid et mort'. And finally a poem 'From Victor Hugo' (1902 – at age twelve), copied out later by Ainslie, which features a conversation between the grave and the rose and again is concerned with death and with the Hope of Glory (all in D9/1 RPTC).

Though too much should clearly not be made of all this, death is a strange preoccupation for a child and the range of examples given shows that the phenomenon cannot be dismissed as simply instances of Robertson writing 'to order' for family occasions, as only death and loss are covered. The important point is that if he was subconsciously drawn to a concern with death at this stage, it was death seen within the context of conventional Christian belief. The place of this observation in the overall scheme of the argument will become clear.

VI

In 1902 Dennis achieved second place in the election for King's Scholars at Eton College, Windsor – despite the fact that he qualified in terms of age by only a few days. This meant that he had won a place by competitive examination at the country's leading public school and so was entitled to have his fees paid. Henceforward he would live in the College in the care of the Master in College in a hot-house atmosphere of competition and hard work. Here he would be separated as a 'Colleger' from the other and far more numerous group of Eton boys who paid the fees and were called Oppidans because they dwelt in boarding-houses in the town, in the care of house-masters or dames.

There is agreement among commentators that Robertson's six years at Eton were both happy and outstandingly successful. His colleague and friend J.R.M. Butler wrote:

> he was one of the brilliant band of scholars and poets clustered round Cyril Alington, then Master in College. He became Captain of the School, winning the Newcastle Scholarship [awarded for success in classics] and, among many prizes, one for a Browningesque poem on the San Francisco earthquake. (Butler, 1963, p. 40. For information and assessment on Dr Alington and his time, see Card, 1994, ch. 7; also Ollard, 1982, ch. 7)

There seems every justification – echoed by other commentators – that in Dennison's words:

> In later life he always recalled his schooldays with affection and gratitude, and his election as a Fellow of Eton in 1948 was one of the honours which he most prized. (Dennison and Presley eds, 1992, p. 16)

The reasons why he would have enjoyed Eton are not hard to find. An ancient foundation (fifteenth century), with beautiful buildings and surroundings, many traditions and ceremonies and strongly associated with the governing classes, Eton would have appealed both aesthetically and to his strongly conservative cast of mind. Similarly, the idea of living in a well-defined and regulated environment, with intelligent and motivated boys against whom he could comfortably compete, and of indulging his inherited talent for writing verse, both serious and light-hearted, must have been at that time utterly congenial to his nature. If there was a serpent in this paradise it was the requirement to take part in games, the public school icon that has blighted the life of many a scholarly but unathletic boy. In 1923 Robertson wrote to Ainslie recommending that he enter his son for a scholarship at Eton. This clear endorsement of the school is not affected by the proviso he included:

hoping you may send James for an *Eton* scholarship, – he would be happy there, – happier than I was, with his fast bowling . . . I noted your cricket scores with pride, I can't think how it's done. Please God I may never have to play again. (Dennis to Ainslie, 6 August 1923, A1/13/20 RPTC)

But games were, of course, a universal phenomenon and, on top of its many other attributes, Eton had the advantage of being entirely his own, in the sense that it was not Cheltenham (his father's school) nor, more particularly, was it Winchester (his brother Ainslie's school). The importance of this fact would have become apparent to him in retrospect.

Also what has not previously been remarked is that the time he spent at Eton covered the six difficult years of transition from childhood through puberty to early maturity and thus may not have been uniformly untroubled. The life-problem he was to face at university, stemming from questions of the ultimate meaning and purpose of life and the suitedness of his own nature to come to terms with them, may already have begun to reveal itself, though only perhaps in a diffused way, filtered through the protective screen of conventional beliefs and the institutional framework of the school. Only when stripped of these supports in the freer world of Cambridge would full realisation break upon him. This in itself would enhance the golden quality of his earlier years.

Of the greatest interest for present purposes about Robertson's time at Eton is the way in which the schoolboy foreshadows the man: the way in which the interests, attitudes and anxieties he reveals during his schooldays uncannily predict those which were characteristic of his later years. In the poems of the period that survive among his papers, the older, public Robertson is found in a schoolboy who is resolutely and unquestioningly conservative, a classicist rather than a mathematician, a poet, a talented amateur actor, not a games player. There is also the first intimation of the private Robertson, who is wistfully nostalgic, tortured and ultimately tragic.

VII

The poems date from the period 1907–8, when Robertson was seventeen and eighteen years old respectively and in his two final years at school. In their subject-matter they reflect the typical concerns of the maturing schoolboy's daily round: preferences among school subjects, attitudes to games, school food, private reading, the habit of the daily newspaper, deeper human stirrings, the loss of security. The interest, of course, lies in Robertson's reaction to them (the references are to D9/1 RPTC).

In 1907 Robertson wrote 'Two pieces of doggerel' for the *Eton College Chronicle* (D9/1/15-18 RPTC: 'printed copies lost'). One of these contains a comprehensive statement of the outlook of the public Robertson, who presents himself as a complacent admirer of the status quo both locally and nationally and oh so comfortable within the reassuring familiarity of established institutions. A note of caution must be sounded as the author claims to be fourth from bottom in class, but this may have been included simply to complete the picture of languor and apathy. The drawling remainder is certainly consistent with other forms of evidence of Robertson's political and social views. Though there is an element of facetiousness concerning school life (a trait for which he had been censured by his father some years before: see Revd James to Dennis, 5 November 1902, A1/1/2 RPTC) there is no detectable irony. See, for example, the following extract:

> I read some politics – the 'Star'
> I purchase almost nightly;
> And I am sure that riches are
> Distributed quite rightly;
> My country's happy state to me
> A tranquil joy affords;
> I venerate the monarchy,
> And like the House of Lords.
>
> I think our Eton system's good,
> My tutor is a dear;
> I gladly eat my daily food,
> And drink my daily beer;
> And when men say the soup must go,
> Or threaten Monday's veal,
> I thank my stars that I have no
> Iconoclastic zeal.

These attitudes expressed, however flippantly, when he was seventeen became characteristic of him and changed only in their hardening. In the austerity of post-1945 Cambridge, John (Lord) Vaizey remarked that Robertson 'saw reds under all non-Etonian and some Etonian beds' (Vaizey, 1977, p. 17). Of particular interest for present purposes is his lack of 'iconoclastic zeal': this was to be a constant feature of his approach to economics and gave rise to his so-called 'evolutionary' style of economic theorising which marked him off so clearly from the revolutionary Keynes.

The same 'piece of doggerel' also contains a statement about Robertson's attitude to games. Note again the tone of languid superiority he affects – not unworthy of the Western Brothers; and though the superiority might be held to stem from his desire to make light of a deficiency, the languid manner was evident to at least one of his students at Cambridge half a century later (Marris to Fletcher, 7 April 1995):

> I have been known to make a run,
>   I sometimes catch a catch,
> But I could never see the fun
>   Of playing in a match;
> I am not covetous for fame,
>   Or eager to be known;
> I have no wish for praise or blame,
>   If I am left alone.

The other of the 'pieces of doggerel' is interesting in as much as it gives voice to the other side of Robertson's affected superior attitude towards games. Here we have the wistful regard of the bookish scholar for the life of the athlete, the man of action. Securely set on the road to success by sensibly studying classics, Robertson nevertheless feels able to indulge himself with a dream of escape from the duteous life into another self. We hear in the following extract the authentic voice of the Mole contemplating Toad's motoring career or Ratty's expert handling of the sculls:

> But mostly neath the summer sun,
> When life seems rather dull and flat.
> I dream of what I might have done
> If I had been an athlocrat.
>
> They tell me that athletic skill,
> Is almost sure to turn the head,
> That Greek and Latin verses will
> Stand me at last in better stead.
> And yet . . .
>
> But though it be an empty feat,
> As I am told to stroke an eight,
> I can't but think it would be sweet
> To help to win the Ladies' Plate.
> [rowing-prize at Henley Regatta]

Robertson gave an indication of his attitude to mathematics, namely, all very clever but not for him, in a poem published in the *Eton College Chronicle* for June of the following year. This piece may be seen to be of the same genre as, and precursor to, the overfamiliar and rather ponderous 'Non-econometrician's Lament'. This, because Robertson became a professional economist, is clearly thought more appropriate. Also, Robertson published it as an addendum to one of his later collections of economics essays (Robertson, 1956).

Nevertheless, 'Thoughts Suggested by the Tomlin [sic] Examination' (for the Tomline (mathematics) Prize) is a more substantial, ingenious and interesting piece. Comparing this written at age seventeen, with the 'Non-econometrician's Lament' written many years later, makes it clear that Robertson did not develop as a poet.

Of the two great disciplines of the time, mathematics and classics, Robertson shows great respect for and appreciation of the first but accepts that, as in the case of games, here is something beyond his grasp. Unlike games, however, mathematics had more practical relevance to his career in economics and he was to become painfully aware of his deficiency in this respect:

> Let others rack uneasy brains and try,
> To chase the shadowy and retreating π;
> Climb with Eucleides to fame's lofty ridge,
> And tempt the flooring of the Asses' Bridge;
>
> . . .
>
> With too presumptuous eyes affect to see,
> The falling stone's kynetic energy;
>
> . . .
>
> Control the projectile's aerial range,
> Mark sadly how velocities will change;
>
> . . .
>
> Measure the impact of a sturdy blow,
> And chide the idle tap's unequal flow;
>
> . . .
>
> Discover lightly and with graceful ease,
> The lurking sine of eighty-five degrees;
>
> . . .
>
> Talk gleefully of dynes, and daily troll,
> How g grows greater as you near the pole: –
>
> . . .
>
> For these high matters is my brain too weak,
> I bow to Allcock but I study Greek.
> (*Eton College Chronicle* 25 June 1908, in D9/4/1 RPTC)

VIII

Robertson's private self is represented in part by a clutch of three poems dating from 1907: 'George Eliot', 'Bradfield – The Antigone' and 'To Kenneth Grahame'. These poems are important because taken together they provide an account of Robertson's view of the problem of life and its solution. It is a view that Robertson held at the age of seventeen and continued to hold throughout his life. The formula it contains is precisely the same as that provided by the *Alice* evidence which we consider below, in Chapter 11. That is, that life is nasty and brutish (a 'bitter way') and, above all, short; the blissful afterlife is no more than a myth; it is our duty (the duteous life) to carry on regardless and to serve our fellow men according to our calling; our salvation lies in the present, through love in human relationships; comfort can be found in a nostalgic yearning for a past, pain-free golden age. Love is superior to nostalgia but not everyone is able to find love, in which case the golden age assumes greater importance.

This was the case for Robertson, who over the years both lost the remnants of inherited belief and came to accept that a loving relationship of the conventional kind was denied him and that in the circumstances of the time an open, loving relationship of an unconventional kind was also impossible. This was the tragedy and the source of unhappiness of the private self. When the professional difficulties began in the 1930s over the dispute with Keynes (a public problem with private implications) the public self moved into alignment with the private self.

In 'George Eliot', Robertson sees the author as teaching someone who is, in Philip Larkin's phrase, 'less deceived' about life how to cope with an ultimately 'meaningless' existence by seeing wisdom in the hidden lives of ordinary people: 'She taught us by their blindness how to see' (a point we take up again in different terms in Chapter 12, below). The problem itself is stated succinctly in the latter half of the poem:

> She taught us though our ancient faith be vain,
> With selfless hearts to serve humanity
> To brighten each for each the fleeting day,
> And, without hope or fear of things to be,
> To tread unfalteringly the bitter way.
> (1907, in D9/1/20 RPTC)

In 'Bradfield – The Antigone' it is love that conquers pain and grief and is a salvation – providing a kind of immortality echoing Auden's 'We must love one another or die' and Larkin's 'What will survive of us is love':

> But he of all most happy is whose heart,
> Is true and tender, who has felt the glow,
> And shed the blinding tears of love, and trod
> The thorny path of bitterness and woe;
> Whom from his love nor death nor sin can part
> Most blest is he and like of unto God.
> (1907, in D9/1/19 RPTC)

The third poem, 'To Kenneth Grahame', is of importance on two counts. First, because it celebrates the less positive, regressive strategy of finding comfort in nostalgia for a lost state of happiness or contentment, which encompasses a simple, rural, childlike vision of escape. In addition, the mention of 'gently-gliding days', recalls the river of *Wind in the Willows* (by Grahame) and here there is a direct parallel with the *Alice* world of Lewis Carroll (C.L. Dodgson) in which the myth of a past golden time and its historical equivalent, the famous river trip from Oxford to Godstow on 4 July 1862, plays a key role (see below, Chapter 10). In Robertson's view, the world that Kenneth Grahame conjures is:

> The mirror of our own past golden age,
> O! could we but return to that old time,
> Ere we were tangled in this troublous maze,
> When life was whole and simple and sublime,
> When sorrow quickly came and quickly went,
> And all the gently-gliding days were blent,
> In the long glory of a golden haze.
> (D9/1/29 RPTC)

IX

The poems quoted above were written during Robertson's adolescence, itself a time of uncertainties and anxieties. Even making due allowance for this, however, the evidence they contain is far too consistent with other sources for it to be taken other than seriously. At this stage the 'troublous maze' in which Robertson felt himself 'tangled' seems a rather unfocused and indeed generalised problem. As he became more aware, however, he began to identify present problems with his own circumstances, and in the following year, the year in which he left Eton for Cambridge, he gave vent to his worries in more personal terms.

The evidence for this is provided by the beginning of the manuscript of a novel entitled 'The Curse of Electra' written (probably) in 1908 (in D9/9 RPTC). Though it is claimed to be only the beginning of a novel – and endorsed by Robertson, in Latin, 'The rest is wanting' – it is, in fact, complete in itself.

It is a most interesting document, consisting of seven and three quarter quarto sheets of neat, legible writing. Told in the first-person singular, it recounts an incident in the life of a child of a family of the Robertsons' position in society, upon which a curse has fallen such that (significantly) 'it should not marry, nor leave any seed to inherit the land'. Here is one aspect of Robertson's fate.

The other aspect is revealed by an incident in which the child is deprived of its sense of ultimate security. Apart from the child, two other characters appear: his elder brother, Noel, and his nurse-maid, Emily. 'Noel', we might surmise, is Dennis's eldest brother Ainslie, who represents conventional behaviour, the path of duty and family precedent, and in whose footsteps Dennis is expected to tread. 'Emily' would be Dennis's nurse-maid Gertrude Spooner, who was with the family from 1881 and to whom Dennis was very close. In correspondence she addressed him as 'My dearest (Chicken) Dennis'; and he addressed her as 'Dearest Old Fox' (see A1/5 RPTC). Emily/Gertrude represents comfort and security in childhood.

The narrator tells us that from his earliest days he seemed to bear an enormous burden on his shoulders – 'the weight of the entire world' – and that he suffered 'many terrors . . . with a troubled mind'. These problems gave rise to sleeplessness, and relief, therefore, could be found in sleep. Although he used it sparingly, the infallible means by which he could get to sleep was through the ministrations of Emily. A sense of urgency is introduced by the consequences of a game of hide and seek with his brother, in which Noel is the hunter and the narrator the hunted. The feelings of fright that this induces turn to 'genuine terror' when the game rouses more elemental forces. The narrator resorts to the familiar remedy, his 'last line of defence', but it fails to work and from that time:

> the innate optimism of youth was first thoroughly shaken and it first clearly occurred to me that perhaps after all it was not inevitable that everything should always come right in the end.

We may interpret the meaning of this embryo novel as follows. The timing is significant: Robertson had recently won his major scholarship to Trinity College, Cambridge, as had Ainslie before him, and was, therefore, duteously following-on and so fulfilling family expectations. He had reached an age, however, at which he realised that he was different from Ainslie and that he must find a path of his own whereby he would be able to reconcile the divergent claims which, he felt, were being made upon him. Consequently, this essay in self-analysis possibly marks the beginning of the distinction between the duteous self and the desired self. At the same time, because the realisation of how he might be different brought deep anxiety, at a time when the ultimate security of childhood had slipped beyond his reach and the buttressing of conventional belief had fallen away, this essay also marks the beginning of the search for some position of certainty upon which to build his life and work. Because of 'The Curse of Electra' he is denied the anodyne of Everyman in coming to terms with a 'meaningless' and 'purposeless' world and must instead look to the past: for personal reassurance to the fictional world of *Alice*; and for professional reassurance to the work of revered predecessors. This latter implies, note, that certainty is handed down from one generation to another by means of a sort of apostolic succession.

X

Though always the scholar and never the sport, Robertson nevertheless achieved success at Eton in ways other than through his books, and it is fitting that we should end on a positive note. He was editor of the *Eton College Chronicle* and preserved for posterity two out of the many editorials he wrote for what was a weekly newspaper (see A2/9/1,2 RPTC). He rose to be Captain of the School and so began a public career which was to reach its apogee at Cambridge. He also made his mark as an actor, revealing a considerable talent and beginning an association with the amateur stage which lasted into his later years.

In the programme of events for Eton's Fourth of June celebrations (which commemorate the birthday of George III, a great benefactor) for 1908, Robertson as Captain of the School has his photograph on the front cover and also appears in the 'Programme of Speeches': in Part I as Euripides in a scene from Aristophanes' *The Frogs*; and in Part II as the White Queen in a scene from *Alice Through the Looking Glass* [sic] by Lewis Carroll. Also in Part II he gave a rendering of 'The Last Tournament' by Tennyson. His name is conspicuously absent from the programme of sporting events (in Al/1/48 RPTC).

Robertson's appearance as the White Queen was a notable event and was referred to by a student journalist three years later at the height of his career in the Cambridge Union as: 'his first, and, perhaps, his most striking histrionic success' (*Granta*, 21 October 1911, in A3/2/1 RPTC). In his obituary memoir of Robertson over half a century later in 1963, J.R.M. Butler described the performance as 'memorable' (Butler, 1963 p. 40). It is the first occasion on which Robertson's name is publicly associated with *Alice*, though in future years his references to the *Alice* books would become characteristic and, indeed, legendary.

4. The land of lost content

I

In 1908 Robertson crowned an outstanding career at Eton by winning a major scholarship to Trinity College, Cambridge. There followed what might be seen as a re-run of his success at school, complete with dazzling examination performances, scholarships, triumph as an actor and achievement of high public office, but played out on the broader stage of one of the ancient universities.

As scholar, actor, poet and debater, the public Robertson was universally fêted, admired and envied. But in these years also, Robertson was confronted with the reality of his life-predicament and in seeking to come to terms with this he formed a life-view which would govern his approach to his activities, professional and private, in the decades ahead. Though he sought to escape, via ameliorants or, more fundamentally, into a variety of personae, he would come progressively to accept that the supposed avenues of escape were so many blind alleys. As acceptance increased, hope diminished until, with the cataclysm of the Keynesian Revolution, the public Robertson would change from being successful, happy and admired to being unsuccessful, unhappy and treated, in some quarters, with derision and even contempt.

That Robertson was academically successful at Cambridge is confirmed by the ample recognition he received. In addition to his entrance scholarship to Trinity and various College prizes, Robertson was awarded the Porson [University] Scholarship in 1910 (named after Richard Porson, 1759–1808, Etonian, Trinitarian and Regius Professor of Greek), and in the same year was placed in the first division (of three) of the first class of Part I of the Classical Tripos. It was at this juncture that he switched to economics, for which he was supervised by the young J.M. Keynes. In 1911 he was awarded the Craven [University] Scholarship and in 1912 was placed in the first class in Part II of the Economics Tripos.

It was an impressive tally of honours. Robertson's sole check was to be unsuccessful with the fellowship dissertation he submitted to Trinity in 1913. Instead, he was awarded the Cobden Club Prize (triennial, last awarded 1913) for the piece, which was successful after revision and resubmission the following year.

Indirect evidence of Robertson's intellectual stature is provided by the variety and extent of the non-academic activities he pursued in tandem. As a writer during these years Robertson published poems in various Cambridge magazines, and we shall examine some of these for the interest of their contents, but official recognition of his talents came with the award of the Chancellor's Medal for English Verse (for best ode or poem in heroic verse) in three successive years: 1909, 1910 and 1911.

Robertson also continued with his (more time-consuming) acting career and scored a notable success on making his début in November 1909 with a part in the triennial Greek Play. The essence of the Cambridge Greek Plays was that actors spoke classical Greek 'simply and unaffectedly as if it were the speaker's own language' (*Cambridge Review*, 8 June 1910, F1/1 RPTC). The production for 1909 was Aristophanes' *The Wasps*, with music specially written by Ralph Vaughan Williams (including the famous overture), performed at the New Theatre, Cambridge.

Robertson, in the part of Philocleon, was (with others) congratulated by the *Cambridge Review* for his speaking of Greek (8 June 1910, in F1/1 RPTC); while as to his acting abilities, the *Daily Graphic* reported that it was 'generally agreed that the best piece of acting was that of D.H. Robertson as "the old Philocleon"' (30 November 1909, in F1/2,3 RPTC). There were similarly good reviews in the *Morning Post*, the *Saturday Review*, the *Westminster Review* and the *Pall Mall Gazette* (preserved in F1/6, 7, 8, 9 respectively, RPTC). Also in the audience was A.C. Benson, Master of Magdalene College, Cambridge, who recorded in his diary at the time that Robertson was 'good'; and later as having 'made such a success of the Wasps by his excellent acting' (v. 108 ff. 54, 75, BDMC). Even two years later a writer in the *Granta* could recall the detail of Robertson's performance: 'none but a good dancer could have capered so ludicrously as he contrived to do in the last scene of the Greek Play' (21 October 1911, in A3/2/1 RPTC). The significance of this confirmation of the promise shown at Eton would not have been lost upon Robertson, who would see it as proof that he was talented far above the ordinary for an amateur player. Its effect would be to raise his expectations of the part acting might play in his scheme of life, as we shall see.

He had by this time joined the Amateur Dramatic Club (ADC) and only a few days after *The Wasps* production showed his versatility by taking part in a smoking concert in which he played, in lighter vein, the part of the Master of Queen's Hall in the Club's production of *Fellow or Felon, or The Master and the Miscreant: A Tragic Melodrama in Two Acts*. Robertson later endorsed the cast list to indicate that he had, like others, played 'in his original part' (ADC: Programme, Michaelmas Term, 4 December 1909, F2/3 RPTC).

After Robertson switched to the Economics Tripos his confidence seemed to increase and his public exposure grew in proportion. In 1911 he was on the committee of the ADC and took the leading part (of Lord Trumpington, Prime

Minister and First Lord of the Treasury) in the Club's *The Shame of the Shelford's: A Play in Two Acts*, by William Brown. In the same year he became President and received the approval of the *Cambridge Review* for his innovatory style (in F2/2 RPTC).

These smoking concert appearances were successful and widely remembered though, perhaps, of lesser importance compared to the classical roles such as that of Philocleon. It was not until 1914 that he played a part of comparable stature – and another upon which his pre-war acting reputation chiefly rests – namely, that of Subtle in Jonson's *The Alchemist*. Here he attracted the attention of no less an authority than Sir Arthur Quiller Couch (Professor of English Literature at Cambridge from 1912), who in an article on the three conspirators wrote:

> [Subtle] . . . (I observe the silence of the Programme on the real names of the actors) was presently taking his lines at great speed in the true parsonic accent. (*Cambridge Review*, 11 March 1914, F3/1 RPTC)

He didn't please everybody, however. His colleague A.E. Housman, writing to the Trinity classicist A.S.F. Gow, remarked that he 'did not think Dennis Robertson really satisfactory as Subtle' (in Maas ed., 1971, p. 133), though his is the only recorded negative comment.

II

Received opinion has left an abiding impression of Robertson as someone who was sensitive, shy and retiring and this sits oddly with the record of his stage career. And while the more extreme of the contributors, such as H.G. Johnson who has portrayed Robertson as virtually incapacitated by shyness (Johnson and Johnson, 1978, pp. 136, 138–9), can be safely dismissed as purveyors of hostile caricature, even Dennison, Robertson's confidant, has expressed surprise that 'someone who was normally so reserved' should have been a 'keen and accomplished actor' (Dennison, 1992b, p. 18).

There is certainly an apparent contradiction here but the explanation might be that Robertson became more overtly shy during the latter part of his life and that this became the basis for commentators' impressions. And while it is said that people become more shy with age, an interesting surmise might be that the phenomenon observed is really a symptom of the realignment of the public self with the private self. There is support for such a view in an illuminating remark of John (Lord) Vaizey who detected in Robertson's demeanour in post-World War II Cambridge an element of (not very adequately?) 'suppressed shyness' (Vaizey, 1977, p. 17).

Certainly, in his earlier years Robertson's public life was not marked by any evidence of shyness. And though an acting career is often seen as an attempt at (over-)compensation by the painfully shy, any application of the argument to Robertson's case would also have to take account of his public life off-stage, including a penchant for the adversarial atmosphere of organised debate. This refers to his membership of the Cambridge Union (debating society and gentlemen's club), in which he was active during his undergraduate and graduate years. He participated in debates and, in the more expansive period after his move to economics, he held the offices of Secretary, Deputy President and President of the Society, in one year, during the Lent, Easter and Michelmas Terms of 1911 respectively (see Cradock ed., 1953, p. 184).

Stanley Dennison (1992b, p. 18) has noted that Robertson and Keynes had 'genuinely beautiful speaking voices and perfect natural articulation'. And although A.C. Benson recorded in his diary an incident, in May 1911, in which Robertson was eliminated in the early stages of a public speaking competition (the Winchester Reading Prizes), for which Benson was one of the judges (v. 121 f. 10, BDMC), the reports of the Union debates kept by Robertson clearly indicate that he was an effective and popular speaker. Appreciation of his talents spread wider than Cambridge, the *Granta* reporting that: 'As an orator, Mr Robertson enjoys the rare distinction of popularity both in the Cambridge Union Society and in another place [that is, Oxford]' (*Granta*, 21 October 1911, A3/2/1 RPTC). In fact, the first report of a debate that Robertson preserved was one in which he participated at the Oxford Union in February 1910, in which he spoke for the motion 'That this House sets a higher political value on the Nationalist than on the Imperialist spirit.' Of his performance in the debate the *Oxford Magazine* said:

> Mr Robertson was vivacious with constant flashes of humour and a vivid faith in his cause. He has returned from a success at Oxford to an even greater – the Porson [Scholarship] – at Cambridge. (17 February 1910, A3/1/4 RPTC)

In Cambridge, in the same year, he spoke against the motion (symbolically perhaps, in view of his later opposition to 'Keynesianism'): 'That a regard for practical efficiency is a more important factor in national well-being than a regard for moral principle' (7 June 1910, A3/1/9 RPTC).

In Oxford again, in June of the following year, he spoke for the motion (though not a 'whole-hogger'): 'That this house is of [the] opinion that the British nation is degenerating.' Robertson's argument, which is of a piece with his views on social deprivation and unemployment, was that the nation was trying to make a silk purse out of a sow's ear: seeking to improve the lot of the race without first improving the race itself. The *Oxford Magazine*, in reporting the debate, commented that:

> Mr Robertson handled the difficult and thorny question of a declining birth-rate
> with ease, ability and tact. We were pleased to welcome him again; we have not
> forgotten his former speech, and it is to be hoped that he will be able some day to
> pay a third visit to Oxford.   (8 June 1911, A3/1/11 RPTC)

Such an expression of warm appreciation by the Oxonians would have given
Robertson particular pleasure, for reasons we shall explore below.

In December 1911 Robertson as Retiring President moved: 'That this
House desires to express its undiminished confidence in His Majesty's
Government.' In speaking in favour of the motion Robertson expressed
opinions which again revealed his deep-seated conservatism. He argued that
for the modern Liberal Party 'the catchword of *laissez-faire* had passed and
that crimes wrought in the name of Liberty were not today wrought by them'.
He saw Liberalism 'as the conservator not the innovator, champion not of
change but of continuity, guardian of certain things of immense value to the
country: principles of aristocracy, national supremacy and good order'
(A3/1/1 RPTC).

It was a speech that recalled his Eton poem written in favour of the status
quo – a poem, incidentally, with which he was now popularly associated at
Cambridge, thanks to an article in the *Granta* which quoted the lines:

> Our country's happy state to me
> A passive joy affords
> I venerate the Monarchy
> And like the House of Lords,

before commenting that: 'These are hardly the sentiments of a president of the
Liberal Club' – an office Robertson currently held (*Granta*, 21 October 1911,
A3/2/1 RPTC). They were, however, we might add, sentiments expressive of
Robertson's innermost self and spoke of the enduring rock-like basis on which
he felt he must conduct his life and thought.

By contrast, Robertson's winning style as a debater owed nothing to brute
force and fury and everything to the 'good manners' and 'sweet reasonableness' that in the debate he lauded as 'British traditions'. The comments made
by the Editor about his performance recall Samuelson's observation of fifty
years later, that Robertson:

> had the rare vice of being a charming writer [speaker]. He would sneak up on the
> unwary reader [listener] and gain his acquiescence by a siren song. The man could
> almost make you believe in such absurd things as cardinal utility.   (Samuelson,
> 1963, p. 518)

As in print so in speech it would seem. But note how the following remarks
are altogether kinder and free of reserve. Note again that the subject is the

pre-watershed (Keynesian Revolution) Robertson rather than the post-watershed Robertson of Samuelson's day:

> The retiring President was in his most characteristic and most charming mood. He surrendered even more than usual to his opponents, but his sweet reasonableness left a more persuasive impression than many more wholehearted and one-sided speeches could have done. The House will miss him. (Debate 5 December 1911, A3/1/1 RPTC)

Thereafter, if we are to judge by the incidence of the reports of debates collected by Robertson, he spoke but seldom – and the House did indeed seem to 'miss him'. When in February 1913 he spoke against the motion 'That this House would rather sacrifice all other literature than the Works of Shakespeare', the Editor of the *Cambridge Review* (18 February 1913, in A3/1/13 RPTC) regretted that 'Mr Robertson comes out of his tent too seldom'. Finally, with thoughts of war in the air, Robertson spoke in April 1913 against the motion 'That this House would favour the adoption of Compulsory Military Training for Great Britain.' The Editor of the *Cambridge Review* was again appreciative of his performance but regretful of his too infrequent appearances:

> Everyone must have been grateful to the Ex-President for bringing out the real points at issue – alas that he must be styled a 'rara avis'. (29 April 1913, in A3/1/2 RPTC)

III

How is this falling away after a period of intense activity to be explained? It is as though Robertson, having made the transition from classics to economics, rejoiced in the new persona he assumed along with his new subject and exploited the release (escape) it brought. But then, as the novelty wore off and his problems reasserted themselves, he drew in his horns again. Whatever the explanation, in Robertson's public life the wave gathered, mounted to a crest and then collapsed.

The crest of Robertson's wave was 1911, an *annus mirabilis* in which his undergraduate public self reached the glittering zenith of its success. In that one year, Robertson, as though in fulfilment of the rightness of his decision to seek a new self, held the principal public offices open to an ambitious undergraduate and was acclaimed for his academic, literary and theatrical successes. In addition to being a scholar of the grandest and richest college in the University – and a I:i in Part I of the Classical Tripos to boot – he was, successively, Secretary, Vice-President and President of the Union, he was

President of the ADC and of the Liberal Club. He triumphed in debate, both at Cambridge and at Oxford. He was awarded the Craven Scholarship. He won the Chancellor's Medal for English Verse for the third year running.

As though to cap it all, Robertson was featured in an article in the *Granta*, in October, on 'Those in Authority'. He is designated 'Presidential Man' and:

> a splendid specimen of the type . . . [the] sort of man whom everybody loves and admires in such a way as to make him president of as many societies as is convenient . . . Rather an alarming person he sounds, and, indeed we have met many persons not intimate with Mr Robertson who have professed themselves abjectly terrified . . . [no need for such feelings]. For the tremendously important fact about him is that he is one of the heroes of 'The Golden Age' turned outwardly Olympian, while still preserving all the charm of those most delightful children. (*Granta*, 21 October 1911, A3/2/1 RPTC)

There is a sense in which this last is a shrewd and insightful observation, though entirely sincere and ingenuous. Its significance will become apparent.

The article is headed by an 'elegant' photograph of the twenty-one year old 'Presidential Man . . . by nature fitted to preside, whether it be over the Union, the A.D.C., or the fortunes of his country'. The president depicted is no hearty, back-slapping, 'flesh-presser' but an intense and serious young man of slender build, withal an air of authority, that prefigures his life in uniform. He stares, unsmiling, into the camera, his hair already receding at the temples, and lurking in his eyes a haunted look. The private self stares out of the public self: the inner man from the outer.

For, with Robertson, all was not as it seemed. Beneath the apparent glamour of his public success he was struggling to resolve an inner crisis. It was a struggle that would, in these critical formative years, determine his outlook, the set of his mind, for the rest of his life. The crisis, in brief, involved his having to come to terms with the idea of living a transient, mortal life without the comfort of religion and without that anodyne of Everyman: conventional requited love. Robertson sought escape from his unsatisfactory self by way of an ideal persona in which he could 'find' the self in which he could feel comfortable. To do this meant taking leave of his past-given self and seeking the true self as he saw it. Here he faced a dilemma. Iron-bound duty, a major component of the past-given self, held him in thrall and produced in his strategy a search for compromise, in company with a yearning for complete escape from the cage of duty. In the public Robertson, the duteous self warred with the desired self; while behind, forever urging resolution, lay the immiserated private self.

Evidence for the existence of a state of conflict in Robertson's public self is readily available because, appropriately enough, Robertson made it public. Although a scholar of Trinity, Robertson spent a 'large proportion' of his time during the pre-1914 years in King's and was recognised as being one of the

'King's metics': that is, those who were members of other colleges but spiritually felt their home to be in King's (Wilkinson, 1980, pp. 65, 90). In 1911, at the height of his public success, Robertson made known his feelings of bitterness at the inappropriateness of his membership of Trinity as compared to King's and at the circumstances which had led him to choose wrongly. In the very first of six articles he contributed to the King's College undergraduate magazine *Basileon*, Robertson wrote, in a piece entitled 'As It Strikes an Outsider':

> to those that can content themselves with the mild excitement of the observation of delightful people in the most beautiful acres of England, I need only say that, as I walked rather drearily down King's Parade that night, I cursed the fortune which had compelled me to live in a suburb instead of in the great and shining Metropolis of the Universe. (*Basileon* no. 13, June 1911, p. 10. An extended version of this passage is printed in Wilkinson, 1980, p. 65 but wrongly attributed to the 1919 issue)

Nor was this an aberration, a temporary disaffection. In 1913, in the last item he contributed to *Basileon*, he wrote, as though in valediction, a piece in blank verse entitled: 'Why One Does not Go to King's, by An Outsider'. In this, in addition to a list of entirely trivial reasons for not going to King's (for example: 'Because at Trinity there is a fountain that plays all day ... Because at Trinity *all* the porters wear top hats on Sunday'), he gives the one big reason for not having gone to King's: 'Because one missed one's opportunities' (*Basileon* no. 15, 13 June 1913, p. 10).

That Robertson should have felt such dissatisfaction with his life at Cambridge seems extraordinary; even more so that he should have made that dissatisfaction public. It is a picture that conflicts completely with the hearty accounts of received opinion which depict him as the natural product of the 'great tradition'. How are such feelings to be accounted for? The answer becomes clear as we delve deeper. The two colleges represent the two warring sides of Robertson's public self: the duteous self and the desired self, the self he felt himself compelled to be and the self he felt himself truly to be. Once this idea is established much else can be explained on the same basis – and in particular the decision of Robertson the gifted classicist to switch to economics for Part II of the Tripos.

These matters will be explored below, but first we must recall that behind the conflicts of Robertson's public self lay the promptings of the private self: the seat of his ultimate problem, his life-view. For this, Robertson appropriately provided no direct public evidence, though strong indicative public evidence does exist, as we shall see. He did, however, reveal his difficulties to a much older man and senior member of the University who duly recorded his impressions in his diary.

This man was A.C. Benson, Master of Magdalene College, and, though Robertson did not know it, one of the world's great diarists. His biographer, David Newsome, provides the following summation of his achievement in this respect:

> The diaries of Arthur Christopher Benson comprise one of the most extensive and detailed private records of a man's thoughts and observations of his times that has ever been preserved. In all they run to one hundred and eighty volumes and provide (with the single exception of four blank years during a period of mental breakdown) a continuous chronicle from the summer of 1897, when Arthur Benson was thirty-five and a housemaster at Eton College, until his death, as Master of Magdalene College, Cambridge, in June 1925 at the age of sixty-three. The whole record amounts to more than four million words. (Newsome, 1980, p. 1; see also pp. 385–7)

Benson's involvement in a number of circles at the top of late Victorian and Edwardian society (Church, Monarchy, Eton, Cambridge and so on) meant that his diary should be regarded as a 'sensitive' document. After his death it was sealed up in a specially constructed crate in the Old Library at Magdalene and embargoed for fifty years, with only innocuous selections made available for publication. Newsome's biography was the first study undertaken on the basis of free access to the diaries in their entirety. Newsome also compiled an index of the entries, which he presented to Magdalene for the use of readers. This index has since been supplemented by another, by Walter Hamilton.

These indexes record entries relating to Robertson between 1909 (the year after Robertson went up) and 1924 (when he was a well-established economics don), with a large gap between 1913 and 1923 inclusive. Benson was renowned for the accuracy of his recall and, despite a weakness for sometimes recording gossip as fact, his impressions are to be relied upon as authentic (see Newsome, 1980, p. 6). The picture he paints of Robertson is consistent and unambiguous and centres on the stark contrast between Robertson's (outward) intellectual achievements and his (inward) emotional turmoil. Most important of all for present purposes is Benson's impression that Robertson, in the full flush of his young manhood and with honours thick upon his head, should feel so utterly bereft of hope and of purpose.

In the following sequence, references are given to Benson's diary (BDMC) by the relevant volume number and folio or page number. On Friday 3 December 1909 Benson went to tea with Robertson in his rooms at Trinity (Master of a college goes to tea with an undergraduate! Tea, incidentally, became Robertson's characteristic mode of entertainment, as against breakfast, lunch, sherry, dinner or supper). Benson found him: 'such a clever creature, son of R of Haileybury, acts in Wasps, gets every sort of prize and scholarship – yet is boyish and unaffected'. At the same time Benson was puzzled to find:

An odd melancholy discontented morbid strain in him – and a certain pleasure in introspective talk, most unlike what I should have expected from his mild and ingenuous (almost rabbit-like) face and gentle demeanour – he seemed dissatisfied and to be looking forward to nothing.   (v. 108 p. 63 BDMC)

A week later, on 10 December, the pair walked beside the river to Clayhithe, and again Benson noted the contrast:

Curious to find this brilliant and successful creature, who has just made such a success of the Wasps by his excellent acting bemoaning his futility and his introspective habit – his dissatisfaction with everything. I wonder what strange weakness lies behind it all.   (v. 108 f.75 BDMC)

Early in the New Year, Benson received some inkling of the extent of the problem after reading some poems Robertson had left for him. He also began to see that it stemmed from Robertson's make-up; that it was a product of his *temperament*:

They filled me with sorrow. I can't make out what the tragedy has been but there *has* been a tragedy. This dissatisfaction and unhappiness became plain to me. It makes me wretched to think of a creature suffering so, especially this extraordinarily able, brilliant and naturally ingenuous boy. I hope I may be able to do something, but I fear it may be *temperamental*. Why must these ghastly elements creep so insidiously into lives and burrow there like worms?   (v. 109 f. 64 BDMC; emphasis added)

On 7 February 1910 they again walked beside the river, Benson clearly expecting that they would be discussing Robertson's latest revelations. He was to be disappointed:

He had written me the most intimate letter, revealing the devastating emotions of his heart and soul, to which I had replied as kindly and straightforwardly as I knew how. And then the little wretch meets me with the face of a baa-lamb and is absolutely silent, takes up no subject, starts no hare, just murmurs politely – while I talk like a skipjack on a thousand things – till weariness of the world and life and my companion falls on me . . . what is the use of trying to make friends with the young if they leave you to do all the talking.   (v. 110 p. 1 BDMC)

There are three points of interest here. The first is Benson's use of zoological figures of speech in referring to Robertson. Here it is 'baa-lamb' but usually it is, as at their first recorded tea together, that Robertson is 'rabbit-like'. For example, on Friday 11 February 1910, Robertson 'came to dinner, like a little rabbit' (v. 110 f. 9 BDMC); in the spring of 1911, when Robertson 'called and had tea' he was again 'rabbit-like' (v. 120 f. 39 BDMC). Benson had certainly caught a characteristic feature; and Robertson's photograph, taken in later life and used by Lionel (Lord) Robbins in his autobiography (Robbins, 1971, facing p. 129) gives him unmistakably the appearance of a startled rabbit. The most important parallel here is with the White Rabbit in Lewis Carroll's *Alice's Adventures in Wonderland*, who is said to represent Carroll himself and who reappears in *Through the Looking Glass* in the guise of the White Knight. The significance of all this will become apparent in Chapters 10 and 11 below. Another reference is to Robertson's psychological problems; Robertson refers to these, following a distressing period when a long-standing malady caused problems in 1933, as the 'ghost-rabbit' which he thought was 'in his hutch again, though God knows whether he ought to be' (letter to Keynes, 22 October 1933, KPKC; quoted in Moggridge, 1992, p. 601d).

Second, this last is one of several of Benson's exasperated references to Robertson's refusal or inability to talk – or at least to sustain a conversation. Given his many public appearances at this time, together with his reputation in later years for good talk and 'effortless captivating wit' (Lee, 1963), Robertson's silences must be seen as a manifestation of his decision to reveal to Benson his desolate inner self – the self he kept hidden from the world at large and possibly revealed to no one else.

In October 1910 Robertson joined Benson for a 'quiet dinner in Hall' but 'his idea of company is to sit silent and wait till I speak. He raises no questions and drops everything promptly; and so one gets tired of jawing' (v. 116 f. 8 BDMC). Later, towards the end of the year, Benson confessed to having

> a curious half-psychological shrinking from him, and he simply can't or won't talk. He never starts a subject or continues it, and I don't see why I should be treated as a kind of *cow*, to be milked into a pail.   (v. 117 f. 28 BDMC)

Winning the Craven Scholarship seemed to raise him somewhat, for in 1911 he looked 'bigger and stronger', though the restoration of his power of conversation did little to please Benson who now found him 'didactic' (v. 119 f. 23 BDMC). The tonic worked only temporarily, however, and two entries in the spring spoke of Robertson as 'Rather silent, and never I think starting a subject' (v. 120 f. 39 BDMC); and as having 'views, and a clear mind and a power of expression, but his mind seems to be fatigued, and he drops a subject helplessly' (v. 121 pp. 4–5 BDMC). Again in February 1912 Robertson looked 'stronger and better' and Benson 'was glad to pick up an end with him' (v. 128 p. 29 BDMC); but a week later Benson found matters at dinner 'rather sticky, D.R. doesn't help things along' (v. 128 p. 34 BDMC).

It was the same in 1913 when Robertson had graduated and was engaged with his fellowship dissertation. On two occasions at dinner, in the spring and autumn respectively, Benson was still complaining that: 'D.R. is clever but it's rather *sticky* work talking to him. The cart suddenly halts in a rut and one can't get it on' (v. 137 p. 48 BDMC); and though Robertson was 'pleasant and in a way sprightly', he still had his 'intolerable habit of dropping everything sharply, so that it's rather wearisome to talk to him, because one has to bear the whole initiative' (v. 141 p. 11 BDMC).

It is worth dealing with this point at some length as it provides such a revealing picture of Robertson's other side, his private self, in stark contrast to the public figure and successful actor that everyone knew and loved.

The third point arising is in a sense complementary to the last: just as it was to Benson that Robertson presented his desolate emotional side in dumb-show, so it was to this most sympathetic confidant of attractive young men that Robertson progressively revealed himself in written form: first with the poems, then with the 'most intimate letter' (both in February 1910), before finally discarding the seventh veil in March 1910 with:

> a rather wild and hysterical note about himself and his tendencies – a surprise, I admit; but the curious daring frankness of the note amazed me even more. (v. 110 f. 51 BDMC)

By 'his tendencies' we may infer that Benson refers to Robertson's revelation that he was homosexual. This is probably the first direct intimation by Robertson of his innermost secret to any living soul. He had been preparing Benson for this, his great unburdening, but the older man was plainly surprised. Benson seems at no time to have made the connection between Robertson's 'tendencies' and the sense of tragedy, futility and hopelessness to which he gave expression.

This is possibly because Benson's own romantic feelings gave him plea-sure. He once said to Frank Salter that 'it is an ill time with one when one's pulse does not beat a *little* faster when someone draws near'; and later agreed with D.A. Winstanley that 'to be a Don and not to care romantically for the young men was a very chilly affair' (BDMC, April 1910, quoted in Newsome, 1980, p. 250). Earlier, in 1908, Benson had attended a King's 'Comby', an informal smoking concert put on by juniors in King's after Founder's Feast and attended by seniors, and was 'surprised (not shocked) at the openness of the display of affection between couples' (Wilkinson, 1980, p. 51).

But for Robertson, his 'Victorian' upbringing, the albatross of duty he forever wore round his neck, and the sense of impropriety in a society in which homosexuality was regarded as deviant and immoral – and was downright illegal – would have removed any sense of pleasure he might have felt at being a member of a smaller all-male world in which homoerotic feelings and even display were widespread and accepted. And we should recall that this was not the extent of Robertson's 'problem' but must be seen in the context of his loss of the faith in which he had been raised, and the loss of a sense of ultimate security as evidenced by the fragment 'The Curse of Electra'.

Also one wonders how many of the 'couples' witnessed by Benson in King's were merely passing through a phase, which would in time give way to more conventional sexual attachments and marriage. This, of course, is what happened with Keynes, who found conventional love and happy marriage after a cavalier and promiscuous homosexual career (see Moggridge, 1992, pp. 169–71, 214–16, 354, 838–9, pls 9, 10). For Robertson, one suspects that, in the pre-war world, a sense of pleasurable adventure was simply not possible: he was too much bound by the chains of the past. After the war, when his behaviour seems to have been more observably homosexual, his amorous pursuits could lead him into scrapes. David Newsome included Robertson in a list of those whom Benson castigated for making 'an exhibition of themselves in their search for romantic relationships [and who] all, at one time or another, had their knuckles rapped for falling victim to the seductive charms of boyish beauty' (Newsome, 1980, p. 367). How successful these adventures were is not recorded (see, however, Chapter 6, below), but ultimately Robertson was to settle for tea, talk, kindliness and wit.

The evidence regarding Robertson's private self afforded by Benson's diary is supported in a more oblique and allusive way by the poetry Robertson wrote at this time or later on reflection. This reveals an outlook shaped by the knowledge that life is short and that death is the end – there is no Hope of Glory; that the inability to find purpose and fulfilment in the face of death as extinction is a temperamental problem and, therefore, a personal tragedy; that there is tragedy also in the inability to find love – and here feelings of guilt about the reasons for this (homosexuality) introduce notions about a sense of sin to be expunged.

Also, at some stage, Robertson came to accept that the force of destiny (the weight of inherited characteristics) is too strong to be escaped by individual effort and individual choice and that, therefore, the shape of our lives is given – for better or worse.

Overall, there is a deterioration in Robertson's outlook as compared to his schooldays. Certainly, smug contentment and gentle wistfulness are gone; but so also is the robust determination 'To tread unfalteringly the bitter way'. Instead, there now yawns desolation and hopelessness. No matter how much he piled up academic success and won personal popularity, the necessity of coming to terms with the reality of his own nature – of being loveless – rather than romantically shedding 'the blinding tears of love' brought feelings of despair. There is also important confirmation of the shift of perspective towards (regressive) nostalgia for a lost golden past.

IV

Leaving aside the Chancellor's Medal poems, which were formal, public and written on set themes, the earliest undergraduate poem to survive among the

Robertson Papers at Trinity College, Cambridge, is 'A Sonnet of Dancing', dating from 1908, the year of matriculation. Although the suffering expressed is relieved by an admixture of romanticism, as with the Eton poems written only a year earlier, the references to 'despair', being 'desolate' and the 'wilderness within' seem particularly appropriate in the light of the Benson evidence:

> I drain this cup of strange experience,
> The body's rapture and the soul's slow ache
> Hark to the sudden sobbing of the flute,
> Comminglingly triumph with a fierce despair
> .   .   .
> And Oh my God! The wilderness within,
> The heart that worshipped and is desolate.
> (D9/1/23 RPTC)

From the pain of unrequited love (specific or generalised?), we turn to the subject of death and the comfort to be derived from the immortality of art. In 'In Memoriam GM and ACS', written in 1909, the year of Robertson's first recorded meeting with A.C. Benson, he mourns the death of George Meredith and Algernon Charles Swinburne but rejoices that the power of these two lovers of life to inspire and sustain is preserved in their poetry, even though the artists themselves have been vanquished by the grave. The importance of this poem for present purposes lies in its recognition of death as 'bleak oblivion' – not as the gateway to paradise – and of the transcending power of love and, therefore, the important part it plays in human life. Finally, we should notice that Robertson's admiration of Swinburne is relevant in the light of Keynes's reference to the poet, when chiding Robertson during their controversy over the *General Theory* (see below, Chapter 25):

> How have they left us desolate, and we
> Mourn for the grace and glory that have been.
> Yet not so desolate, if but some breath of Swinburne's flaming soul,
>   Some surge and swell
> Of Meredith's strong laughter linger still,
> Because the misanthrope, unlovely death,
> And frost of bleak oblivion cannot kill
> Those who have loved mankind and life so well.
> (D9/1/25 RPTC)

In 'Songs of Night and Day', written in 1910, Robertson returns to the insistent theme of unrequited love. Although the object of Robertson's yearning remains anonymous, the gnawing emptiness of a solitary night-time (night which 'should ease a lover's sorrow', see Housman, 1896, XI), seems more immediate and focused:

If there had been but a word from you
As the torn sun sank to bed,
Some whisper of hope that I heard from you
Some light, slight thing that you said!
But the sun sank and is dead.

If there had been but a thought from you
Borne on the wings of the night,
A cry that the wind had caught from you
A murmur of pain or delight!
But the stars are blank and bright.
(D9/1/26 RPTC)

The nature of the love for which he yearns is indicated by a poem entitled 'Communion'. It is undated but was included by Robertson in a collection he made for possible publication, under poems of 'Love' rather than of 'Religion'. In this poem Robertson seems to reflect the change of attitude towards homosexual love that was abroad in Cambridge from the first decade of the new century (see Wilkinson, 1980, p. 51). Centred on the Conversazione Society (the Apostles) and led by Lytton Strachey and Maynard Keynes (though Robertson was not elected until the 1920s), the appreciation of beautiful young men shifted from the cerebral, Platonic level to the more tangible and satisfying currency of physical consummation. In placing homoeroticism in a Christian liturgical setting, Robertson's poem has much in common with G.M. Hopkins's 'The Bugler's First Communion' and Wilfred Owen's 'Maundy Thursday'. The nature of the communion Robertson seeks is clear and reveals a familiarity with Church terminology that is wholly appropriate to a son of the vicarage:

Hands lay apart: lips never kissed:
There was no touching but of mind.
You gave me healing Eucharist,
But gave it only in one kind.

So though your thoughts walk bare with mine
I still must cry what church has said:
'Let there be served a little wine
As well as good white wheaten bread.'
(D9/3/7 RPTC)

With recognition of his true nature and its associated desires, there followed also a sense of guilt and sin together with a wish to be whole again. In 'Synthesis', printed in the *Cambridge Review* in February 1914 (see D9/4/3 RPTC), Robertson seems to express his belief in the unity, coherence and harmony of the universe. To the pattern that emerges, like a natural law, the individual must conform in order to be whole. Robertson sees himself excluded because of the flaw in his make-up, and by interpreting this flaw in terms of the Christian concept of sin (not unreasonably, given the times) he determines to seek 'redemption' by the renunciation of 'sin'.

This poem, retitled 'Synthesis – A Mood', was later included in the collection intended for possible publication in book form and is designated a poem of 'Religion'. As compared to the earlier, *Cambridge Review* version, Robertson has sought to reinforce the idea of there being a spirit of unity in all existence:

> The sundered members of the hyperbole
>> Are bended now towards a concentric round:
> The shattered mirror of my life grows whole,
>> The world's disordered beat serene and sound.
>
> He dances in the engine wheels, his hand
>> Is evident in the market and the mine,
> His is the laughter that can understand
>> The jests of drunken men for his the wine.
>> .   .   .
> Wherefore since one thing lingers yet within
>> Which for his vast embrace is yet too gross
> I will root out this body's gaping sin,
>> And build the broken curve, and clasp him close.
> (D9/3/24 RPTC)

V

That the natural harmony of all existence, the *anima mundi* that Robertson senses, owes nothing to a conventional Christian view of God is revealed by a poem published in the *Cambridge Review* in June 1914. 'Lines suggested by a Sermon on the Loss of the Empress of Ireland, 1914' was also included by Robertson in the collection destined for a possible slim volume and classified under poems of 'Religion'.

Here Robertson rejects the idea that one's safety on a sea voyage should be dependent on the whim of a God who is fickle enough to allow one shipload of passengers a safe passage while allowing another shipload to perish. Instead, the God in which Robertson would place his trust would be the product of intelligent contrivance: a well-found ship, equipped with all modern safety aids and officially inspected:

> But I (who do not understand)
> Should like to take this God in hand
>> .   .   .
> I'd like to build him out of boats

> And human arms and brains and throats,
> Give him a wireless voice and wings
> Covered with lights and bells and things,
> And pound him at the Board of Trade
> Until he's well and truly made.
> If I have got to go to sea
> That is the kind of God for me.
> (D9/3/22,23 RPTC)

But to reject the idea of a personal God, to whom representation can be made to sway the course of things, is to reject the idea that we live in a planned and directed universe. When Robertson lost the faith in which he had been raised he henceforth lived in a universe whose unity and harmony were but cold comfort in their indifference to his fate. If the natural processes represented a kind of certainty and continuity which were somehow reassuring in their freedom from discretionary power, they were at the same time unfeeling, inexorable and ultimately 'meaningless'.

What the 'Empress of Ireland' poem is actually saying is: would that it were so, that we *could* so order our lives; but as Robertson sought repeatedly to escape into a variety of new personae and found himself blocked at every turn, so he became increasingly fatalistic and placed increasing reliance on the only alternative avenue left to him: retreat into nostalgia, the myth of a golden past.

Robertson's view of the immutable power of fate and the entirely arbitrary, from the individual's point of view, distribution of attributes, is given in the last of the three poems he included in the 'Religion' section of the fair-copy collection. 'The Demiurge' (the creator of the world in Platonic philosophy) is undated but its uncompromising tone denotes it a poem of conviction and experience. It eloquently elaborates the notion of Robertson's 'Calvinism', of which he spoke in a letter to Keynes in August 1937 (17 August 1937, L/R/134, KPKC). It is worth quoting in its entirety:

> There sat a troll in his little den,
> Busily forging the souls of men:
> 'Hark!' said he, 'how my hammer rings!
> Some shall be beggars and some be kings.
>
> 'But whether he lives in pomp and pride,
> And sleeps by his chosen lady's side,
> Or whether he wanders in rags and mire,
> And frets with unfulfilled desire.
>
> 'None of them all, whate'er his state
> Can lose his nature and change his fate

Or buy his quittance or sell his soul,
- And that is the joke of it!' laughed the troll.
D9/3/25 RPTC)

To later observers as much as to Benson, to whom he directly communicated his distress, it must seem strange that Robertson, so well endowed intellectually, to whom academic success came easily and who gathered prizes 'as it were bread' (v. 120 f. 39 BDMC), should have felt bereft. Perhaps it was that Robertson privately discounted areas of his life in which success came easily, in comparison to areas in which he felt himself denied. In the face of the great indifference of the universe it was his inability to find love that hurt – and rankled most. See, for example, Robbins's insightful observation that Robertson was 'obviously craving affection' (1971, p. 221). It was one of Robertson's 'admirable' qualities, that despite his 'profound sense of the harshness of human destiny . . . he would never yield to cynicism or defeatism' (Butler, 1963, pp. 41–2). Nevertheless, it is all too plainly the case that Robertson believed that he had 'missed life's best', and in a poem that he set at the head of the little collection assembled in the copybook for possible publication he recognised the importance of love and the sense of loss its denial brought him. The evident absence of any hope beyond death makes the significance of the loss unmistakable:

> What shall we have to gaze upon
>   Whom Love passed by?
> The brows of brave men that we meet,
> The eyes of children in the street
>   And the large sky.
>   .   .   .
> What shall be given us to drink
>   Who craved Love's dreams?
> A bottleful of salted tears,
> And the rich juice of bruisèd years,
>   And quiet streams.
>
> How shall we win at length to sleep
>   Who missed Life's best?
> They weave us death who spun us birth;
> The winds accept us, and the earth
>   Shall yield us rest.
> (D9/3/3 RPTC)

Confirmation that the poem has the significance we have suggested is given by the title, in classical Greek. This can be translated as 'The Next Best Way' (as sailors use oars when they cannot use sails). It means that in his life Robertson pursued a second-best strategy: denied that which he most desired, he made the most of that which he could have.

VI

To solve the problem of the private self, Robertson sought the 'ideal' arrangement of his public self. Here the situation was complicated by the incessant
struggle between the inherited duteous self and the desired true self. At
university this conflict was personified by Robertson's attitudes towards
Trinity College and King's College respectively. To understand this it is
necessary to understand the differences in character between the two colleges:

> King's stood for the Muses *en masse*. It was reported in other colleges to have
> celebrated a Bump Supper by marching around the College singing the chorus from
> a Greek play. Even if the story was only *ben trovato*, no one . . . would have told it
> of any other college . . . King's looked up to Trinity as the great college it was.
> Much larger than the rest . . . it also had overwhelming academic superiority.
> (Wilkinson, 1980, p. 36: includes the report of a speech by G.M. Trevelyan, Master
> of Trinity)

These differences and the physical proximity of the two colleges brought forth
feelings of rivalry. George Rylands, who was an undergraduate at King's in
the 1920s and later an English don at the same college, remembers that
Kingsmen thought Trinity rather dry, severe and stiff – though academically
unchallengeable – whereas King's was more open, outgoing and liberal. 'We
were', he said, 'free spirits: artistic and literary and romantic' (interview,
17 February 1994). Apart from Ryland's Cambridge circle, centred around the
Marlowe Society and the ADC, there were links through both Rylands and
Keynes with Bloomsbury and the world of literature, painting and the ballet;
while in the previous generation there were Rupert Brooke and his circle, a
circle which represented poetry and the theatre and which gave birth to the
Marlowe Society.

In addition, King's was set apart – and the contrast would have seemed
particularly marked in Trinity – in that it was thought to have more in common
with an Oxford college. Rylands suggested that this view existed though he
considered that it was not in fact the case (interview, 17 February 1994). That
the view had currency, however, is confirmed by Wilkinson, who has noted
without demur that: 'Members of Oxford colleges seem to find it more akin to
theirs than do most other Cambridge colleges' (Wilkinson, 1980, p. ix).

Now we begin to see why King's would have been so congenial to
Robertson and why he would have spent so much time there before 1914 when
he was a 'King's metic'. The writer of the eulogistic article in the *Granta*
('Presidential Man') in 1911, when Robertson was at the apogee of his public
career, noted that: 'almost the only person who has really roused him to wrath
was the unfortunate creature who accused him of being Oxonian at heart'
(*Granta*, 21 October 1911, A3/2/1 RPTC). But how percipient was this

unknown observer! Robertson the published and prize-winning poet, the out-standingly talented amateur actor, who saw himself as at heart a free spirit – romantic and literary – was in this sense 'Oxonian', in the same way as King's.

As a member of Trinity with one foot in King's, Robertson was not at all unusual nor would he have felt out of place, for if the proximity and the differences between the two colleges caused feelings of rivalry, they also gave rise to strong connections and joint activities:

> The connections between King's and Trinity had long been close. Their members combined in the T.A.F., Chit-Chat and even Philatelic Clubs, and later in the Decemviri, a debating society. (Wilkinson, 1980, p. 35)

Of the last Robertson was certainly a member. In 1910 he rode one of the twelve runners in the Decemviri November Race Meeting. On this occasion the public Robertson was as conservative as ever, being mounted on the blood horse 'Union Jack' and wearing colours of red, white and blue (G11 RPTC).

We might also mention here the possibility that Robertson would believe King's to be a society more tolerant of homosexuality. As we have seen, King's had a reputation for overt and flamboyant homosexual behaviour (see also Wilkinson, 1980, *passim*) and Robertson may have thought that in such company the psychological strains upon him would have been less – or indeed, that here he might more readily receive communion in both kinds.

VII

Given Robertson's evident dissatisfaction with his lot in feeling that he had been denied membership of the college which he felt best reflected his nature, how was it that he found himself at Trinity? Received opinion is of no help. Hicks, for example, simply states that: 'A Classical scholarship at Trinity (Cambridge) followed naturally' (Hicks ed., 1966, p. 10). But in what sense did it follow 'naturally'? Eton's sister foundation at Cambridge was not Trinity but King's, and this could perhaps be said to be the natural destination for Eton boys, though the matter was by no means clear-cut:

> The old circle by which King's College was peopled exclusively by King's Scholars from Eton had long been broken by ... [Robertson's] time, and even when it existed there had been boys who had gone to other colleges, both at Oxford and Cambridge, either by choice or because there was no vacancy at King's ... Oppidans had always attended a variety of colleges in both universities.... (Hatfield to Fletcher, 1 December 1994)

However, there were reasons why Trinity could be seen as the more appropriate choice for Robertson. The first concerns the relative status of scholarships awarded at Trinity and King's. Although King's had admitted non-Etonians from the 1870s, the College still retained closed scholarships for Eton boys alone. Hence the award of an open scholarship at Trinity could have carried more prestige for the academically outstanding (especially given Trinity's academic reputation, as noted above). Such a suggestion would find support on both the Eton (Hatfield to Fletcher, 1 December 1994) and the King's sides. L.P. Wilkinson has noted that:

> The Etonians who came to Cambridge mostly joined one or other of these two Colleges. Indeed the cleverer ones tended to go to Trinity . . . For after the establishment of open scholarships it was natural for masters at the school who had an allegiance to neither to steer the brighter boys who wanted Cambridge through these to Trinity, leaving the close scholarships at King's as a cushion for the second best.   Wilkinson, 1980, pp. 35–6)

There was, second, the financial consideration. For an outstandingly able boy from a poor clergy family, the prospect of a major scholarship would have been a definite inducement. In addition, third, there was a family precedent. In 1899 Ainslie Robertson had won a major scholarship in classics to Trinity, had enjoyed a successful career there and had duly graduated with a first. If Ainslie could achieve success at proportionately smaller cost to the family budget, then the pressure was on Dennis to do the same.

VIII

The sense in which it would seem 'natural' for Robertson to go to Trinity should now be clear. What should also be clear is why, despite the College's eminence, he should resent his situation so bitterly and long to be elsewhere. In the circumstances of his going there Trinity came to represent the demands of duty, the constraint of external circumstance and, ultimately, the force of destiny from which he could not escape.

Robertson's resentment of Trinity and of duty is reflected in his resentment of Ainslie, who represented both of these. Ainslie was everything that Dennis was not and Dennis both envied and scorned him (see above, Chapter 3). Dennis's attitude to Ainslie is indicated by the amendments he made to the draft obituary that he prepared jointly with his niece Jean Bromley (he designated himself 'chief nagger to recording angel': see Al/21 RPTC). For example, where Jean Bromley had written that Ainslie had been 'Manager' of the Booth Line Steamship Co. Ltd, Robertson had queried this and suggested substitution of 'a manager', which was probably more accurate but also ensured that credit was not received where it wasn't due. Similarly, where Bromley has written that 'Substantial as his achievements were in the business world . . .', 'Substantial' has been replaced by 'Important' but then Robertson has suggested replacement by the rather deprecating 'Strenuous as were his labours . . .'.

The most interesting point concerns Robertson's comments about Ainslie's degree. In a few waspish lines he tells us that, though good, Ainslie is not in the same league as himself:

> Yes, he got a lst class all right. True it was in Part I; but in his day (and mine) Part I was a full 3-year, degree-giving exam, Part II only to be taken by aspirants for don-hood. True also the lst class was divided into 3 sub-classes, and he was a I,ii not a I,i. But a I,ii was a first all right!   (Robertson to Bromley, 14 May 1961, A1/21 RPTC)

Finally, in a letter to the Editor of the *Liverpool Daily Post*, Bromley writes that she doubts 'whether my late uncle, Sir Dennis H. Robertson of Trin. Coll., Cambridge, ever sent you the *curriculum vitae* which we prepared' (27 January 1965, RPTC): a curious oversight and one that is quite in keeping with Robertson's rather peevish attempts to tone down the record of achievement of someone who seems to have been very much the elder brother, very much his father's son.

But even as he raged at the circumstances and the 'fortune' that had forced him to accept them, his feelings of bitterness may have been intensified by the tension between the apparent possibility of escape into circumstances more in tune with his nature, and the suspicion that the possibility of escape was in fact a mirage. As life unfolded it would be made plain that he must live by his intellect and not by his art; and in any case duty was too powerful a keeper to be overthrown.

Like his contemporary A.E. Housman who, when young, had lived in Worcestershire (Bromsgrove) but looked towards Shropshire (see, for example, Housman to Martin in Maas ed., 1971, p. 347), so Robertson lived in Trinity but looked towards King's. In Housman's *A Shropshire Lad*, Shropshire became an idealised fantasy-land for whose 'blue remembered hills' Housman could yearn in his years of London exile. It was an image none the less potent because he knew that it was a 'land of lost content' to which he could escape only in his dreams (references to Housman, 1896, XL).

So it was with Robertson, who was always free to visit King's to observe the 'delightful people' and to walk those 'most beautiful acres in England'; but at the same time he could never aspire to the vision of escape it represented. King's was Robertson's fantasy-land, his 'land of lost content' and in this it represented the self he yearned for: the self he could never be.

IX

Robertson's year of greatest public success in Cambridge, 1911, followed almost in affirmation of the rightness of his decision to switch from classics to economics in 1910. 'Why did he move?' asks Hicks rhetorically, before answering:

> One can only conjecture, but it is not hard to conjecture. An intellectual, but with a conscience that rode him more strictly than those of most intellectuals, he sought the field for his talents where he could be of most service. (Hicks ed., 1966, p. 10)

There is evidence to show that this is at least part of the answer. Whatever information Hicks had obtained on his own account when researching the article, he had the written confirmation from Jean Bromley that:

> It is fact that social conscience led D. to the economics Tripos: 'to be useful' a constant preoccupation. (Bromley to Hicks, 19 September 1964, G11/6 RPTC)

There is also the evidence of A.C. Benson, who in August 1911 recorded in his diary that Jim (J.R.M.) Butler had told him that 'Robertson (D) was almost too tolerant, and had an immense idea of the value of work and the duty of service' (v. 123, p. 59 BDMC). Then we have the evidence of Butler himself that Robertson had a practical interest in social questions (Butler, 1963, p. 40). Finally, there is Dennison's comment that:

> there was increasing interest among the younger generation in economic and 'social' affairs with a desire to understand what was involved and possibly discover solutions to the many problems facing society. (Dennison, 1992b, p. 17)

We can certainly discern here the influence of Robertson's need to appease the demands of duty and what in modern parlance would be seen as a desire for 'relevance' in one's studies. In addition, such a move was by no means unprecedented, for Robertson was after all only one of several eminent economists who turned from the conventional paths of classics or mathematics to the young and exciting discipline of economics (for example, Marshall, Pigou, Keynes, Austin Robinson).

Nevertheless, in the light of the picture we have built up of Robertson, it is evident that this cannot be the whole answer. The switch involved *giving up classics* as much as it involved embracing economics, and in the context of Robertson's life the first had as much significance as the second. This was in fact Robertson's first attempt at escape. By 1910 he had, first, been taught classics at home by his underemployed father; then he had been taught classics for six years at Eton; then he had been supervised for two years as a classical scholar at Trinity. George Rylands, to whom Robertson was close in the 1920s, surmises that by that time one would have had enough and be ready for a change (interview, 17 February 1994). Unlike Austin Robinson, however, who rebelled against his college's requirement that he should adhere to the terms of his classics scholarship instead of pursuing his new interest in economics (in Moggridge ed., 1974, pp. 99–100), Robertson dutifully completed the course, like the blood horse he was. And this gives us the clue. By 1910, Robertson had done his duty: to his ex-classics-don father, who had similarly triumphed; to his school, where he excelled as a classicist; to his family, in treading dutifully in the footsteps of Ainslie (and obtaining a better degree); and finally to his college, for which he was a model and altogether outstanding student. Having thus *done* his duty, Robertson got out as early as he decently could.

But having thus escaped from the tunnel of duty in which he had been so long confined, whither should he turn? In striking out an independent line, with what persona should he clothe his public self in order to meet the urgings of his private self? In the struggle for his public self between duty and desire, duty prevailed and Robertson compromised: he would establish a new self but allow it to reflect notions of duty, usefulness, service and relevance to problems of the world. Art could be served on a part-time basis.

As a choice it must have seemed inspired. The evidence of the two great texts he studied over the summer of 1910, Adam Smith's *The Wealth of Nations* and Alfred Marshall's *Principles of Economics* (see Dennison, 1992b, p. 17), would convince him that he would find the subject congenial. Moreover, it would strengthen his links with King's, for his supervisor was to be J.M. Keynes. And the events of the following four years – a first in Part II of the Economics Tripos in 1912, the award of the Cobden Prize in 1913 and, to cap all, his appointment to a teaching fellowship in the subject in 1914 – would only serve to confirm his expectations.

Yet he *had* compromised, and the evidence of Robertson's continued unhappiness shows that, in failing to break clear of the chains which bound him by seeking to fulfil the desires of what he regarded as his true self, Robertson had done little to solve his problem. In truth he could not, though this would not be beyond doubt for almost two decades. Worse, the years would also reveal that his ideal compromise, his *modus vivendi* and principal intellectual activity, would at last turn out to be a false trail. Both because of changes in the nature of the subject itself and because of the Keynesian Revolution, his career as an economist would lead to the destruction of the safety barrier between his private self and his public self and hence to the immiseration of the latter.

X

But in the years before 1914 none of this was visible; and though Robertson must have known that he had not solved his problem and that he still yearned for the vision afforded by King's, he must also have comforted himself with the reflection that he had done the best he could, in all the circumstances: he had gone as far as he could go.

Following acceptance of the revised version of his dissertation, Robertson was elected to a fellowship at Trinity in 1914. It was indisputably a fitting climax to a scintillating career at school and university and even Robertson was able to hint at a sense of achievement:

> – re fellowship. It's satisfactory to know one has done a decent job of work. I'll let you know if I have any report of it. The market was lightened by young Thompson (J.J.'s son) [J.J. Thompson: eminent Cambridge physicist] going to Corpus (en route for the army!) but I dare say there was some competition. (Dennis Robertson to Ainslie Robertson, 14 October 1914, Al/13/2 RPTC)

When Housman was elected to a fellowship at Trinity, on being appointed Kennedy Professor of Latin in the University in 1911, he thanked his new colleagues for the honour they had done him by recalling the words of Lord Macauley concerning the eminence of the office:

> Macauley used to rank a Fellow of Trinity somewhere in the neighbourhood of the Pope and the Holy Roman Emperor: I forget the exact order of the three, but I know that the King of Rome was lower down, and His Most Christian Majesty of France quite out of sight. (A.E. Housman to H.M. Innes, 21 January 1911; quoted in Page, 1983, pp. 94, 219n. Not included in Maas ed., 1971)

Robertson's election was announced in *The Times* for 13 October 1914. On the cutting which he kept he wrote: 'was admitted in uniform – with sword' (G11, RPTC). For, following the outbreak of World War I in August, Robertson was already in the army and his career as a don was postponed for the duration. In the event he had to wait five years before beginning his life as a senior member of the College, but unless we deal with the fact of his election at this juncture the significance of the timing will be lost. Like the true scholar he was, however, he took care to lay the foundations of that life even in the midst of war. He wrote up his dissertation for publication and it duly appeared, destined to become a classic, as *A Study of Industrial Fluctuation* (Robertson, 1915). He also abstracted some of the results of his research for a paper which he read before the Royal Statistical Society and which was then published in the Society's *Journal* (Robertson, 1914).

Nevertheless, it was the war that was to dominate his immediate future and it was the war that constituted the next important phase of his life.

5. A good war

As with his acting career, commentators have expressed surprise and some amusement at the apparent incongruity of one of Robertson's temperament having volunteered for military service. 'Enlistment', said Dennison, 'was perhaps unusual for somebody so unmartial and gentle' (Dennison, 1992b, p. 20).

Both Dennison and Hicks also reported that in the period prior to the war Robertson was simultaneously a member of the Officer Training Corp (OTC) and of the Cambridge University [anti-war] War and Peace Society. Hicks's information came from a letter from Jean Bromley in which she says that her father (Ainslie) had reminded her that 'Dennis was a pacifist demonstrating in Trafalgar Square' (19 September 1964, G11/6 RPTC). Stanley Dennison indicates the extent of Robertson's involvement as being more than perfunctory, in that he represented the War and Peace Society at a conference at Le Touquet organised by Norman Angell (Dennison, 1992b, p. 20). Robertson himself provided clear evidence of his commitment to the cause. On the day after war was declared he wrote to his brother Ainslie that:

> I was working tooth and nail up till mid-day yesterday for neutrality – lobbying in the H of C [House of Commons], getting up the Belgium neutrality problem with Charles Trevelyan, thinking Editors, wringing money from rich men etc. I believe even now my heart is with Morley.   (5 August 1914, A1/13/5 RPTC)

He was later to provide the same correspondent with a list of reasons justifying his chosen course of action (see the letter of 3 February 1916, A1/13/5 RPTC).

J.R.M. Butler attempted to resolve the apparent contradiction implied by these disparate loyalties by seeing Robertson as being against war and working actively for peace, while preparing to do what was contrary to his nature in the face of the inevitable:

> No one could have hated militarism more whole-heartedly or looked less soldierly, but he prepared himself for the impending war by joining the cavalry squadron of the OTC. . . .   (Butler, 1963, p. 20)

But what curious behaviour. Surely the proper course for such a person as

Butler depicts would have been service with the Friends' Ambulance Unit when the occasion arose (like his colleague A.C. Pigou) rather than training for the army in peacetime. Butler's assessment reads like a neat *ex post* rationalisation that is at one with received opinion: that Robertson's call to arms was both incomprehensible and slightly ridiculous. In fact it was neither of these, as we shall see.

With respect to appearance, Robertson's photograph in uniform in 1915 shows him as a quite dashing figure (with moustache) and with an authentic subaltern's bearing. The impression is borne out by a later photograph of February 1918 in which he appears, mounted, with his brother officers under the Middle Eastern sun. Rather than the somewhat comical figure that even friendly commentators delight to paint him, Robertson was to prove himself an effective and courageous officer (though, it must be admitted, one who never rose above junior rank).

Also, although it is possibly correct that Robertson joined the OTC to prepare himself for the 'impending war', we should notice that his amateur soldiering began some time before war was actually imminent. He had, in fact, been a member of the OTC since at least 1911 (see the article in *Granta*, 21 October 1911, A3/2/1 RPTC, which speaks of him as 'an enthusiastic cavalry-man'). Subsequently there is a letter to his mother showing him involved in summer manoeuvres in 1912: 'We slept in barns' (7 September 1912, A4/3/4–5 RPTC); and A.C. Benson reports that he came across him mounted on 'a roaring horse' whilst taking part in a practice battle in November of the same year (v. 134, p. 27, 26 November 1912, BDMC).

Might we not see this equestrian sequence as being of a piece with his riding in the Decemviri steeple-chase as early as November 1910? In other words is there not justification for regarding his training with the OTC as more than a precautionary measure? Was it not in fact another of Robertson's exploratory attempts at escape – or at least one of his ameliorant adventures? The *Granta*'s description of him not as a reluctant hero but as an *enthusiastic* cavalryman gives us the clue. Also Butler admits that Robertson 'enjoyed the humours of camp' (Butler, 1963, p. 41); his letter to his mother of September 1912 shows him tired but happy (A4/3/4–5 RPTC). Finally, in celebration of what in later years Robertson would come to regard nostalgically as a golden episode, he wrote a long elegiac poem, 'Salisbury Plain, 1912', in which elements both of adventure as release from the quotidian and of preparing oneself to do one's duty find their place – *and in which the former predominates*. Note, however, how Robertson recognises that, as escape, the army can be no more than a diversion, a leaven, and that, as noted in the previous chapter, it is by his intellect that he must both live and make his contribution to life:

How will it be when we are middle-aged
A dozen years ahead . . .

.   .   .

Shall we forget in those prosaic days
How we rode forth our amateurish ways
And stormed the folly-wood and held that bridge
And charged a convoy from that distant ridge?

.   .   .

Surely peace claims us first:
Yet if fate send the worst
And the shrapnel-cloud of madness burst
Out of the leaden sky,
Who knows that even I
Who am fitter to work for England with my brain
And think for her and write for her
Than ride for her and fight for her,
May not come forth and join you once again
In memory of those days upon the plain? .
(In copy-book, D9/3/8 RPTC; emphasis added)

And this was the formula that was repeated on a larger scale in the war: observance of the requirements of duty, in company with a sense of adventure; a means of escape for a captive free spirit.

Interestingly it is Hicks, the Robertson biographer who gives the impression of having had the role thrust upon him, who explicitly mentions the commonplace idea of Robertson's war service as providing the opportunity 'to satisfy his sense of duty' (Hicks ed., 1966, p. 12). On the other hand, it was George Rylands, the King'sman, who was very close to Robertson in the 1920s, who independently confirmed the notion of Robertson's military career as being, in part, a romantic episode: a big adventure (interview, 17 February 1994).

There is support for this idea in an article Robertson contributed to *War and Peace* in March 1915: 'A Reminiscence by a Territorial Officer', in which he reviewed attitudes to war and suggested reasons why it might seem attractive:

If you want to kill for ever the itching for war, you must try to make peace a little less respectable and more spirited. For all your fine metaphor, a self-acting machine is *not* such fun to handle as a rifle, nor a Guardians' [Poor Law] meeting so exciting as a bayonet charge. To many thousands active service with all its discomforts and horrors comes in the guise of a welcome relief from the uncongenial slavery of the counting-house and the factory. You must enquire whether desire for *adventure* as compared with desire for *domination* does not play a much larger part than you had realised in that very complex attitude of mind which you describe rather perfunctorily as 'militarism'. (D5/4/1 RPTC; emphasis in original)

This piece also shows, incidentally, evidence of Robertson's open-eyed realism regarding human (including economic) behaviour.

II

One writer, Sir Frank Lee, has claimed that the experience of two wars left Robertson with 'a sense of tragic waste and loss' (Lee, 1963, p. 312; see also Chapter 1 above). But as our argument has developed it has become clear that such feelings stem from other, inward, causes and all the available evidence indicates that, at least in the case of his active-service war, 1914–19, the period of hostilities acted as a sort of tonic and in some respects seems to have eased his symptoms.

This outcome would not have been possible if Robertson had not had a good war, and in this respect Hicks was not a million miles from the truth when he qualified his statement that the war enabled Robertson 'to satisfy his sense of duty' with the observation that circumstances enabled him to obtain satisfaction 'without continual danger' (Hicks ed., 1966, p. 12).

These circumstances were a combination of the nature of his duties, namely, transport officer, and good luck in his service postings. Although it was not uncommon for army transport to be under fire, personnel were not as a matter of course placed in direct contact with the enemy. Second, Robertson was exceptionally lucky in being sent to secondary theatres where casualties were relatively light. In combination this meant that Robertson avoided the trenches of the Western Front, because his regiment was chosen to reinforce the Gallipoli operation; but he then avoided the carnage at Suvla Bay by being detained in England with the transport. On joining the 'remnants' of his regiment in Egypt, he was lucky not to be included in detachments from the Egyptian Expeditionary Force sent to take part in the ill-fated Nivelle Offensive in France; or to be sent to Mesopotamia, so that he not only avoided the drawn-out horror of Kut el Amara but also the abortive attempts at its relief. This last was a distinct possibility, as a letter from his sister Gerda makes clear (22 March 1916, A1/11/16 RPTC).

Nevertheless, he still saw action – on a manageable scale – and was even awarded a very respectable decoration for the part he played. Overall, he acquitted himself honourably and well and returned with his physical and mental capacities unimpaired. As usual with Robertson, however, success was not unqualified and along with his honours and happy associations he retained his doubts.

For present purposes a detailed history of Robertson's war service would be inappropriate. Instead, we can focus here on three episodes as illustrative of the experience of war as a factor in Robertson's life and outlook. These are: (a) enlistment; (b) his brush with the Civil Service; (c) the award of the Military Cross.

III

With respect to the circumstances of his joining up, received opinion has Robertson preparing himself for war by training as a cavalryman before making the curious transition on the outbreak of war to service with an infantry regiment – and not even then, to say the least, one of the most famous:

> on 4 August 1914, he . . . enlisted as second lieutenant in the 11th Battalion of the London Regiment (Finsbury Rifles). (Dennison, 1992b, p. 19)

The assumption is apparently that all is explained by the fact that he subsequently served as Battalion Transport Officer. But it all seems rather bathetic after 'those days upon the plain', in which he 'rode forth' and 'charged a convoy from that distant ridge' ('Salisbury Plain', 1912, in D9/3/8 RPTC).

What becomes clear is that Robertson received his posting due to a combination of circumstances: his own indecision due to conflicting advice from his family (see his letter to Ainslie of 14 October 1914, A1/13/2 RPTC) together with the intransigence of the military authorities:

> The War Office bungled my commission, and sternly refused to make amends. So here I am, horseless, with one of the more mediocre London territorial battalions. (Letter to Keynes, 19 November 1914, L/R/6 KPKC)

The Finsbury Rifles, the 1/11th Battalion of the London Regiment, were a battalion of the 2nd (London) Territorial Division. Their drill-hall was in Penton Road, near to Pentonville Prison, and these Saturday-night soldiers were locally, and alliteratively, known as 'The Pentonville Pissers' (Carver, 1978, p. 5).

It did not seem an auspicious beginning for a member of the Cambridge University Cavalry Squadron and at first it was an uphill struggle. As Battalion Transport Officer he wrote to Ainslie:

> trying to get level with the heritage of weeks of incompetence and neglect and lack of discipline . . . the animals [are] a 'sorry menagerie' at present due to skin diseases and lameness of various kinds. . . . (23 February 1915, A1/13/3 RPTC)

Conflicts of temperament brought forth irony. To Ainslie he wrote in May: 'I do most genuinely love my cockneys, or most of them – such gentlemen, and so alive' (9 May 1915, A1/13/4 RPTC). However, Robertson's attitude to 'the Regiment' softened as time went on and whenever separated from it on other duties was eager for news of its fortunes (see the letters to his mother of 19 October and 17 November 1917, A4/3/4-5 RPTC).

IV

The course of Robertson's war was shaped by changes in the British Order of Battle. In 1915 the 2nd (London) Division was broken up. One brigade was sent to France but the brigade of which the 1/11th Battalion was a part (the 162nd) became part of the 54th (East Anglian) Territorial Division, which was based at Hatfield (see Becke, 1936, pp. 128–31). It was here that Robertson remained when troops of the Division left for Gallipoli in the summer. Here he had leisure to deal with pre-publication queries regarding his forthcoming book (*A Study of Industrial Fluctuation*) and to extend an invitation to Keynes to visit 'this jolly place' for a 'walk' and 'lunch and tea' (letter, 6 June 1915, L/R/8–9 KPKC).

Over Christmas he was in hospital, ill with jaundice, but fully expected after recovery and leave to rejoin 'the remnants of my regiment, now in Egypt' (letter to Keynes, 13 January 1916, L/R/10–11 KPKC). In February, however, he was whisked away to work in the Ministry of Munitions. It is clear from a letter from one of his men, Sergeant J.A. Kendrick, that the move was unexpected and unsettling:

> it is getting very trying after the other units going, and then for you to have to leave us so suddenly. I must admit I personally do not feel the same as when you were here. . . . (14 February 1916, A4/2/9 RPTC)

To Robertson also it came as a shock. On 28 February, when he was at last at sea and on his way to Alexandria, he wrote to Gertrude Spooner, devoted family servant: 'I daresay you will have heard . . . that I had another unexpected week at home, which was nice, though it was not a very quiet one' (28 February 1916, A1/5/7 RPTC). However, a motherly letter from his sister Gerda to Ainslie Robertson gives a somewhat less bland view of events and one, most likely, nearer to the truth:

> the Army Council has overridden the M of M and allowed him to go . . . Anyhow his conscience is now clear, which with him I suppose is the only thing that really matters; but of course the other work would have been extremely interesting, as he saw from his day at it yesterday and [he] knows he would have done it well. He says he has lived years in this week and you never saw such a harassed face. . . . (17 February 1916, A1/13/7 RPTC)

And there are, of course, no prizes for guessing why that was. While Ministry work would have satisfied the needs of the most devoutly duteous, it could not provide the element of escape that Robertson needed to balance his more conventional side. No matter how 'interesting' the 'other work' was (was an attempt made to mollify the recalcitrant?), Robertson could only have felt stifled. Though he served in the Treasury in the 1939–45 war, he was then much older and decidedly 'unmartial', and even then it was not a very satisfactory episode (see below, Chapter 7).

In 1916 things were very different and escape was still a possibility. Faced with the routine of the Civil Service Robertson fled back to the army. Like General Charles George ('Chinese') Gordon, who preferred to face fever-ridden swamps and rebel armies rather than the dining-tables of London hostesses, so Robertson opted for sand-flies and bullets – and the 'animal work' he found so fulfilling – rather than tolerate committee rooms, calculations and inter-office memos. This was, of course, the same Robertson who in later years only agreed to serve on public committees with great reluctance and after much persuasion and who got out as quickly as he could.

The experience took its toll, as a letter from Gerda to Ainslie makes plain:

> I can't begin to describe yesterday but from this letter you will gather what sort of state he was in! However, we did our best to enliven him and S [Sheila, Robertson's other sister] and I conducted him dressed in packs, – water bottle, pistol etc etc to the train 12 midnight at Paddington. We soon found the section and Kendrick awaiting him, and as he approached along the platform they struck up three cheers for him, which must have helped him, – and touched his old sisters greatly. They were genuinely elated to see him and said they had felt no heart in going – So he went off into the night. . . .   (18 February 1916, Al/13/8 RPTC)

He was 'off' to Devonport, en route for Alexandria and service in Egypt. Whether his conscience really was clear by this time is a moot point. A letter written after his arrival hints at the need for self-justification. Robertson contrasts his own life of ease with the pressured world of Whitehall and blames his decision to escape on 'a system that orders one's life remorselessly in the smallest detail, and then suddenly leaves one with a power of choice which one doesn't want and has almost forgotten how to use' (letter to Ainslie, 7 March 1916, Al/13/9 RPTC).

Robertson then moved to Mena Camp near Cairo to rejoin his regiment (see letter to Ainslie, 24 March 1916, A1/13/10 RPTC). At the beginning of April the 54th Division took over the southern section of the Suez Canal Defences (the 162nd Brigade at El Kubri, north of Suez; see Carver, 1978, p. 21; Becke, 1936, p. 131). The letter Robertson wrote to Keynes shortly afterwards reveals how strong an aftertaste the Whitehall episode had left. It expresses feelings both of relief and of resentment – not unmixed with guilt at having escaped so precipitately from what was clearly a summons to public duty:

> one can enjoy oneself quite a lot; and I came out with such rage and bitterness in my heart for various reasons that I was determined to! . . . Such distractions [as Cairo and Gizeh, Sakhbara etc.] have so far kept at bay the feelings of disappointment at finding that (1) my transport job and therefore (2) the company

of my 35 selected ruffians which were the deciding factors in making me reject the solicitations of the Hotel Metropole [Civil Service], are a wash-out in this land of camels and light railways . . . and I am beginning to feel rather bitter at finding myself again a sweating and rather out-of-date platoon commander, with 8 months seniority and experience lost.

However nobody with life [and] a full complement of limbs intact has much to complain of these days; and I am almost boredom proof now . . . only feeling a little guilty when I think of all of you who are working your eyes out in London, as well as the concentrated hell of the last few weeks in France.   (7 April 1916, L/R 14–15 KPKC)

Robertson felt 'rather out-of-date' because while he was detained at home the action at Suvla Bay had changed the make-up of the 'regiment'; though he had missed the danger he had also lost the opportunity for advancement:

It is queer coming back to the regiment, – rather like going back to Eton and finding one's fag in Pop etc: most of my particular friends are killed or invalided home.   (7 April 1916, L/R 14–15 KPKC)

It is also clear that he felt disorientated at having been deprived of the anchor of his new life: the contact with animals that his transport work had involved:

One misses terribly the animal work which is always real work and a guarantee of not getting far from commonsense, however remotely connected with beating Germans.   (7 April 1916, L/R 14–15 KPKC)

By August, however, matters had improved. Robertson again had his transport job and with it his link with reality:

I continue to live the life of a combined country squire and Carter Patterson agent . . . on the longer moves I acquire suzerainty over some score of camels, but meanwhile find that detailed attention to leather, wood and the muline digestion, not to mention the Cockney temperament gives quite a good deal of work in this climate and successfully plugs the loopholes of thought. But now and again one feels both unheroic and useless to a rare degree . . . One reads as in a dream of events in France. . . .   (Robertson to Keynes, 15 August 1916, L/R 16–17 KPKC)

Nevertheless, Robertson could feel reassured that the civilisation they were fighting to preserve continued unimpaired, with Quails à la Möise and strawberries on the menu for 'a very pleasant O.E. [Old Etonian] dinner for the 4th of June' (Robertson to Keynes, 15 August 1916, L/R 16–17 KPKC).

At this time also the battle of Romani removed any direct threat to the Suez Canal and marked the beginning of the Turkish withdrawal into Palestine. In March of the following year the Turks established themselves on a defensive line from Gaza to Beersheba, and the British attempts to dislodge them from this position determined Robertson's war for 1917.

V

There were three battles of Gaza: in March, April and October–November 1917. Robertson took part in all three in his role as transport officer (latterly for a machine-gun company) and for his exploits in the first battle, officially dated as 26 and 27 March (see Becke, 1936, p. 131), he was awarded the Military Cross (MC). In considering the award it will help to bear two points very clearly in mind: the difficulties of the transport work itself, and the vital strategic importance of the commodities transported, particularly water. With respect to the first, animal transport presented its own peculiar challenges. Michael (Field Marshal Lord) Carver in his biography of Allan (Field Marshal Lord) Harding (Harding served with Robertson and became a lifelong friend) describes an incident in the campaign as follows:

> Harding's machine-gun company consisted of four sections, each of four Vickers machine-guns. Their transport was provided by mules brought from the Argentine, while the supply transport was provided by camels. The mules greatly disliked the camels and, to avoid trouble, were normally kept up wind of them. On the final night march they found themselves downwind of a supply column going in the opposite direction. Chaos ensued as the mules scattered over the desert but they were reassembled and 162 Brigade had its machine-guns in time for the start of the battle. (Carver, 1978, p. 24)

Carver is also explicit about the importance of the availability of water as a determinant of events in a desert region. In planning the attack on Gaza, for example, it was decided that if the town had not fallen by nightfall the attack should be called off, both because Turkish reinforcements were approaching but also because 'water . . . would only be available for men and horses alike if Gaza itself, with its wells, were captured' Carver, 1978, p. 25; see also pp. 28, 29).

The reason it is necessary to keep these points before us is that in dealing with the matter of Robertson's award of the MC writers have either been reticent or dismissive. Dennison, his staunchest champion, merely records that 'He had been awarded the Military Cross earlier in the year' (Dennison, 1992b, p. 22). Sir Frank Lee and Austin Robinson make no reference to the award. On the other hand, Hicks, tight-lipped, concedes that: 'There were moments of danger for one of which he was awarded the Military Cross' (Hicks ed., 1966, p. 12). H.G. Johnson notes that: 'He had served in the First World War and been awarded the Military Cross though nobody ever spoke about this and I never found out for what act of valour he received it. It certainly was not anything he ever talked about (Johnson and Johnson, 1978, p. 136). Unusually, Samuelson reports the award without qualification and very interestingly draws attention to a point mentioned by no one else:

> He was awarded the Military Cross, and according to rumor [*sic*], came close to
> receiving the Victoria Cross.   (Samuelson, 1963, p. 519)

The interest of this point is that in 1917 Robertson's manner of informing
his family of the MC caused confusion, and subsequent letters find him
apologising shamefacedly for leaving open the possibility that it might have
been 'a VC or a DSO' (letter to Ainslie, 9 July 1917, A1/13/13 RPTC; see also
the letter to Gerda, 24 May 1917, A4/1/9 RPTC).

J.R.M. Butler, as though entering into a private joke with his departed
friend, recalls that:

> he was given charge as battalion Transport Officer of a motley 'circus' of mules,
> camels and donkeys and for his distinguished work in this capacity he was awarded
> the MC – a fact which in after life he did his best to conceal.   (Butler, 1963, p. 41)

One feels there should be at least three exclamation marks at the end of that.
But in fact the suggestion of concealment appears to be more than polite
affectation. Jean Bromley, in chiding Hicks for his lack of generosity in
dealing with the affair, also refers to it:

> Father [Ainslie] considers D's war service was more heroic than you make it sounds
> [*sic*], and he acted with great bravery in bringing up water to front lines, for which
> he was awarded the MC (D himself never referred to this).   (19 September 1964,
> G11/6 RPTC)

There is also the evidence of Robertson's *Who's Who* entry for 1963, in which
no mention is made of the award. This, of course, would be compiled from
information chosen and supplied by Robertson himself. The item is, however,
included in the entry in *Who Was Who, 1961-1970* and it is clear from the
difference in print colour that an extra paragraph has been added to the entry
by an unknown contributor, who has wrongly dated the award to 1916.

Why did Robertson seek to conceal a signal honour? Modesty may have
played a part but the probability is that it had something to do with the grounds
upon which the award had been made. Shortly after the news reached him he
wrote to Gerda:

> You will have heard by now of my birthday present . . . and will know better than
> most how hot and uncomfortable I have been feeling these two days, and with what
> regrets for things left undone and false impressions given; and how truthfully I
> should like to be able to pass it quietly on to the doers and endurers of some of the
> things I have seen and heard of the last two months. . . . (24 May 1917, A4/1/9
> RPTC)

That justification in some sense seemed called for, is shown by a letter from
Sergeant Kendrick in which he testifies that he 'can positively state of his

pluck and daring' in leading a camel water-convoy to the relief of the Battalion:

> with great risk and nerve strain almost to breaking point he succeeded in reaching the new area of our boys sometime before midday – to find every bottle empty and everyone praying for one of the greatest necessities in the country, namely 'Water'. (Kendrick to Constance Robertson, A4/1/8 RPTC)

The official citation was published in a supplement to the *London Gazette* of 14 August 1917. It read:

> For conspicuous gallantry and devotion to duty. As regimental transport officer he took the supply of food, water and ammunition into his own hands and organised it with the greatest success, working day and night with most untiring energy and showing complete disregard for fatigue or personal discomfort.   (4th Supplement, 16 August 1917, to *London Gazette* of Tuesday, 14 August 1917, p. 8381)

Here was ample recognition that Robertson had done his duty honourably and well but perhaps he feared it did not quite have the ring of martial zeal that would be expected – as, for example, the citation for the award of the MC to the war poet Wilfred Owen undoubtedly did:

> For conspicuous gallantry and devotion to duty in the attack on the Fonsomme Line on 1st/2nd October 1918. On the Company Commander becoming a casualty, he assumed command and showed fine leadership and resisted a heavy counter attack. He personally manipulated a captured enemy MG [machine-gun] from an isolated position and inflicted considerable losses on the enemy. Throughout he behaved most gallantly.   (Document reproduced in Hibberd, 1992, p. 174)

If the two citations could have been exchanged it might have pleased Robertson and also Owen's family. That this is true of the latter is confirmed by the presence of a falsified version of the citation among the family papers, which makes Wilfred's act of gallantry appear less bloodthirsty and more in keeping with his mother's vision of him as a Christian gentleman (see document reproduced in Hibberd, 1992, p. 174. The falsified version is quoted as genuine by Bell ed., 1985, p. 351 n.2)

VI

Finally, as further support for the argument pursued here that Robertson's 'sense of tragic waste and loss' (Lee, 1963, p. 312) did not derive from his years of active service, we might note the way in which he recalled them in after years. In addition to the warmth of the letters he exchanged with some of the men with whom he served, his relationship with George Rylands in the

1920s included a holiday in Egypt to see the sights, together with fond reminiscences of life lived camping in a wadi (interview, 17 February 1994).

Most potently there is the poem 'Retrospect Gaza, March–April 1917', which, according to a note he appended to it, he wrote in 1931. The dating in the title indicates that it refers to the First and Second Battles of Gaza. There are five stanzas, two of which will illustrate both the strengths and the limitations of Robertson's versifying and the mixture of danger, beauty and adventure that predominated in his memories. Overall the effect is warm and nostalgic:

> I wish I could hear them again tonight
> Those sounds so harsh and sweet:
> The yelp of the guns that lurked unseen,
> And the chant of the homesick fellaheen,
> And the deadly raider's droning flight
> And the plash of camel-feet.
>   .   .   .
> But I'm glad that I felt it even I,
> – The thrill as we left the sand
> At four o'clock on a breathless morn,
> And rode amid poppies and standing corn,
> And crossed, as the sun shot up the sky,
> The edge of the Promised Land.
> (In copy-book: final corrected version, D9/3/16 verso RPTC)

With whatever qualification, Robertson's military service satisfied most of his criteria for success and happiness. There was the sense of duty well performed combined with the care and comradeship of men, together with the element of escape involved in the romance of faraway places and the thrill of adventure. With the war into its final year, his 'moments of danger' behind him and before the doubts about the course of his future life began to nag, Robertson caught the essence of the whole experience in a letter to Ainslie:

> The days slip by and here I am still in kindly Cairo . . . A wonderful country. I have had a pretty good time in this war!   (27 January 1918, Al/13/16 RPTC)

6. Infirm glory

I

As the war went on, Robertson began to give thought to the time when its protective bonds would be loosened and he would be left to shape his own destiny. He had evidently had misgivings about the post-war implications of his work for neutrality since early 1916 (see the letter to Ainslie, 3 February 1916, Al/13/5 RPTC). Later, however, it was the question of the career itself that gave cause for concern, as his correspondence shows. Perhaps the most interesting finding is that it was by no means a foregone conclusion that he would go back to Cambridge or even that his future would lie in the academic sphere. Note the considerable emphasis laid on the scale and regularity of remuneration as criteria. In May 1917 Gerda wrote to him:

> I can't help you over it because if you are vague as to what your future is tied up in I am much vaguer. But I shouldn't have thought you got £300 from Trinity nowadays. (6 May 1917, Al/11/20 RPTC)

In December 1918 he told Gerda that he was 'still in the dark' about his future (8 December 1918 A1/11/23 RPTC) and even by the end of March 1919, when peace was more than four months old, all was doubt and speculation:

> I simply can't pledge myself to go to Cambridge without knowing if there is a prospect of an assured income there, and would rather look for a regularly (if not extravagantly!) paid job under the WEA, and live in London. (30 March 1919, Al/11/24 RPTC)

By this time he was with the army of occupation in Constantinople, centre of the defeated Ottoman Empire. But most extraordinary of all, with demobilisation well advanced and Robertson's own release in sight, he had still not settled on what to do. In April 1919 he wrote to Ainslie:

> May begin starting to get away in a week or two . . . but going to be a *very* slow business . . . I don't know any more what to do when I get back to England – and don't much care, I've had no single word from any living soul at Trinity! (20 April 1919, Al/13/19 RPTC)

If Robertson were contemplating escape from past associations, the fluid conditions at the war's end would provide the ideal opportunity. No positive ideas are expressed, however, and the tone is one of resignation. Perhaps inevitably, therefore, he did go back to Trinity and to all the duteous obligations it represented, both past and future. A College memoir of 1957 says that he returned in the summer of 1919 (*Trinity Review*, 1957, p. 23; copy in G11/5) and he at last took up the fellowship he had won five years before. College teaching began with the Michaelmas term, and in November he wrote to Gerda: 'I lectured this morning inter alia on emigration to the colonies' (20 November 1919, Al/11/26 RPTC).

Robertson was back where he belonged. What was to follow was a decade of developments, which, in broad terms, were predictable on the basis of trends we discerned earlier. While Robertson would continue to enjoy academic success and to receive acclaim for his appearances on the amateur stage, he would also experience emotional turmoil and feel the elusiveness of love. There would be attempts at escape, both as a palliative to provide temporary relief (successful); and, possibly, as a more permanent solution to his life's problems (unsuccessful).

We shall examine the characteristic features of Robertson's life in the 1920s, as a follow-through of the formative influences identified earlier and as factors relevant to an understanding of Robertson's approach to economics. These, together with the literary evidence explored in Part II, will provide the basis for the exposition and interpretation of Robertson's contributions to the theory of fluctuations and money, which were the principal product of the period, which form the subject matter of Parts III and IV.

II

It must always be borne in mind that intellectual achievement came easily to Robertson: he could not have accomplished what he did if it were not so. This facility allowed him to reconcile the demands of duty – to concern himself with matters he genuinely thought were important and useful – with the promptings of desire. He was thus able to maintain a substantial flow of high-quality work, while at the same time keeping up other activities to compensate for the feeling that, aesthetically, economics left much to be desired.

This was of particular importance in the decade following Robertson's return to Cambridge in 1919, during which he continued to make positive contributions to economics, elaborating and extending his theory of industrial fluctuation, and before he turned critic and sceptic. It was a period of growth and professional achievement, during which he acquired an international reputation. It has been estimated that Robertson reached the height of his professional fame in the mid-1930s (see Samuelson, 1963, p. 520; also

Deutscher, 1990, quoted in Moggridge, 1992, p. 598), but even in the 1920s he ranked sixth in a citations league table of monetary economists (Moggridge, 1992, p. 598).

Of the two textbooks he wrote in quick succession in the Cambridge Handbooks series (*Money*, 1922, and *The Control of Industry*, 1923), *Money*, in particular, stood the test of time and in later editions (from 1928) came to embody the essence of his thought on money and the trade cycle. This was also the decade of the theoretically innovative but 'unreadable' *Banking Policy and the Price Level* (1926), the bones of which, in demystified form, he restated in 'Theories of Banking Policy' (1928b). There was also a succession of contributions to other areas of economics, which he published as articles in leading journals (see Dennison's bibliography, in Dennison and Presley eds, 1992, pp. 216–17).

In addition, the busy professional economist was in demand on matters of more immediate concern. In 1921 he was invited to serve on a subcommittee that the British Association had set up to consider the question of policy on the currency and the return to the gold standard.

His counsel was also considered worthy of the Tuesday Club, a private dining club whose members, drawn from the universities, City, public service and journalism, met for uninhibited discussion of economic and financial questions at the Café Royal in London. He became a member in November 1922, 'the only one of Keynes's younger Cambridge colleagues to do so until Richard Kahn joined nearly twenty years later in April 1941' (Moggridge, 1992, p. 597). In 1923 he joined Keynes in running the Cambridge end of the London and Cambridge Economic Service in the production of the *Monthly Bulletin*. In the 1920s also, until 1928, he maintained his links with the Liberal Party, giving lectures at the annual Summer Schools, such as that of 1923 to which we refer below, and, from 1926, helping to prepare material for the Liberal Industrial Enquiry, which produced its report, *Britain's Industrial Future*, in 1928 (Dennison, 1992b, p. 24; Butler, 1963, p. 41). He also contributed 'to various discussions and publications of the Royal Institute of International Affairs' (Butler, 1963, p. 41). The period was suitably closed by the presentation of his written 'Memorandum of Evidence' to the Committee on Finance and Industry (the Macmillan Committee) in 1930, together with oral evidence on questions arising therefrom.

Above all perhaps, in view of subsequent events, the 1920s were the decade of collaboration with Keynes. It was in fact a somewhat short-lived phase, with Robertson all too soon feeling that he must distance himself in order to survive. Nevertheless, while it lasted it was a time of growth. As they read each other's drafts and wrote their books in parallel, so Robertson could feel that he was swimming with the tide and that by engaging with Keynes he was engaging with life.

As Robertson's prominence as an economist increased so he received wider recognition within Cambridge, with a succession of University posts of increasing seniority, which he held in addition to his fellowship at Trinity. In 1924 he was appointed University Lecturer, after funds became available to expand the teaching staff, and from 1928 held his lectureship under the title of Girdler's Lecturer (named in recognition of the financial assistance given by the Girdler's Company), before being made Reader in 1930 (*Cambridge Historical Register: Supplement 1921-30*, pp. 25, 31, 356). And so at the end of the decade, the year in which he gave his expert evidence before the Macmillan Committee, he attained the highest academic post at Cambridge, short of the Professorship of Political Economy. This was currently held by A.C. Pigou who had succeeded Marshall. Robertson would himself hold the Chair from 1944.

III

In parallel with his professional career, Robertson also increased his reputation as an amateur actor and these years saw the fullest flowering of his talent. Three Shakespearean roles in particular: Pandarus (*Troilus and Cressida*), Shallow (*King Henry IV*, Part II), and Menenius (*Coriolanus*), became associated with his name but he distinguished himself in a variety of other parts as well. These included: Silenus in Euripides' *The Cyclops*, Corbaccio in Ben Jonson's *Volpone*, Li, the Head Eunuch in Lytton Strachey's *The Son of Heaven* and, in a College revival of *Fellow or Felon, or The Master and the Miscreant*, he again played the Master of Queen's Hall College.

As before the war, the performances were greeted with critical acclaim and there was general recognition that his abilities were considerably beyond what would be expected of an amateur player (all the following reviews: F3/5, 4 and 11, 6, 3, 2 RPTC respectively).

The tone was set by the critical reception for Robertson's Pandarus in the Marlowe Society's production of *Troilus and Cressida* in 1922, a play that successfully captured the mood of disillusionment in post-war Britain (Rylands, interview February 1994). It was first staged in Cambridge in March and Robertson's performance was universally applauded. The *Granta* considered that 'Pandarus was excellent throughout and couldn't have been better', while to the *Cambridge Review* 'Pandarus and Ulysses seemed . . . quite brilliant' (both 10 March 1922). The next day the *New Cambridge* was similarly enthusiastic but more specific:

> Pandarus was Pandarus in voice, in gesture – we thought the woodenness was more effective than any freer use – and in appearance – this latter a triumph; and his final

outburst of savagery 'put this in your painted cloths' – capped this play of disillusionment most perfectly. (11 March 1922)

A week later the *Outlook* struck a slightly different and more telling note for Robertson, in that it compared his performance to that of other members of the cast:

> Much the best – indeed a really fine – piece of acting was Pandarus who was almost too good, since he was in a completely different class from the other performers and tended to make them look more amateurish than they really were . . . The Marlowe Pandarus gave a deep, subtle and extraordinarily amusing performance. (18 March 1922)

It was a notice that might turn any amateur actor's head – or set his sights on a higher station.

In June the play was staged in London and though the notices in the national press were less effusive (*The Times* could only manage: 'Nestor, Pandarus and Ajax were as amusing as they always were', 22 June 1922), the *Daily Telegraph* echoed the judgement of the *Outlook* concerning the relative value of Robertson's performance:

> Apart from the commanders; of the others perhaps the most striking performance was the Pandarus of Mr D.H. Robertson who undoubtedly made plausible the most cruel of all the caricatures of Shakespearian comedy. (22 June 1922)

Important as this success was in shaping Robertson's views of his potential as an actor, there were others. At the Liberal Summer School held in Cambridge in August 1923, the serious business of improving society was preceded by a performance of *The Cyclops* of Euripides. Robertson demonstrated his versatility by contributing to both. In *Lord Oxford's Letters to a Friend*, the Liberal peer (Herbert Asquith) wrote: 'this morning I went to one of the lectures in the Summer School on "Trade Cycles" by Robertson (who played Silenus yesterday)' (8 August 1923, A11/2 RPTC). It must have been an impressive double-bill, as Robertson noted that: 'The old man [Asquith] was [?] genial, and kind about my paper – the only one except Maynard's which he attended' (10 August 1923, A1/13/21 RPTC).

The events were dutifully noticed by the *Nation*, which said of Robertson (combining praise with a rare note of reserve):

> Mr D.H. Robertson (distinguished alike as classic, economist, actor and Liberal) played the part of Silenus with excellent spirit, though one would have liked to see a shade less of refinement and a shade more of bibulous animalism in his manner. (11 August 1923, F4/2 RPTC)

One suspects, however, that Robertson was not over-endowed in the 'bibulous animalism' department.

As different again was his part as Li, the Head Eunuch (and head of the cast-list), in Lytton Strachey's *The Son of Heaven*. *The Times* (14 July 1925) was blandly approving of his performance but Desmond MacCarthy in the *New Statesman* made the crucial distinction between his performance and that of his fellows:

> The amateurs did very creditably . . . Mr Denis [sic] Robertson's Li (Head Eunuch in the Palace) was the best performance. (18 July 1925, F4/6 RPTC)

As late as 1930 when he played Corbaccio in Jonson's *Volpone*, Robertson could still charm the critics. The *Cambridge Review* thought his performance 'excellent . . . When reading the will he was superb' (2 May 1930, F4/5 RPTC).

His last performances, at least of which he kept record, seem to have been in 1932, when he again played Pandarus in *Troilus and Cressida* at the Festival Theatre (though the *Cambridge Review* only noticed it as 'a play of disillusionment': 13 May 1932, F4/1 RPTC); and the Master of Queen's Hall College in a May Week Concert perform-ance at Trinity. After that his acting career seems to have come to an end – for possible reasons which we shall examine below – though he did contribute to the Shakespeare recordings for the British Council (organised by George Rylands and the Marlowe Society) in the late 1950s.

In recollection, Robertson's contemporaries came to discern certain characteristics in the roles he played, which taken together provide useful insights into the actor himself. To Austin Robinson he 'excelled in humorous parts'; while to his friend at Trinity J.R.M. Butler:

> he came to specialise in old men's parts . . . [though] All his ancients, deservedly or not, became rather sympathetic characters. . . .   (Butler, 1963, p. 40)

One role in which these features are combined and which may be seen to characterise Robertson himself is that of Mr Justice Shallow in Shakespeare's *Henry IV, Part 2*. He played the part in the late 1920s, alongside (Sir) Michael Redgrave (a lifelong friend, then an undergraduate at Magdalene) as Prince Hal and Donald Beves as Falstaff and gave, as Butler remembers, 'a really moving rendering' (Butler, 1963, p. 40; see also Dennison, 1992b, p. 18; Robinson, 1963; notices and other items in the Robertson Papers F3/8–14 RPTC). The significance of this will be explored in Chapter 12, below.

IV

Economics and the stage were not the whole of Robertson's life and he found time for other interests and activities.

In 1926 he was at long last elected into membership (at the age of thirty-six!) of the Society of Apostles, the secretive Cambridge Conversazione Society, founded in 1820 and attracting to itself in each generation those members of the University considered to be the brightest, most interesting, amusing, physically attractive and generally congenial to the existing members. Membership of the Society over the years has included names both distinguished and, sometimes, notorious: for example, Alfred, Lord Tennyson, Roger Fry, Lytton Strachey, J.M. Keynes, George Rylands, E.M. Forster, Ludwig Wittgenstein; but also Anthony Blunt and Guy Burgess. An invitation to join has been seen as a significant cachet (see Deacon, 1985, pp. 200–5).

It seems extraordinary that Robertson's invitation should have come at such an advanced age, when most prospective members were sought out in their first year at University. Moggridge (1992, p. 183) thinks that the occasion was Keynes's restructuring of the Society after World War I. However, if the date of election, 1926 (given by Skidelsky, 1992, p. 273; Deacon, 1985, says only 1920s) is correct, it would coincide with publication of Robertson's *Banking Policy and the Price Level* (*BPPL*) and thus come at the end of a period of close association with Keynes. It would also come at a time when Robertson's friendship with Rylands, an existing member, was well established. For Robertson, the late call to mingle with the young, brilliant and beautiful must have come as refreshment indeed. When he had originally been considered for membership, in 1908, Keynes had thought there was 'a good deal in his favour, but a little pudding-headed perhaps' (quoted in Moggridge, 1992, p. 183).

Finally, we might mention his years of service as Librarian of the Marshall [economics] Library from 1925 to 1931. This was the Faculty Library established in 1925 by Marshall's widow Mary Paley Marshall 'largely', according to Dennison (in Dennison, 1992b, p. 6), 'with Alfred's books'. Robertson's seems to have been a part-time, supervisory, advisory and responsibility-taking role, with Mary Marshall doing the actual work of issuing books and so on (there is a picture of her busy with the card-index at the age of ninety-two in Keynes, *CW* X 1972, opposite p. 240).

In 1931 Robertson wrote to his nominal assistant saying that he intended to give up the Librarianship. Her reply draws attention to a warm, reassuring component in Robertson's personality, visible to some through direct contact but more widely known through his writing, especially the handbooks *Money* and *The Control of Industry* and in some of the collected essays, which should not be lost sight of:

Ever since we started . . . it has been such a comfort to know that you were there, and that nothing could go wrong when I had you to consult, and you have been so very kind and helpful . . . I could not understand how you managed to fit in this bit of work as long as you have (hope you can look in from time to time) as it would be too sad to lose sight of our kind librarian.   (9 March 1931, C1/8 RPTC)

V

In these years, therefore, Robertson's public self seemed to have found its equilibrium, balanced successfully between duty and desire, between economics and the stage. But as always with Robertson, things were not as they seemed. Behind the professional success, the kindly helpfulness and the humorous stage roles at which he 'excelled' lay the still unsatisfied demands of the private self.

Economics had seemed the ideal compromise, between the need to escape into a new self while still observing the prerogative of duty. Outwardly it was a great success – especially when swimming along with Keynes – but even in the 1920s Robertson had doubts that all would be well. This was partly due to the changing nature of the subject itself, which increasingly offended his aesthetic sensibilities (later it would be connected with the threat posed to his security by the revolutionary Keynes). Even more so, however, the change of persona had failed to solve the problems of the private self – as well it might – but being a compromise it appeared that it was the choice of economics that was to blame. Had he, it seemed, but gone the extra step and followed the demands of the desired self, all might have been well. As it was, the manifest success of his career on the amateur stage, with his own performances recognised as being in a different class from those of fellow players, must needs keep alive the thought of final escape. In the midst of apparent success Robertson still looked to his 'land of lost content'.

If we leave aside the question of Robertson's growing alienation from economics until the next chapter, we can explore here the nature of Robertson's situation as it revealed itself in the 1920s and the way in which he attempted to come to terms with it.

VI

It has become clear (Chapter 4, above) that the missing element in Robertson's life was love; he was denied the loving relationship that is Everyman's instinctive means of coming to terms with mortality. In its place Robertson could only substitute, although there is evidence of a female attachment (see the letter from Gerda, 18 July 1920, A1/11/35 RPTC), infatuations with attractive young men. One of these relationships, both because of its importance in Robertson's life and because there is evidence available, will be looked at more closely. This is the relationship with George Rylands which began in the 1920s when the latter was an undergraduate at Cambridge.

Like Robertson a King's Scholar at Eton, George 'Dadie' Rylands went on to a career that might have been planned by Robertson's desired self. He won a scholarship to King's, read English, took a first and then, whilst writing his fellowship dissertation in London, worked for Leonard and Virginia Woolf at the Hogarth Press (see, for example, Lehmann, 1978, pp. 4–5, 7). He returned to King's in 1927 as Fellow and Lecturer in English Literature, bringing with him links with what must have seemed to an economics don chafing in Trinity, the exotic artistic world of Bloomsbury. During the inter-war period Rylands was the dominant figure in Cambridge drama: an innovative actor-director and leading light of the Marlowe Society and the ADC.

When Rylands went up in 1921 he stunned Cambridge with his good looks – including his famous yellow hair – and quickly captured the hearts of those who were wont to 'care romantically for the young men'. Robertson was one of the smitten and he duly set off in pursuit.

Looking from Trinity towards King's, Robertson must have seen in the young Rylands a vision of himself as he would like to have been, his desired self made flesh. His cause was helped by their shared interests; most notably, of course, the theatre but also English literature, especially poetry. The metaphysical poets were very popular at the time and Rylands, who was to become a very considerable book-collector, received from Robertson for his twenty-first birthday the two-volume Nonesuch edition of John Donne.

There were also related activities, including walking tours: on the Housman trail to Shropshire (in September 1923, the year of Silenus and the Liberal Summer School); and (in 1926) to the Hardy country, where they had tea with Thomas Hardy at Max Gate (Rylands had family connections with the neighbourhood of Stinsford, where Hardy grew up). Also Robertson entertained Rylands with nostalgic tales of his war service and these memories gave rise (in March–April 1927) to a 'very happy' holiday in Egypt, during which '*inter alia*' they visited Luxor (Rylands, interview, 17 February 1994; see also Robertson to Rylands, 27 April 1927, RPKC).

Problems arose, however, on account of the nature of Robertson's feelings and the terms on which he expected them to be reciprocated. Though they had much in common, Robertson was but one of many admirers and had to compete for attention. Given the depth of his feelings – 'he was', recalls Rylands, 'in love with me' – he expected to have Rylands to himself. But Rylands, who by his own account had a much wider circle of friends, both men and women (he was at one time 'very close' to the novelist Rosamond Lehmann), was unable to comply. The result was that during Rylands's undergraduate years, Robertson was importunate, while Rylands was bowed down with the demands of the various rivals.

Apart from the recollections of Rylands himself, our windows on this fragment of history are Benson, who recorded some events and impressions in his diary and letters written by Robertson to Rylands.

With respect first to Benson, the difference from the entries to which we referred in the previous chapter is that Benson is now a participant – a contender for Rylands's affections and one, moreover, who expected to be worsted. This may have coloured the terms in which his observations were couched.

At dinner at the end of 1923, all was sweetness and light. Benson found Robertson 'very pleasant indeed and full of talk', as he 'told me much about Rylands' (v. 170 p. 29 BDMC). In January of the following year, however, he had Rylands himself to dinner, who complained that he was suffering from depression and had been on-and-off for two years and that he wanted to leave Cambridge. The reason was that:

> He couldn't bear all the claims made on him by W [D.A. Winstanley] and D.R. [Robertson]. They expected him to be always cheerful. (31 January 1924, v. 173 p. 17 BDMC)

In February he recorded: 'who should we meet but Rylands . . . closely and secretly attended by D. Robertson' (5 February 1924, v. 173 p. 27 BDMC). Similarly, two days later he noted that:

> I saw Rylands stalking about, followed by the wizened and sinister form of D. Robertson . . . [Winstanley] thinks R [Rylands] too much beset by the Lucas folk [the brothers D.W. and F.L. Lucas] and DR [Robertson]. I think I shall have to give up all idea of seeing much of him, though he is woefully attractive to me. But I can't be just another competitor, an elderly incubus. (7 February 1924, v. 173 p. 31 BDMC)

Robertson's jealousy and possessiveness drove him to behaviour that Benson considered dishonourable. Rylands, preparing himself for Finals (after what Benson considered to be too much time spent on the theatre and associated socialising) saw it as just one more turn of the screw:

> Dadie to dinner . . . wretched about his Tripos. He told me that my last silly letter to him was found on his table by Dennis and *read* by him. This does seem to me quite unpardonable . . . How *can* a man do such things? Or having done it, how can he confess it? (15 March 1924, v. 174 pp. 44–5 BDMC)

Indignation lingered and a week later, after visiting D.A. Winstanley in King's, Benson again reflected that:

I don't feel rigid about many things but reading other people's letters seems to me an offence against honour.   (23 May 1924, v. 175 p. 2 BDMC)

The mood also led to analysis of the defects in Robertson's character that gave rise to such behaviour:

[Winstanley's] belief was that D [Robertson] claimed the complete possession over his friends, about their parts and about their bed.   (23 May 1924, v. 175 p. 2 BDMC)

Rather curious phraseology, but given the context – of Robertson's amours – not inexplicable. The important thing of course is that it confirms Rylands's own account of Robertson's possessiveness.

This idea, that for Robertson love and exclusive possession were inextricably linked, evidently struck a chord with Benson who brought it out again in July after Rylands had graduated, as commentary on Rylands's further account of Robertson's antics. This entry also gives an insight into Robertson's outlook on life at that time:

D. [Rylands] talked but restlessly – told me of Dennis' persecution and the row at Cambridge in which D. [Robertson] accused him of cruelty and said 'Don't make life harder for me than it is'. I don't doubt that Dennis loves, but he also annexes and thinks he has a *right* to possess.   (24 July 1924, v. 175 p. 54 BDMC)

The row was evidently about Rylands's wider associations: the friends with whom Robertson did not wish to share him. In the previous month, the occasion of Rylands's departure from Cambridge gave rise to anguished scenes as Robertson contemplated the loss of Rylands and also, perhaps, the loss of any control over his activities:

Then Rylands came – very radiant [after award of his first in the Tripos], in silvery grey, and entertained me by accounts of *six* successive leave-takings with Dennis Robertson who seems half-crazy. They don't *say* anything. DR sits and moans and his head rolls on his shoulders.   (16 June 1924, v. 175 p. 23 BDMC)

After an interval of seventy years Rylands affirmed this impression of Robertson's possessiveness. He recalled that the relationship came to an end in the late 1920s, after his return to King's as a don, when Robertson, consumed by jealousy and unwilling to share Rylands with anyone else, decided that if he couldn't have Rylands totally he wouldn't have him at all – and summarily broke it off (Rylands, interview 17 February 1994).

Note also the interesting parallel to be drawn here – and one to which Rylands would give credence – between this episode and that involving the breach between Robertson and Keynes. This provides a previously unconsidered perspective. The explanation would thus be that in addition to Robertson's need to become independent of Keynes – to escape in order to preserve his individual identity – there was a further element that came into play later as Robertson grew jealous of Keynes's relationship with those positive lovers of life and art, Joan Robinson and Richard Kahn.

The testimony of Rylands and Benson finds support in Robertson's view of matters, graphically recorded in the letters he wrote to Rylands during a passionate and stormy nine-year affair. These depict a Robertson often in turmoil, sometimes suicidal, ever jealous, whose emotional and physical demands led to tensions and to mutual recriminations. Robertson finally broke off the relationship in 1930 following his discovery that he did not hold the special place in Rylands's affections he felt was his due.

The twenty-four letters that survive in the Rylands Papers illustrate quite clearly the nature and degree of Robertson's needs and the burdens he placed on those called upon to meet them. The following extracts convey the flavour of the whole (all in RPKC). With respect, first, to the nature of the relationship, Robertson was at pains to emphasise aspects other than the purely fleshly:

> [7 August 1930]
> . . . I think you misjudge if you think I could have remained in thrall all these years if I hadn't been drawn to you by your character as well as by your charm and your beauty and dreaded losing contact with it . . .

Nevertheless, communion was to be in both kinds and this seems to have come as something of a shock to Rylands at first intimation. Note the self-assertive tone (rare in Robertson) of the following plea in justification:

> [No date]
> . . . I felt it fair that you should know that I had felt quite sure that as a result of what I said in London you were expecting the second request, – that it wouldn't come as a shock or a treachery. – There seems to me nothing broken . . . Only a bubble burst. The clue, as so often, in my hoarding of words. 'When the other person enjoys it, one responds physically, and enjoys it oneself' . . .

Even so, Robertson was to feel pangs of guilt:

> [23 December, year unknown]
> . . . Don't make me feel more like a thief than you need, for I don't believe that on balance I am one . . . but I am grateful to you for your gentleness to the law-breakers in these latter times . . .

He was even capable of compassionate self-restraint, albeit only on a temporary basis:

[31 March 1930]
... Your time in London being so short, I had made up my mind not this time to allow myself to make emotional or physical demands. It is possible that that decision makes me constrained and grey in manner without my knowing it, - if so, you must try to overlook it as the lesser evil, - you will quite often enough be called on to bear the greater ...

It was also clear that Robertson suffered greatly for his passion:

[11 December 1926: from the British Legation, Bangkok, during the Asian tour]
... This is the third year running, to go no further back, that in spite of very great efforts of self-mastery, a row with you has made great havoc for weeks on end with my powers of reading and of general receptivity and of give-and-take of happiness with my family and friends ... Don't think I'm trying to land all the responsibility on you: I know very well that my physical hunger, and my obstinacy in refusing to part, and my moody and melancholic temperament must bear their full share ...

Despite this, the relationship with Rylands provided a lifeline for Robertson, especially at times when his perennial sense of pointlessness and hopelessness was most acute:

[no date]
... You have done me great service in bringing me to London, - thereby giving me more weapons to fight with against sloppiness, and against the deep and terrible desire to be dead (I don't use these words lightly) which grew and grew on me last term, and especially last Sunday. I'm terribly grateful to you for facing being sometimes with me here ...

But helping Robertson along life's way was, for the helper, to follow a path strewn with thorns. For example, the regressive element in his make-up could never let bygones be bygones and he sought always to be picking over the bones of old quarrels, speaking in one letter (27 April 1927) of the need for 'history extras'. There was also the problem of Robertson's possessiveness (he read other people's letters to Rylands to him: see 27 April 1927; see also Benson, above) and perpetual tension regarding Rylands's other relationships. But it was Robertson who ended the affair when, during a particularly excoriating soul-baring session, he discovered that he dwelt but in the suburbs of Rylands's good pleasure. He refused any compromise solution and offered only the hope that eventually things would come right:

[18 September 1930]
... I can't persuade myself that any truthful letter which you could write now could undo what you did - what you meant to do - in that conversation, - namely forcing me to realise how little you regard yourself as having got out of our relation ...

[9 October 1930]

... during that conversation you couldn't bring yourself to qualify in any way the picture which you drew of my unsatisfactoriness as compared with other people, both as friend and 'lover'. But I do accept absolutely the truth of what you now say: and it both comforts me inexpressibly that you should say it, and also causes me deep distress: for I know that it means that I *am* doing you immediate injury on the balance of insisting on complete separation . . .

[Also from 9 October 1930]

... I think it *does* offer the *best* chance of eventually attaining to the balanced and immutable friendship of which you speak . . .

VII

Rylands's close relationship with Robertson, in all its aspects, both happy and stormy, gave him a unique insight into Robertson's problems in the 1920s, which can be summarised as follows. He had, thought Rylands, what we would call an inferiority complex. His homosexuality, in the climate of the 1920s, made life difficult, as he couldn't 'be himself'. In addition, he thought of himself as old and as unattractive. The unfavourable self-image was completed by Robertson's growing consciousness that he couldn't do maths. Overall, the effect was that Robertson thought of himself as a failure.

If we take the components of Robertson's inferiority complex and consider them in the context of evidence of his activities in the 1920s we can obtain a composite picture of Robertson the man and his dilemma.

Consider first the question of Robertson's age. Robertson thought of himself as old and there is in one sense justification for his view. This is because in, say, 1923, the active young don who had just dashed off his second classic textbook since the war and whose career seemed only recently to have begun, was in fact thirty-three. His four years as an undergraduate, his two years as a research student and, most important, his five years in the army, had all combined to make him 'old'.

It is true that, in the same year, Robertson was described by Lord Oxford as 'a youngish don from Trinity' but the Liberal leader was then over seventy and to other contemporaries Robertson had by the 1920s taken on the appearance of an intellectual sage.

Lionel (Lord) Robbins, friend and admirer of Robertson, wrote:

I am not clear when first we met – I think it was in Hugh Dalton's company *in the twenties*. There was *already the characteristic appearance*, the diffidence of manner, the hunched shoulders out of which there emerged, like that of some peculiarly gifted turtle, the nearly bald head with the face of a thinker . . . (Robbins, 1971, p. 221; emphasis added)

In April 1927 at the time of Robertson's return from his tour of Asia, Keynes wrote to his wife that Robertson looked 'only moderate – rather older, *very* bald, with the bones of his skull showing more than they did . . . very Chinese' (27 April 1927, quoted in Skidelsky, 1992, p. 283).

The interesting point is that the 'characteristic appearance' was evident in the 1920s, and that thirty years later the same features were still evident – down to an almost exact zoological parallel. Corin Redgrave, the son of Robertson's long-time friend, Michael Redgrave, wrote in his biography of his late father:

[Plato's *Symposium*]: it was all about love between men. It looked not unlike my father's world, I thought, peopled by a cast of beautiful young men and older men, and one old man who was infallibly wise [Socrates] and so repulsively ugly that he was almost sublimely attractive.

In this company Corin accorded Robertson the dubious honour of being cast as Socrates in his attempt to match the *Symposium* with his father's friends:

[Robertson] often came to stay. He was a bachelor with a bald head which poked in and out of his shoulders like a tortoise. He was a distinguished economist, appointed about this time by the government to head a brains trust of three advisers to the Treasury. The press instantly dubbed them 'the three wise men' [the Cohen Council on Prices and Productivity, 1957–8] so that in that respect at least this was suitable casting. (Redgrave, 1995, p. 111)

The related question of Robertson's unattractiveness may turn on his looking old and bald, but it may equally be the haunted, worried look that is detectable in photographs from Eton onwards that is the crucial factor (a photograph from the 1920s from Rylands's collection – showing Robertson as Treasurer of the A.D.C. (during 1923–4 when Rylands was President) – may be added to the list). Attractiveness, one suspects, is not dependent on physical features alone but comes from within and Robertson may have felt that he radiated the wrong signals.

If we now put together the idea of Robertson's thinking of himself as old and unattractive, with a life-view that sprang from his consciousness of 'the harshness of human destiny', we obtain a novel insight into his acting career. For, if we recall that 'at Cambridge he came to specialise in old men's parts', and that, furthermore, 'his ancients, deservedly or not, became rather sympathetic characters' (Butler, 1963, p. 40), we realise with a shock that in these roles *Robertson was playing himself* – the self he saw and didn't wish to be – and through them appealed to the audience (to the world) to look kindly upon him. It is an insight that complements Robbins's observation that Robertson's manner in everyday encounters revealed him as 'obviously craving affection' (1971, p. 221) and Vaizey's that he was 'easy to like but hard to persevere with' (Vaizey, 1977, p. 17).

In political terms Robertson, like Keynes, was always considered a Liberal, though he ended his association with the Party and with politics in 1928 (Dennison, 1992b, p. 24). By temperament, however, he was deeply conservative and this should be kept in mind when assessing the claim quoted without comment by Skidelsky (1992, p. 22) that he be included in a tightly knit group of Liberal radicals. Conservatism was a constant in Robertson's make-up, in parallel with his obligation of duty.

Conservatism is a trait discernible, as we have seen, from his time at Eton (see Chapter 3). As an undergraduate he had spoken, in the Union Society debates (see Chapter 4), of Liberalism as the conservator and not the innovator, the champion not of change but of continuity, guardian of certain things of immense value to the country, which included – and was mentioned twice – 'good order'.

In the 1920s, Robertson had lost none of his certainty on this score, and in a leader which he wrote anonymously for *The Times* on 25 February 1924 he attacked the actions of the Guardians of the Poor in the London borough of Poplar, whom, he thundered, must not be allowed to use local rates to supplement Poor Law allowances, even if the order forbidding them had not been enforced. Visions of apocalyptic consequences both financial and constitutional were conjured up if the practice were to receive any form of official recognition:

> It requires an assurance that neither the Cabinet nor any individual member of it harbours any design of establishing a costly millennium by administrative order behind the back of the House of Commons.   (D5/7/1 RPTC)

Though this does not, of course, mean that Robertson's concern was misplaced.

It is difficult to know how much Rylands's recollection that Robertson was conscious of his deficiency in mathematics (a suggestion that sprang unbidden and unprompted from Rylands: interview 17 February 1994) refers to the 1920s. To whatever extent, it does indicate the fragility of Robertson's economics persona as a means of escape and self-assertion. The knowledge that he would not be able to become master of all aspects of his chosen discipline would emphasise his dependence on the working relationship with Keynes, as a sign that all was well. As the relationship between them became increasingly oppressive and he sought to break away, there would be growing pressure for him to take the extra step to satisfy his desired self and so make escape complete.

VIII

But first there was a sort of trial run, a prolonged absence from Cambridge that was not required by work or military service. From August 1926 until April 1927 – a period of more than eight months – Robertson obtained leave of absence to undertake a tour of Asia. The result was a kaleidoscope of sights and experiences that made a big impression on him and brought him genuine feelings of happiness and escape.

First there was the brashness and invigorating novelty of the Russian communist state, with a glimpse of Lenin's 'white and waxy little body'. Then the Trans-Siberian Railway, in the company of 'a very nice, humorous and well-read C of E parson teaching English in Pekin [*sic*]'. In Manchuria there was the English Club at Mukden: 'a ghastly atmosphere of gin-and-bitters, golf tournaments, appalling women and the sanctity of "British Interests"' (letter to T.H. Marshall, 2 October 1926, L/R/28–31 KPKC).

After twelve days in Japan, during which he visited *inter alia* the ancient cities of Kyoto and Nara (where the university had a 'wonderfully well equipped Economics Department and Library'), Robertson travelled on to China. Here perhaps more than anywhere else his aesthetic sense was engaged, so much so that he extended his stay by two weeks: 'I am so happy and interested here . . . I find it all fascinating aesthetically and deeply interesting politically' (letter to Archie Rose, 18 October 1926, L/R/34–8 KPKC). There were visits to the Great Wall, the Ming Tombs and to Peking, of which he wrote to Keynes: 'You must come here sometime – its one of the supremely undisappointing places of the world – like the Acropolis' (13 October 1926, L/R/22–27 KPKC).

Then on through China: Nanking, Shanghai and Canton, after which he 'traversed Indo-China [saw] the ruins of Angkor . . . [then to] Bangkok . . . hurtled through Malaya [on to] Ceylon [and] South India'. Here he experienced

> the most fantastic episode of my wanderings hitherto, a visit to the Laccadive Islands with the Inspecting Officer [for which they were rowed ashore in island boats, accompanied by fireworks and singing]. Altogether a delightful little Odyssey . . . (Letter to Keynes, 15 January 1927, L/R/39–44 KPKC)

The delightful memories endured, and in 1931 Robertson recounted his adventure in a broadcast talk 'A Visit to the Laccadive Islands', which was printed in the *Listener* and included in *Essays in Monetary Theory* (Robertson, 1940).

The tour was altogether an unforgettable experience but what in the end was the reason for his going? Dennison (1992b, p. 23) says that Robertson 'felt in need of a break' and Hicks seems to endorse this view in that the tour takes place 'after *Banking Policy* was off his hands' (Hicks ed., 1966, p. 17). Alternatively, letters Robertson wrote to Keynes and others contain references to his looking into economic activity in the various countries visited, though more often fascinated by the politics (letters to Keynes, 13 October 1926, L/R/22–27; and to Archie Rose, 18 October 1926, L/R 34–38 KPKC).

But these reasons by themselves seem a rather flimsy pretext in view of the unusually long duration of the 'break'. The fact that he failed to obtain an Albert Kahn Travelling Fellowship to finance the trip seems to support this assessment. Nevertheless Robertson thought it worthwhile to go anyway and to fund the jaunt from private sources. Dennison (1992b, p. 23) says he financed himself. Cairncross has asserted that Keynes paid (in Harcourt ed., 1985, p. 135). However, in a letter which he wrote from Peking to (C.A.W.) 'Archie' Rose, a businessman whom Robertson had known as an advanced student at King's during 1911–12, Robertson seemed to suggest that Rose had provided the necessary assistance:

> I tell you these odds and ends just to show how enormously I'm appreciating my stay here, and I owe it all to you.   (Letter of 18 October 1926, L/R/34-38 KPKC)

Though equally the assistance may have been confined to arrangements for staying in Peking.

Whoever put up the money, Robertson went – and probably for a number of reasons. First, there is no doubt some validity in the idea that Robertson felt the need for a refreshing break. The fact that the Albert Kahn Travelling Fellowships existed seems to point to the fact that the value of a sabbatical year was recognised and we recall that Robertson had been hard at work since the autumn of 1919, seven years earlier.

Second, these exotic interludes had become quite the fashion, and Rylands (interview February 1994) believed that this may have played a part in persuading Robertson. During the period 1911–12, for example, Goldsworthy Lowes Dickinson undertook an Eastern tour, financed by a Kahn Fellowship, upon which he wrote a report for the Trustees under the title *The Civilisations of India, China and Japan*. Dickinson traversed much the same ground as Robertson, but in the opposite direction, beginning with India and ending with the Trans-Siberian Railway back to Europe (Proctor, 1973, pp. 177–88).

Third, there was another fashion which may have had a special importance in Robertson's case. This was the notion of having a break away from Cambridge as a means of becoming 'semi-detached' from Keynes. This is because Keynes, for all his stimulative powers in advancing economic discourse, was also a very demanding colleague whose powerful intellect and personality could all too easily subjugate and hold in thrall those around him.

Austin Robinson has warned against the dangers of keeping too close to

Keynes and of the benefits of the new perspective lent by a period away (in M. Keynes ed., 1975, p. 11). He himself spent two years in India as tutor to the Maharaja of Gwalior for this very reason. But as such he was gainfully employed, and for Robertson to have gone without payment must indicate that he felt the need to be an urgent one. Hicks's observation that Robertson had gone 'after *Banking Policy* was off his hands' points obliquely to the reason. Writing the book with Keynes's 'collaboration' had been a bruising experience for Robertson and he responded in two ways: first, by writing his book in a private, inaccessible style; and second, by detaching himself physically from Keynes's stifling presence. The two still remained friendly and co-operative but from now on Robertson would plough his own furrow.

Finally, there is the notion of escape on a larger scale: to advance the desired self at the expense of the duteous self. This was, as we have argued, a perennial consideration but the matter possibly became more urgent under pressure from two sets of influences. First, the realisation that he could no longer be at one with Keynes threatened his link with 'life' and at the same time weakened the support he derived as an economist from their collaboration. Second, there was also a positive pull from the acclaim he received as an amateur actor of quite unusual powers. In concert these forces would encourage him to take the final step. For this the Asian trip could perhaps be seen as a trial run, a break during which the future might be considered, free from the sway of the usual constraints.

IX

There was no discernible change in the pattern of Robertson's life following his return to Cambridge, and here we might quote Stanley Dennison as a reminder of what that life largely consisted of:

> In the Michaelmas term 1927 he was again lecturing on Principles for Part I of the Tripos, doing his stint of College teaching, and producing a steady flow of articles, book reviews, lectures for conferences, as well as pursuing his other interests, including acting. (Dennison, 1992b, p. 24)

The long vacation of the following year found him occupied with a major revision of *Money*, to take account of *BPPL*, in time for the new academic year:

> I'm hard at work rehashing 'Money', and find some trouble, as I expected, in not being too full of information and too difficult . . . [the publisher] wants to have the books in the shop windows by the beginning of term. (Letter to Keynes, 27 July 1928, L/R/45-7 KPKC)

However, in the same year, Robertson scored another notable success on the stage, as Menenius in Shakespeare's *Coriolanus*. The *Cambridge Review* (9 March 1928) drew an appreciative parallel with Robertson's performance as Subtle in *The Alchemist* a decade-and-a-half previously. If he was waiting for some final stimulus to make good his escape, this was it. The exact turn of events is difficult to establish but the evidence is as follows.

It was Rylands's belief (interview 17 February 1994) that in the late 1920s Robertson had gone to Stratford to be auditioned with a view to becoming a professional actor. It was a belief he affirmed in a subsequent letter:

> I think he was interviewed at Stratford by Glen Byam Shaw (dead some time ago) – probably after his success as Pandarus in 1922 and Menenius in 1928. (Rylands to Fletcher, 7 April 1994)

There is, however, a problem of dating. Glen Byam Shaw (1908–86), actor and director, made his first stage appearance only in 1923 and did not direct his first independent production until after World War II. He became co-director with Anthony Quayle of the Shakespeare Memorial Theatre in 1953 and director in 1956.

At the critical time, therefore, he would have been too junior to have undertaken a convincing assessment. The point is not lost, however, because other evidence suggests that Rylands had correctly identified but run together two separate incidents. The first is referred to in a letter of January 1929 from his sister Gerda, who seeks to comfort him in his anguish over a part in a play. While not completely explicit, it is clear that the play was King Lear; that Robertson had had to agonise over a decision connected with it; that having decided, he was then desolated by having to watch somebody else in the part:

> I am dreadfully sorry for your disappointment over Lear as also to hear you have had another catarrh – no wonder after that awful black Thursday up here. You must have felt rather crazed trying to settle finally for or against and it will be almost too much for you to have to watch the young man doing it . . . who can foretell whether you decided wisely? Probably I think you have, so try not to have regrets all this next month 'It'll all be the same 100 years hence' but I do feel for you and you must now somehow take to playing the piano to make up! (22 January 1929, A1/11 RPTC)

With regard to the second incident, it is clear that Robertson never entirely gave up the vision of theatrical success on a wider stage than that afforded by Cambridge. His contact was Anthony Quayle, with whom he had played in *Troilus and Cressida* in Cambridge in 1932 (with Quayle as a young professional). In January 1949 Quayle wrote to invite Robertson to Stratford and included a rather diplomatic response to what seems to have been a previous question from Robertson:

Do come to Stratford this summer: I really am sure you would enjoy it and it would be such a joy to see you again, and I shall then take you up very seriously over the question of your coming to play as a guest artist. I shall never forget your performance of Pandarus and I know I shall never see a better.   (2 January 1949, A7/109 RPTC)

This in itself is of great interest, but of more immediate concern is Robertson's later endorsement: 'But alas! In 1959 his successor [Byam Shaw] rejected me!'

Here then is explicit rejection, and by Byam Shaw, that could have given rise to feelings of having received 'a dreadful blow – another indication that he had failed' (Rylands interview, 17 February 1994). It was an incident that became known only to a small circle, as is indicated by a letter from Jean Bromley commenting on a draft obituary sent by Hicks:

> I am doubtful about the reference to the audition at Stratford. Dennis told very few people about it, as it was a great disappointment about which he felt deeply and I think he would have preferred it to be forgotten.   (Bromley to Hicks, 19 August 1963, in G11 RPTC)

What then are we to make of the first incident? The evidence of Gerda's letter together with the testimony of Rylands would suggest that Robertson had at least considered choosing to give up academic life and economics to satisfy the demands of the desired self. Also, this was ten years before he was allegedly driven from Cambridge in the wake of the Keynesian Revolution. Though there is no explicit element of rejection here, might we not see in Robertson's decision to withdraw evidence of the triumph of duty over desire?

As a tailpiece we might notice another rejection that Robertson had received two years before. On a letter from Rylands himself in 1957 Robertson had written, evidently mortified: 'He had *sacked* me from the part of Menenius on his BBC recording of "Coriolanus"' (A6/5 RPTC). Given that it was his performance as Menenius in 1928 that, according to Rylands, had tipped the balance in favour of escape, this must be accounted the unkindest cut of all.

PART II

The Mirror of Literature

7.   A literary economist

It has become customary to describe Dennis Robertson as a 'literary' economist, though we should notice that the term has been applied to him in two quite different senses: pejoratively, to imply that he lacked capacities thought necessary to the modern economist; approvingly, to imply that he possessed capacities thought to be all too often absent in the modern economist.

The first of these turns on the question of the use of mathematics in economic analysis, and here writers have differed in their view both of the extent of Robertson's deficiency in this area and of the effect it had on his contribution. In fact Robertson did utilise mathematical expressions as an expository device and aid to his argument but in doing so only excited the contempt of serious practitioners. Hicks refers to his algebra as being 'flat-footed' (Hicks ed., 1966, p. 21); while Samuelson regrets that in *BPPL* his 'elementary mathematics is not presented gracefully' (Samuelson, 1963, p. 518).

What comes over strongly from the context of the remarks is that writers believe that Robertson's *attitude* to the use of mathematics is wrong. In fact, in his lectures to the undergraduates Robertson took an inclusive, broad-church view on the use or non-use of mathematics in economics (see Robertson, 1963, p. 26). Nevertheless, it is this question of attitude that provokes their ire. Hicks speaks of Robertson's '(rather flaunted) lack of mathematics' (Hicks ed., 1966, p. 21); while Samuelson regrets that 'his inability to understand what $e = 2.718 \ldots$ meant, he wore throughout his life as a badge of honor [*sic*]' (Samuelson, 1963, p. 519).

Robertson himself did nothing to allay his critics' suspicions in this respect. His disdain for techniques and modes of expression in which he had little natural facility (see his poems at Eton, Chapter 3 above) – but for which he felt considerable distaste – is evident throughout his writings. His chosen technique – to dismiss with gentle, mocking humour – is probably the aspect that infuriated his targets most of all. Nevertheless, he was professional enough to do what was considered absolutely necessary, though at the same time maintaining a proper distance. In 1954, at the beginning of his Stamp Memorial Lecture, 'Wages', in what may be considered a vintage effusion, Robertson told his audience that:

> If you feel moved to buy the printed version, you will find at the end a little nosegay of figures, culled in the garden of the Central Statistical Office but arranged, with some defiance of the warnings of the gardeners, by my own fumbling fingers. You will also find a humble and non-quantitative example of the kind of criss-cross contraption without which no self-respecting paper on economics is now complete, and which is known, I believe, as a matrix. I shall allude to these things later, but the things themselves are fit only for the eye, not for the ear.   (Robertson, 1954, p. 5)

In a note to the revised edition of December 1954 Robertson warned the reader that:

> The fingers mentioned on the opposite page proved to be even more fumblinger than I feared! The nosegay has now been skilfully refashioned by Mr A. Adams and Mr P.R. Fisk of Cambridge, with generous assistance from the compassionate gardeners (who very reasonably point out that they are not yet in a position to grow roses without thorns) . . .   (Robertson, 1954, p. 5)

Commentators' perception of the reason for Robertson taking the attitude he did is to accept that, while conceding his lack in this respect, he genuinely feared that over-reliance on mathematics – and quantitative models – would impoverish the subject and lead to incorrect analysis. Hicks says that Robertson was 'opposed to the *reduction* of economics to mathematics' (Hicks, 1981, p. 885; emphasis added); while Austin Robinson sees Robertson's efforts being directed to 'the puncturing of over-ambitious and over-simplified generalisations by the more mathematically minded model makers of his subject with whom he had little patience and sympathy' (Robinson, 1963). Goodhart noted how 'Dennis the classicist and humanist, enjoyed poking fun at some of the pretensions and jargon of the subsequent generations of more mathematical economists' (Goodhart, in Presley ed., 1992, p. 10).

But here the question of 'attitude' takes a new turn as, in the eyes of his admirers, Robertson possessed greater mathematical expertise than the extent of his use of it in his professional work would indicate:

> [though it is] obvious that Dennis was more proficient at Maths, and certainly at understanding the mathematical analysis of others, than he liked to let on, he viewed its increasing use with considerable reservation. He felt that the need to reduce complex affairs to a simplified and tractable mathematical system tended to lead economists to concentrate unduly on a limited set of explanatory factors. (Goodhart in Presley ed., 1992, p. 11)

Similarly Dennison discerns here the exercise of self-denial in the interests of furthering economic understanding:

He was particularly distrustful of mathematical models, especially when they were used for 'forecasting' in precise terms the course of events. He disclaimed any knowledge of mathematics, though he was not quite so ignorant as he made out, and his scepticism did not spring from inability to use this tool, but a belief that it was an inappropriate instrument for understanding economic phenomena, based as they were on human actions and human responses to changing situations. (Dennison, 1992b, p. 8)

Such caveats aside, however, there is a residual feeling, in both the opposing and the friendly camps, that Robertson's failure to employ mathematics more extensively deprived him of full recognition for his contributions. H.G. Johnson, as part of his portrayal of Robertson as a generally pathetic figure, speaks of the problems caused by the inability of 'a subtle but hopelessly literary mind to tackle serious problems' (Johnson and Johnson, 1978, p. 144). More specifically, Samuelson, in regretting Robertson's lack of facility in mathematics, does so because he

can justly claim to have been an originator of the period analysis (i.e. dynamic difference equations and the qualitative analysis of market 'days'), which became in the 1930s so useful a tool in the hands of Lundberg, Hicks, J.M. Clark, Metzler, and others. He also made claim – with more than an epsilon of justification – to having been an originator of the geometric progressions that Harrod, Domar and others have made so famous in the golden age we live in. (Samuelson, 1963, p. 518)

While for Goodhart there is genuine regret that:

I have to comment that his inability, or unwillingness, to use maths at certain points in his expositions was a significant weakness . . . if only Dennis had been able to use maths to formalise his own model, and to make it more widely accessible, he might have been able to take a more positive approach to setting out his own vision of the economic system, instead of appearing, from the 1930s onwards primarily as a critic, reacting to the agenda of others, notably of course, Keynes. (Goodhart in Presley ed., 1992, pp. 11–12)

Which is both an acknowledgement, in line with our findings of the previous chapter, that Robertson 'couldn't do' maths and a survey of symptoms which could be seen as stemming from that deficiency. Although the attribution of causation involved is correct, the questions raised about the medium in which economic ideas should be expressed, namely, the failure of Robertson to make his ideas more widely accessible and his failure to set out a positive view of his own system instead of setting up as a resident critic of the mainstream economics profession, are more complex issues and are clearly bound up with the flow of our overall theme.

Before turning to these more complex issues, however, we might look briefly at the mathematical context in which Robertson made his decision to become an economist in the years prior to 1914.

II

When Robertson began his study of economics in 1910 the prospects for the non-mathematician must have seemed bright enough. The two works that Robertson 'read and digested' during the summer of that year and from which 'throughout his life, he constantly refreshed his memory' (Dennison, 1992b, p. 17), Adam Smith's *The Wealth of Nations* and Alfred Marshall's *Principles of Economics*, offered ample evidence of the scope available for good writing and for purely literary exposition and polemic. True, Marshall provided diagrams to help elucidate a point here and there, but it was intended that the argument should never rely upon them. Mathematics was excluded from the text. Marshall believed that:

> The chief use of pure mathematics in economic questions seems to be in helping a person to write down quickly, shortly and exactly some of his thoughts for his own use: and to make sure that he has enough and only enough, premises for his conclusions (i.e. that his equations are neither more nor less in number than his unknowns).   (Marshall, 1890, preface)

Marshall's reassurances were not confined to his textbook for students. In 1898 he had plainly stated in the *Economic Journal* that:

> vast and subtle mathematical engines working out large volumes full of mathematical formulae . . . cannot be applied to economics. The most helpful applications of mathematics to economics are those which are short and simple, which employ few symbols; and which aim at throwing a bright light on some small part of the great economic movement rather than at representing its endless complexities.   (Quoted in Pigou ed., 1925, p. 313)

Even better, and nearer to Robertson's time, he had written to A.L Bowley in 1906:

> I had a growing feeling in the later years of my work at the subject that a good mathematical theorem dealing with economic hypotheses was very unlikely to be good economics: and I went more and more on the rules – (1) Use mathematics as a shorthand language, rather than as an engine of enquiry. (2) Keep them till you have done. (3) Translate into English. (4) Then illustrate by examples that are important in real life. (5) Burn the mathematics. (6) If you cannot succeed in 4, burn 3. This last I did often.   (Quoted in Pigou ed., 1925, p. 427)

Best of all, in the same letter, Marshall exhorts Bowley to 'do all you can to prevent people from using Mathematics in cases in which the English Language is as short as the Mathematical' (quoted in Pigou ed., 1925, p. 427).

Altogether, the mathematical requirements seemed to pose no real obstacle to progress in economics – especially to one who was widely regarded as among the most intellectually gifted of his time. Furthermore, the tenor of Marshall's remarks seemed to indicate that mathematics was to be regarded as a solitary vice – an aid to an economist's private devotions – rather than a professionally imposed *pons asinorum* or exclusive code.

Even so, Robertson might well have reflected that both his life-long idol and exemplar, Marshall, and more immediately his director of studies (and when he came to write his dissertation, his supervisor), Keynes, had both been mathematicians before they had become economists. This might suggest that there was perhaps something in the mathematical inclination and training that would shine through one's prose to convince others to take one seriously. As Edgeworth later reflected about Marshall's work:

> Eagerly studying these writings [*The Pure Theory of Foreign Trade and Domestic Values* and *The Economics of Industry*] I discerned a new power of mathematical reasoning not only in the papers bristling with curves and symbols, but also in certain portions of the seemingly simple text book. With reference to such passages, writing in the year 1881, I characterised the author by a phrase which he himself acknowledged to be appropriate, '*bearing under the garb of literature the armour of mathematics*'. The phrase might be applied to many passages in the text of the *Principles of Economics*.   (Quoted in Pigou ed., 1925, p. 66; emphasis added)

At the time, however, there was no sign of the future mathematisation of the subject or indication that the use of mathematical tools would become a benchmark of professionalism. And perhaps Robertson quieted any misgivings he might have had with the thought that Pigou ('The Prof') came from a history/philosophy background and had written a thesis on 'Browning as a Religious Teacher' *and* had won the Chancellor's Gold Medal for English verse. If he did, he would have been misled: Pigou came to regard mathematics as a prerequisite for the practice of economics – on the ground that it would discourage charlatans.

III

Robertson, therefore, began his professional career with what some would regard as a built-in disadvantage – and by the time he came to know George Rylands in the 1920s he was very conscious of his deficiency (see above, Chapter 6). There is evidence also that Robertson was not taken wholly seriously as an economist, as will be shown; and while this phenomenon may obviously be related to the approach to economics he did *not* take – that is, he did not typically work with mathematical models – this may not be the whole story. It is an important part of our overall argument to suggest that (negative) attitudes to Robertson may also be related to the approach he *did* take: that is, to adopt a conscious 'literariness' in his work.

It would be wrong, however, to see the matter in terms of simple alternatives: of Robertson adopting a literary approach because he is denied mathematics. There is more to it than that. Robertson's fastidiousness in the matter of his dealings with mathematics and statistics (the 'criss-cross contraption' and 'little nosegay of figures' of the 'Wages' lecture) was but a facet of a wider – and growing – distaste for the currency of modern economic discourse. Though Robertson continued to regard economics as important because of its relevance to an understanding of real-world problems – and therefore worthy of his best efforts – he found its subject-matter alien to his own nature and less than satisfying aesthetically. It was in his efforts to make his professional work *palatable* that Robertson was to provoke questions regarding the seriousness of his commitment. It is to a consideration of this second sense in which Robertson became known as a literary economist that we now turn.

For the bulk of his economic writings, Robertson sensibly capitalised on his natural strengths: command of language; a fluid and elegant writing style; wit and verbal dexterity; an extensive knowledge and appreciation of English and classical literature. It is an aspect of Robertson's work recognised by all sides and raised by his supporters to the level of a positive virtue. Goodhart, in his Centenary Lecture, described Robertson as 'a master craftsman in the use of English' and praised him for the 'carefully-wrought elegance and lucidity of his work [which] makes it a great pleasure to re-read' (Goodhart, in Presley ed., 1992, pp. 9, 10). Austin Robinson recalled his writings as 'brilliant', 'penetrating' and 'epigrammatic' (Robinson, 1963). Sir Frank Lee considered that his style 'kept to the end its own particular cadence, colloquialism and feline grace' (Lee, 1963).

Hicks considered his contributions 'outstandingly well written, in a style peculiarly his own which won the affection of many of his readers' (Hicks, 1981, p. 885). An anonymous writer in the *Trinity [College] Review* revealed his own preferences when he wrote:

> Amongst economists, he is perhaps most envied for his wit, his economy of words and his feeling for the English language – qualities which many economists have every reason to envy. (*Trinity Review*, 1957, p. 23 in G11/5 RPTC)

Dennison, as might be expected, is the most fulsome in his tribute:

> As a writer he is famous for the elegance of his style; it has often been said that in his hands economic literature becomes English literature. He had complete mastery

of language and his writing is clear, concise and vigorous with constant felicitous touches and memorable phrases, and the whole illuminated by his delightful wit. Many of his essays (particularly those, intended for a wider audience than professional economists) are worth reading for these qualities alone, and no doubt they are often so read. (Dennison, 1963, p. 43)

These appreciative remarks, included by Dennison in his obituary notice in 1963, were, with the exception of the pious hope expressed in the final sentence, repeated in essence in his article on Robertson for the *International Encyclopaedia of the Social Sciences* three years later (Dennison, 1968, p. 530).

Overall, therefore, Robertson became known as a literary economist, both in the sense that he made little use of mathematics in his work and in the more positive sense that language was his natural medium and that through his use of language his corpus of economic writings acquired the qualities of a work of art. In what follows we shall not dwell upon his mathematical deficiencies but, rather, explore the meaning and implications of his literariness as being the true embodiment and expression of the man.

As part of this we shall show that there is a third way in which Robertson may be regarded as a literary economist. That is, through his widespread use of literary quotations: from the classics, the Bible, Shakespeare, poetry; but, above all, from Lewis Carroll's *Alice* books. Writers have often made reference to this practice, especially with respect to those from Lewis Carroll, but they have not realised its significance. The references Robertson used were not such as might be cribbed from a dictionary of quotations and scattered like confetti for effect. All stem from his familiarity with and understanding of the works concerned. Robertson used quotations and allusions to season his work for his palate: that is, to make economics more aesthetically acceptable than either (in his eyes) its subject matter or, later, its typical mode of expression could justify. In doing so Robertson provided invaluable clues to his fundamental outlook on life and to his approach to his work.

IV

Robertson served his apprenticeship as a writer of economics in the preparation of his fellowship dissertation, in the period following his graduation in the summer of 1912. This was the work that was ultimately published as *A Study of Industrial Fluctuation* at the end of 1915. Reading it now one can only feel astounded that the first version was submitted to the examiners as early as the summer of 1913 (see Keynes to Robertson, 28 September 1913, C2/1 RPTC). Robertson had used empirical data to examine the phenomenon of fluctuations in the activity of individual industries and then used the results to arrive at an explanation of fluctuations in the economy as a whole (see below, Chapters 14, 15).

The examiners were duly impressed by his industry as gauged by the quantity of raw material he had processed and by the originality of his conclusions. They were less impressed with his method (the form in which his argument progressed), and the submission failed. With this version, however, he won the Cobden Club Prize for 1913 – the last year in which it was awarded (it was established in 1876; from 1898 it was worth £20 plus a silver medal). Robertson then revised the dissertation in the light of advice from Pigou and Keynes (respectively one of the examiners and his supervisor) and his submission was successful in 1914.

Given the amount of praise that has been heaped upon Robertson for the quality of his economics writing (recall, for example, Goodhart's commendation of the 'carefully-wrought elegance and lucidity of his work', in Presley ed., 1992, p. 10), it is instructive to read the reactions of Pigou and Keynes to this early work. And here note how the comments of these two inheritors of the Cambridge tradition complemented each other: the one dealing with 'architecture' – the structure of the work; the other with 'art' – getting one's message across.

Pigou, writing in 1913, recalled the strictures of his great teacher, Alfred Marshall, concerning the stages in the process of forming an economic argument:

> (1)   You have collected an astonishing amount of material [but it is] at present . . . mainly a great mass of raw material. Marshall used to instruct one that the *bones* of a piece of work, which was really one's own production, grew gradually and then the whole thing came together round them. You haven't yet got the bones; you haven't thought through the material. The next stage is to sit and stew on all these facts and partial explanations until some coherent unity grows up and the separate facts fall into their proper place. I often used to find that notes of *consecutive* events disappeared altogether in one's final writing; your histories of the various products . . . were originally the raw material on the strength of which a theory was made, and, *when* it was made [would become] illustrations of it. This *using* of materials is, of course, the really difficult thing and you have hardly touched it yet . . .
> (2)   I think that in the process of stewing it would be much better if you took a *positive* rather than a critical line i.e. try to set out positively a theory of your own, criticising other people only so far as it helps that.   (Pigou to Robertson, 1913, C1/2 RPTC

Robertson evidently took the advice to heart, for in the Preliminary Chapter to the published version he counselled that:

> A word remains to be said as to the method of discussion adopted in the following pages. The ideal method of economic exposition is perhaps to elaborate an independent constructive theory, treating the results and suggestions of others as

material for incidental rejection or as buttresses to afford incidental support and introducing facts rather as illustrations than as the formal groundwork of generalisations. While I have tried in the main to follow this method, it has not seemed to me entirely applicable [because of the present state of the study of fluctuation]. (Robertson, 1915, p. 9)

When Pigou received his copy he thought that it was:

enormously improved since its Cobden Club form . . . In Part I you have completely mastered your material, and I think it is very good indeed. (Pigou to Robertson, January 1916, Cl/3 RPTC)

Nevertheless, though his advice had plainly been acted upon, Pigou perceived that the process had not been carried far enough:

Part 2 is, of course, concerned with more difficult things. This is very ambitious, I think, and heroic, but the troops are still rather conscripts. It's sometimes, on a first reading anyway, *very* difficult to follow and the trees sometimes obscure the wood. I think if this blasted war ever ends and you have time to work over your ideas, you will get something less like a greater number of *little* boxes and more like a skeleton organised round a few connected *big* boxes. (Pigou to Robertson, January 1916, C1/3 RPTC)

The manuscript of the *Study* was read for Macmillan by Keynes who recommended that they publish it 'without delay'. The letter he wrote to Robertson in May 1915 comments on the work in terms almost identical with those used by Pigou:

It is immensely improved since I last saw it; and it will be accepted, I believe, as a most brilliant and important contribution to the subject. It is a great thing to be able to *improve* a first draft so much – it's one of the big tests of the capacity to do real work . . . (Keynes to Robertson, 30 May 1915, C2/1 RPTC)

Even so, there was room for improvement and Keynes, writing as one who was supremely gifted in the art of writing economics, offers advice which reads strangely in the light of Robertson's subsequent reputation:

I think you haven't yet discovered the 'art-form' best suited to you. You know how to write and how to construct economics. But the two things are not yet harmonised, except occasionally. And the next step is to learn to write so as to compel people to listen to you; and I believe you are capable of that. (Keynes to Robertson, 30 May 1915, C2/1 RPTC)

Note Keynes's two recommendations: to discover one's own individual and therefore natural (expressive of self) style of writing economics; and to become a persuasive writer so as to command attention and to get one's ideas accepted. The two are not, of course, necessarily compatible. While both Robertson and Keynes became renowned for their own highly distinctive and extremely enviable writing styles, they differed fundamentally in their approach to the question of persuasion – a difference which in turn accurately reflected the divergence in outlook on life of the two men. This point will be developed further below.

V

The *Study* was an important work for Robertson. The 'laborious' (Robertson, 1915, p. xxi) wrestling with intractable empirical data, yielded a theoretical structure which formed the foundation for his professional life's-work. Thirty-two years later he was to refer to the *Study* as 'my only real book', which dealt with what he thought was not only the 'most interesting' subject for study in economics but also the only one to which he had made any contribution (in a speech to the Faculty Board in 1946, B2/3 RPTC).

In addition to its importance for Robertson's subsequent work, its significance in a wider context was recognised by others, and in 1948 it was reissued by the London School of Economics as Number 8 in their Series of Reprints of Scarce Works on Political Economy. Here Robertson rubbed shoulders with McCulloch, Malthus, Mill and Pigou. As Keynes's comments of 1915 make clear, however, it is not the book of Robertson-the-exemplary-stylist; it is not the one to which Robertsonians typically refer the reader; it is not the one to which the eulogistic epithets recorded above typically apply. The nature of the subject-matter, the 'considerable amount of honest sweat' Robertson expended in forcing 'these facts and figures' to yield their message, the necessity of leaving the process sufficiently on view so as to satisfy the examiners, together with the fact that Robertson had not yet found his voice, all combined to produce a dull and difficult book in which the prose style rises above the pedestrian only occasionally (quotations from Robertson, 1948, p. viii).

Opinion at the time of publication was mixed. *The Times* of 28 January 1916 found it 'highly technical and obscure in both treatment and style'. The *Saturday Westminster Gazette* of 19 February 1916, by contrast, after, admittedly, a longer period of reflection, found it a 'masterly survey of a question hitherto as obscure as any in the whole range of economics'. However, though it considered that Robertson possessed 'intellectual clarity' it made no reference to his writing style. A few weeks later, *The Economist* for 11 March (pp. 509–10) thought the book 'altogether an exceedingly able and sound piece of work, distinguished by strong common sense and great logical acuteness [but was at the same time] highly technical, and demands of the reader considerable familiarity with the methods of the Cambridge School of Economics' (D7/1–3 RPTC).

Where the writing does noticeably improve it is associated with a lightening of treatment due to the inclusion of a literary reference. This is shown, for example, in his discussion of the plethora of existing explanations of industrial fluctuation, in which he introduces his first quotation from *Alice* to make the point that this

> does appear to be a case in which, in the deathless words of the Dodo, everybody has won and all must have prizes in the sense that almost all the writers who have made any serious contribution to the study of the matter appear to have had a considerable measure of right on their side. (Robertson, 1915, p. 1)

It is also found in his consideration of the concept of over-investment:

> It is clear then that we must be on our guard against condemning as over-investment what is really only unavoidable preliminary investment upon an exceptionally large scale. We must be careful not to blame the Swiss Family Robinson for sitting down to make bows and arrows instead of catching the cassowary – a swift-footed bird – by putting salt upon its tail. The period of gestation cannot be shortened except at the cost of a miscarriage. (Robertson, 1915, p. 286)

The metaphor continues, and we learn about the possibility of over-investment under the influence of inertia, over-optimism (hubris!) and all the competitive tensions inherent in the contemporary state of industrial organisation:

> At the same time there seems little reason to suppose that the process of investment is eventually checked at the ideal moment. It seems clear . . . that as a rule the happiness of the family through time could be increased if some of them, instead of making bows and arrows, were to pursue the eggs or the young of the cassowary, which can be caught with the hand, or even to dance and sing for the edification of the rest. But they are obsessed by the danger of being unarmed: they keep the extent of their preparations dark from one another; and they forget that (especially if they enjoy the advantage of electric light) one bow and set of arrows can be made to go further if they work in shifts than if they all want to use them at once. Further, there is a tendency among them to suppose that their existing bows and arrows with which they have been accustomed to shoot cassowaries in Cocoa Nut Grove will be ineffective now that the herd has migrated to Silver Creek. Finally, as a matter of fact, a number of the family are not engaged in making bows and arrows at all, but in constructing an island railway capable of transporting the corpses of a hundred cassowaries as yet unhatched. (Robertson, 1915, pp. 186–7)

Another notable passage occurs during his questioning of the received wisdom that stability of economic activity can be secured by way of the maintenance of a stable price level and that this can justify a concomitant degree of monopoly power in an industry. Robertson argues that, on the contrary, experience suggests that the market produces better results than discretionary control. It is here that he makes the first of three references in his published books and volumes to a line from the Sonnets of Michael Drayton (Elizabethan poet, 1563–1631). We shall return to Drayton in the next chapter:

> A new stage of the problem arises when by some means over-investment in the sight of God has been converted into over-investment in the sight of man and the spirit of enterprise is dead or dying. In this stage it is urged upon the combinations that 'from death to life they might him yet recover' by a policy of vigorous price-reduction; and the 'cost' theorists are loud in their complaints against the Steel Trust, which after the 1907 crisis refused to submit to any reduction of prices till February 19, 1909, and against the Raw Iron and Coal Cartels, which by the device of two or more year contracts maintained prices throughout 1900–1. Yet even in this stage it seems quite likely that the snake of investment mania has been scotched, not killed: and that the head if not the heart of the Steel Trust deserves more credit for attempting to prevent the American people from wasting their scanty stores of real capital on further construction in 1908 than for its self-denying ordinance in 1901, or for the lowering of prices in 1909 which prepared the ground for the meretricious and disastrous little iron-spurt of that year.   (Robertson, 1915, p. 245)

The last noteworthy passage to which we shall refer is Robertson's valedictory flourish in the Conclusion, in which he raises the question of the ethics of secular growth. That is, he raises the question of how far it is justified to limit the material welfare of the present generation in order that generations yet unborn may reap the benefit. If writers are seeking a passage to quote in connection with the *Study*, this is the one they choose: from the anonymous reviewer in the *Saturday Westminster Gazette* mentioned above, to Hicks in his 'Memoir'. This is because it is the most striking passage in the book, though only linked to the main body of the argument through a 'last-minute' questioning of one of the assumptions. It has been quoted, as it were, out of context – or at least without its significance as a clue to Robertson's ultimate concerns being made plain. This is a task for Chapters 16 and 17 below, where the passage will be considered again:

> What is meant by the most desirable distribution of the community's income through time? Is the assumption valid upon which western civilisation seems to proceed, – that it is desirable so to manipulate one's income-stream that it shall flow in with an ever-rising tide? From some points of view the whole cycle of industrial change presents the appearance of a perpetual immolation of the present upon the altar of the future. During the boom sacrifices are made out of all proportion to the enjoyment over which they will ultimately give command: during the depression enjoyment is denied lest it should debar the possibility of making fresh sacrifices. Out of the welter of industrial dislocation the great permanent riches of the future are generated. How far are we bound to honour the undrawn bills of posterity, and

to acquiesce in this never-closing hyperbola of intersecular exchange? Shall we sacrifice ourselves as willing victims to the

> Urge and urge and urge
> Always the procreant urge of the world?

Or shall we listen to the words of one of the wisest of English philosophers, who counsels us to eat our grapes downwards, and who always washed up the knives first in case it should please God to take him before he got to the forks? The question is one of ethics, rather than of economics: but let us at least remember that we belong to an age which is apt to forget the οὗ ἕνεκα among the ὧν ἄνευ οὐ, and immolate ourselves, if we must, with our eyes open and not as in a trance. (Robertson, 1915, pp. 253–4; see also below, pp. 226)

Finally, we might anticipate what is to come, by noticing that evidence of Robertson's training as a classicist is visible throughout the book, with twelve instances of quotations from the classical Greek or other references to the ancient world. This practice of classical quotation is a marked feature of the early, pre-war work though it drops sharply away subsequently. Robertson obviously assumed that his readers, and in particular his examiners, would be sufficiently familiar with the medium not to require translation. It does, however, create problems for most modern readers.

VI

After Robertson returned from the war in 1919 he embarked upon a spate of writing which resulted, principally, in the publication in quick succession of two introductory textbooks: *Money* (Robertson, 1922) and *The Control of Industry* (Robertson, 1923). These were volumes in the series of Cambridge Economic Handbooks, which was conceived and planned by Keynes. The series was intended, in the words of Keynes's famous 'Introduction to the Series':

> to convey to the ordinary reader and to the uninitiated student some conception of the general principles of thought which economists now apply to economic problems.

Because of their brief:

> The writers are not concerned to make original contributions to knowledge, or even to attempt a complete summary of all the principles of the subject. They have been more anxious to avoid obscure forms of expression than difficult ideas; and their object has been to expound to intelligent readers, previously unfamiliar with the subject, the most significant elements of economic method. (Keynes in Robertson, 1922, pp. v, vi)

Assignments to write the individual volumes were shared out by Keynes. The contributors were all engaged in teaching at Cambridge and an early list shows *Money* as being assigned to Robertson, though he was not a monetary specialist (Keynes is said to have been too busy, though whether this was the whole story is questioned below, in Chapter 19). *The Control of Industry* was, however, assigned to Barbara Wootton, but when she dropped it Robertson seems to have picked it up as a not altogether welcome chore.

These books became standard texts and established Robertson's reputation as a successful, popular writer of economics. Though they were rattled off as tasks, in double-quick time, the tone is relaxed, warm and reassuring, as though Robertson were purveying conclusions arrived at after a lifetime of gentle mulling. The reader is convinced that here is a guide to be trusted. No hint appears of the emotional turmoil that marked his private life.

They are also noteworthy as the first vehicles on a considerable scale for quotations from Lewis Carroll's *Alice* books, with which Robertson opens each chapter or – in later editions of *Money* – part chapters. Each quotation is chosen with an unerring eye for its appositeness. Charming and whimsical, this feature plays a part in creating the character of the books and in endearing them to the reader, which should not be underestimated. The whole *Alice* question is dealt with in Chapters 10–12, below.

VII

Money was Robertson's first attempt on any scale to present serious ideas in popular form and the result was enormously successful. Readers seemed astonished at the innovation in style. Robertson revealed a truth hitherto unsuspected: namely, that economics could be fun. When Pigou received his copy he wrote:

> The whole thing is extraordinarily brilliant and charming – I never looked to be 'entertained' by a book on Money. And its all done in a way that will make people think for themselves. Altogether a very fine flower for the Cambridge School. (C1/4 RPTC)

The reviewer in the *Pall Mall Gazette* made essentially the same points:

> He entertains as he enlightens, and so makes what in some hands is the dullest of all sciences really interesting . . . Mr Robertson's method is easy to understand and is expressed in familiar words but is none the less scientific on that account.   (D7/4 RPTC)

All, therefore, depends upon the individual economist and the way he handles the important ideas of his subject. Robertson the alchemist turns to gold that which others are incapable of recognising as base metal.

Money is the epitome of the Robertson style: witty, elegant and amusing; authoritative and wise (and notwithstanding the essays collected in subsequent volumes that would have to be included in any characteristic Robertson 'canon'). The following passages both illustrate that style and show how successful Robertson was at explaining the principles of the subject. Page references are to the first, 1922, edition.

Here, first, is Robertson elaborating the qualifications to that 'dowdy but serviceable platitude' (p. 34), the quantity theory of money. The quantity of money available is not the same thing as the quantity of money in existence, and the difference is important for the value of the monetary unit:

> First, the relation between the quantity of money and its value, like all other relations, must be taken to apply relatively to some period of time – let us say a week. But during that week some of the pieces of money in existence will not be available for work; they may be holiday-making in my pocket, or taking a prolonged rest-cure in the bank or even being 'cooled a long age in the deep-delved earth'. On the other hand, some will be available twice or thrice or many times, and will be used in one short week to discharge a number of quite separate transactions. Some pieces of money are very agile, like pieces of scandal, and skip easily from one person to another: others are like an old lady buying a railway ticket – one would think that they had lost the power of locomotion altogether. This truth is often expressed by saying that we must take account not only of the total quantity of money, but also of its average 'velocity of circulation'. And though we have found it convenient to approach it by a different route, it is precisely analogous to the truth that in estimating the demand for money we must take into account not only the volume of goods to be disposed of within a given time, but also the frequency with which each of them changes hands. (p. 35)

And here is Robertson explaining the different kinds of money by carrying on a conversation with a Treasury Note, or 'Bradbury' (Treasury notes were issued in 1914 in lieu of gold coin and circulated alongside Bank of England notes until 1928). Robertson treats the note like a 'botanical specimen' in order to distinguish between legal tender (Bradbury) and optional money (Maria Theresa dollar and the notes of the US National Banks):

> When I was travelling with an officer in the Middle East a year or two ago, I met a very interesting lady called a Maria Theresa dollar. She said that she had been travelling in those parts for nearly two hundred years without any Government passport at all, but that everybody seemed pleased to see her, because she was made of such good silver, and looked so kind and homely. She said she could not see any point in being legal tender: she had always got on very well without it, and she seemed to regard it rather as a mark of ill-breeding and of not being quite sure of oneself. I believe I have some cousins in America too – the notes of the National Banks – who go about without any help from the Government, and seem to get on

all right. But personally I believe in being legal tender. These are queer times, and people sometimes get funny ideas into their heads; and if anything *should* happen – well, I've got my orders and that clears *me*, as we used to say in the Army. (pp. 41–2)

However, while there may have been no 'armour of mathematics' beneath Robertson's prose, there is a tight logical structure devised by his razor-mind. His tendency to create taxonomies was a valuable asset – when writing a textbook – but the unwary reader who has progressed easily through the seemingly undemanding argument, collecting terms and definitions along the way, is suddenly confronted with a summation that sends him turning back to find out how he missed the steps in the argument. The following passage seems to foreshadow aspects of *Banking Policy and the Price Level* published four years later, though it can in no wise match the leaden complexities of the later work:

We have throughout spoken of the relations between bank money and *common* money. But wherever legal rights and obligations are spoken of, the reader can make a gain in accuracy by substituting 'legal tender' for 'common money'. As regards actual practice, the pools and streams of common money consist in Western countries partly of subsidiary money and (in some cases) of token optional money. But the quantity of subsidiary money is everywhere regulated by Governments, on the basis of their experience of the habits of their peoples, in some relation to the quantity of legal tender. And the quantity of token optional money (where such exists) is also, as we shall see in a moment, regulated with reference to the quantity of legal tender. What we have therefore in effect discovered is that the volume of bank money is regulated with reference to the volume of legal tender.   (p. 59)

It all follows through, of course, but constitutes a sudden tightening of the exposition – a hint of intellectual steel beneath the surface gaiety.

As a final illustration, we have Robertson explaining the role of a falling price-level in a depression. His proposition is that, rather than simply functioning as a symptom of depression, it is also 'an active agent in increasing its severity and prolonging its duration' (p. 162). Prosaic analysis of economic concatenation is transformed into an irresistible piece of drama by the veteran of Gaza, 1917:

A downward swoop of the price-level reveals like a flare a line of struggling figures, caught in their own commitments as in a barbed-wire entanglement. Not one of them can tell what or how soon the end will be. For a while each strives, with greater or less effectiveness, to maintain the price of his own particular wares; but sooner or later he succumbs to the stream, and tries to unload his holdings while he can, lest worse should befall. And right from the start he has taken the one step open to him; he has cut off the new stream of enmeshing goods, and passed the word to his predecessor not to add to his burden. So the manufacturer finds the outlet for his wares narrowing from a cormorant's gullet to a needle's eye, and he too takes what steps occur to him. If he is old and wily and has made his pile he retires from business for a season, and goes for a sea-voyage or into the House of Commons. If he is young and ambitious or idealistic he keeps the ball rolling and the flag flying as best he can. If he is an average sort of manufacturer he explains that while he adheres to his previous opinion that the finance of his business is no concern of the working-classes, yet just so much financial knowledge as to see the absurdity of the existing Trade Union rate is a thing which any workman should possess. In any case,

> Early or late
> He bows to fate,

and restricts in greater or less degree the output of his product . . . And men trained and (within limits) willing to work find no work to do, and tramp the streets with the parrot-cries of journalists about increased output ringing in their ears, and growing rancour in their hearts. (pp. 162–3)

The impression left from a reading of *Money* is that instances of good writing, so rare in the *Study*, have now become the norm.

VIII

The Control of Industry, though never as popular as *Money*, is a fitting complement to it and shines with its own, though lesser, lights. Some representation is, therefore, required of this other expression of Robertson's period of positive, confident writing in the first half of the 1920s. Here, for example, is Robertson explaining that the advantage of the large firm over the small firm stems partly from the greater scope for specialisation. Page references are to the 1924 reprint of the *Control of Industry* (*COI*):

It is just worth noting, by way of example, that in retail shop-keeping the specialized shop window plays something of the part played by the specialized machine in manufacture. Everyone can tell the difference in effectiveness between the elaborate series of tableaux of hothouse flowers, ladies' blouses and so forth which goes to make up the frontage of a big Department Store in London or New York, and the higgledy-piggledy profusion of cheese and candles in the single window of the village shop. (p. 22)

Or Robertson explaining the realities of the 'uncoordinated nature of capitalism':

Here and there, it is true, we have found islands of conscious power in this ocean of unconscious co-operation, like lumps of butter coagulating in a pail of buttermilk. The factory system itself, while it involves endless specialization of the work of ordinary men, involves also deliberate co-ordination of their diverse activities by the capitalist employer; and the head of a single big business today exercises a width and intensity of industrial rule which a Tudor monarch might have sighed for in vain.　(p. 85)

And here is Robertson expressing social concern in teasing out the qualifications to 'Capitalism's Golden Rule . . . that where the [entrepreneur's] risk lies, there the control lies also' (p. 89):

> But finally, there are many persons – more persons than not – who incur risks of an important kind without acquiring any share in industrial government. The whole body of manual workers launch not indeed their material capital, but the strength of their arms and the skill of their hands in ventures over the issue of which they have no control . . . To thousands who have felt the rod of unemployment and to millions who live beneath its shadow, the statement that the capitalist bears the sole risks of industry and naturally therefore wields the sole control, comes with a bitter and provocative irony.　(p. 92)

IX

The success of the Cambridge Economic Handbooks stemmed in part from the skill with which the writing was tuned to the tastes and background of its intended readership. Keynes's 'ordinary reader' and 'uninitiated student'; his 'intelligent readers, previously unfamiliar with the subject', were in the 1920s and much later restricted to an educated few. This is certainly true of Robertson's contributions, which would be best appreciated by those whose mental furniture had most in common with his own. This can be shown by reference to the examples Robertson uses to illustrate his arguments, as well as by the tone of the literary quotations and allusions. In *Money*, in instances where the characters referred to are not merely cyphers of their own trade ('Mr Orangeman and Mr Eggman', pp. 87–9; 'Mr Super-Selfridge', pp. 72–9) but assume recognisably normal names, it is the classless 'John Smith' who is seen paying by cheque (pp. 3–4). By contrast, the two men who go to the Derby with a barrel of beer are not named, let us say, Lytton, Austin or Maynard but proletarian 'Bob and Joe' (pp. 35–6).

Similarly, in the *COI*, Robertson concludes that a more optimal form of industrial organisation would involve collectivist forms as well as the dominant form – free enterprise capitalism – which would itself have to become more responsible and more responsive. Thus none of the world's extant economic philosophies offers a complete prescription – and salvation must be sought in hope-inspired pragmatism. Note, however, who are here seen as the weak links in the process:

> Fettered by the insufficiency of the earth and the chronic disappointingness of human nature, Society stumbles clumsily forward on the only half-realized quest for

a more sensible and kindly way of conducting its affairs. In the economic world, as in the spiritual world with which it is so perplexingly intertwined,

> There is no expeditious road
> To pack and label souls for God
> And save them by the barrel-load.

But if we are neither false to our visions nor moderate in our hopes we need not despair of witnessing the slow growth of something worth calling Freedom in industrial affairs: even though we know that in any society which we are likely to live to see, old Bill Bailey will continue to think more about his early broccoli than about the mysteries of cost-accounting, and young Alf Perkins to take more interest in the prospects of Manchester United than in those of cotton cultivation in equatorial Africa. (p. 169)

But what when we have a society in which the caricatures 'old Bill Bailey' and 'young Alf Perkins' themselves will expect to go to university (one as a mature student)? What would they make of Robertson's texts? With the advent of mass higher education, the correspondence between 'uninitiated student' and the educated mind stocked like Robertson's could no longer be assumed. The appeal of the books must then decline.

The idea that the appeal of Robertson's work would decline as the audience for which it was intended declined is of considerable importance, because throughout his career he wrote for essentially the same audience, namely, the senior and junior members respectively of an educated intellectual elite. Furthermore, just as the *Study* provided the basis for his life's work on fluctuations, so *Money* was the work in which he established the characteristic style of writing to which he (with notable exceptions) subsequently adhered.

This style had certain features which delighted many and brought him a loyal following. By the same token, however, it repelled many more; because those who found Robertson's style uncongenial increased in importance as time passed, the consequences for Robertson's reputation as an economist suffered accordingly. There were two principal manifestations of this: (a) potential readers of his writings were discouraged so that Robertson is not as well or widely known as he might have been; (b) during his lifetime Robertson was not treated with the level of seriousness as an economist that his contribution would seem to justify.

These negative consequences of Robertson's adoption of his characteristic style will be examined in Chapter 9, after we have first examined the features of the style itself.

8. The Robertson style

I

Robertson's characteristic style possessed five main features. We shall examine each in turn.

The first and most obvious is that with which we are already familiar: that is, that Robertson's approach to economic analysis was not overtly 'scientific' (and was often explicitly sceptical of the value of 'scientific' methods) but was consciously literary. Because Robertson was as consistent (taking his career as a whole) in his style as he was, by common consent, consistent in the content of his work, he became prey to changing fashions – as much in approach as in doctrine.

Stanley Dennison has railed against what he regarded as almost a conspiracy to exclude Robertson's work from university economics courses in the period since 1945 (see above, Introduction; for a sceptical view of this position see Howson, 1993, pp. 1083–4). But with the triumph of Keynesian economics, which eclipsed alternative systems in Britain for almost four decades after 1936, the rise of the techniques of model specification and empirical testing to which 'Keynesian' demand management policies gave such a fillip, together with the accompanying mathematisation of the subject, Robertson's ideas and methods would appear decidedly dated and indeed 'quaint'. Not only were his *ideas* seen to fail, in the above sense, in comparison with Keynes's but they were presented in a form which appeared to be at odds with the temper of the mainstream.

The era of mass higher education has also brought a change in ideas about the process of efficient learning. The modern textbook's approach (following the example of the Americans, who preceded the British along this path) tends towards a rather cut and dried but highly effective formula. For each topic there is an introductory survey and concluding summary. Stated propositions or principles are highlighted in heavy type or featured in 'boxes'. Points are illustrated with diagrams and equations. The language is limited and technical and examples are determinedly drawn from popular culture. Overhead transparencies accompany the text. All is geared to clarity and directness of exposition and to ease of assimilation.

In comparison, Robertson's treatment, though he does use rubrics at the heads of each section of a chapter, can appear to the uninitiated as a discursive and allusive ramble, with principles explained by way of parables (named as such in *Money*, 1922, p. 130), such as Bob and Joe and the barrel of beer, pp. 35–6; Mr Eggman and Mr Orangeman *et al.*, pp. 87–9; the stone-rich islanders of Uap, pp. 130-1 (all in Robertson, 1922). The steps of the argument can appear as elusive as the goods in the Old Sheep Shop in *Through the Looking Glass*, which vanished whenever Alice looked directly at them. One is reminded here of Keynes's warning regarding Marshall's *Principles*, which was one of Robertson's twin exemplars, that:

> A student can read the *Principles*, be fascinated by its pervading charm, think that he comprehends it, and, yet, a week later, know but little about it. (Keynes, *CW* X p. 212)

Though, in the case of Robertson, the student would at least remember (the presence of) the *Alice* quotations – a point to which we shall return. A Robertson text requires a particular cast of mind as well as persistence if it is to yield its full bounty.

There is also the question of the appropriateness of the language of metaphor. To the student (defined in the broadest sense) trained in modern economic method, Robertson's description of the Treasury bills held as liquid assets by the banks as 'ripening claims to common money – the chirruping as it were of hosts of unborn Bradburys' (Robertson, 1922, p. 114) might appear unbecomingly whimsical. And this could also be said of less anachronistic examples, such as the explanation of the velocity of circulation by way of reference to 'pieces of scandal' and the 'old lady buying a railway ticket' (p. 35); or the description of a person's current account at the bank as his '*chequery*, because it is both a breeding-ground and a homing place for cheques, as a rookery is for rooks' (p. 50); or the assurance that paper notes may be converted into gold as having 'the same kind of soothing effect as the sound of church bells in the distance, and . . . equally unprovocative of action' (p. 60). Which all goes to show how much the 'scientific' economics student misses – and, possibly, how much he or she is thereby diminished.

A further point is that Robertson's characteristic style of exposition, given its target audience, assumes command of a larger vocabulary than does the typical modern text. Pitfalls can, therefore, arise when the readership is wider than envisaged. In one copy of *COI* examined by the present writer, in the passage:

> The maw of Marketing, with its handmaiden Advertisement, absorbs a proportion of those resources which may indeed be necessary to the effective working of the whole arrangement, but which could scarcely strike an unprejudiced observer as anything but wasteful and excessive   (p. 87),

an unknown hand has written above the word 'maw', the word 'law', thus substituting for the unfamiliar the inappropriate.

II

The second feature of Robertson's style – another aspect of his conscious literariness – is his rather ostentatious use of literary quotations and allusions. These occur throughout the corpus of his writings, to a greater or lesser degree, and serve both as a means of illustrating a point and, for the reason that a housekeeper might put scented lining-paper in a drawer: to impart to the contents a fragrance which they would not otherwise possess; or that a gentleman might keep a nosegay of sweet-smelling herbs constantly about him when dealing with 'trade'. For our purposes they provide valuable clues to Robertson's outlook on life and the basis of his approach to economics. The justification for this is that Robertson freely chose them and so could say, with Montaigne, that though he has 'gathered a posie of other men's flowers . . . the thread that binds them is mine own'.

A guide to the principal sources of quotations and allusions contained in Robertson's published books is provided in the table printed as an appendix to this chapter. Titles, whether of monographs, collections of essays or lectures, are listed in chronological order with separate entries for the principal later editions of *Money*. The references themselves are grouped under six heads representing sources or categories, arranged in alphabetical order as follows: Alice, Bible, Classical, Poetry, Shakespeare, Other. That these particular heads have been chosen and that some are more specific than others may appear arbitrary but can be justified on the grounds either of frequency of occurrence and/or of their significance in some sense in Robertson's life. Thus 'Alice', encompassing references both to *Alice's Adventures in Wonderland* (*AAW*) and *Through the Looking Glass* (*TLG*), is included both because of its high incidence *and* because of its great significance as a clue to Robertson's life-view. This latter aspect will occupy the whole of Chapters 10–12.

(i) The *Alice* references make their first appearance on page 1 of the *Study*, but it is in *Money* and *COI*, with which Robertson established his characteristic style, that they become a 'trademark'. There are quotations at the head of each chapter and, in later editions of *Money*, part chapters. In the Preface to the revised edition of *Money* (1948), Robertson wrote that:

> Thanks, as I am constantly being informed, mainly to its chapter-headings, this book, in spite of not having been revised since 1928, still finds a market. (Robertson, 1948, reset in 1959, p. ix)

Money, however, also had *Alice* references in the text: one in 1922, six in 1928 and eight in 1948. Thus *Money*, the exemplar of the quintessential Robertson style, has nineteen *Alice* references in its final version.

Of Robertson's other books, *BPPL* (1926) is uniquely devoid of references in the text – the significance of which will be examined below – but has a single quotation from *Alice* on the title page. This practice, of putting an *Alice* quotation on the title page to stand sentinel over what is to follow and to supply the key to the prevailing theme of the book's contents, is also followed in: *Economic Essays and Addresses* (of Robertson's section – he was joint editor with Pigou, 1931); *Economic Fragments* (1931); *Essays in Monetary Theory* (1940); *Utility and All That* (1952); and *Lectures on Economic Principles* (1963). It was also followed by Hicks in the collection of Robertson's essays he edited as *Essays in Money and Interest* (1966). This volume should really be seen as a new and enlarged edition of *Essays in Monetary Theory* and Hicks uses the same quotation.

What has impressed and delighted discerning readers is not just the *Alice* quotations themselves but also their *appositeness* in the context in which they appear. It has not hitherto been remarked, however, that Robertson was quite prepared to change his *Alice* references between editions of *Money* and to use the same quotations in different contexts.

For example (all *Alice* references to Martin Gardner's (1970) critical edition of the works), in the 1922 edition, Chapter III, 'The Quantity of Money', is headed by the White Knight's comment, regarding the song he is about to sing, that: 'It's long . . . but it's very, very beautiful' (*TLG*, p. 306), referring presumably to the length of the chapter that follows and to the intrinsic merits of the material or of Robertson's exposition. In the 1928 edition, the section dealing with the gold standard is hived off into a separate chapter. The old Chapter III now has at its head the Gnat's question regarding the naming of insects, and refers presumably to the multiplicity of kinds of money to be described:

> 'What's the use of their having names,' the Gnat said, 'if they won't answer to them?'
>
> 'No use to *them*,' said Alice; 'but it's useful to the people that name them I suppose.' (*TLG*, p. 222)

The new chapter, dealing with the (causal) relationship between the quantity of gold and the price level, is headed by the interchange between Alice and the Red Queen, regarding causation:

> 'The cause of lightning,' Alice said very decidedly, for she felt quite sure about this, 'is the thunder – no, no!' she hastily corrected herself, 'I meant the other way.'
>
> 'It's too late to correct it,' said the Red Queen: 'When you've once said a thing, that fixes it, and you must take the consequences.' (*TLG*, p. 323)

The first part of the quotation is referred to twice in the text of the ensuing chapter and the second part is also used on the title page of *Lectures on Economic Principles*.

The White Knight, banished from *Money*, nevertheless makes two entirely successful appearances in *COI*. Chapter IX 'Collectivism and Communism', is headed by the quotation in which Robertson casts doubt on the likelihood of an ultimately desired outcome, the collectivist ideal, ever being realised:

> 'Well, not the *next* day,' the Knight repeated as before: 'not the next *day*. In fact,' he went on, holding his head down, and his voice getting lower and lower, 'I don't believe that pudding ever *was* cooked! In fact, I don't believe that pudding ever *will* be cooked! And yet it was a very clever pudding to invent.'   (*TLG*, p. 305)

He also appears at the head of Chapter X, 'Workers' Control', in the scene in which he tells Alice of his technique for getting over a gate, given that his head is high enough already and the difficulty is with his feet. His solution – with implications for the organisation of society of a move to workers' control of industry – is to put his head on the gate and then to *stand on his head*.

In the 1922 edition of *Money*, Chapter IV, 'Bank Money and the Price-level', is headed by one of the Duchess's 'morals' from *AAW*: 'And the moral of that is – The more there is of mine, the less there is of yours.' In the 1928 edition this chapter disappears but some of the material is incorporated into the new Chapter V, 'Money and Saving'. This is headed by the 'moral' quotation, which now seems more appropriately employed.

Another of the Duchess's 'morals' occurs at the head of Chapter VII in *COI*, 'A Survey of Capitalism':

> ''Tis so,' said the Duchess; 'and the moral of it is Oh! 'tis love, 'tis love, that makes the world go round!'
>
> 'Somebody said,' whispered Alice, 'that it's done by everybody minding their own business!'
>
> 'Ah, well! It means much the same thing,' said the Duchess.   (*AAW*, pp. 120–1)

Robertson also refers to it in the essay 'What Does the Economist Economise?', reprinted in *Economic Commentaries*, where he describes *Alice* as 'another of my favourite sources of wisdom' (Robertson, 1956, p. 154).

The first *Alice* quotation that occurs in the Robertson canon: the Dodo's pronouncement that '*Everybody* has won, and *all* must have prizes' (*AAW*, p. 49), occurs on the first page of the *Study*; but also crops up in *COI* at the head of Chapter XI, 'Joint Control'.

Chapter II of *COI*, 'Large-scale Industry' is headed appropriately by the quotation concerning the White King's commitment to the principle of specialisation and the division of labour:

'I only meant that I didn't understand,' said Alice. 'Why one to come and one to go?'

'Don't I tell you?' said the King impatiently. 'I must have *two* – to fetch and carry. One to fetch and one to carry.'   (*TLG*, p. 280)

Robertson also makes reference to this passage in his 1928 lecture and essay 'Theories of Banking Policy' to illustrate the point that the process of money creation by banks necessarily requires two parties to the transaction: 'one to lend and one to borrow' (in Robertson, 1931, p. 98; and Hicks ed., 1966, p. 26).

Finally, we might refer to the *Alice* quotation that stands on the title page of Robertson's shortest, most forbidding book – and one which is otherwise a literary wasteland – *BPPL*. In choosing this quotation, Robertson seems to confirm our view that the style in which he wrote the book, which is of pivotal importance in the elaboration of his basic theory of fluctuation, sounds a note of revolt: the first blast of the trumpet against Keynesian domination:

'She's in that state of mind,' said the White Queen, 'that she wants to *deny something* – only she doesn't know what to deny!'

'A nasty vicious temper,' the Red Queen remarked.   (*TLG*, p. 319)

Needless to say, it turned up again – in 'The Trade Cycle: an Academic View', 1937 (in Hicks ed., 1966, p. 94).

(ii)   The second category of references is labelled 'Bible' and encompasses those made to the Authorised Version of the *Bible* (1611) and the *Book of Common Prayer* (1662). It is included to demonstrate that though Robertson had early lost his faith, he was familiar with the contents of these two books – as befits a son of the vicarage. The early books of the Old Testament, the Psalms, St Luke's Gospel and St Paul's Letter to the Galatians are featured. The number of references is consistently low throughout.

(iii)   The 'Classical' category is included because of Robertson's training in the classics, at school and at university prior to his switch to economics. As the table shows, the initial flurry of references in the *Study* was not repeated after the war. Classical references were subsequently few except for the high incidence in *Economic Fragments* (1931). This exception is explained by the inclusion of early pieces, written from 1913 onwards. One of these references, shown in the table as an addition to the twelve of Robertson's own, is to 'Marshall's favourite motto: *Natura non facit saltum*'. This, together with the only other classical reference to which we shall devote any attention, that to Heraclitus, the sixth-century BC Greek philosopher, provide clues to Robertson's thought.

The small number of classical references as compared to *Alice* references is not without significance, in that it can be seen as reflecting Robertson's escape from old constraints and the establishment of new 'philosophies' for a life-view.

H.G. Johnson, in paying tribute to Robertson's intellectual stature but questioning his commitment to economics (a point to which we return below), assumed that his heart 'really lay' in the classics in which he had been trained. We shall argue that Johnson's error is to confuse commitment with style, but the truth that resides in the idea of his 'heart' being elsewhere is that Robertson's approach to economics was governed by his life-view; and his life-view is indicated by his literary references. Hence the predominance of *Alice* references as compared to classical. In the most positive period of his writing Robertson established not only his characteristic style but also his characteristic philosophy.

(iv)   The category 'Poetry' refers to quotations from poems, either unadorned or in parody, that the present writer has been able to identify. Shelley, Keats, Clough, Whitman, Belloc and the Bolshevik poet A. Gastev all make their appearance; while there are no less than three references (in various versions!) to a couplet from Michael Drayton's 'Sonnets'. This appears first in the *Study* (1915, p. 245); then in his Memorandum submitted to the Macmillan Committee in April 1930 and reprinted as 'The World Slump' in *Economic Essays and Addresses* (1931, p. 124); and finally in 'The Trade Cycle in the Post-war World'. This last, a misquotation by design, was reprinted in *Economic Commentaries* (1956, p. 86). The use of this quotation, which in its literal form runs,

> Now if thou wouldst, when all have given him over,
> From death to life thou might'st him yet recover,
> (Drayton, Sonnets: 'Idea', lxi)

seems, from the contexts in which it is variously used, to indicate concern for man's innate preoccupation with the achievement of immortality through human artifice. Given the fact of mortality, immortality can apply only to the race and not to individual members of it. In the *Study*, Robertson, who had no issue and, given the circumstances of his life, saw no prospect of it, drew attention to the cost inflicted on the living by the pounding, driving, blind compulsion to provide for the future. Was this, he tentatively asked, the only way to arrange the distribution of income through time? Might there not indeed be a better way, one that allocated more of the fruits of economic enterprise to the comfort of our own mortal span? This is an issue we shall explore at length in Chapters 16 and 17, below.

(v) Inclusion of 'Shakespeare' as a separate category reflects Robertson's distinguished career as an amateur actor and his commitment to the Marlowe Society, under the auspices of which many of the plays were performed or recorded. There are Shakespeare references scattered throughout Robertson's works from the *Study* to *LEP*, though two books, *COI* and *BPPL* have none. Robertson shows familiarity with eight plays: *Hamlet, Macbeth, Lear, Antony and Cleopatra, Merchant of Venice, Julius Caesar, Measure for Measure* and *Twelfth Night*, the first four of which receive multiple references. There are no references to *Henry IV, Part 2*, in which Robertson scored a notable success as Shallow, possibly because the associations came too close to home. We shall look at this at length in Chapter 12, below.

On the other hand, there are two references to Ben Jonson's *The Alchemist* which recall his role as Subtle in the pre-war production. Both appear in pieces written prior to the 1920s (in Robertson, 1931, pp. 221, 258).

(vi) The 'Other' category is necessarily a residual, to which all references which do not find a place under the other heads (or which the present writer has failed to identify!) are consigned. The list of writers gathered under this head indicates erudition and catholicity of taste and includes Ben Jonson (as indicated above), Dr Johnson, Samuel Butler, Rupert Brooke, H.G. Wells, Kipling, G.B. Shaw, Conrad, Swift, Lamb, Dickens, Milton, Carlyle, Victor Hugo, Rousseau and Sinclair Lewis.

III

The third feature of Robertson's style to which we should draw attention – and the one for which, after quotations from *Alice*, he is best known – is his use of neologism. By this we mean his practice of inventing new words or using existing words or phrases in a novel way as a means of communicating his economic ideas. It is this feature in combination with his habit of literary quotation that makes Robertson utterly distinctive as a writer of economics. In Robertson's hands, neologism is of a completely different order from, say, Keynes's use of new terms such as 'multiplier', 'liquidity preference', 'user-cost' or 'marginal efficiency of capital', in that it produces an effect which is at once lighter in tone, witty, whimsical and even homely.

This feature first emerged in Robertson's style-setting books of the 1920s. In *Money* – and this despite a mock admission that 'it is a bad and foolish practice as a rule to create new names for common things' – Robertson cleverly makes clear the dual aspect of a bank deposit by referring to the deposit against which a customer draws cheques as his 'chequery', as noted earlier:

Because it is both a breeding-ground and a homing place for cheques, as a rookery is for rooks. We shall speak then of an individual's chequery, but of a bank's deposits. The total of individuals' chequeries is the same thing as the total of bank deposits. (1922, pp. 49–50)

Similarly, in *COI* he describes one kind of industry which naturally tends towards monopoly: 'rail and tram transport, the supply of water, gas and electricity, the telegraph and telephone', as the 'octopoid' industries, because they employ a 'large and widely ramifying plant' (1923, p. 114). The effect of Robertson's usage is, as before, to render the concept involved instantly intelligible and approachable by means of a familiar image.

We might also mention his explanation of the relationship between the demand for money and the velocity of circulation by comparing the behaviour of money to that of a bird. Thus we have 'money sitting' as compared to 'money on the wing': a metaphor that immediately indicates the essential nature of the concepts involved and prepares the reader for a technical explanation.

Then there is an example of Robertson following the practice of Lewis Carroll, who was the inventor of the 'portmanteau' word, which was so named· because, 'you see it's like a portmanteau – there are two meanings packed up into one word' (Humpty Dumpty, of 'slithy', in *TLG*, p. 271). In the same way Robertson coined the word 'Ecfare' as a shorthand way of referring to, in Edwin Cannan's phrase, 'the more material side of human happiness'. That is, he used a new word 'partly for brevity and partly in the hope of craftily dispelling the notion that the phrase "economic welfare" is bulging with ethics and emotiveness' (from the eponymous essay of 1950 reprinted in *Utility and All That*, 1952, pp. 29–30).

As an ironic comment on Robertson's famous, or notorious, addiction to the practice of neologism, the following is instructive. In his 'A Survey of Modern Monetary Controversy' of 1937, Robertson makes the following statement concerning the touchiness of some writers respecting their favoured forms of expression, not intending (presumably) that the strictures should apply to himself:

I pass to the second class of differences, those which I have called differences of expression – though I am afraid there is no doubt that some of those who recognise here their own views will resent hearing them described in this way, since to themselves their own mode of language has quite naturally come to seem the ark of the covenant, essential to the exposition of the truth as they see it. (Robertson, 1940, p. 137)

Against this passage an unknown hand, fully appreciative of the irony, has written 'Whacko!'.

We must, however, finish by referring to the case in which Robertson uses neologism to the extent that it becomes virtually a private language and in which the effect created goes against much of what was said earlier in praise. This is the case in *BPPL*, and in particular Chapter V, dealing with 'The Kinds of Saving'. Because this book is also the prime example of the third feature of Robertson's style, we may defer examination until we are prepared for a dual approach.

IV

The fourth notable feature of Robertson's style is that he wrote not only with elegance and precision but also with economy. That is, no matter how relaxed or discursive his prose appears to be it is also concise: polished to the extent that all surplus words are brushed away. About the effect of this, however, it is possible to be somewhat ambivalent, though here, as ever, Stanley Dennison entertains no such doubts. Shortly after Robertson's death he wrote admiringly that Robertson was 'a master of compression; every sentence is important, and many of them contain as much as most economists get into a paragraph.' To the enthusiast there was no concern that the consequence of this would be that:

> It is often necessary to read and re-read before one perceives to the full the powerful and subtle mind, and the strength and symmetry of the analytical scheme, which lie behind the seemingly simplest of propositions or gentlest sallies of wit. (Dennison, 1963, pp. 43–4)

Three years later Dennison again referred to Robertson's writing as being known for its 'conciseness' but also for its 'clarity'. Unfortunately, the two qualities are not always perceived as being equally in evidence and the result is that Robertson's ideas become less than readily accessible to both junior and senior economists. The Rt Hon. Sir Terence Higgins MP, recalling his days as a pupil of Robertson admitted that:

> some of us had some trouble with Dennis Robertson because the exposition was so brilliant, but also so condensed, that one had to read every sentence many times before one understood anything at all about what he was trying to say. (In Harcourt ed., 1985, p. 139)

The truth is that *Lectures on Economic Principles*, described by one reviewer, with justification, as embodying the 'definitive Robertson' position (*The Economist*, 1963, p. 936) were, as the undergraduate lecture notes they purported to be, something of a fraud as they routinely included verbatim chunks of Robertson's journal articles and lectures to professional audiences. The above writer is surely not the only one to have been mystified. In fact the profession too had 'trouble' with Robertson's 'conciseness', most notoriously in the case of *BPPL*, as mentioned earlier. Here the negative aspects of Robertson's style triumphed completely over the positive to produce the extraordinary paradox of the famed master of economic literature as English literature writing a book of key importance in the elaboration of his theory of fluctuation in a style that has been pronounced 'almost unreadable'.

Criticism of the style of *BPPL* began early, with Keynes, who had collaborated with Robertson and commented on earlier drafts. It is clear that he found the Robertson version heavy going. At the end of September 1925 he wrote to Robertson: 'I like this latest version though God knows it is concise' (Keynes, *CW* XIII pp. 39–40). At the proof stage he wrote:

> It will be interesting to see whether anyone, and who, will when it is published see what you are driving at. You'll be lucky if you get five understanding readers within two years; after that there will be lots. (Keynes, *CW* XIII pp. 40–1)

In commenting approvingly on the partial accuracy of this prediction, Dennison wrote:

> In the first comment Keynes was right, as shown by various reviews, not one of those now available showing any grasp of the argument [footnote reference to that written by the hapless J.C. (Lord) Stamp]. The second was too optimistic, as for over sixty years many economists have found it very hard going and confessed failure fully to understand. (Dennison, 1992b, p. 33)

The question that springs to mind, of course, is: would Robertson have been pleased? The correct answer should become apparent as we proceed.

One of those who laid claim to finding it 'very hard going' was Paul Samuelson who, in his obituary of Robertson, gave prominence to the notion that the style was so bad that senior economists were physically incapable of reading the book through:

> *Banking Policy and the Price Level* (1926), which many would regard as Robertson's greatest work, is almost unreadable. Professor John Williams used to be able to say without shame that he had never finished reading it, because every few years, when conscience drove him to make the effort, he always got to the same page 40 at which the frailty of the flesh took over. Hoping to benefit by his example, I tried as a student to read it backwards but not with greater success: at page 103 minus 40, I too conked out. If we should ever meet in the Pullman club car an explorer who began his climb at page 40, the three of us might be able to gauge the book's greatness. (Samuelson, 1963, p. 518)

Similarly, Richard Kahn, looking back to the period of the making of Keynes's *General Theory* had to admit that: 'Robertson's *Banking Policy and the Price Level* I found completely unintelligible' (Kahn, 1984, p. 171).

Passages from the book itself will illustrate the problem to which commentators refer. Examples can be found in Chapter 20 below.

V

How is the phenomenon of *BPPL* to be accommodated within the general view of Robertson's writing as elegant, lucid and charming? Dennison, of course, sees no problem at all – except as it lies in the eye of the beholder – but otherwise the practice seems to have been one of omitting mention of the book when discussing style (for example, Goodhart, 1990, in Presley ed., 1992, pp. 8–34) or of treating it as an aberration, an inexplicable exception to the rule (for example, Samuelson, 1963, p. 518). Neither of these provides a satisfactory solution, and to suggest one we need to take into account Robertson's relationship with Keynes.

Received opinion sees *BPPL* as being written midway through the 'happiest decade of his scholarly life; [when he was] working closely with Keynes in a mutually productive relationship' (Samuelson, 1963, p. 519); the 'great days of the nineteen-twenties, when he and Keynes were going forth together' (Hicks ed., 1966, p. 21) and so on. This view sits rather oddly with the other view of Robertson as the ultra-scrupulous and sensitive scholar, whose sense of rectitude forced upon him the thankless and emotionally draining role of 'keeper of [Keynes's] conscience' (Austin Robinson, in M. Keynes ed., 1975, p. 13; in Patinkin and Leith eds, 1977, p. 32; in Harcourt ed. 1985, p. 132).

The truth is, probably, that after only a few years of 'collaboration' with Keynes, that is, commenting on each other's work and stimulating each other's ideas but publishing *nothing* under joint authorship, Robertson began to feel the rub of the yoke and decided – as did others – that to survive as an independent spirit he would have to break away and establish a position 'semi-detached' from Keynes. Austin Robinson wrote candidly and with feeling that:

> I, like a few others, stayed on in Cambridge and became his [Keynes's] very much junior colleague. It was at this stage of achieving maturity that some of us, at least, found the necessity to stand back, to escape from our self-imposed surrender and to try to see him more objectively . . . to stand back and to get out for a period from under his shadow. What was more important was that most of us, having recovered our own initiative, came back and learned a more independent, a less subservient, relation . . . when I look at my friends and colleagues I cannot help cataloguing them into those still in the phase of uncritical adulation, those struggling for independence and those who have won through. (Robinson, in M. Keynes ed., 1975, p. 11)

Thus Keynes must be seen both as the great enthuser, inspirator and invigorator of other people's work: carrying them forward on his own rushing tide; but also as the deadly Upas Tree, in whose shade all else withers and dies.

For Robertson the act of defiance involved both writing *his* book in *his* way and, then, physically removing himself by embarking on an eight month tour of Asia, as we have seen.

VI

Matters came to a head during the process of writing *BPPL*, which was referred to at the time as Dennis's 'egg' (Keynes also referred to his own work-in-hand at that time – the *Treatise* – as his 'egg'). Laying the 'egg' proved to be a painful business when assisted by Keynes, who formed decided views on the direction the book should take. And here, note, we are not concerned with the question of the extent or content of Keynes's input, which cannot in any case be finally determined (see Keynes, *CW* XIII p. 29). What does concern us is the nature of the relationship between the two as revealed by the *tone* of Keynes's letters to Robertson, of Keynes's letters to his wife Lydia and of Robertson's replies to Keynes. Note the senior–junior, leader–follower, active–reactive, character of the comments and exchanges.

JMK to LK, 18 May 1925:

> This afternoon I sat in the garden, reading the proof sheets of Dennis's egg which is now in print. But I still don't like it – I can't help it – so I went round to tea in his room and criticised and bullied him; and I thought he seemed very sad. It would be better, I think, to let him print it as it is and say no more.   (In Hill and Keynes eds, 1989, p. 325)

And again four days later, JMK to LK, 22 May 1925:

> Then to the garden to read more of Dennis's egg. It won't do *at all* – I'm *sure* it's wrong; so afterwards I went round to bully him again and almost to say he ought to tear it up and withdraw it from publication. It's dreadful. When I've finished this letter, I shall write to him about it.   (In Hill and Keynes eds, 1989, p. 327)

It is clear, however, that Robertson realised that in his new book he had grasped at ideas of great importance both for his own work and for the development of the subject – no matter how imperfectly he had expressed them or how uncomfortably they sat with Keynes's own lines of thought. Though confessing himself consumed with doubt, he tenaciously held his ground in the face of Keynes's attack and even tentatively suggested that Keynes's own thinking had perhaps hardened into a rigidity that prevented him from appreciating the originality and subtlety of Robertson's new departures.

DHR to JMK, Sunday [May 1925]: 'It is an attempt to explain to myself at least, why I am still inclined to go ahead and publish . . . .' He explained the dilemma as follows:

> I am afraid of being swayed into publishing by the desire to avoid disappointment and loss: but I am also afraid of being swayed against publishing by my tendency to believe you are always right! Sometimes when I have stood out against this weakness, I have been justified! I think it just possible that you have reached such clear conclusions on the matters in hand, and got your own apparatus of words and thoughts for dealing with it so fixed, that you find it harder to follow the exact shades of my argument than somebody approaching it with a less committed mind, and that what seem to you howlers may be only differences of emphasis and methods of approach. In any case I feel the truth about the whole matter is so obscure and uncertain that it isn't wicked to publish what doesn't pretend to be final truth. I am so unconfident that I should always like to put at the top of everything that I write 'Nobody must believe a word of what follows'; and I think that almost *va sans dire* in books on the trade cycle, and that I would rather write a preface to that effect than not publish at all! Is that a hopeless frame of mind?   (In Keynes, *CW* XIII pp. 30, 33)

Keynes, however, remained unconvinced. JMK to LK, Monday 25 May 1925:

> When I got back I found a long letter from Dennis pleading for his egg. I think I shall tell him that, before he decides to publish he ought (1) to allow a little time to pass for reflection, and (2) to get another opinion besides mine.   (In Hill and Keynes eds, 1989, p. 329)

Accordingly, he wrote to Robertson telling his errant pupil that he was not 'of course' obliged to abandon his position 'unless, or until' he came round to Keynes's way of thinking, though not to do so would involve hazard and he should, therefore, employ safeguards.

JMK to DHR, 28 May 1925:

> I have now read carefully the rest of the book, and also your letter, and remain just as unhappy about the whole thing as I was before. Of course, I don't think you ought to yield to my criticisms unless, or until, you are convinced by them. But I think that you ought to let some little time for reflection elapse before committing yourself, and also to get another opinion.   (Keynes, *CW* XIII p. 34)

In the end, however, Robertson's tenacity was justified – as perhaps was his assessment of the cause of Keynes's difficulties with the book – when Keynes suddenly began to see the light. JMK to LK, 31 May 1925:

> this morning I worked again at Dennis's egg. I think I have discovered what is true in it and see how to express it correctly – it is very interesting and new and important, but it wasn't right as he wrote it. Then I went round to talk with him about it and left him what I had written to think over.   (In Hill and Keynes eds, 1989, p. 332)

Until finally, JMK to LK, 1 June 1925:

> Dennis and I have at last come practically to agreement about what is right and tasty in the egg and what not – which is a relief.   (In Hill and Keynes eds, 1989, p. 333)

Robertson then revised the book in the light of Keynes's criticisms and it was upon receipt of the new version that Keynes was taken aback by what was apparently an abrupt change of style. JMK to DHR, 25 September 1925:

> I like this latest version, though God knows it is concise . . . My general impression is that the ideas in your head are very important and very necessary to the clarification of our minds, but that, when you have got the matter *quite* straight, the whole thing can be put *much* simpler and shorter.   (Keynes, *CW* XIII pp. 39–40)

At proof stage Keynes could report that finally, enthusiasm had replaced criticism and doubt. JMK to DHR, 10 November 1925:

> I have now finished your proofs . . . I think that your revised Chapter V is splendid, – most new and important. I think it is substantially right and at last I have no material criticism. It is the kernel and real essence of the book.   (Keynes, *CW* XIII p. 40)

VII

But it is the style of the book that immediately commands attention: almost brutal in its stark inaccessibility. Features which were barely hinted at in previous books – compression and neologism – are here carried to the furthest and most cryptic extent. Given that Robertson knew very well how to write an accessible book, we must conclude that he *intended* that the book be obscure and difficult (see Robertson, 1926, p. 4; also below, Chapter 19).

Consider the circumstances. He was convinced that he had grasped at ideas of fundamental importance. But it was all so complex and tentative and Robertson was so unsure of himself that he felt that he had to accept the wholesale intrusion of Keynes, his mentor, in order to feel confident enough to go ahead. There are several aspects to this. First, Robertson and Keynes were routinely 'collaborating', so it was natural that Keynes should be involved. Second, he was here chasing elusive ideas in the very area in which Keynes himself was working – hence again the 'collaboration' – as Robertson intimated in the Introductory Chapter 1 when he referred to (what was expected to be) the imminent appearance of Keynes's 'own version of the Theory of Credit' (Robertson, 1926, p. 5; it actually appeared in 1930 as the *Treatise*). Third, this did not happen in the case of the *Study*, except as regards form, and Robertson instead found his own way. He was, in that book, however, doing something rather different: reviewing alternative theories of the cycle on the basis of data from individual industries.

Though Robertson presumably felt that he had benefited from Keynes's participation, did he perhaps also feel resentful at the extent of Keynes's intrusion? Did he, in fact, feel invaded, occupied and oppressed? He acknowledged Keynes's contribution in the famous passage in *BPPL*, which may now be read in a new light:

> I have had so many discussions with Mr J.M. Keynes on the subject-matter of Chapters V and VI, and have re-written them so drastically at his suggestion, that I think neither of us knows how much of the ideas therein contained is his and how much is mine.   (Robertson, 1926, p. 5)

In regard to the style, however, he would assert his independence. Flinging aside elegance, charm and wit, Robertson gave full sway to his extraordinary verbal dexterity to make a protest about the conditions under which the book had won its way to the press. And here we might note that Humpty Dumpty put it even more pithily:

> 'Impenetrability! That's what *I* say!'   (*TLG*, p. 269)

And with that, Robertson took himself off to Asia.

VIII

This was not, however, the end of 'collaboration'. The editors of Keynes's *Collected Writings*, for example, use Robertson's acknowledgement to Keynes in the 1928 edition of *Money* as an indicator that 'the collaboration between himself and Keynes was fruitful and close':

> My debt to Mr J.M. Keynes, already very large when the first edition of this book was published, has reached a sum which is no longer capable of expression in words. There is much in this book especially perhaps in Chapter VIII ['The Question of the Cycle'], which ought scarcely, even in such a book as this, to see the light of day over any other signature than his until his forthcoming work on the theory of money has been published.   (Keynes, *CW* XIII p. 51)

Such evidence of continuing collaboration should not be seen as undermining the conclusions reached above regarding the significance of Robertson's style in *BPPL*. First, because the provenance of Chapter VIII stretches back through his 1928 article 'Theories of Banking Policy' to *BPPL* itself, and the wording of the acknowledgement reflects this – with the same effect as before. Second, Robertson paid similar tribute to Keynes in his Preface to the ninth edition of

Money, except that the 'sum . . . no longer capable of expression in words' has become:

> The immeasurable debt which both the original and the 1928 editions of this book owed to Mr J.M. Keynes has not been diminished by the lapse of time.

And this was written in October 1937, more than a year and a half after the publication of the *General Theory*, when the (professional) breach between them was no longer in doubt.

What the publication of *BPPL* marks, then, is not the end of 'collaboration' (in the sense of Robertson supplying copious comments on Keynes's work-in-progress) – it would continue until the divergence of Keynes's ideas from Robertson's own rendered the concept meaningless – but, rather, Robertson's rejection of the idea of domination by Keynes.

It will become apparent that the book as published was important on several counts. First, it contains the essence of Robertson's thinking on matters which were later to lie at the heart of the Robertson–Keynes controversy. Second, it proclaimed the wholehearted co-operation and agreement of Keynes himself – and established a shared position from which Keynes rather than Robertson could be seen to depart. Third, it was nevertheless indubitably Robertson's own work, written in a private language that defined and enclosed a private universe. Fourth, the book, therefore, provided a secure repository for the title deeds of his theoretical position, the road to understanding and, therefore, criticism of which lay shrouded in defensive obscurity.

IX

The fifth and last feature of Robertson's style which may be distinguished is its 'donnishness', a term that is intended to convey the idea that it is marked on the one hand by intellectual acuity, learning and discrimination; and on the other by detachment and remoteness. It betokened him the essential critic and the perfect book reviewer. But in comparison with Keynes, who was incidentally the 'world's best biographer' according to Robertson and, we might add, a masterly reviewer of books into the bargain, Robertson's writing lacks the vitalising element of *urgency*. He is ever willing to point out the folly and futility of the approach taken by others to economic analysis: recall his dismissal of Paul Samuelson's use of technical language with the comment 'we all have our funny little ways of putting things' (Robertson, 1952, p. 40), or of the efforts of the economic forecasters as 'all largely a matter of guess-work after all' (Robertson, 1952, pp. 60–1). He is even willing to set out his own position in terms of his own choosing. However,

Robertson's published writings reveal no evidence of a compulsion to reach out and convince; no burning desire to convert. He had, that is, no fire in his belly.

If by virtue of injudiciously formulated economic policies the world should choose to take itself to the Devil, Robertson will be happy to enumerate both causes and consequences. What he will not do is to bombard those whose hands are on the levers with streams of unsolicited polemic in the hope of guiding them instead to the Promised Land (cf. Keynes, below, Chapter 23). It was a trait for which he came to be known and, combined with other features of his style, affected the way he was regarded by those charged with actually running affairs. For the moment we might just note that Robertson was aware of the way others saw him, as is revealed by a letter he wrote to the Chancellor of the Exchequer to intimate that he intended to decline his invitation to become a member of the proposed (Cohen) Council on Prices, Productivity and Incomes. DHR to P. Thorneycroft, 2 August 1957:

> my mind is moving strongly in the direction of feeling that I must decline. I know the criticism to which this lays me open from the P.M., yourself and Mr Governor, that I am aways sniping on the sideline but unwilling, when given the opportunity, to do a responsible job of work. (Quoted in Dennison and Presley eds, 1992, p. 95)

There are three considerations here. The first is that advocacy of policy initiatives involves engagement with the machinery of government and Robertson abhorred committee work, as we have seen (see also Bradfield to Fletcher, 23 January 1998). The second is that Robertson held a clearly stated view of the economist's proper function *vis-à-vis* government. In a passage of his essay 'On Sticking to One's Last' (Robertson, 1952, pp. 64–5), that function is limited to the provision of expert advice and to warning and specifically excludes any attempt to lead by the nose:

> I do not want the economist to mount the pulpit or expect him to fit himself to handle the keys of Heaven and Hell. I want him to be rather brave and rather persistent in hammering in those results achieved within his own domain about which he feels reasonably confident, not too readily reduced to silence by the plea that this, that or the other is ruled out of court by custom, or justice, or the temper of the age. But in the last resort I want him, too, to be rather humble – humbler than some of his great predecessors were disposed to be – content to bow to judgment of the prophets or even the men of affairs if he is convinced that his case has been properly understood and fairly weighed. In fine, I like to think of him as a sort of Good Dog Tray rather than as a Priest for Ever after the Order of Melchizedek.

Finally, Robertson's conservative temperament made him sceptical of the efficacy of central planning and the apparatus required to administer it, as the following illustrates:

It is of course easy for academic persons with infinite leisure – or so it is commonly supposed – to pick verbal holes in documents drafted by overworked civil servants and initialled by distracted ministers. But it is not, I think, surprising that the amiable woolliness of this particular document should have occasioned some bewilderment. Nor was that bewilderment allayed by the explanation given soon afterwards by a very highly placed person indeed of the precise manner in which, in respect of its most crucial aspect, this co-operation of the beplanned people with the planning Government was expected to implement itself. (Robertson, 1952, p. 50)

And so on: though Robertson wrote extensively on policy questions he wrote as a critical commentator – an academic sceptic – rather than as a passionate advocate of positive policy.

X

There was, of course, a 'positive' period in Robertson's writing, and we have emphasised it when selecting passages for illustration of style, but even during that phase Robertson was never the radical campaigner. Political affiliations were dropped at an early stage and Robertson brought his ideas to birth in an 'evolutionary' spirit of continuity and development. All too soon, however, as Samuelson noted:

a new note enters into Robertson's writing which was to remain until the end – a querulous note of protest over the pretensions and correctness of so-called new ideas and a somewhat repetitious defence of earlier wisdom . . . I mention it because it is there, recognised by foe, friend and Robertson himself and it may put readers off unduly. (Samuelson, 1963, p. 520)

Samuelson allows that this 'Robertsonian querulousness was not, . . . on reflection sterile'. Points made by Robertson would have been regarded as valuable had they come from Keynes's supporters. This does not, however, alter the case. It was still comment; it was still criticism. Robertson had no programme of his own. In later years admirers would urge him to make a positive contribution. Why did he not, for example, complete the task he had begun with the *Study* and with *BPPL*? To one such exhortation Robertson replied:

I'm afraid there is no chance of my responding to your challenge and trying to produce a full length synthetic Theory of Money or Fluctuations or What-you-will. I'm too old and too lazy! But even if I were younger and less lazy, I think history had made it impossible. I believe that once Keynes had made up his mind to go the way he did it was my particular function to . . . [elucidate and criticise the details of his work] . . . and to go on pegging away at them (as is still necessary). It will not be easy for *anyone* for another twenty years to produce a positive and constructive work which is not in large measure a commentary on Keynes, - that is the measure of his triumph. For me, it would now be psychologically impossible, and the attempt is not worth making. (Private letter of D.H. Robertson to T.J. Wilson, 31 October 1953, quoted in Danes, 1987, p. 210)

For Robertson the psychological obstacle posed by the Keynesian Revolution was real enough. It marked, as we noted earlier, the transition between the successful and happy public Robertson and the unsuccessful and unhappy public Robertson. Thus did 'donnishness' turn sour.

Another suggestion was that Robertson should assume the mantle of his revered master Alfred Marshall by writing the modern equivalent of the *Principles*. In a long review of *Utility and All That* written in the Indian *Economic Weekly* in 1953, the same year in which Robertson wrote his response to Wilson's overtures, Bhabatosh Datta provided a valuable insight into the way Robertson was viewed by someone remote from the strife on the other side of the world. His remarks are worth quoting at length:

There has never been anyone like Robertson in the world of economists. Marshall, Pigou and Keynes, Hicks and Joan Robinson, all won their position by the positive contributions they made; Robertson won his largely by saying 'No'! . . . It is for many years now that Robertson has been writing from his position as a censor. His positive contributions almost all came out in his younger days . . . There is a danger in all this, likely to arise from what is Robertson's great virtue - persuasive writing . . . all but the careful reader is likely . . . to be carried away by the impression that there is nothing really valuable in the new developments . . . It is for this one longs for a full positive treatment of the major problems of economics by Robertson . . . It is only Robertson who has read everything and understood everything and it is he alone who can undertake the task of presenting a new Principles of Economics in which all that is valuable in all that has been written before has been assimilated and yet a consistent, systematic and complete analysis has been perfected. If Robertson would do this his achievement would be comparable not to what Keynes did in 1936 but to a much greater thing - to what Marshall did in 1890. (Datta, 1953, pp. 695, 697-8, in D7/6 RPTC)

Despite such entreaties, however, for Robertson the Keynes who had died in 1946 lived on in spirit to make it 'psychologically impossible' for him to contemplate the construction of a major synthetic work; and continued to obtrude himself like King Charles's head into the books Robertson did write (as with Mr Dick in Dickens's *David Copperfield* - an allusion Robertson himself used in *Utility and All That*, 1952, p. 32, and in correspondence with Hawtrey). The new edition of *Money*, published in 1948, has an extra chapter, 'Problems of Words, Thought and Action', in which Robertson appeals directly to his gentle reader, in tones of unrestrained querulousness, to acknowledge the justice of his case:

Mrs Robinson, having explained in the passage which I have quoted how the amount of saving and the amount of capital outlay, being defined so as to be identical, must always at every level of income indeed be equal, goes on a few pages later to explain (the italics are mine) how 'the increase in incomes must necessarily continue *up to the point at which* there is an addition to saving equal to the additional [capital] outlay.' Reader, do you see what has happened? An assertion that two quantities are by definition identical has been transmuted into an assertion that the establishment of equality between them is a *condition of equilibrium*. It seems to me that this is very confusing, and that I have not been unfair in comparing economists who write in this way to a naturalist who, having defined an elephant's trunk and its proboscis in identical terms, should then go on to explain the profound biological forces which tend to adjust the size of the trunk to the size of the proboscis. (Robertson, 1948, pp. 175–6)

Evidence of his preoccupation can also be found in the nearest thing to a comprehensive and connected survey of economic theory that Robertson produced, his *Lectures on Economic Principles*, initially published in three volumes, in 1957, 1958 and 1959, after he had ceased to give the lectures. The last volume, which deals with money, reveals the extent of his obsession with Keynes and the impact of his ideas on economic theory. In a series of lectures intended for all candidates for Part II of the Economics Tripos, Robertson does not hesitate to play the partisan, exposing what he regards as the shortcomings of Keynesian economics and the iniquities of its exponents. The Rt Hon. Sir Terence Higgins MP, who attended the lectures was clear that:

he was desperately anxious that the undergraduates all understood what Keynes was trying to say, not least I think to explain where he thought Keynes had got it wrong . . . It was, I think, a remarkable experience for us but it did perhaps colour for us, the undergraduate view at that time towards Keynes, because Keynes at that time had departed from the scene. (In Harcourt ed., 1985, p. 139)

To close this section we turn to the views of a member of the Cambridge School who saw from the inside that the contrast between Robertson the pure scholar, detached and aloof, and Keynes, the campaigning journalist and true political economist, is complete. This was Austin Robinson, who was Robertson's pupil for a time and, later, a friend and colleague of both Robertson and Keynes. Several times and in very similar terms in his writings, he approached the subject of the difficulties between the two men and the differences of temperament that lay behind them (see M. Keynes ed., 1975, pp. 13–14; Patinkin and Leith eds, 1977, pp. 31–2; Harcourt ed., 1985, pp. 132–3). The following is the most vivid account:

Keynes was always the applied economist; he was always trying to identify a practical problem, to work out what he thought were the intellectual and practical issues involved in solving the practical problem; and then he wanted to go ahead and persuade people and to secure action. Dennis Robertson was the exact opposite of that; he was the perfect academic; he wanted to be right in the minority of one and had no particular anxiety to see his particular solutions of problems adopted and applied by governments. Keynes wanted to get agreement; Dennis Robertson was a person who did not sell agreement. (In Harcourt ed., 1985, p. 132)

To illustrate his impression of Robertson, Robinson recalled a telling incident. This concerned the dilemma that arose when a decision had to be made regarding the signing of the door into the new home of the Marshall Library:

> I proposed that Marshall Library should be inscribed on the upper bar of the door; Dennis Robertson and Piero Sraffa, both wanting to be right in the minority of one, argued for having it on the lower bar of the door. So I said 'yes, you have agreed, we now go ahead'. But that involved them both becoming members of the majority, and that was a thing of which they were wholly incapable. Dennis retired to the Orkneys; Piero retired to Genoa, and I was left to solve the problem of the door. (In Harcourt ed., 1985, p. 133)

XI

As a comment on the previous section, we should make clear that although Robertson's writing lacked urgency, it was not without its sharp side. That is, despite the impression of gentleness and kindliness recorded by his pupils and friends, he was not also helpless in controversy. The suggestion that he might be arose in the turbulent circumstances of the aftermath of the Keynesian Revolution in Cambridge. Joan Robinson has recorded her indignation at H.G. Johnson's portrayal of Robertson as 'a pathetic figure', utterly without resource in the face of the Keynesian onslaught. In particular, Johnson had referred to the essential one-sidedness of any contest in stand-up debate between the two in the following terms:

> Well take – on the one hand – Joan Robinson, whose forte in life has been standing up in front of audiences and announcing her political conclusions (with much economic nonsense) without feeling any compunction about it; and – on the other hand – Robertson who had to write out every lecture in order to give himself confidence to deliver it. This was certainly no contest; it was a giant challenging a baby to a boxing match. (Johnson and Johnson, 1978, pp. 138–9)

In arriving at this conclusion, Johnson attributes to Robertson the characteristic of being 'very aloof about relationships with other people and . . . not cut out for the rough life of politicking behind the scenes or for public debate'; while at the same time accusing Joan Robinson of bad behaviour:

> She – I would not say necessarily consciously – certainly used the attitudes of the opposite sex towards her as an excuse for behaviour which often would not have

been acceptable from a male economist, I mean in terms of distorting arguments and abusing the privileges of academic discourse. (Johnson and Johnson, 1978, p. 138)

On this view, therefore, it must be concluded that Robertson chose the wiser course in declining the invitation to public debate. He would in any case have realised that the real battleground lay elsewhere – in the written word – rather than in verbal point-scoring in front of the undergraduates. But what of Joan Robinson's scepticism regarding the accuracy of Johnson's portrayal? In other words, was Robertson really as helpless as Johnson makes out, or was he, rather, adept in employing the most effective tactics available to him in the circumstances? Our consideration of the evidence on Robertson to date would indicate that the latter might be nearer the mark.

Consider that in 1923, on the occasion of the Liberal Summer School, Lord Oxford (Herbert Asquith) wrote in his 'Letters to a Friend' that Robertson 'came well out of the heckling afterwards' (8 August 1923, A11/2 RPTC). Consider also all the evidence detailed in Chapter 4, that Robertson was in fact a skilled debater well able to tune his subtle song to the ears of his listeners and the needs of the occasion. Consider, third, that Robertson was not averse to the adversarial approach to economic discourse. Well into the crucial transition phase between Keynes's *Treatise* (1930) and the *General Theory* (1936), Robertson had declared himself to Keynes as being positively in favour. DHR to JMK, 1 April 1933:

> I hate always to appear in print as a controversialist with you, but it is because of the inexhaustible suggestiveness of the *Treatise*. And I don't see how progress is better to be made in these fundamental matters than by public discussion between the $\frac{1}{2}$ dozen people who are wallowing in them. (Keynes, *CW* XXIX, pp. 16–17)

Consider finally that Johnson's claim that Robertson needed to write out his lectures in full (and rewrite them every September) as a means of giving himself the confidence to deliver them is nonsense. The plain fact is that Robertson, being a consummate amateur actor, would consider it natural to work from a full script; and being the complete professional scholar, he was constantly revising and polishing his work with a view to publication.

Robertson was shrewd enough to understand the implications of the Keynesian Revolution, both for economics and for himself: namely, that he could not confront it head-on but only in detail. He was therefore, pursuing a rational strategy to maintain his position intact and not funking the issue due to shyness or an oversensitive fear of strife. Recall the letter to Wilson quoted above with Anyadike Danes's inserted parenthesis:

I believe that once Keynes had made up his mind to go the way he did it was my particular function to . . . [elucidate and criticise the details of his work]. . . and to go on pegging away at them.   (Danes, 1987, p. 210)

His admission in that letter, that it would 'now be psychologically impossible' to produce an alternative positive view to challenge Keynes, was a reflection not just of the immensity of Keynes's 'triumph' as he stated, but also of the nature of the threat posed by the Keynesian Revolution to his own security.

Robertson's capacity for combat is evident from his writing. Though his approach is often infinitely more subtle than that of his opponents, he is nevertheless willing to wound. Of his *modus operandi*, Samuelson wrote, with obvious reference to his literariness: 'What others had to steal by the bludgeon of matrix calculus, he deftly purloined by the stiletto of wit' (Samuelson, 1963, p. 518).

Accordingly, he eschewed the dubious privilege of an opportunity for verbal debate with Joan Robinson and settled instead for comments in print that were calculated to provoke fury in their target:

Only Mrs Robinson, I think, still finds the concept of loanable or investable funds so obscure as to compel her to perform prodigies of self-stigmatisation and expectoration.   (Robertson, 1963, p. 376n.)

He does not, of course, when occasion arises, shrink from being more directly critical, as in 'Wage Grumbles' (1930) in which he describes Mrs E.M. Burns's essay on 'Productivity and the Theory of Wages' (London Essays in Economics) in comprehensively condemnatory terms: 'the whole article is in truth an almost unique museum of muddle' (Robertson, 1931, p. 45). There are, also, the comments on mathematicians and model-builders referred to earlier.

But it is Samuelson's idea of the 'stiletto of wit' which is more acute as a guide to the man. It is the idea of the smiler with the knife which conjures the darker strains that would be consonant with our knowledge of Robertson as a 'cat-person'. He kept a cat in his college rooms (the animal was granted free passage by means of a flap in the door: Butler, 1963, p. 41; Goodhart, 1989, p. 106, and in Presley ed., 1992, p. 13; Bradfield to Fletcher, 23 January 1998) and was himself according to John (Lord) Vaizey, who knew him in post-war austerity Cambridge, 'feline' in nature (Vaizey, 1977, p. 121). The same adjective was also used by Sir Frank Lee but in respect of his style of writing (Lee, 1963, p. 312). 'Feline' conveys a combination of ideas: some of warmth and gentleness, others of detachment, stealth and menace. A dictionary definition of 'feline amenities' is 'veiled spite' or 'women's innocent seeming thrusts' (*Concise Oxford Dictionary*, 1951, p. 435).

Though Vaizey, in another place, varies the zoological metaphor and refers to him as 'waspish', as does incidentally Robertson's niece Jean Bromley (see Vaizey, 1977b, p. 17; and Bromley to Hicks, 19 September 1964, in G11/6 RPTC), it is 'feline' that is more appropriate – and for further reasons which will become apparent. As Alice observed of the Cheshire Cat:

> It looked good-natured . . . still it had *very* long claws and a great many teeth, so . . . it ought to be treated with respect. (*AAW*, pp. 87–8)

APPENDIX

Source:	Alice	Bible	Classical	Poetry	Shakespeare	Other
Industrial Fluctuation (1915/1948)	1 (page 1)	0	12	3/4	1	3
Money (1922)	9 (8 chap. heads)	2	2	2	2	2
Control of Industry (1923/1960)	11 (all chap. heads)	1	1	2	0	4
Banking Policy and the Price Level (1926)	1 (on t.p.)	0	0	0	0	0
Money (1928)	15 (9 chap. heads)	1	1	2	2	2
Economic Essays & Addresses (with A.C. Pigou) (1931)	2 (1 on t.p.)	1	0	1	0	1
Economic Fragments (1931)	1 (on t.p.)	4	12 + 1	3	1	13
Essays in Monetary Theory (1940)	9 (1 on t.p.)	2	4	1	3	1
Money (1948)	19 (11 chap. heads)	2	1	2	3	2
Utility and All That (1952)	11 (1 on t.p.)	2	0	3	1	4
Britain in the World Economy (Page-Barbour) (1954)	0	0	0	0	2	1
Economic Commentaries (1956)	2	3	0	3	2	3
Lectures on Economic Principles (1957, 8, 9; 1963)	3/5	0	1	0	4	5

9. The style that was the man

I

Robertson's adoption of a consciously literary style of economic writing was bound to have an effect on the way that he was regarded as an economist. As we have seen, the stylistic features developed in the 1920s produced a body of work, much of which is worth reading for these features alone. But this in itself might create a problem with a subject that increasingly saw itself as a first cousin of the natural sciences rather than, say, of a Macauleyan approach to history. What the adverse consequences actually were is a matter of conjecture but the indications are that Robertson's style could have led to his contributions being less well known than perhaps they ought to have been, because of what, to the more conventionally trained or minded, would have appeared a very diffuse and inexact method of presentation. It is also likely that he was treated less seriously as an economist than his ideas and his industriousness would perhaps warrant.

II

With regard to the first, it is clear that Robertson felt that he had often anticipated ideas which were later hailed as the innovations of others. He several times drew attention to instances in which his pioneering work had gone unnoticed. For example, in the New Introduction to the 1949 reprint of the *Study*, he saw it as his duty to the editors of the London School of Economics Series of Reprints to point out instances in which his thinking, as expressed in the book, had been in advance of more famous victories.

One instance is that Robertson believed that in the *Study* he had in one respect anticipated Keynes's *General Theory*:

> it seems worth mentioning in view of a prevalent tendency to suppose that the behaviour of 'output as a whole' first attracted the attention of economists in the 1930s [that Robertson had himself almost forty years earlier chosen] *real national income* . . . as the thing whose fluctuation is to be the primary object of study. (Robertson, 1948a, p. ix)

In selecting this measure Robertson had been building on work already extant

('Part IV of Pigou's *Wealth and Welfare*, 1912, was in my hands') and this, in his view, rendered the Keynesian claims to originality seem even more presumptuous.

In a similar manner he upbraided Lord Beveridge for his belief that he had discovered

> an important *and hitherto almost wholly neglected element* in the causation of the trade cycle . . . the relation between primary producers and the industrial users of their products. (Beveridge, 1944, quoted in Robertson, 1949b, p. x; emphasis added by Robertson)

This belief, which implies ignorance of the work of pioneers in the field, such as 'the Jevonses father and son', is rendered, Robertson thought, 'rather more surprising than it would anyhow have been' by the fact that Robertson had himself included 'a very extended and meticulous discussion' of the matter, extending to 'about one third in bulk of the whole book' in the *Study* and had epitomised it later in *BPPL*. Therefore:

> Surely his excellently phrased suggestion, that 'one of the main secrets of the trade cycle is to be found, not in bankers' parlours or the board rooms of industry but on the prairies and plantations, in the mines and oil-wells', was not quite such a new idea as he seems to have thought. (Robertson, 1948a, p. x)

Another instance of Robertson's claim to prescience is his use in the *Study* of the concept of 'effort-demand' (discussed below in Chapters 14 and 15), which though criticised 'may not have been so wide of the mark' given the contemporary interest in incentives and 'inducement goods'.

Robertson's preoccupation with the notion that his contributions often went unnoticed found its most overt expression in a talk given informally at university seminars in the USA, published in 1954 (and reprinted in Hicks ed., 1966, pp. 234–44). It is also used piecemeal in *Lectures on Economic Principles* (*LEP*): see, for example, pp. 421–2. This is from 'Thoughts On Meeting Some Important Persons':

> One of the signs of senility, especially among academic persons, is a tendency, if they are introduced to somebody who has attained distinction in the world, to look him up and down, cudgel their memories, and finally to frame a greeting in some such words as these: 'Ah, so it's *you*, my boy. Why I knew you when you were quite a little feller. Well done, my lad – I'm glad you've had such good luck, and become such an important person.' When this tendency reaches pathological strength, it develops an element of hallucination, and leads the sufferer to treat the distinguished stranger as his own son. (In Hicks ed., 1966, p. 234)

But, of course, it is 'parentage after the spirit, not after the flesh' that Robertson has in mind. The three distinguished but long-lost sons to whom he gives greeting are theoretical concepts first developed by himself but which 'have come to play a prominent part in the recent developments of dynamic economics' in the hands of others. In the case of each of the concepts: autonomous investment, the Domar Equation, the Kalecki Effect, Robertson helpfully explains how its provenance includes his own original thought, hitherto neglected. Only the Kalecki Effect, which involves support for Robertson's accustomed belief that saving has independent power to generate investment, is of interest for present purposes; it appears again in Chapter 28 below.

III

The second possible consequence of Robertson's literary approach – that he was treated with less seriousness as an economist than he deserved – is bound up with the idea that he himself did not take his economics sufficiently seriously. Though palpably unfair in the light of Robertson's contributions to economic debate, there is yet a grain of truth that needs to be teased out and placed in its proper context. For whatever the malice or misapprehension of others concerning the reality, Robertson played a fully culpable role in the creation of the appearance. Concerning the charge itself, H.G. Johnson, remembering Robertson in post-1945 Cambridge, judged that:

> His attitude towards economics was pretty much of a gentleman's attitude and an Establishment attitude . . . His attitude towards economics was that it was something one did lightly. (Johnson and Johnson, 1978, p. 136)

Then why was Robertson doing economics at all? Johnson had clearly seen that there is a point to be made here but did not pursue the matter further.

For others, actions spoke louder than words: and here we go outside Cambridge and into the public domain. During the years of his war service, 1939–44, Hicks tells us that:

> He occupied the position of economic adviser to Sir Frederick Phillips, Third Secretary, in charge of overseas finance; that is to say, of watching, and so far as possible controlling, the balances of payments (the separate balances of payments) with the individual non-sterling countries with which trade was still open, with a view to the management of the nation's dwindling gold and foreign exchange reserves. (Hicks ed., 1966, p. 18)

Hicks is quick to reassure us that:

> It was a task which required far more economic judgement than might appear at first sight; its importance to the nation does not need to be underlined. There were *some*

who thought that in this specialised task he was being underused; but he did not think so himself. It was an important service, and he was glad to do it.   (Hicks ed., 1966, p. 18; emphasis added)

But here again is the condescending tone that marks the whole 'Memoir', and Hicks's reassurance is not wholly convincing.

One of those who did think that Robertson was underused was Lionel Robbins, who provided one source of the information upon which Hicks based his account. L. Robbins to J.R. Hicks, 28 September 1964:

> for a very long time he was given work to do which was very definitely below his capacity [Robertson spent long days working out arithmetical calculations and commented plaintively] 'Yes and the trouble is that my calculations are very often wrong.'   (In G11/24, 25 RPTC)

And unfortunately Robertson's actions in other matters served only to support the general view. Dennis Proctor to Jean Bromley (8 January 1968):

> I must confess that I regarded his occasional interventions in matters with which I was concerned more as pungent *marginalia* than as constructive contributions, and I should not myself have found too much fault with this particular passage in [Hicks's 'not very satisfactory and indeed, intolerably condescending in places'] memoir.   (G11/10, 11 RPTC)

Eventually Robertson was to escape the drudgery of the balance of payments computations, when he was sent to Washington as part of the British delegation charged with negotiating post-war financial arrangements. Here again, however, he was undervalued by his superior, (Sir) Frederick Phillips. L. Robbins to J.R. Hicks, 28 September 1964:

> even Phillips, who had an eye for what was going on in economics, under-rated Dennis' potentialities *vis-à-vis* the Americans; and I remember a feeling of some embarrassment at being put up to speak - with Redvers Opie - at discussions at which Dennis was one of the party without specific assignment.   (G11/24, 25 RPTC)

Proof of the veracity of Robbins's assessment is provided by a letter from Robertson to his sister Gerda of 27 June 1943, which reveals that Phillips had had to return home for a few weeks and that Robertson had *not* been left in charge: 'I am torn between being offended at not being left in charge and relieved at not having to make the effort! The latter predominates on the whole . . .', though it did convince him that his true home was in academia and not in public affairs (in A1/11/61 RPTC).

IV

At long last Robertson got his chance, as a member of the delegation for the Bretton Woods negotiations, and made a great success of it by Robbins's account, being 'second only to Keynes in the importance of what he did and in the impact he made on the international assembly' (Robbins to Hicks, 28 September 1964, G11/24, 25 RPTC). However, the wording of Robbins's letter suggests that even Keynes, who led the delegation and knew him as well as any, had to be 'persuaded' to name Robertson as one of its members.

Even in his hour of triumph and when again working with Keynes and with the prospect of full reconciliation before him, an incident occurred which was to dash the cup from his lips and to inflict a hurt which ever after affected him. This incident, details of which Robbins did not think should be published – so no hint of it is present in Hicks's memoir – may possibly have taken a worse turn than would otherwise have been the case, because it seemed to confirm the doubts about Robertson that Keynes clearly harboured. One can only wonder. The problem arose as follows.

No sooner had Keynes hailed Robertson's achievement in a letter to his mother with the famous eulogy: 'Dennis Robertson is perhaps the most useful of all – absolutely first-class brains do help!' (J.M. Keynes to F. Keynes, 25 September 1944), than a misunderstanding over a negotiating position (Robertson believed that Keynes was in agreement) led Keynes into an outburst that set all at nought again. Back in London he announced to the Chancellor of the Exchequer, without warning and in Robertson's presence, that 'he had been betrayed by his delegate on this particular clause and the matter must be taken up forthwith with the Americans' (Robbins to Hicks, 28 September 1964, G11/24, 25 RPTC).

Robertson's innocence in the affair was explained to Keynes, who accepted that it 'must all have been a muddle after all' (it was Robbins who did the explaining, by letter). But Keynes with his 'characteristic nonchalance' failed to communicate his new understanding to Robertson, who was left to nurse his hurt. He never spoke of the matter and ever after, thought Robbins, 'anything to do with his recollections of Keynes seemed so obviously agonising to him' (Robbins to Hicks, 28 September 1964, G11/24, 25 RPTC). The possibility is, of course, that this incident *ex post* coloured Robertson's view of Keynes's real regard for him during their controversy over saving, investment and the rate of interest. It could thus be the effect of this incident that was 'grinning through' to cause Robertson pain when his pupil Charles Goodhart, in his undergraduate innocence, had suggested that his controversy with Keynes had been 'exciting' (see Goodhart in Presley ed., 1992, p. 15).

Even when any possible personal animosities and differences of opinion about economic theory, policy and philosophy are taken into account, there remains a large measure of scepticism to be explained. The most likely explanation of this phenomenon lies in Robertson's style as an economist. The very features that made him 'the most deeply loved economist of his time' (Lee, 1963, p. 312, repeated in Butler, 1963, p. 44) caused him to be thought not wholly serious: one who did economics 'lightly'.

V

W.H. Auden's jibe that 'deliberately he chose the dry-as-dust' would probably be as unfair applied to Robertson as it was to its target, Robertson's Trinity colleague, A.E. Housman ('A.E. Housman' in Auden, 1966, p. 126). Still, duty should not be too enjoyable, and in settling on economics Robertson had chosen a subject as alien from his nature as could be imagined. The questions with which it dealt seemed to mock the man he was. Robertson was no practical economist actively engaged in the increase of his wealth. He was not addicted to speculation and pronounced himself too incompetent and bored to bother with the rigmarole of moving his capital out of equities and into Consols in the face of an expected fall on the Stock Exchange:

> [I find] all this getting in and out of things rather boring, even when it comes off, which with me it generally doesn't!   (Robertson to Keynes, 27 July 1928, asking for his advice in the face of a recommendation from his brokers: in L/R/45–7 KPKC)

Similarly, he managed no enterprise and sat on official bodies only with the greatest reluctance, as we have seen. In all this, of course, he was completely different from Keynes, the all-round purposeful economiser.

The problem can only have been exacerbated by the changes in the language and methodology of economics that gained ground during his lifetime. While economics had seemed a game for ruffians played by gentlemen, Robertson could feel at home among its practitioners; but with the rise of the mathematical model-builders and the econometricians, it increasingly seemed a world that was not his own.

It is true that others of his kind existed in this world and continued to thrive. Austin Robinson was, like Robertson, a classics scholar with a (Christian) conscience. Inspired by listening to Keynes's lectures on the iniquities of the 'Peace' of 1919, he perceived the relevance of economics to the solution of the pressing problems of society. He was never, however, a detached and clinical dissector of the world's foibles and foolishness. Instead, although his training in economics had been much like Robertson's, he became one of the most practical of applied economists. His progress was greatly helped both by his membership of the majority party in the Keynesian Revolution and by his supreme gift for administration, which gave him power in the Cambridge Faculty, in the Royal Economic Society and the International Economic Association, and rather more than a foot in Whitehall and the world beyond (see Robinson, 1992; and Cairncross, 1993).

Another case is that of Joan Robinson, who aspired to the ranks of the Great Economists but who was never criticised for her lack of mathematics. It was a lack of which she was conscious and to compensate for which she had to 'think very hard'. Though there is no suggestion that she was intellectually more able than Robertson, she was more positive, forceful and life-loving. An independent spirit, she determinedly pursued her own line and campaigned always for acceptance of the views she espoused. The only one of the Keynesians to give a clear and explicit statement of Keynes's central theoretical relationship involving investment and saving (see Robinson, 1937), she clashed bitterly with Robertson. After Keynes's death she, typically, did not choose to live off the glory of the Great Age of which she had been a part. Nor was she constrained by the need for a safe and secure anchorage in the past. Instead she carried the theory forward in directions not envisaged by Keynes.

Finally, we might mention G.L.S. Shackle, who also was admired for the quality of his writing. This, together with his well-recognised, prodigious intellectual capacity, allowed him to pursue his insistent theme: of the problems posed for economic behaviour by the constraints of time, uncertainty and the need for decision, outside the mainstream preoccupations of the profession. Like Robertson, Shackle had a profound knowledge of English literature but did not make the mistake of allowing this to obtrude itself into his economic writing and so make it 'charming'.

VI

It may have been that, as in the specific case of mathematics, Robertson was unduly reassured as to his own future peace of mind by having Keynes as his director of studies and later as his dissertation supervisor. Keynes, the fellow of King's (the college of 'free spirits'), combined an intense interest in economic questions with a commitment to *avant-garde* thinking in philosophy and the arts. Despite his enormous professional output, Keynes never allowed economics to occupy more than a part of his life and was equally at home in the world of literature, painting and the ballet. However, Robertson might have been less reassured had he been able to dip into the future and read Keynes's approval of Marshall's choice of preparatory reading for his life's work:

He had painful recollections in later days of his tyrant father keeping him awake
into the night for the better study of Hebrew, whilst at the same time forbidding him
the fascinating paths of mathematics. His father hated the sight of a mathematical
book, but Alfred would conceal Potts' Euclid in his pocket as he walked to and from
school. He read a proposition and then worked it out in his mind as he walked along,
standing still at intervals, with his toes turned in. The fact that the curriculum of the
Sixth Form at Merchant Taylors' reached so far as the Differential Calculus, had
excited native proclivities. Airey, the mathematical master, said that 'he had a
genius for mathematics'. Mathematics represented for Alfred emancipation, and he
used to rejoice greatly that his father could not understand them. No! he would not
take the scholarship and be buried at Oxford under dead languages; he would run
away – to be a cabin-boy at Cambridge and climb the rigging of geometry and spy
out the heavens.   (Keynes, *CW* X pp. 163–4)

Or even worse, to glimpse the famous passage in which Keynes pigeon-holed
the future scope of the professional economist's work:

do not let us overestimate the importance of the economic problem or sacrifice to
its supposed necessities other matters of greater and more permanent significance.
It should be a matter for specialists – like dentistry. If economists could manage to
get themselves thought of as humble, competent people, on a level with dentists,
that would be splendid!   (Keynes, *CW* IX p. 332)

Though keeping firmly in mind, of course, that Keynes's own approach was
the antithesis of 'dentistry'.

VII

Robertson embarked on his life as an economist from a variety of motives in
which conscience and duty as much as the desire for escape played their part.
It is also clear that increasingly he found economics aesthetically unsatisfying.
Even before the millennium of Keynes's dentists the indications are that
Robertson found it necessary to filter economics through a protective gauze of
his own manufacture. Hence the private language and hence the literary
references and quotations that he scattered like sanctuary stones, or charms to
keep evil spirits at bay, throughout his work.

It was not that Robertson thought that economics was something one did
lightly: he treated the intellectual challenges posed by economic problems
very seriously indeed. The lightness of touch which characterises much of his
work is a revolt against the brutish nature of the subject matter for one of
Robertson's essentially artistic temperament.

Hence the vicious circle. Robertson had chosen economics in part to satisfy
his sense of duty. To make the subject palatable he played his strong suit and
took the literary approach. By taking this approach he was thought to be not

wholly serious and was, therefore, underestimated as an economist. As the years advanced and economics changed, the circle tightened. And yet most humiliating of all, it was not upon the reef of mathematical or quantitative economics that Robertson's ship was wrecked but rather on that of the Keynesian Revolution, written in Robertson's own language and dealing with matters close to his heart. This was irony indeed.

VIII

Robertson's stylistic trait was recognised by Dennison, who clearly approved but was at the same time anxious that people should be aware of the distinction between presentation and substance. In commenting on Robertson's account of pre-1914 military manoeuvres he noted that:

> This lightness of touch was typical, and could be deceptive. For as in much else, including his Economics, he could be most serious when apparently most flippant. (Dennison, 1992b, p. 20)

Or again, when remarking appreciatively on Robertson's 'provocative' criticisms of the efforts of builders of growth models, Dennison points out that they were delivered with that 'lightness of touch and almost sly humour which were hallmarks of his deadly seriousness' (Dennison, 1992b, p. 29).

Dennison gives no reasons for which Robertson would have adopted this tactic but it should be clear from the argument to date that style and content are not separate entities but are intimately related. Robertson's style is a form of self-expression and provides a guide to his real nature. In turn, Robertson's nature shaped his economics. To demonstrate this dual relationship will be the task of the chapters that follow. For the moment we might just notice the words of Samuelson, who wrote with perhaps a degree of unconscious percipience, as a sub-heading to a section of his obituary that:

> [It is] The Style That Is the Man. (Samuelson, 1963, p. 518)

IX

It is now clear that mathematics was only a symptom, a particularly disagreeable aspect, of a more general distaste. Robertson was, therefore, the more ready to recognise any gleam of light in the dark. In reviewing Lionel Robbins's *The Great Depression* in 1935, he remarked on its 'high intellectual and artistic quality' and commented that 'Books on economics which have also the stirring quality of a work of art are not so common but that all economists should join to give them welcome' (Robertson, 1940, p. 169). In general, however, there was little enough to rejoice about on this score, as Robertson hinted throughout his career. The first such hint in his published work comes in the form of the quotation from *Alice* that appears at the head of Chapter 1 of *COI*:

> 'Ahem!' said the Mouse with an important air. 'Are you all ready? This is the driest thing I know. Silence all round, if you please.' (*AAW* p. 46)

In his review in *Economic Fragments* (1931) of Henry Ford's book *My Life And Work* he suggests that 'most of us I imagine, agree with Professor Pigou that economic science would be a dreary affair if it promised us light only and not also a hope of fruit' (Robertson, 1931, p. 205). In the same place he also advances the opinion that 'It may be worth reading and writing dull books in order to promote the happiness of the human race' (Robertson, 1931, p. 205).

In the preface to *Utility and All That* Robertson warns the reader that '[Some essays] while not highbrow by modern standards, are probably of a different order of stodginess from the rest' (Robertson, 1952, Preface). In *LEP* he has Makower and Marschak writing a 'somewhat crabbed' article; and John Neville Keynes as having written a 'dry' book (Robertson, 1963a, p. 335).

Robertson became explicit about the nature of economics as a subject when delivering the Page-Barbour Lectures at the University of Virginia in 1953. Economics, he told his audience, was 'a drab and crabbed specialism compared with most of those which occupy the attention of learned persons and fire the imagination of the intelligent public' (Robertson, 1954, p. 9).

Robertson's definitive statement of his view was made in *LEP* (1963a), the preface to which he signed only a few weeks before his death. Economics, he told his undergraduate audience:

> is a branch [of objective study] which in sheer intellectual interest is inferior, or so I think most people would admit, to many others which are open to our pursuit. When one considers the wonders of modern physics or the glories of ancient Greek or modern English literature, one is driven to the conclusion that as an intellectual pastime economics is rather a drab and second-rate affair. If it is worth pursuing – and it certainly *is* – it is mainly worth pursuing not for its own sake, but with a practical object. (Robertson, 1963a, p. 14)

In expressing these views, Robertson was only reflecting in more extreme form (because of his essentially artistic nature) a more widespread view of economics held by its then gentlemanly practitioners. F.H. Hahn has argued that prior to World War II, economics was 'still very much a British subject with a recognisable British tradition'. One of the distinctive characteristics of this tradition was a belief that:

The study of economics is not to be regarded as an end in itself. It lacks the beauty of mathematics or art or the possibilities for precision and prediction of physics. The main motive for its study must be the improvement of the condition of mankind. (Hahn, 1990, p. 539)

This, of course, was Robertson's view and 'to be useful' was the duteous irritant that goaded him into becoming a professional economist. Despite the abrasions inflicted on his sensitive temperament by the nature of the material, he was perfectly able to make the crucial distinction (see the extract from *LEP*, above) between that which is dull and alien and that which is nevertheless of consequence and, therefore, worth doing regardless. This point is illustrated by passages from the introduction to his lecture 'Utility and All That':

To the idiot [Robertson was addressing his fellow idiots] who is happily absorbed in the tasks of practical life, whether in making money or doing good or both, most of what I have to say will be of repellent aridity.

However, he goes on to assure his audience that 'my report, though arid, is on the face of it of some importance' (Robertson, 1952, p. 13).

10. Robertson through a looking glass

I

Questions raised by Robertson's prominent use of *Alice* quotations in his work can be dealt with under four headings, as follows. First, the *association* of Robertson the economist with the works of Lewis Carroll. Second, the *importance* Robertson accorded these works. Third, the *identification* of Robertson with Lewis Carroll himself. Fourth, the *significance* of Carroll's works for Robertson and by extension, therefore, for an explanation of the relationship between Robertson and his economics.

II

The *association* of Robertson's name with the works of Lewis Carroll is well established, having been attested to by the economics profession over many years. As long ago as November 1932 Keynes, in commenting on the manuscript of Joan Robinson's new book 'Monopoly' (*The Economics of Imperfect Competition*), wrote to his publisher:

> I think that the quotation from Sylvie and Bruno should be deleted, not because it is not apposite, but because Dennis Robertson really must be considered to have a patent in quotations from Lewis Carroll in economic works. (Keynes, *CW* XII p. 867)

In 1953, Alvin H. Hansen and Richard V. Clemence wrote in their introduction to one of Robertson's essays they were reprinting:

> Professor Robertson is moreover an authority on the works of Lewis Carroll. The aptness of his quotations verges on the incredible, and provides an example of monopoly resting on superior talents. (Hansen and Clemence eds, 1953, p. 166)

In the obituary that he wrote on Robertson in 1963, Samuelson spoke of his subject as being 'well remembered for his quotations from Alice in Wonderland' (Samuelson, 1963, p. 518).

Hicks in his 1966 'Memoir' of Robertson, commented on *Money* that it was 'so attractive a work (with a tone that was set by the 'Alice' quotations at the heads of the chapters)' (Hicks, 1966, p. 13).

Similarly, in the next decade, T.E.B. Howarth wrote in his account of the Cambridge economics faculty between the wars that 'Robertson wrote a very well-received, but highly traditional book called *Money* in 1922 with quotations from Alice in Wonderland as chapter headings' (Howarth, 1978, p. 138). The same example was mentioned by Mark Blaug in his *Great Economists Before Keynes* (Blaug, 1986, p. 205) and by H.G. Johnson in *The Shadow of Keynes* (Johnson and Johnson, 1978, p. 136). It was, moreover, a practice that found favour with the book's readership, as Robertson himself noted in his preface to the fourth edition of *Money* published in 1948:

> Thanks, as I am constantly being informed, mainly to its chapter-headings, this book, in spite of not having been revised since 1928, still finds a market . . . Anyway, there are still the chapter-headings – and two more of them. (Robertson, 1948, p. ix)

In 1983 the Rt Hon. Sir Terence Higgins MP in recollecting visits to Robertson's rooms at Cambridge spoke of there being 'little Alice in Wonderland figures all around' (in Harcourt ed., 1985, p. 140).

In 1990, in his Robertson Centenary Lecture delivered before the Master and Fellows of Trinity College, Cambridge, Goodhart described Robertson's practice of using Alice quotations as 'one of [his] trademarks' (in Presley ed., 1992, p. 9).

Finally, Robertson's colleague at Trinity J.R.G. Bradfield included *Alice* among the four aspects of his recollections of Robertson that came most readily to mind:

> *Alice in Wonderland* Dennis's great virtue to a non-economist was that he could illustrate most of the important principles of economics by reference to the story of Alice in Wonderland. This, to my mind, is the index of a really great academic – namely that he can explain highly complex concepts in simple, every day language which can be understood by the non-specialist (admittedly of course at a superficial level); and it is even better when the explanations are in terms of something like Alice in Wonderland which sticks in the mind. (Bradfield to Fletcher, 23 January 1998)

III

With regard to the *importance* that Robertson attached to the works of Lewis Carroll, the question that must be asked is whether Robertson was simply following fashion. Did he merely float on a tide of enthusiasm for the *Alice* books? It was a tide that had ebbed in the early years of the century but it returned to the flood towards the end of World War I, as many sought refuge from the current horrors in the reassuring images of childhood (*Alice* was, for example, featured in R.C. Sherriff's play set in the trenches, *Journey's End*). Certainly, Robertson may have found comfort in exile in Egypt in reading *Alice* as he found it in reading Wordsworth (see Robertson to Keynes, 7 April 1916, in L/R/14–15 RPKC), but the books were not for him a new discovery. He had acted the part of the White Queen whilst at Eton (see Butler, 1963, p. 40) and there is a reference to *AAW* on the first page of *A Study of Industrial Fluctuation* (1915) which was written before the war began.

Nevertheless, after the war intellectual fashion followed popular fashion and it is true that Robertson's most intensive use of *Alice* quotations, in *Money* (1922) and the *Control of Industry* (1923), coincided with a similar upsurge among academic philosophers. Peter Heath, for example, has spoken of there being, in that profession, a 'growing propensity to quotation (dating from the early 1920s onward)' (Heath, 1974, in Bloom ed., 1987, p. 51). R.B. Braithwaite, a Cambridge philosopher who was later to be strongly identified with the Keynesian camp, clearly had Robertson in mind when he wrote in 1932 (the year of Keynes's letter to his publisher, mentioned above): 'Indeed in Cambridge it is now *de rigueur* for economists as well as logicians to pretend to derive their inspiration from Lewis Carroll' (Braithwaite, 1932, p. 177).

On the basis of the range of topics referred to by Heath and Braithwaite, it is also clear that Robertson's interest in the *Alice* books went beyond the intellectual: that there was something much more profound involved. H.G. Johnson caught the flavour of it when he wrote that the practice of quoting *Alice*, 'truly reflected his character: whimsical, somewhat withdrawn and very shy' (Johnson and Johnson, 1978, p. 136). He could sense that this literature spoke to Robertson's condition in some particularly appropriate way but he did not realise how deep the correspondence was.

For Robertson, the practice represented far more than just another example of what we might term Serious Thinker's Whimsy: that is, the quirk in behaviour that in an otherwise remote figure fulfils both the popular notion of the 'eccentric professor' and provides a point of contact in everyday experience between the life of the ivory-tower don and that of the ordinary man. A good example is that of the late Wykeham Professor of Logic at Oxford, the apparently austere author of *Language Truth and Logic*, A.J. Ayer. Ayer was given a human face for the general public when it was revealed that he was known as 'Freddie' and that he supported a well-known football team (Tottenham Hotspur). Something of the sort doubtless operated in Robertson's case with his practice of introducing quotations from what the majority of his readership would regard as classic books for children. But Robertson's understanding of the *Alice* tales would be much deeper than theirs and his involvement with them more personal.

That the economics profession recognised that Carroll's works were *important* for Robertson is clear from the Hansen and Clemence quotation given above, which describes him as an 'authority' on the subject. Professor T. Wilson, a friend and admirer of Robertson over many years and a Robertson scholar, spoke of him as 'one so devoted . . . to the works of the Reverend Charles Dodgson' (in Harcourt ed., 1985, p. 126). Lionel (Lord) Robbins, another friend and admirer, went so far as to describe Robertson as having 'an *equal* admiration of Lewis Carroll and the classical literature which was his first love ere he turned to economics' (Robbins, 1971, p. 221; emphasis added).

However, just how important the *Alice* books were to Robertson and why they were important has not hitherto been recognised. We might, therefore, end this section with a question. In his Centenary Lecture, Goodhart quotes the story, possibly apocryphal, of the Indian student who, noting that the *Alice* books were quoted so many times in Robertson's work, wrote to ask whether they were set books. What we shall attempt to establish in this chapter and the next two is what the answer to that question should have been.

IV

(i) When reading the *Alice* books it is very easy to slip into the belief that they were written by Robertson himself, so closely has he come to be *identified* with them and so nearly do they seem to reflect his temperament as we know it from other sources. This sense of identity is reinforced when we go on to consider the parallels that exist between Robertson's life and that of the real author of the *Alice* books, the Reverend C.L. Dodgson. These parallels explain very clearly why Robertson would have found Dodgson such a sympathetic writer and why he became so devoted to his books. To study the life of Dodgson and the circumstances in which he came to write the *Alice* books is to gain a unique insight into the life of Robertson, the reasons why he became identified with the *Alice* books and, most important, the nature of the relationship between Robertson the man and Robertson the economist.

(ii) Lewis Carroll was the pen-name under which the Reverend Charles Lutwidge Dodgson (1832–98), Victorian clergyman and Oxford don, wrote his *Alice* and subsequent 'nonsense' books (Lutwidge = Ludwig = Lewis; Charles = Carolus = Carroll; Dodgson often reversed his initials as a child). In its general circumstances his life uncannily prefigured that of Robertson. He, like Robertson, came from a background that was scholarly and clerical and spent his childhood in a country rectory (vicarage in Robertson's case). He too was descended from a family with a tradition of service to the Church – but also to the state rather than to education (see especially Bakewell, 1996, ch. 1). His father, like Robertson's, was a classicist and clergyman of the Church of England. He attended one of the great public schools, Rugby as against Eton, and achieved distinction in the classroom rather than on the playing field (see Hudson, 1976, pp. 53, 64, 81). He was strong in classics (like Robertson) but stronger in mathematics (unlike Robertson). He was an undergraduate at the grandest college at Oxford (Christ Church) as Robertson was at Cambridge (Trinity). He, similarly, was duly elected to a fellowship of his own college (called a studentship at Christ Church) and remained there as a don for the rest of his life, occupying college rooms of some grandeur. During their careers as scholars and teachers both men served as librarians: Dodgson for his college library, Robertson for the Marshall Library (see the letter from Mary Marshall of March 1931, in A7/84 RPTC).

(iii)   These strikingly close parallels define the ambience within which both men lived and worked: but of greater significance for present purposes are the parallels between the set of personal characteristics each exhibited. For both Dodgson and Robertson there are parallel contrasts and contradictions that both reveal the underlying complexity of each man's character and give evidence of the life-circumstances with which each strove to come to terms. The characteristics in question (passing over the more commonplace and less significant) belong together as a group and are in fact properly seen as alternative manifestations of the same phenomenon.

By complexity of character we mean, on a non-expert level, that there is evidence in each man's make-up of contrasting and contradictory elements; that conflict resolution will lead to repression and the manifestation of the repressed elements in some form. Success and happiness become a function of the manner in which the problem is resolved, a process in itself, of course, constrained by the problem it seeks to solve. Both Dodgson and Robertson were faced with fundamental problems of life and both showed great courage in facing up to them. In this respect, however, we shall argue that Dodgson, using methods which even then seemed singular and would now seem bizarre, was more successful than Robertson, whose approach was essentially derivative and indeed second-hand.

That Dodgson's character was 'exceedingly complex' was acknowledged by his kindly and eminently reasonable biographer Derek Hudson, who noted that his self-discipline and self-control, which gave the appearance of great steadiness, 'disguised a precarious balance and much inner tension'. He was, Hudson believed, 'richly endowed emotionally but at the same time emotionally immature' (Hudson, 1976, p. 159). Hudson also believed that there was 'some justice' in the Freudian interpretation of Dodgson as being 'strongly repressed', so long as the doctrine is applied cautiously and 'not with prurience but with love and understanding' (Hudson, 1976, p. 128). Though he was intellectually curious and wished to be useful (like Robertson) and to do good, 'in great issues . . . his need for certainties kept him cautious and conservative . . . the dynamic qualities of the reformer were missing' (Hudson, 1976, p. 75). In other words, though well disposed and generous in his personal sphere, he accepted the status quo and followed wholeheartedly the conventions of Victorian society. Like Robertson, he was no iconoclast.

Similarly, though Dodgson, like Robertson, had a reputation for being very shy and retiring, he too by contrast was naturally attracted to showmanship and the world of the theatre (see Hudson, 1976, pp. 46, 79, 134, 139, 175; see also Bakewell, 1996, p. 58; and Clark, 1979, p. 13). Mark Twain found him the shyest grown man he had ever met (Greenacre in Phillips ed., 1972, p. 317); but he was also, like Robertson, noted for his wit and verbal dexterity. However, as against Robertson's 'genuinely beautiful speaking voice and perfectly natural articulation' (Dennison, 1992b, p. 18), Dodgson's shyness was accompanied by a painful stammer which made formal public speaking, whether for lectures or sermons, a considerable strain. Therefore, the difference between them lay in the kind of showmanship to which they were attracted and in the manner of their involvement with the theatre, as we shall see.

Also, Dodgson like Robertson had an artistic temperament, which could in principle have been developed to provide a self-satisfying life of indulgent self-expression and creativity. However, he was also 'endowed with a most exacting conscience . . . set himself the highest standards of personal conduct and was incessantly engaged in a struggle for perfection . . . an artist had been mixed up with a puritan' (Hudson, 1976, p. 101; also Clark, 1979, pp. 146-7; with respect to Robertson, see Rylands to Fletcher, 7 April 1994). But it was in his possession of a social conscience that Dodgson truly paralleled Robertson, for he was one of those 'who were artists at heart but whose energy and compassion carried them far into fields of public or patriotic service' (Hudson, 1976, p. 84). In this respect the impression is that it was via the father in each case that the sense of duty was instilled.

(iv)   The most obvious and, for present purposes the most significant, parallel of contrasts is that Dodgson, like Robertson, combined literary interests and activity with a professional life devoted to precise scholarship in his chosen subject. He was also, like Robertson, extremely industrious, only more so. The difference between them comes in the range of material they produced and the consequent variation in quality. Dodgson, for his part, put out a great variety of publications, from professional treatises through the well-known children's stories to games, puzzles and university ephemera. Robertson's published work, being more narrowly focused, was of a more consistent quality.

The importance of this point is that we are used to thinking of Robertson as being, by the standards of economists, literary. By this we mean that his professional books and papers are marked by elegance and precision of expression and that they are studded with literary references and quotations (as we have seen above, Chapter 7). But apart from a small collection of poetry, published and unpublished, together with a few journalistic efforts, Robertson's literariness was confined to the medium in which he presented his thoughts on economics. In other words, the way in which Robertson combined literary work with precise scholarship was to employ the one in the service of the other, both because of his lack of and distaste for mathematics and as a way of making a somewhat dry and unromantic subject more palatable.

In this sense Robertson had no literary reputation distinct from his professional work. On the other hand, in professional terms Robertson was hailed during his lifetime as one of the world's great economists (see again Hansen and Clemence, 1953, p. 166) and he has a place in the history of economic thought. Taken together, it is likely that his literariness endeared him to certain sections of the economics profession in the same proportion as it alienated him from others. To a wider audience it gave him a voice that was unique among economists, albeit one that was not entirely his own.

Though his use of *Alice* quotations enhanced his appeal as a writer, the very 'aptness' of those quotations, which verged on the 'incredible', meant that the appeal of Robertson was derived in no small measure from the timeless appeal of the *Alice* books themselves. Robertson and the *Alice* books became so closely identified that it is difficult to imagine the corpus of his work without their mediating voice. But in no sense can Robertson be accused of literary parasitism. It is rather that in Lewis Carroll he found the writer who spoke most truly to his condition and from whom he derived the philosophy of life he so desperately needed. Indeed, we shall argue that it is only through Lewis Carroll and *Alice* that we can come to understand Robertson and his approach to his work.

In employing his literary talents in the service of his professional work, Robertson was unknowingly following the example of Dodgson's father, Charles Dodgson Senior. Dodgson himself, on the other hand, deliberately pursued a literary career distinct from but in tandem with his mathematical work. It is of great significance that he should have done so, both for his own reputation and for our understanding of the Dodgson and Robertson life-view.

(v)   In comparison with Robertson, Dodgson's professional standing during his lifetime was altogether on a lower level. Though well known through his textbooks and numerous other publications, he was not considered to be engaged in work of fundamental importance. This was partly a function of his training which, though rigorous, was narrow and unimaginative. In his mathematical work Peter Heath has judged him as follows:

> An inveterate publisher of trifles, he was forever putting out pamphlets, papers broadsheets, and books on mathematical topics, but they earned him no reputation beyond that of a crotchety, if sometimes amusing, controversialist, a compiler of puzzles and curiosities, and a busy yet ineffective reformer on elementary points of computation and instructional method. In the higher reaches of the subject he made no mark at all, and has left none behind. (Heath, in Bloom ed., 1987, p. 45)

The problem seemed to be, as Tony Beale has argued (in Gray ed., 1992, p. 295), that Dodgson lacked both the stimulation of greater minds, so often necessary as the spur to scholarship in mathematics, and the essential personal quality of singlemindedness. With the *hint* of a *constraint* (see the emphasis added to the following passage) that could equally be applied to Robertson, Beale writes:

> His interests were wide and although his mathematical training is evident in all his work, his application was always at an elementary level. His determination to understand every *step* of an argument and to go from the beginning to the end, with strict logical precision [the 'step-by-step' approach], often left him with a walnut size problem which he had cracked with a sledgehammer. (Beale, in Gray ed., 1992, p. 298; emphasis added)

In the same vein he claims:

> It is also doubtful whether he had the kind of mind for really original mathematics. In all his work he pursued the solution of the problem with relentless logic, starting always from premises which could be shown to be true. (Beale, in Gray ed., 1992, p.298)

However, Dodgson's interest in puzzle and paradox had its serious side, and Peter Heath has argued that as compared to his mathematics, 'in the infant science of mathematical logic his place is a notch or two higher' (Heath, in Bloom ed., 1987, p. 46).

(vi)   Dodgson's 'extra-mathematical reputation' was of course that which he made with his highly successful 'nonsense' books for children, written under the name of Lewis Carroll. These were, in order of publication and, significantly as we shall see, in declining order of popularity: *Alice's Adventures in Wonderland* (1865); *Through the Looking Glass and What Alice Found There* (1871, dated 1872); *The Hunting of the Snark* (1876); *Sylvie and Bruno* (1889); *Sylvie and Bruno Concluded* (1893). There was also a mass of lesser works and ephemera. The most important of the *oeuvre* by a considerable margin are the *Alice* books, referred to henceforth as *AAW* and *TLG* respectively. They are the works with which the name of Lewis Carroll is chiefly associated and are the only ones to which Robertson makes reference. For this reason they will receive most attention in what follows.

The tremendous success of the *Alice* books – in time they would become established as a source of quotation and reference on a par with the Bible and the works of Shakespeare – made Lewis Carroll a household name at home and abroad (Levin in Phillips ed., 1972, p. 176). At the same time C.L. Dodgson remained largely unknown outside professional circles, his college and university. In particular his colleagues at Christ Church found the contrast between the shy and unobtrusive mathematics tutor and the world-famous author difficult to understand and there was some resentment. 'It was', comments Hudson, 'the old situation of the prophet who is not without honour save in his own country' (Hudson, 1976, p. 175). Interestingly the same comment was made in identical terms about Robertson by a friend who drew the contrast between the world recognition he achieved as an economist and the rejection and hostility he experienced at Cambridge (see Proctor to Bromley, 8 January 1968, G11/10, 11 RPTC).

(vii)   Dodgson found fame with his fanciful work because he possessed the genius to draw on the means by which he came to terms with his life-situation to create works of art of imperishable merit. The implication is that it is by way of *Alice* that we find our way to Dodgson, for as Hudson has recognised: 'The "Alice" books were in some degree an autobiographical miscellany, woven together with extraordinary skill: an Odyssey of the subconscious' (Hudson, 1976, p. 73).

Robertson, by identifying with Dodgson and by finding solace, as it were, second-hand in his works, by the same token indicates the nature of the life-situation in which he, Robertson, must live and work and the nature of the fundamental concerns and constraints that shaped his approach to his work. By interpreting the works of Dodgson we shall obtain a unique insight into the works of Robertson.

(viii)   As a preliminary, we must introduce at this juncture a parallel between Dodgson and Robertson that has not so far been considered: namely, that both men remained unmarried; but that both, by contrast, desired love and affection in their lives and sought to find it. The significance for present purposes lies in the manner in which they did so. And here again we shall find that it was Dodgson who showed the unmistakable, if extraordinary, originality of genius while Robertson, whose talents were more narrowly focused, could only find refuge at second hand.

There was, it must be allowed, an attractive alternative to marriage available to both men. By remaining single they were able to live in college in conditions of comfort and dignity. Both chose to do so and for the rest of their lives their colleges became in a very real sense their *alma mater*. For Dodgson, indeed, given the period in which he lived, to remain unmarried (and to proceed to Holy Orders) was a condition of his retaining his life-studentship – a not inconsiderable incentive. Nevertheless, it was always open to him to marry and then to be presented to a college living, a route his father dearly wanted him to follow (and one which Robertson's father was to follow after the episode at Haileybury; see above, Chapter 2). But Dodgson's shyness and his serious stammer meant that life as a parish priest could hold no real attractions for him and he never proceeded beyond deacon's orders.

But college, as a society of bachelor dons, for all its attractions, was necessarily monastic in character and there were deeper reasons why neither attempted to find love within a marriage. For Robertson, the ultimate bar would have been his sexuality, which led him by way of compensation into infatuations with young men. These were necessarily unsatisfactory not only because the times were not ready for such liaisons but also because they could not provide a stable source of the affection that, in the words of his friend and ally, Lionel Robbins, he 'so obviously craved' (Robbins, 1971, p. 221). Nevertheless it would seem that Robertson did require the protective love of a woman, as the closeness of the relationship with his mother, to whom he was devoted, and with his sister Gerda, who acted very much as a confidante, would indicate.

In this last, Robertson closely paralleled Dodgson who, though not homosexual, similarly exhibited symptoms of emotional immaturity, as his biographer has noted:

> He was a man *who carried his childhood with him*; the love that he understood and longed for was a protective love. He had a deep instinctive admiration for women, yearning for their sympathy and often finding it. But it is probable that he could not reconcile in himself love and desire. . . . (Hudson, 1976, p. 159; emphasis added. See also Bakewell, 1996, pp. 39, 74, 98, 139, 245)

Dodgson's past-fixation was a determining impulse in his life and its influence was to increase as the years went by. For Hudson, the damage was wrought by the humiliation suffered at public school by a shy and sensitive boy who was then faced with the sudden death of the mother whom he greatly loved (Hudson, 1976, p. 66).

One does wonder, however, whether this diagnosis gives sufficient weight to the effects of puberty and to the increased awareness of one's life situation that growing up can bring. Certainly for Robertson, whose change of outlook during these years seems so closely to parallel that of Dodgson, the period was of crucial importance. Something, which we must assume was the growing realisation of the nature of his sexuality and apparently in conjunction with his loss of security and loss of faith, transformed the happy and self-valuing schoolboy into the intellectually brilliant but emotionally desolate undergraduate (see above Chapter 4).

For Robertson as for Dodgson, awareness brought regret for the future and nostalgia for the past. But was there *nothing* to look forward to? Here at least there seems to be a clear distinction between them. Dodgson was an ordained deacon of the Church of England and had for the future the comfort of the Christian Revelation. Robertson, by contrast, though he came from a clerical family, had lost his faith and had no Hope of Glory. As a colleague wrote of him: 'For all his gaiety and wit he had, as his poems printed and unprinted bear witness, a profound sense of the harshness of human destiny' (Butler, 1963, p. 42).

Is this the point of departure between the two and if so how is it to be accounted for? In fact the position is not as clear-cut as it appears and closer examination reveals a fundamental similarity of view. Most important is the evidence afforded by Dodgson's fanciful writing and in particular by the *Alice* books. To the extent that these can be seen as 'an Odyssey of the subconscious', they provide a true guide to his deepest feelings (see Hudson, 1976, p. 73; see also Bakewell, 1996, p. 100).

(ix)   A knowledge of the circumstances in which Dodgson came to write the *Alice* books is of material importance for an understanding of what the books contain, what they 'mean' and their significance for Robertson. As a preliminary to an examination of the circumstances, we should notice that so far in the story neither Dodgson nor Robertson have found the love they desired. The love, that is, that encompasses personal affection, the urgings of sex, the need for mutual support and society, the requirements of Christian obligation and, in a larger and less well-defined way, a defence against uncertainty and fear of the unknown.

Neither, in fact, was to do so – in the recognised sense of finding requited love in intimacy with another adult person. Robertson's long-running, though necessarily furtive, relationship with Rylands brought him release but was racked by storms and always rather one-sided. Both instead sought a substitute in the company of young people (the importance of their being young will be discussed below). For Robertson this meant his pupils at Cambridge who, in the nature of students, came up year-by-year and were always youthful and who never grew old. Also, through his stage activities, it meant the actors of the Cambridge Amateur Dramatic Club (the ADC) and the Marlowe Society. Rylands recalled that 'he found the players and members of the ADC and Marlowe D.S. very *lively* and *congenial* and *friendly* and *young!*' (Rylands to

Fletcher, 7 April 1994; emphasis in original). And finally, it meant finding love at one remove, by sharing in the fruits of Dodgson's own solution to the problem.

Dodgson's solution, which was altogether more successful than Robertson's in meeting his particular needs, drew on his extraordinary capacity for communicating with and entertaining children. From his early twenties onwards Dodgson cultivated the society of a series of 'child-friends', mostly girls as he considered boys 'an unattractive race of beings', and these friendships became the mainstay of his existence. 'Children are three-fourths of my life', he once wrote, and he was certain that there was nothing so much worth having as 'the heart-love of a child'.

He also understood, however, that because there are 'few things in the world so evanescent as a child's love' (Rackin, in Bloom ed., 1987, p. 125) and because child-friends grew up so quickly – he lost interest in them as they reached puberty – new recruits had constantly to be found. These he sought from among the families of friends and acquaintances and from children he met on train journeys, in the street or on the beach. The practice raised eyebrows then and would be utterly inconceivable now, but for Dodgson it was a means of salvation. With children at least he could relax and be his own natural self. And note here the closeness of the parallel with the case of Robertson, of whom Austin Robinson wrote:

> To the last Robertson got much pleasure, as he had as a younger man, from the society of the young. He was at his best and happiest among a chosen group of the ablest of the younger economists. These he knew intimately and with them, unaffected by doctrinal divisions, he could be wholly natural and at his ease. (Robinson, 1963)

Child-friends could, of course, provide only a partial solution to Dodgson's problem and the real nature of his relationship with them is controversial (see Hudson, 1976, p. 67; Bakewell, 1996, p. 245; Coveney in Gray ed., 1992, pp. 329, 334).

Nevertheless, as a result of these relationships Carroll/Dodgson produced literary works that became a source of delight for the world in general and a source of inspiration and of solace for those who found in his *Alice* books a philosophy with which to approach the inescapable problems of life – and death.

The means Dodgson used to entertain his child-friends were those with which he had beguiled his brothers and sisters (particularly his sisters, as there were ultimately seven of them) at home as a boy: conjuring tricks, puzzles, sketching and above all story-telling. He had an inexhaustible supply of stories with which to spellbind his child-listeners. Over the years these extempore stories lived and died 'like summer midges', until one particular incident served to pin them down and to preserve them for posterity. These stories were the beginnings of the *Alice* books and, therefore, the incident itself and the events surrounding it have great symbolic and explanatory interest.

V

The inspiration and eponymous heroine of the *Alice* books was Alice Liddell, daughter of Henry Liddell, Dean of Christ Church (cathedral and college). The incident was the famous river expedition of 4 July 1862, when Dodgson together with a colleague, Robinson Duckworth, fellow of Trinity College, rowed the three Liddell sisters up the Thames to Godstow for a summer picnic (see Batey, 1980, pp. 14–21). Alice was not the first of his child-friends and this was not the only river trip with her, but it was to be distinguished for all time when Alice asked Dodgson to write out for her the stories with which he had been entertaining them: 'Alice's adventures'. Dodgson undertook to do so, and by November had accumulated enough material to begin preparation of a formal manuscript. This, written in his own autograph and illustrated with his own sketches, he had bound up into a volume entitled *Alice's Adventures Under Ground* (*AAU*) for presentation to Alice Liddell. This volume, which he later published in facsimile and which has more recently been reissued by the British Library (with an interesting foreword and useful introduction, [1886] 1985), was to be the preliminary version of *Alice's Adventures in Wonderland*.

At the time, Dodgson did not mark the events of 4 July 1862 save by a routine account in his diary; but seven months later, as their significance began to dawn upon him, he added to the entry the words: 'on this occasion I told them the fairy tale of Alice's adventures underground' (see Gardner ed., 1970, p. 21 n. 1). Over time his sense of their importance seemed to increase and the account he wrote of them twenty-five years later is both deeply nostalgic and redolent of those things that meant most in his life:

> Many a day had we rowed together on that quiet stream – the three little maidens and I – and many a fairy tale had been extemporised for their benefit . . . yet none of these many tales got written down: they lived and died, like summer midges, each in its own golden afternoon until there came a day when, as it chanced one of my little listeners petitioned that the tale might be written out for her . . . Stand forth, then, from the shadowy past, 'Alice', the child of my dreams. Full many a year has slipped away since that 'golden afternoon' that gave thee birth, but I can call it up almost as clearly as if it were yesterday – the cloudless blue above, the watery mirror below, the boat drifting idly on its way, the tinkle of the drops that fell from our oars, as they waved so sleepily to and fro, and (the one bright gleam of life in all the slumbrous scene) the three eager faces, hungry for news of fairy-land. (Lewis Carroll, 1887, quoted in Gardner ed., 1970, p. 21–2)

Dodgson's recollection of the afternoon as 'golden' is amply borne out by the testimony of his companions (see the quotations in Gardner ed., 1970, p. 22).

However, when enquiries were made at the Meteorological Office in 1950 it was discovered that the official records of the weather at Oxford, 'cool and rather wet', did not bear out the unanimous recollections of the boating party (see Gardner ed., 1970, p. 22; Hudson, 1976, p. 114; Gordon in Phillips ed., 1972, pp. 99). But though the facts seem to spoil a neat story, they do in fact give it added significance. The explanation for the discrepancy might go as follows (but see also Bakewell, 1996, p. 115, who is inclined to accept the participants' accounts as factually true).

Dodgson seems to have taken on the task of writing out 'Alice's Adventures' with no great eagerness and his enthusiasm for the project only increased when he began to glimpse its literary possibilities. The more he poured himself into the *Alice* books, the more significant they became to him – and with them, also, the significance of the 'golden afternoon'.

Therefore the actual weather conditions on the day are of little importance – there was evidently confusion with other similar days when the sun had blazed – but it became increasingly important to Dodgson that the *Alice* books should have originated in the events of a 'golden afternoon'. It became, in other words, a *myth*. The tales of Wonderland *had* to be conceived under summer suns and Dodgson took care to enshrine the myth for posterity: first in the dedication of *AAU*; then in the introductory poem to and in the conclusion of *AAW*; then in the introductory and concluding poems of *TLG*; in the prefatory poem to *The Hunting of the Snark* (*Snark*); and finally in the article of 1887, quoted above.

What remains from all this is that Dodgson originated the myth of the golden afternoon and that presumably he had reasons for doing so. The reasons are bound up with the message or meaning of the *Alice* books and the part they played in his life and, by extension, in the life of Robertson and others who identified with Lewis Carroll and found solace in his philosophy. It is to this topic, the last of the four headings specified above, that we turn in the next chapter.

11. Alice's evidence

Any idea that Lewis Carroll's *Alice* and other 'nonsense' books are simply books for children – as that term is usually understood – is dispelled by evidence of the literary and scientific interest lavished upon them. Professional philosophers, literary allegorists and Freudian psychoanalysts have all attempted to find meaning below the surface chaff of the narrative and there is now a considerable critical and interpretative literature.

Many of the most interesting and useful contributions have been gathered together in three volumes of readings, to which reference has already been made in the previous chapter: these are Bloom ed. (1987); Gray ed. (1992) and Phillips ed. (1972). Also extremely helpful are Martin Gardner's *The Annotated Alice* (1970) and the same editor's *The Annotated Snark* (1974). In addition we shall make much use of Elizabeth Sewell's seminal and highly suggestive study *The Field of Nonsense* (1952).

II

The idea of the *Alice* books as texts possessing logical and philosophical interest has already been introduced and here we might reinforce the point by adding Peter Heath's assessment:

> The notion that *Alice* is a grown-up book is certainly nothing new. Many readers find this out for themselves and the fact has long been familiar to various sections of the academic world, including professional philosophers and logicians. Fiction, of course, is normally of no interest to philosophers – any more than facts are – but *Alice* is a book they can all understand, and many of them find it compulsive reading. Their habit, however, has been to keep this news to themselves, as if slightly ashamed of it, and to notify their addiction only by a growing propensity to quotation (dating from the early 1920s onwards) and by the occasional insertion of a discreet article in a learned journal, remote from the vulgar gaze. (Heath, in Bloom ed., 1987, p. 51)

As an example of a 'discreet article in a learned journal' by a professional philosopher, that by R.B. Braithwaite is particularly appropriate. The 'insertion', in the *Mathematical Gazette*, was entitled 'Lewis Carroll as a

Logician' and included 'some discussion of the logical points involved in the solipsism of the Red King, the monism of the Other Professor and the nominalism of Humpty Dumpty' (Braithwaite, 1932, p. 174).

However, beyond establishing the point that the 'more popular view of [*Alice*] as a mere farrago of amiable nonsense', is wrong; and that 'not only is it *not* nonsense [but] also contains, by implication, a great deal of excellent sense' (Heath, in Bloom ed., 1987, p. 51), we have no further interest in the philosophy of the books as that term would be understood by a professional philosopher. What we do have a great deal of interest in is the 'philosophy' of the canon in the sense of the message it contains regarding the universal human condition: the life-view of those who must ultimately face death.

In seeking Carroll's philosophy we shall have little to do with psycho-analysis, though the field has proved a fertile one for initiates, and their constructions are ingenious and interesting (see, for example, the group of papers gathered in Phillips ed., 1972). Nor shall we look for any deliberately concealed comment on burning contemporary issues; or seek elaborate, allegorical references to leading individuals and ideas of the day (see, for example, Jo Jones and Frances Gladstone, *The Red King's Dream*, 1995). Instead, we shall offer an interpretation that proceeds directly from the following: first, what we know of Dodgson/Carroll: his temperament and characteristics of behaviour, together with the events of his life; second, the background to the anxieties of the age in which he lived; third, what we find in the books themselves, bearing in mind the circumstances in which they came to be written.

At a superficial level and as a counterweight to overblown flights of fancy, Derek Hudson's assessment of his subject's creations cannot be bettered:

> The 'Alice' books may be explained as the original work of a mathematician and logician, interested in the precise meaning of words, who was at the same time a genius of invention and poetic imagination with a love for children and a gift for entertaining them.   (Hudson, 1976, p. 157)

There is, of course, more to it than this and more to it than is allowed for by the philosopher's contention that the books constitute a joyous logician's playtime. The best clue to what that something more might be is given by Elizabeth Sewell's celebrated study, *The Field of Nonsense* (1952), which, though it ultimately misses the point, nevertheless still provides the most useful analytical framework for an approach to the interpretation of *Alice*. By the same token it provides an understanding of the thought processes of Dodgson and Robertson and, by extension, of the central issues dividing Robertson and Keynes.

III

Sewell's study explores the meaning of 'nonsense' by reference to the works of the leading 'nonsense' writers: Lewis Carroll and Edward Lear. In the exposition and criticism that follows, all references are to the original 1952 edition.

We begin with language because language is a principal means by which the mind makes sense of ideas and events. Nonsense, therefore, is 'a collection of words . . . which in their arrangement do not fit in to some recognised system in a particular mind'. It is nevertheless 'a structure held together by valid mental relations' (p. 4). Nonsense is orderly. Both Carroll and Lear relished order in their lives and 'if a work of art is co-natural with the mind of the artist, then nonsense may be orderly too' (p. 45, see also Guiliano, in Bloom ed., 1987, p. 110).

The form of order that nonsense assumes is that of the game. Language is reorganised not according to the rules of prose or poetry but according to those of play, with the 'game as an enclosed whole, with its own rigid laws which cannot be questioned within the game itself'. The benefit to the player of this particular game is that by allowing oneself to be bound by the system's laws one can 'attain that particular sense of freedom which games have to offer' (p. 26).

This freedom, we might add, is of the kind which stems from the limitation of the range of problems and outcomes which have to be faced and can be seen, in economic terms, as representing the distinction between risk and uncertainty (Frank Knight's classic distinction: see Knight, 1921, pp. 19–20; and Knight, 1921, Chapter VII). Sewell puts it as follows:

> It is essential to the working of a game that the mind should feel safe inside it. It is this sense of safety which the game's rules and limitations are intended to ensure, making a game more certain than life can be.　(p. 66)

However, nonsense as game limits possibilities and maintains order not only through the rules under which it operates but also, and of particular interest for present purposes, through the form of its construction, *in the sense of the relation between the whole and its parts*. This is a point upon which Sewell lays considerable emphasis, twice stating in identical terms that:

> This universe . . . must never be more than the sum of its parts, and must never fuse into some all-embracing whole, which cannot be broken down again into the original ones. It must try to create with words a universe that consists of bits. (p. 53; see also p. 98)

Moreover:

> The emphasis must always be on the parts rather than on the whole . . . Part must

be separate and distinct from part, wholes must be analysable into parts and the total construction must be no more than a detached product of the conscious mind which must never identify itself with its production in any way. (p. 98)

In *TLG*, the White Queen asks Alice: 'What's one and one and one and one and one and one and one and one and one and one?' The fact that Alice cannot answer the question is unimportant, as it is not the total but the composition that matters:

for this is to be the composition of the universe of nonsense, a collection of ones which can be summed together into a whole but which can always fall back into separate ones again. (p. 98)

Thus the maintenance of a universe of nonsense as game and the promise of freedom and safety (a haven from life's realities) that it provides depends on the assurance that the whole can never be more than the sum of the parts. This we may interpret as meaning, with one eye on what is to come, that the separate elements of a chosen universe when summed together will produce an outcome that is predictable.

We say 'chosen universe' because we enter into the game voluntarily, playing because we choose to take advantage of the benefits obtained from doing so. Often games simulate aspects of life itself but with the benefit of having the issues simplified, the rules of conduct specified and the range of possible outcomes strictly limited. It follows that if game-playing is voluntary, we are free to choose games that best suit our own situation – or temperament. By extension we ourselves may specify the rules and the outcomes.

We need not, negatively, specify exclusions, for the danger may lie in the unknowable, or the uncertain. Instead, positively, we may specify a known world of risk but no uncertainty and in which wholes as outcomes are not merely not 'beyond the grasp of logic' as Sewell would say but, more restrictively, which proceed directly from the sum of the elements in a way that is predictable and acceptable in that they do not threaten the integrity of our chosen universe.

These ideas, which are of the utmost importance, will form the basis of our interpretation of Robertson's approach to economics.

IV

Integral to Sewell's thesis (see pp. 46, 53, 99) is the Manichean idea that order and disorder co-exist in the mind and that nonsense as game must engage with and overcome disorder as opponent by the establishment of a universe of order. Disorder is the antithesis of order and breaks out in situations in which the power of logic is weak and discreteness breaks down: that is, situations governed by unconscious states of mind or by the emotions.

The first category is represented by dream-states in which all is fluid and, therefore, uncontrollable (p. 36). In the extreme form, nightmare, the orderliness of logical relations is swamped as the mind attends to all possible relations simultaneously. Instead of one and one and one, nightmare produces one big One (pp. 50-1).

Closely akin to dream is poetry, which makes extensive use of imagery and figurative speech to produce an underlying unity through the establishment of 'a multiplicity of irrational relations and [which is] perceived by the dream faculty of the mind' (p. 112).

In the second category lie the emotions, which may be engaged in several ways to produce relationships destructive of nonsense. One, the strict avoidance of which Sewell regards as a matter of 'real importance' (p. 107), is beauty, which poses a double threat: first, by weakening a participant's detachment and indifference by its invitation to 'some kind of union with the beautiful object' (p. 107); second, the essence of beauty is due proportion, which means that each *part* must bear a fitting relation to the *whole*. As a consequence the mind perceives more than a sum of ones: it sees *organism* rather than organisation. (The relevance of this point to the wider argument will be made clear in Chapter 24, below, where it is related to the philosophy of G.E. Moore, which had a profound influence on Keynes and his circle.)

The agent most destructive of nonsense in Sewell's catalogue is love. Love is to be regarded as particularly dangerous because it is 'supremely unitive'. Love has 'special affinities with poetry and in its wilder manifestations, with madness'. Love 'demands subjection of the whole individual – partly suppressing the logical intellect' (p. 153). Sewell judges that in the *Alice* books 'the game continues unaffected by love' (p. 154); see also Rackin, who endorses Sewell's argument (in Bloom ed., 1987, p. 111). In *AAW*, for example, Carroll protects his nonsense by introducing a symbol of love, the Queen of Hearts, as a main character but 'turns her into a termagent, shifting the emphasis from the unitive passion of the heart to the divisive one of anger' (p. 154). But the intrusion of love into the later works marks their progressive degeneration as nonsense-works: 'Love begins to creep into the *Snark* and by the time we reach Sylvie and Bruno it is everywhere' (p. 154). Love, like beauty, will play an important part in the argument that follows, both in interpreting Carroll's works and in explaining the life-circumstances of Robertson and Keynes and their approach to work.

In Sewell's thesis, emotion is the 'gate to everythingness and nothingness where ultimately words fail completely' (p. 129) and is alien to nonsense as game. There must in particular be an absence of feeling between player and plaything. Sewell sees this as being achieved by way of two forms of insulation (pp. 138, 143–4). The first is the separation of one part from another within the whole by the exclusion of emotion. She points out that Alice is treated as an object without feeling by the creatures she meets and experiences 'gratuitous and recurring rudeness'.

This is certainly true as far as it goes – we recall in particular Alice's treatment at the hands of the Caterpillar and the Mad Hatter in *AAW*, and Tweedledum and Tweedledee and Humpty Dumpty in *TLG* – and Sewell is correct in saying that no one 'with the possible exception of the White Knight' (significantly as we shall see), shows her any kindness (he is at least 'not unkind'). However, this interpretation does not allow for the possibility that Alice herself may be a sympathetic character, a point we shall find to be of the greatest significance.

The second form or layer of insulation is the dream-state within which the events of the *Alice* tales are supposedly experienced. In Sewell's view, it is the 'true purpose of the Alices' to ensure that the player's mind is isolated from all possible contact with real life. Again we comment that while this is a valid hypothesis it is not the whole story.

If 'everythingness', to which emotion is the gate, is represented by nightmare, 'one big One'; then 'nothingness', which is equally destructive of nonsense and is of particular importance for the present argument, is represented by death: or more precisely, death as extinction. Sewell twice refers to William Empson's assertion that fear of death is one of the crucial topics of the *Alice* books (pp. 41, 124). Other writers have interpreted the *Snark* as an allegory of voyage towards discovery of death-as-extinction. It is very significant that Robertson made no reference to this work supposedly composed solely of pure nonsense.

V

In Sewell's view, the progressive degeneration of the Lewis Carroll canon, which is marked by the inclusion of more and more of the agents destructive of nonsense, is caused by Carroll's attempt to extend the boundaries of the game until it should encompass his whole life:

> because the player cannot live without the sense of safety the game gives, he cannot cope with reality on any other terms than those of a game and so must squeeze everything into this charmed circle where the player is in control.   (p. 175)

The strategy is, of course, self-defeating, for the attempt to achieve total security has the effect of destroying the essential characteristics of the game itself.

Unable to meet the reality of life, Carroll imprisons himself within his would-be game. Here deprived of the normal human response to existence he risks insanity, the condition of which Sewell accuses him (see, for example, pp. 168, 169, 181) and in which assessment she claims the support of other testimony and of a rumour during Dodgson's lifetime that he had gone mad (p. 181).

But this is a harsh judgement, and more so if there is a hint at there being misanthropy in Dodgson's make-up. More just, perhaps, is Derek Hudson's kindly view that he was a 'very brave man' who found himself in a certain life-situation, accepted it and made the best of it:

> The sensitive boy from the Rectory, with his genius and his principles, was allotted no easy task in life. More than once the balance had trembled; he had found the courage to keep it true.   (Hudson, 1976, p. 246; see also p. 159)

Much the same might be said about Robertson, who similarly found himself in a very difficult life-situation but who found the courage to keep going and to use his native abilities to achieve success. Dodgson's achievement was obviously greater because of his genius. Robertson, in working out his own solution, leant on Dodgson, who was the true original. But the one mirrored the other, and the better we understand Dodgson the better we shall understand Robertson.

VI

There is a more fundamental objection to Sewell's thesis. Although the structure or fabric she employs is extremely helpful and apposite, laying emphasis on the relation between the whole and the parts and going one-and-one-and-one, the conclusion itself seems too insubstantial or even trivial. One can readily accept that nonsense as game provides a safe environment in which some of life's battles can be simulated and that by playing the game the mind will obtain relaxation and refreshment. But can this sufficiently explain the appeal of the *Alices* to highly intelligent adults, some of whom see in them not only logical puzzles, whimsical charm and a delicious variety of humour but also a philosophy of life? In this respect we might notice that Roger Henkle has commented on 'the remarkable impact that the Alice books have had upon adult readers for over a hundred years' (in Gray ed., 1992, p. 357).

To see them as embodying a philosophy of life is to put the books on a far higher plane than say, ludo, halma or even chess. It is true that Sewell does indicate that she is thinking in terms of relatively complicated games, but as she still talks about 'men' as pieces, halma or draughts would not in principle be excluded. And what about 'Monopoly', which is undoubtedly a game but which has as its essence the very references to commerce and the law that, for Sewell, so badly mar the *Snark* as nonsense (see Sewell, 1952, p. 149ff.)?

Relaxation and refreshment do not sufficiently explain the appeal of the *Alice* books which provides a degree of warmth and reassurance that seems quite at odds with the notion of love being ruthlessly excluded as a way of creating the conditions for nonsense as game. Donald Rackin has asked:

> why do adult readers today often remember the *Alices*, despite all [the] evidence to the contrary, as somehow warm, even loving, experiences and Alice herself as the embodiment of Dodgson's own later vision of her: . . . 'Loving, first, loving and gentle: loving as a dog (forgive the prosaic simile, but I know no earthly love so pure and perfect), and gentle as a fawn'. (Rackin, in Bloom ed., 1987, p. 113)

Yes, 'warm even loving experiences', despite the fact that Alice is disorientated in time and place, is often lonely, is treated with breathtaking coldness and rudeness, is subjected to death-jokes, and in both books experiences disillusion in her quest.

It is an extraordinary phenomenon but there is a further quality that the *Alice* books possess which gives us the key to the conundrum and which is of particular relevance for the present study. Rackin, in another essay of the same period, refers more explicitly to their therapeutic appeal when he writes of them as having 'become the cherished, sometimes sacrosanct possession of troubled adults' (Rackin in Gray ed., 1992, p. 402). Dodgson and Robertson were troubled adults. The *Alice* books reveal what their troubles were and how they sought to meet them.

The books thus possess a dual character. If we use Sewell's scheme of analysis as a looking-glass, we can obtain two entirely different images. The first, the surface reflection, shows Sewell's nonsense-as-game: a vista of safe, ingenuous, knockabout play that provides a haven from the real world. But when we pass through the looking-glass, all is the same but dramatically transformed. The pieces, the counters, the discrete parts-in-relation-to-the-whole are there as before but their character is entirely different. Now they are seen as dark reality, while the everyday world seems positively bright by contrast. The child sees only the world of play; the adult, troubled and untroubled, sees in addition the darkness of reality.

Because of the dual character of the *Alice* books, the two images can co-exist without invalidating each other and we may pass through and through, from one to the other, as perception varies with temperament or mood.

Where differences may lie is in the reaction to the revelation of dark reality behind the looking-glass. Both Robertson and Keynes were intelligent and perceptive enough to see through to reality but their responses were different. Keynes's was normal and progressive; Robertson's by contrast was abnormal and regressive, like Dodgson's, and there lies the key to our whole argument.

VII

Nonsense as game and dark reality do not enter simply as abstract concepts – like Platonic forms – but find expression in a particular institutional setting. This setting is Victorian society. The *Alice* stories are in fact fairy tales delivered in the similitude of a dream, and awake or asleep we are in a Victorian world. In the (waking) introductory and concluding prose and verse sequences, Dodgson and his illustrator, Sir John Tenniel, locate us in historical Victorian times. In the dream-tales themselves, Victorian society is still there but entirely subverted (see Rackin in Phillips ed., 1972, pp. 391–416). There is in fact a complete contrast between what we actually find in the *Alice* tales and what we are led to expect from a reading of the material that surrounds them.

This contrast between the waking world of Victorian society and the dream world of Victorian society subverted, *together with* the dual character of the *Alice* tales, for which Victorian-society-subverted provides the institutional setting, is the clue to the ultimate meaning of the *Alice* books and, therefore, to their true significance for Dodgson and for Robertson.

Of course, we catch only an oblique glimpse of Victorian society in the waking parts of the *Alice*s, as seen from the viewpoint of a young girl of the solidly middle class, but we can readily reconstruct the rest from the subverted version portrayed in the dream-tales themselves. The offices and institutions of high Victorian civilisation are in place but shown as bumbling and absurd or arbitrary and tyrannical. Worthy, improving and sentimental poems and songs are mercilessly parodied. Though the framework poems are overwhelmingly nostalgic and sentimental, speaking of heart-love, childhood, summer days, summer seas and hazy golden dreams, the tales themselves are, with a single significant exception, loveless, morally void and subject always to cruel chance.

In one crucially important respect, however, there is concurrence between the waking and dreaming parts of the *Alice* tales, namely, in a universal preoccupation with time. The nostalgia of the framework poems, for childhood and summer days long ago is juxtaposed with expressions of regret about time's passing and its ineluctable consequences of ageing, decay and death. This concern – extraordinary in a supposed fun-book for children – is picked up in the tales themselves, which indicate anxiety about the passage of time (for example, in the encounters with the White Rabbit, the Mad Hatter, the Red Queen, the White Queen) and feature death-jokes (the best known occur in the encounters with the Tweedle Brothers, the Red King's dream, and with Humpty Dumpty, who hints at euthanasia).

It is in the light of these considerations that the dual character of the *Alice* books becomes painfully clear. Both *AAW* and *TLG* satisfy sufficient of Sewell's criteria to pass muster as nonsense-as-game. This, given the delightful sense of play they radiate, is at least the effect they have. What is harder to swallow, however, is the idea that love has been deliberately excluded as a *means* of creating the conditions for the very feelings of warmth and reassurance that nonsense engenders.

Might it not be rather that the conditions necessary for nonsense-as-game describe also the characteristics of a natural state that is the obverse of nonsense? We realise, with a shudder, that the one-and-one-and-one of Sewell's nonsense-as-game, the fantasy world in which to seek refuge from the real world, is in fact a horrifying vision of the natural world beneath the veneer of order and civilisation that we impose upon chaos and refer to as ordinary life in the light of common day (see Rackin in Phillips ed., 1972, pp. 391–416).

VIII

To understand how Dodgson came to endue his fairy tales with this darker aspect of their dual nature, we must draw a further parallel between Dodgson and Robertson not referred to so far: that is, that both men in their respective universities found themselves in a cockpit of revolutionary ferment. For Robertson, in the 1930s, it was the Keynesian Revolution. For Dodgson, in the 1860s, it was the scientific revolution that seemed to many to challenge the literal truth of Scripture and therefore the validity of established Christian belief. Jan B. Gordon, referring to Walter Houghton's *The Victorian Frame of Mind*, has pointed out that:

> Once Chambers and Lyell, two geologists, had challenged the theological idea of a Creation in a single instant of time with their Uniformitarian thesis, Victorian England was quite literally cast adrift upon the seas of time . . . The impact of the *Voyage of the Beagle* [1831–6] was not entirely dissimilar, since the concept of the fortuitous mutation implied a certain lack of any orderly progression from a Creation in the past. (Gordon in Phillips ed., 1972, p. 98)

Darwin's *The Origin of Species by Natural Selection* appeared in November 1859 and the famous debate between the naturalist T.H. Huxley and Bishop William 'Soapy Sam' Wilberforce (Dodgson's bishop) took place in Oxford in 1860. Both events, therefore, occurred less than three years before the 'golden afternoon' of the river expedition of July 1862, for which they

provided a very disturbing prelude. Halfway between the publication dates of
AAW and *TLG*, Matthew Arnold's poem 'Dover Beach' (1867) acknowledged
the 'slow withdrawing roar' of Faith.

The effect of all this was to raise a dreadful spectre: that the universe, far
from being created by a loving God who gave it meaning, order and purpose,
was instead meaningless and purposeless. True, there was order of a kind but
it lay only in the realm of physics. All was cold, discrete and morally void.
And if this much could be viewed with a certain amount of detachment, as
posing problems for the scholarly interpretation of Scripture, the implications
could not be, for they applied to each individual personally and profoundly.
Instead of the Hope of Glory and a blissful life after death in Heaven, there
now loomed the prospect that 'the only end of age' was death as extinction.

Instead of a life spent in working out the Divine Will, it was now necessary
to find some means of establishing a still point of reference with meaning for
one's own circumstances and of somehow coming to terms with the idea of
living a life in which one moved from youth to age under sentence of death as
extinction.

The problems that confronted Dodgson as a consequence of scientific
discovery were, of course, the problems of Everyman. But in confronting them
Dodgson had also to contend with the difficulties raised by his own
temperament, for this would determine the way in which he joined with those
'despairing Oxford contemporaries [who] had already turned to love as the
only possible refuge on the "darkling plain" of their faithless age' (Rackin in
Bloom ed., 1987, p. 111). For just as love was the greatest enemy of nonsense
because of its power to fuse separate elements and so break down the structure
of one-and-one-and-one, so it was by the same token the natural means, to
which most ordinary, unreflecting people turned instinctively, of coming to
terms with the cold, discrete reality of the natural world.

IX

Because Dodgson was unable to find love in the usual way, he sought his own
expedient in the cultivation of child-friends, using those talents with which he
was peculiarly well endowed. The *Alice* books were a by-product of this
process and so reveal to us the role that child-friends were to play in
Dodgson's solution to the problem of life and death. It was because they were
the by-product of an essentially abnormal solution to the problem that they
became, as noted earlier, 'the cherished, sometimes sacrosanct possession of
troubled adults' (Rackin in Gray ed., 1992, p. 402).

The child-friends strategy was an aspect of Dodgson's past-fixation, the
ever increasing conviction that happiness is experienced only in retrospect and

that childhood is the golden time of life, the very antithesis of and antidote to age and decay. By associating with the young, Dodgson sought to revivify himself and so stave off the inevitable end. In addition to turning over his stock of child-friends, so that they were always the same age, Dodgson endlessly photographed them (he was a noted amateur photographer) in their bloom-time, knowing that, though the reality fades, the moment lives on in facsimile, the memory refreshed with the camera's eye.

The past-fixation, encapsulated in the idea of the mythical 'golden afternoon' that gave birth to the *Alice*s, also had a nostalgic annual celebration. The sun becomes the emblem of life; the summer's day the Edenic fixed point of the turning year. Its warmth and light represent life as against winter's cold and dark which represent death – so much like the cold, dead universe itself. Each year Dodgson celebrated the return of the sun with a long sojourn at the seaside. His defence against age and death is, therefore, extremely pagan, reflecting the wheel of life, cycle of the year mentality of pre-Christianity, with its belief in the power of warm, eager youth to nourish cold, hopeless age and, each year at the solstices, the festivals of the dying and returning sun.

Because childhood occurs only once, its celebration necessarily involves looking backward, and the question is whether this is to be interpreted as a purely negative response to life. Peter Coveney has drawn attention to a change in attitude to childhood in literature over the course of the nineteenth century:

> In their concern with childhood, Wordsworth and Coleridge were interested in growth and continuity, in tracing the organic development of the human consciousness, and, also, in lowering the psychic barriers between adult and child. For Blake, Wordsworth and, for the most part, Dickens, the image of the child endows their writing with a sense of life, and the same is true of Mark Twain in *Huckleberry Finn*.

By the latter decades of the century, however, we find a wholly different 'cult of the child':

> Writers begin to draw on the general sympathy for childhood that has been diffused; but, for patently subjective reasons, their interest in childhood serves not to integrate childhood and adult experience, but to create a barrier of nostalgia and regret between childhood and the potential responses to adult life.

The danger of this strategy is that it becomes

> a regressive escape into the emotional prison of self-indulgent nostalgia . . . One feels their morbid withdrawal towards psychic death. The misery on the face of Carroll and [J.M.] Barrie was there because their responses to life had been subtly but irrevocably negated. Their photographs seem to look out at us from the nostalgic prisons they had created for themselves in the cult of Alice Liddell and Peter Pan. (Coveney in Gray ed., 1992, pp. 327–8)

Notice here, for future reference, how Coleridge and Wordsworth are seen as adopting a positive, progressive approach to childhood, being interested in 'tracing the *organic* development of the human consciousness' (emphasis added). On the other hand, the approach adopted by Carroll and Barrie is seen as regressive, in seeking to retreat into nostalgia and regret. They are, therefore, not interested in the '*organic* development of human consciousness' but, presumably, in its antithesis.

With respect to Carroll we have identified that antithesis as nonsense-as-game. The maintenance of nonsense-as-game requires, as we have seen, that part must be kept separate from part and that the whole must be no more than the sum of the parts. We shall find that the distinction between this discrete, atomistic approach on the one hand and the organic approach on the other provides an immensely important organising principle, of equal validity in literature and economics.

Notice also that Coveney's assessment of Dodgson's behaviour is rather too bleak, in particular as it implies that Dodgson *chose* to lock himself in a psychic prison. Our own position would be that Dodgson's essentially second-best strategy was successful in as much as, given his circumstances, it allowed him to live a very productive life and gave him happiness of a kind. A much more positive view of Dodgson which also makes allowance for his deep concerns is provided by Michael Bakewell's account (Bakewell, 1996).

This view of Dodgson as a rather more positive figure than that allowed for by Coveney applies also to our assessment of Robertson – but not as much. Because Robertson's devotion to *Alice* was essentially derivative, it involved no actual loving relationship, so that Coveney's strictures apply more appropriately to him than to Dodgson (recall Robertson's poem that describes him as one 'whom love passed by' and its title indicating that he had followed 'The Next Best Way', in D9/3/3 RPTC). He would not have chosen the course he actually pursued had a better one been available and he did make the best of the situation in which he found himself.

The implications of Robertson's outlook for his work, however, were profound and it is in this respect that Coveney's strictures regarding 'regressive escape into . . . emotional prison' strike a responsive chord. It was Robertson's regressive temperament that drove him to seek bedrock in what had gone before and caused him to close his mind to any theoretical development that would undermine the foundations of his economics and with it his own psychic security.

Robertson's inhibiting regression was detected by Keynes with his famous intuition. During the controversy that developed between them, Keynes described Robertson, in his approach to the key questions on which they were disputing, as attempting to creep back into his *mother's womb* (see below, Chapter 26). Consequently, and because his regressive behaviour is, as compared to Dodgson's, unrelieved by positive aspects, it is to Robertson rather than to Dodgson that Coveney's words might be seen to refer when he writes:

> The child indeed becomes a means of escape from the pressures of adult adjustment, a means of regression towards the irresponsibility of youth, childhood, infancy and *ultimately nescience itself.* (Coveney in Gray ed., 1992, pp. 327–8; emphasis added)

X

In interpreting the *Alice* books writers have commented on the abrupt and apparently inexplicable contrast between the framework material, which is replete with intimations of love and of nostalgia, and the bleak inhumanity of the texts of the tales themselves. Donald Rackin, in one of his several essays on the *Alice* books, sees this phenomenon as evidence of Dodgson's falling away from the Sewellian ideal:

> as critics anyway, we must simply declare that the warm (and sometimes sentimental) love which permeates the frame materials of the *Alices* and which is sometimes ridiculed within their narratives has no place there, is finally extraneous, playing no important part in the books' artistic successes [being rather] sentimentally generated flaws in the generally pure nonsense which is their principal achievement. (Rackin in Bloom ed., 1987, p. 114)

Peter Coveney similarly finds the two aspects of the books entirely incompatible. Referring first to the mawkish 'Easter Greeting' inserted in the *Snark*, he says:

> It was extraordinary that the artist Carroll, could distinguish from all this, from the 'delicious dreamy feeling', this 'shame and sorrow', this self-apologia, the valid emotions which went to the creation of the *Alice* books. Every factor which made for weakness became focused into the astringent and intelligent art of *Alice in Wonderland*, so that, in a strange way indeed, the 'dream', the reverie in Dodgson, becomes in *Alice in Wonderland* the means of setting the reader's senses more fully awake. Lewis Carroll is in fact one of the few cases where [D.H.] Lawrence's famous dictum of trusting the art and not the artist happens to be absolutely true. (Coveney in Gray ed., 1992, p. 331)

However, both these interpretations miss the point. It should be clear from all that has gone before that the correct approach is to view each of Dodgson's works as all of a piece, with frame-materials and adventure as each forming part of an integral whole. We have seen that, read as nonsense, the Lewis Carroll canon is subject to progressive degeneration as more and more of the elements inimical to nonsense are allowed to invade the adventures themselves – a development Sewell attributed to Dodgson's attempt to bring more and more of his life within the safe circle of nonsense.

But another way of interpreting the same phenomenon is to say that in successive books the tendency is for framework and adventure to merge and blend. Thus in *AAW*, which was based directly on *AAU* (itself derived from the tales told spontaneously on the river), the dichotomy between loving, nostalgic framework and pure uncompromising adventure is complete. The dichotomy represents (in the adventure) the nature of reality in the post-Darwinian universe; and (in the frame-materials) Dodgson's response to it.

In *TLG* the same formula is applied, except in two respects. First, the message of the books is spelt out much more explicitly in the framework, with the contrasts between youth and age, summer and winter, emphasised. There is a clear reference to the approaching threat of death. The second is that Carroll himself enters the adventure (in the guise of the White Knight: 'It's my own Invention') to plead his case directly with Alice, seeking the assurance of her young love to strengthen him in impotent old age (see Rackin in Bloom ed., 1987, pp. 116–20).

Thus the meaning of it all should now be clear: Dodgson uses the books, first (*AAW*) in the frame-materials, and then (*TLG*) in framework *and* text, to indicate to Alice and other child-friends what is required of them as regards the enormous benefits that youth can confer by supporting age.

We may pass quickly over the *Snark*, with its dread confirmation that death is the end, and over the Sylvie and Bruno books, with their explicit message that the true redemption is love, to consider precisely what it is that youth can give to age. This is the function of the *Alice* adventures themselves.

XI

Just as the purpose of the framework is to explain the nature of the human predicament and the duty of youth towards age, so the purpose of the adventures is to spell out the nature of dark reality and *the attitude necessary to confront it*. Dark reality is, of course, the cold, remorseless, moral void that science has revealed beneath the thin veneer of Victorian civilisation. Because this world is so completely alien, it is described as 'nonsense', 'madness' and a 'curious dream', whereas what Alice actually encounters there is far more real than the completely artificial *imposed* order of everyday life. *It is the way Alice faces up to reality that provides the inspirational element in the books.*

As she progresses through her adventures Alice encounters hostility, indifference, chaos and loss of identity and orientation. She remains indomitable, however, and *in extremis*, when things at last threaten to get out of hand, she abandons polite reasonableness and arbitrarily brings each story to an end by force of will (see Rackin in Phillips ed., 1972, pp. 414–15).

To Dodgson, therefore, Alice is the 'Child of the pure unclouded brow' (*TLG*, p. 173), who, in her youthful innocence and vigour and her ever positive, ever-hopeful approach to life, represents the ideal type of child-friend whose heart-love he will seek to win. It is, therefore, in Alice's behaviour that we find written the formula that Dodgson saw as necessary for all those who come to realise that they must face life without the comfort of religion. This formula says that they must be brave, keep smiling through their tears, impose order and meaning on chaos and meaninglessness, find love.

The third of these is of great practical importance. It implies that Victorian society, with its mores, rules and conventions, exists not by Heaven's Command but because men willed it to be so. Though fabricated and artificial it is always preferable to the howling nightmare of dark reality.

In commenting on the need for human beings caught in the web of purposeless existence to distinguish arbitrarily between what is to be regarded as the world of meaning and what is to be dismissed as nonsense, madness or dream, Rackin has drawn attention to the significance of Humpty Dumpty's exchange with Alice in *TLG*:

> 'When *I* use a word,' Humpty Dumpty said, in rather a scornful tone, 'it means just what I choose it to mean – neither more nor less.'
> 'The question is,' said Alice, 'whether you *can* make words mean so many different things.'
> 'The question is,' said Humpty Dumpty, 'which is to be master – that's all.'

In other words: 'He is master of his world because he *chooses* to be in spite of the actual circumstances' (Rackin in Gray ed., 1992, p. 403).

Are we to submit to the blind forces of chance and give way to despair in the face of chaos, or to be brave and to take responsibility for our own destiny? There is no doubt at all that Dennis Robertson understood very clearly the nature of the choice posed by Humpty Dumpty's words. Nor is there any doubt about the nature of his response: 'he would never yield to cynicism and defeatism. He found comfort in music and his friends' (Butler, 1963, p. 42).

And, we might add, he found comfort in Alice's Positive Attitude in Wonderland.

12. Alice figures

I

It is by reference to *Alice* that we can best explain Robertson's condition. The story of Lewis Carroll and the world he created is an allegory of Robertson's life and the dilemma he faced. The appeal of the *Alice* books for Robertson was twofold.

First and foremost they provided a philosophy of life. Carroll's message was positive and realistic and provided the justification for action and endeavour in the face of the certainty of individual extinction. The maxims were never stated explicitly but were manifested in the behaviour of Alice herself. In this form they constituted a sort of therapeutic pill, rolled in the jam of warmth that the surface text of the books radiated. Many, of course, enjoyed the jam without noticing the pill, or feeling the need of it, but for others the sheer enjoyment that the books provided had to go hand-in-hand with comfort and reassurance and the necessary message with which to steel the heart for the business of life.

The problem is that not everyone is, or can be, an Alice figure, and whether or not they are will determine what they will see or seek in the books: enjoyment and intellectual stimulation or reassurance and escape. Alice figures are progressive in their outlook and see death as completion at the conclusion of a life of fulfilment. Non-Alice figures are regressive in their life-view, see death as the negation of all endeavour and seek escape from reality in the nostalgia of a mythic golden past time. Others perhaps, though they are not Alice figures, carry on bravely, using Alice as a support but all the time maintaining a secure refuge, which nothing must be allowed to challenge or disturb. One such was Robertson, who, as his strategy of escape was frustrated, turned increasingly to the defensive and, in his resistance to the Keynesian Revolution, fought a Famous Battle with Keynes to preserve the foundations of his professional integrity and, by extension, his emotional security.

II

Though Robertson was not himself an Alice figure he was capable of responding to and drawing strength from those who were. The most important

Alice figure in his life was Keynes, with whom he enjoyed a productive relationship in the 1920s but from whose suffocating demands he was forced to detach himself at a time when ultimate escape still seemed a possibility.

Fictional Alice figures were safer and more enduring, and with them Robertson could find release without fear of subjugation. It will be recalled from our review of his acting career that Robertson specialised in old men's parts and that those, friends and colleagues, who knew him best found particular significance in his role as the aged Justice Shallow in Shakespeare's *Henry IV, Part 2*.

This play is of particular interest because it deals with precisely those issues which have emerged from our exploration of the Alice phenomenon in Robertson's life: time, change, age, decay, mortality and the relationship between times past and times future (in interpreting this play the following works are of particular value: Humphreys ed., 1966; Melchiori ed., 1989; Knights, 1959; Traversi, 1957). Our interest is further aroused by the fact that Dodgson/Carroll used references to this play as examples on at least two occasions. First, in *Useful And Instructive Poetry* (1845) when, as an exercise in literary criticism, he imagines that he is the sleeping King, listening to his son Prince Hal's soliloquy and pointing out verbal obscurities and infelicities (see Hudson, 1976, p. 187). Second, in the Preface to the *Snark*, in which he quotes lines from the play and mentions Shallow by name.

III

In *Henry IV, Part 2*, Shallow is a justice of the peace, old and of comfortable means, living a small rural life but touched by matters that shadow larger, national, events. One of the duties of a justice is to find names to fill the muster-book and through this he is again brought into contact, after half a century, with (Sir John) Falstaff, who is recruiting soldiers for the King's service. They recall the uninhibited days of their youth and consider the changes that time has wrought in their lives and those of their contemporaries. Our particular interest for present purposes lies in the approach that Shallow adopts to the universal human predicament of age, decline and inevitable death, regarded in the light of the past events of his life. This is compared with the approach adopted by Falstaff, who has fewer illusions.

Shallow warms his age with memories of youthful profligacy as a law student at Clements Inn (an Inn of Chancery, inferior to the Inns of Court), memories which have usurped the prosaic and unflattering truth. Comedy arises in the discrepancy between his claim that memories of his exploits will linger on at the Inn – 'I think they will talk of mad Shallow yet' – and the ludicrous nature of the exploits themselves: fighting with 'one Sampson

Stockfish, a fruiterer', and in the unheroic names of his fellow 'swinge-bucklers', such as Francis Pickbone and Will Squele. Similarly with his recollections of his sexual prowess. Though he confides that 'I may say to you that we knew where the bona-robas ['smarter whores'] were, and had the best of them all at commandment', Falstaff remembers that Shallow, rather than having the pick of the profession, in fact patronised the lowest members of it, the 'overscutched housewives' ['worn-out hussies', 'deadbeat whores': Humphreys ed., 1966, pp. 96, 98 nn.]. And, in general, Falstaff declares himself astonished at the extent, not merely of exaggeration in Shallow's recollections but of pure invention:

> Lord, Lord, how subject we old men are to this vice of lying! This same starved justice hath done nothing but prate to me of the wildness of his youth and the feats he hath done about Turnbull Street [notorious for thieves and loose women]; and every third word a lie, duer paid to the hearer than the Turk's tribute. (*Henry IV, Part 2*, III. ii. 298–303)

Nevertheless, whether wilful invention, as Falstaff claims, or involuntary assumption of day-dream or wish-fulfilment, these memories provide a warm and reassuring view of the past that enables him to face the future – the winter of life and death itself – with equanimity. Shallow, though seen as foolish and ridiculous, has the inestimable gift of a positive instinct. His 'memories' show an optimistic and joyous, rather than regretful or nostalgic, view of the past that is natural to him. In his old age his zest for life is undimmed and he loses no opportunity for personal profit, whether in the produce of his orchard (pippins of his own 'graffing'), in corrupt dealings with his staff (in supporting the plea of an 'arrant knave'), in cultivating Sir John ('A friend i' th' court is better than a penny in purse'), or in enquiring about the market price of livestock.

At the same time he senses the incongruity of this continued interest and activity, with the knowledge of the harvest of death among those who shared his adventures:

> Jesu, Jesu, the mad days that I have spent! And to see how many of my old acquaintance are dead! (*Henry IV, Part 2*, III. ii. 32–3)

When reminded that 'We shall all follow', Shallow acknowledges the fact but the form of his acknowledgement shows that he approaches the idea of death in a detached, academic way (or as a child would do) that will not allow it to interfere with his enjoyment of life past or present:

> Certain, 'tis certain; very sure, very sure. Death, as the Psalmist saith, is certain to all, all shall die. How a good yoke of bullocks at Stamford fair? (*Henry IV, Part 2*, III. ii. 35–7)

Therefore, Shallow is, in terms of our classification, an Alice figure: a (second-childhood) 'Child of the pure unclouded brow', who in his active engagement in everyday matters shows that life goes on – and must go on – even in the face of death.

This message would not have been lost on Robertson, who would have derived comfort and inspiration from Shallow's lack of paralysis under threat of extinction, and it drew from him his most deeply felt performance. Recall the idea put forward earlier, that in playing old men's parts Robertson was playing himself. In the character of Shallow, his view of himself as old and his need for and devotion to *Alice* are simultaneously realised.

There is support for this linkage of a different kind. In a footnote to the Arden (1966) edition of the play, the editor, A.R. Humphreys, observes that:

> Shakespeare did indeed see life as a ridiculous but fascinating blend; a blend in the present scene [III. ii] of men dying and bullocks sold in the busy market. (Humphreys ed., 1966, p. 98n)

He suggests that:

> This topic may owe something to Ecclesiasticus, XXXVIII 22, 24–5 Genevan, where mortality, bullock-breeding, and rustic simplicity are conjoined. (Humphreys ed., 1966, p. 97)

The Genevan Bible, the work of English exiles, was the most popular available version during Shakespeare's lifetime. The passage in question, from the Apocrypha, runs:

> Remember his judgment; thine also shall be likewise, unto me yesterday, and unto thee today . . . How can he get wisdome that holdeth the plough . . . and his talke is but of the breeding of bullocks?

Very interestingly, this passage, was included in the edited text reading, from Ecclesiasticus 38.25 to 39.10, chosen as the lesson for Robertson's memorial service in Trinity College Chapel on 25 May 1963. The full reading is instructive:

> How shall he become wise that holdeth the plough, that driveth oxen, and is occupied in their labours? He will set his heart upon turning his furrows; and his wakefulness is to give his heifers their fodder. So is the smith sitting by the anvil, and considering the unwrought iron: the noise of the hammer will be ever in his ear, and his eyes are upon the pattern of the vessel. So is the potter sitting at his work, and turning the wheel about with his feet, who is always anxiously set at his work, and all his handywork is by number. All these put their trust in their hands; and each becometh wise in his own work. In the assembly they shall not mount on high;

neither shall they declare instruction and judgment. But they will maintain the fabric of the world; and in the handywork of their craft is their prayer.

Not so he that hath applied his soul, and meditateth in the law of the Most High. He will keep the discourse of the men of renown, and will enter in amidst the subtilties of parables. He will serve among great men, and appear before him that ruleth. He will travel through the land of strange nations; for he hath tried good things and evil among men. If the great Lord will, he shall be filled with the spirit of understanding: he shall pour forth the words of his wisdom. He shall direct his counsel and knowledge, and in his secrets shall he meditate. Nations shall declare his wisdom, and the congregation shall tell out his praise.

The appropriateness of the second part of this for Robertson the honoured scholar and teacher is obvious. For a full picture of Robertson the man, however, we must also consider the first part – and especially if extended back to include the verses specified by Humphreys.

This is because, from the point of view of the present discussion, there is a further dimension of meaning. Not only should we see here the point that, as noted above, life goes on – and must go on – even in the face of death (the continued uses of commerce on the brink of eternity) but, more fundamentally, that there is a cost for having acquired 'wisdom'. That is, the artisan, the craftsman and the husbandman are too preoccupied to acquire 'wisdom' but by the same token they have no empty hours to become prey to anxieties regarding the ultimate 'meaning' of things. They must perforce be Alice figures, carrying on from day to day through good times and bad. Those with the privilege of leisure for thought and contemplation have no such anodyne and must reconcile themselves to their end as best they can.

Now we see how wide is the gulf between Robertson's sensibility and that of Justice Shallow. In playing this role Robertson would have been only too aware of the comfort afforded by Shallow's world. His 'shallowness' can be thought of as his lack of 'wisdom', which is mercifully crowded out by a make-believe past and an unreflecting, quotidian busyness in the present. He would also have been aware that the strength to be drawn from playing this role lay in the fact that Shallow's reference to a past golden age was progressive rather than regressive: a base from which to advance rather than a refuge to which to retreat.

IV

Falstaff, like Robertson, carries the burden of 'wisdom'. By contrast with Shallow he dwells on his age and is, therefore, more sombre. He has no sense of having sated his sensuality in former years, like Shallow, and pursues a more reckless course, hoping thereby to encourage his failing powers (as the ancients lit bonfires to encourage the failing sun at the summer solstice).

Accordingly, he continues to do honour to habitual urges and flirts with Doll Tearsheet (a whore) while regretting that, in Poins' words, 'desire should so many years outlive performance'. Though conscious of death, he resolutely averts his gaze from it. When Doll suggests that it might be time to 'patch up thine old body for heaven', he shows that he finds the subject too painful to contemplate:

> Peace, good Doll, do not speak like a death's-head, do not bid me remember mine end. (*Henry IV, Part 2*, II. iv. 236-7)

He has no illusions and, while acknowledging the 'glories' of former days, he finds they provide neither refuge nor sufficient compensation for present deprivations. When Shallow asks him (III. ii. 191-2):

> O, Sir John, do you remember since we lay all night in the Windmill [a brothel] in Saint George's Field?

He answers (ll. 193-4) with regret: 'No more of that, Master Shallow, no more of that.' His acknowledgement of good times past: 'We have heard the chimes at midnight, master Shallow' (ll. 211-12), implies both bawdy midnights past and the imminence of death to come.

V

Also safer than living *Alice* figures were those who had already completed their earthly journey, leaving behind the example of their lives and, in the case of artists, their works to inspire those who come after. One such figure was the nineteenth-century American poet Walt Whitman, who evidently influenced Robertson's outlook and whose works provide a most revealing clue to the interpretation of his economic writings. The contribution of Whitman's life and work to our understanding of Robertson and of Robertsonian economics is explored in Chapter 16, below.

PART III

Robertson's Economics I: The Foundations

13. Economics and the man

I

Such is the relationship between Robertson the man and Robertsonian economics that by understanding the man we shall better understand his economics. But what sort of economics might we expect from a man of Robertson's temperament? Biographical and literary clues would seem to suggest the following. If this is the only life we have, then economic salvation must be sought in the here and now rather than in some other, for example, abstract or future world. By extension, given Robertson's desire to be 'useful' (see above Chapter 4), this would imply a preoccupation with matters that most immediately affect 'the attainment and ... the use of the material requisites of well being' by the broad mass of mankind engaged in 'the ordinary business of life'. This, of course, was Marshall's definition of economics to which Robertson makes reference three times in his lecture 'What is Economics?', with which he began his second year Principles of Economics course at Cambridge. Robertson considered Marshall's summation 'difficult to improve on' (Robertson, 1963, p. 15) but significantly, as we shall see, he reinforced the idea that it is with the *material* aspects of human welfare that we are concerned (the consumption of goods and services), with a supplementary definition taken from Edwin Cannan (Robertson, 1963, pp. 15–16).

The same evidence suggests that Robertson would not approach the study of economics as a free spirit, able to abandon himself to the flow of the argument wheresoever it might lead; that he would, rather, be constrained by his life-view, which was regressive and which implied the need to keep his work safely grounded in a pre-existing certitude. Consequently, any theoretical development, whether his own or someone else's, which seemed to pose a threat to the security of his intellectual origins, would be shunned or opposed.

On this view, what has been accepted as a commonplace of Robertsonian studies – that his approach to economics was evolutionary rather than revolutionary and exhibits as a consequence a commendable consistency throughout his career – could be rather misleading. For reasons which will become clear, the term evolutionary is not entirely appropriate, being too open-ended a process adequately to describe Robertson's constrained advance.

In tracing the relationship between the man and his economics we shall find that the theme of struggle between the demands of duty and the desire for escape that shaped the course of Robertson's life in general is also evident in the development of his work in economics. And just as in life he sought to resolve the conflict with a compromise, by turning to the study of economics, so, in turn, in his economics, his 'evolutionary' approach meant that he compromised between the possibilities opened up by the logic of his own insights, in leading the way forward from orthodoxy; and his need to retain a reference back to his classical roots. As a consequence, Keynes leapfrogged ahead and Robertson's bid to find fulfilment through economics was defeated by the Keynesian Revolution.

II

The corpus of professional work that Robertson left behind is extensive, for he was industrious and published prolifically. One of Stanley Dennison's signal contributions to Robertson studies was to compile a comprehensive bibliography of his work. On this basis Presley, who collaborated closely with Dennison, has credited Robertson with 'over 100 articles, 30 of which were published in the *Economic Journal,* and 15 books . . . nine books of original material [monographs, handbooks, reports, memoranda of evidence, lectures] plus six books comprising collections of previously published works' (see Presley, 1981, p. 176 and n. 13; Dennison and Presley eds, 1992, pp. 214–24).

The general picture, of around 100 articles, many of which appeared in high-ranking journals, seems a fair representation of his calibre (again, using Dennison's compilation). Presley's emphasis on the *Economic Journal* as a benchmark is acceptable for the period in which Robertson was active, and any charge of parochialism, on the grounds that he published principally in British journals, can be met by pointing to his contributions to the *Quarterly Journal of Economics* and to other overseas publications.

Presley's assessment is also fair with respect to books, except that one of his six volumes of previously published work, *Essays in Money and Interest* (1966), involves double counting (triple in one instance) since Hicks, the editor of the volume, had in fact taken the essays on money and interest from *Essays in Monetary Theory* (1940) and added essays on the same theme from later collections: *Utility and All That* (1952) and *Economic Commentaries* (1956); (see Hicks, 1966, pp. 7–8).

The bibliography also reveals a substantial collection of book reviews, dating from before World War I until almost the end of his life. Here, as with his published articles, though on a greater scale, Robertson demonstrates that his interest and his vision range far beyond the narrowly economic.

Our main interest is, however, with his contribution to economics and here we might note the valuable service rendered by Goodhart who in his Centenary Lecture at Trinity College, Cambridge in May 1990:

> made a tentative allocation of his books and main papers [with some overlap] . . . into five major categories, these being in rough order of the timing in which he first addressed these studies of:
>
> 1. Trade cycles
> 2. Industrial structure
> 3. Monetary economics
> 4. Micro-economics (utility and value)
> 5. Macro-economic commentary and policy advice. (Goodhart in Presley ed., 1992, p. 14)

Such broad categorising does, of course, subsume some individual topics which deserve a mention, such as international trade and payments, but these are minor matters compared with Robertson's major area of concern. What this might be and how it relates to our predictions from Robertson's life-view is the subject of the following chapters.

III

There is little doubt about the area of Robertson's work which the profession has deemed the most important. The dominant view, and the reasons that justify it, are best expressed by Presley in his *Robertsonian Economics*, which focuses on:

> The theory of industrial fluctuation, since this is where the majority of Robertson's writings were concentrated, where he made the greatest impact upon the study of economics and where much of the debate between Robertson and Keynes took place. (Presley, 1978, p. 5)

Presley's treatment, we should notice, covers a variety of topics, including movements in aggregate output and employment; the relationship between saving and investment; the finance of investment; money and the rate of interest; all of which are part and parcel of the explanation of 'fluctuation' in a modern economy. They are also topics which we specified earlier as being of central importance for the study of Robertson in relation to Keynes (see above, Introduction).

Nevertheless, if Robertsonian economics is held to be a manifestation or natural expression of Robertson the man, then perhaps more weight should be given to the views of Robertson himself? Here, fortunately, his views are in complete accord with the dominant view among commentators, as can readily be confirmed from the two explicit statements Robertson obligingly made on the subject. The first is in a speech made, as Chairman, to the Faculty Board of Economics and Politics at Cambridge in 1946:

> Now about the economics of fluctuation. This is where I have to be a little bit personal. To me this has always been the most interesting branch or aspect of economic study. It's the only one to which I have made any contribution; my only real book published (alas) 32 years ago was about the fluctuation of output. . . . (B2/3/2 RPTC)

The second was made in a form that has come to be recognised as the definitive Robertson position, namely, his *Lectures on Economic Principles*, as published in 1963, the year of his death:

> I have now. . . to say something about money, about fluctuations in activity, about 'lapses from full employment' – the subject matter of Marshall's projected volume, never fully brought to birth, on 'Money, Credit and Employment'. If I may strike a personal note, this has always been to me the most interesting part of economics – the only part to which I can hope to be remembered as having made any personal contribution.   (Robertson, 1963, p 325)

Robertson's contribution in this area, the core of which was contained in just a handful of books and articles, was built up progressively, step by step. The first step and the foundation for all later work, was an empirically based 'real' theory of the trade cycle, the outcome of research carried out for his fellowship dissertation during the year 1912–13 and revised for publication as *A Study of Industrial Fluctuation* (1915).

Later steps developed the initial theoretical position by successively incorporating what we have referred to as the key variables – but in such a way that each innovation was made consistent with what had gone before. Money, the theory of which Robertson worked out in the course of preparing his textbook *Money* (1922) was 'reintegrated' (Robertson, 1948, p. xv) into that of the cycle in *Banking Policy and the Price Level* (1926). Monetary factors were accorded a secondary role compared to real factors but played an important part, via movements in the price level, in Robertson's novel analysis of the relationship between investment and saving. The theory of interest came on the scene surprisingly late, in 'Industrial Fluctuation and the Natural Rate of Interest' (1934) and then only as an alternative way of expressing his main theory. This means either that in earlier versions of the theory the role of interest had been tacit; or, and more likely, that earlier and later versions were almost mutually exclusive alternatives.

IV

Robertson's work in the area of economics that had greatest meaning for him will be dealt with in two parts: (a) that which treats of the relationship between the cycle and the trend, based on the ideas and the analysis contained in the *Study*; (b) that which treats of the relationship between the key variables, as evidenced by *BPPL* and subsequent publications.

Robertson did not, of course, write in a vacuum and reference will be made as necessary to the work of other writers. However, there will be no attempt to assess Robertson's position as a member of the Cambridge School (the other members of which included Marshall, Pigou, Lavington, Keynes and, at one remove, Hawtrey) or to survey the work of the School in general. These matters are beyond the scope of the present study but have been ably and extensively discussed by, for example, Bridel (1987) and by Bigg (1990).

14.   *A Study of Industrial Fluctuation*

I

Perhaps the best place to begin our investigation of the meaning and significance of the *Study* for Robertson's life and work is with the title. This has caused difficulties for some writers who have evidently believed that it ought to be slightly other than it is and so have produced an interesting range of variant renderings (see, for example, Backhouse, 1985, p. 186; Blaug, 1986, p. 205; Costabile, 1997, p. 324; Hicks, 1942, p. 57; Hicks, 1981, p. 885; Robinson, 1963; Wilson, 1980, p. 1524; Wilson in Presley ed., 1992, p. 58).

The form chosen by Robertson, presumably with some care as with everything he wrote, was *A Study of Industrial Fluctuation: An Enquiry into the Character and Causes of the so-called Cyclical Movements of Trade*. The ideas he intended to convey by this form of words will become apparent as we proceed, but some preliminary remarks will help to set the scene. First, by the time Robertson began his research in 1912 the conviction that a 'trade cycle' existed had a long history. It can be traced to the latter part of the eighteenth century when political economists began to investigate the apparently regular occurrence of 'commercial crises'. The thought that these were not entirely unconnected discrete events led to attempts to provide a more continuous account, and by the nineteenth century descriptions and explanations of the complete cycle of varying degrees of elaboration were available.

II

To designate variations in the level of economic activity as 'cycles' *connotes* regularity and hence gives rise to the question of causation. It says much for the earnestness of Robertson's approach and of his determination to get to the bottom of things that he subtitled his book, as we have seen: *An Enquiry into the* Character *and* Causes *of the* so-called *Cyclical Movements of Trade* (Robertson, 1915, title-page; emphasis added). That is, both the notion of there being a cycle and the causes of the observed movements of trade must be subjected to scrutiny.

Robertson's approach to the question of the form of the movements is given by the title itself *A Study of Industrial* Fluctuation (Robertson, 1915, title-page; emphasis added). 'Fluctuation' is defined by the *Shorter Oxford Dictionary* (1964) as 'a motion like that of the waves, an alternate rise and fall'; or, 'the action or condition of fluctuating; repeated variation, vicissitude'. We shall see that images of waves and of the sea feature strongly in Robertson's approach. To describe industrial activity as being wave-like is to imply movement and the alternation of ups and downs, but does not commit the writer further. In this context, vicissitude means (*SOD*), 'successive substitution of one thing or condition for another taking place from natural causes'; and '*alternation*, mutual or reciprocal succession, of things or conditions'.

Vicissitudes was a term Robertson himself was to use in the *Study* when, having spent Part I examining the influence of various factors on changing levels of activity in individual industries (notice here Robertson's characteristic procedure of examining the parts as a means of reaching conclusions about the whole), he had to acknowledge the many indications that the 'alleged universality and simultaneity of the so-called general fluctuations of trade are in part a figment of the public imagination', the implication being that 'the vicissitudes of the several industries and groups of industries are in no small measure governed by their own individual idiosyncrasies of supply and demand'.

This could not, however, be the complete story:

> Nevertheless, we are apparently not in a position to deny the existence of something which may fairly be called an *alternation* of general expansion and depression, and of which we have not as yet succeeded in giving a comprehensive explanation. That is the task of the present book. (Robertson, 1915, p. 121; emphasis added)

Yet even when the task ('no light one') was completed and the existence of a general cycle of trade was established, it possessed on Robertson's view nothing of the smooth conformity of the sine wave. It became his settled conviction that not only did the trade cycle differ in timing and amplitude between industrialised countries but that the characteristics of successive cycles in any one country would not be identical (see Robertson, 1952, p. 193). Similarly, the characteristics of the cycle could differ as between the output of capital goods and of consumption goods, the more strongly marked fluctuations in the former playing a key role in Robertson's scheme of thought, as we shall see.

The outcome of Robertson's 'crude and primitive attempt to set theory and history walking hand in hand', with its 'attempt to trace the different consequences, for general activity, of the diverse natures and successive phases of the great innovations – railways, basic steel, electricity, oil', was to leave him with:

an abiding sense of the difficulty of providing, in a world in which so many and such varied changes may be wrought by the wand of Science, neat little models of the trade cycle and (*a fortiori*) [with regard to the recommendation of policy measures] neat little packets of therapeutic pills. (Robertson, 1948a, pp. ix–x)

Robertson's scepticism regarding 'stylised models of the cycle' which later became 'so fashionable', complemented his antipathy to the proliferating breed of econometricians, for whom 'stylised models' were grist to the mill:

I confess that to me at least the forces at work seem so complex, the question whether even the few selected parameters can be relied on to stay put through the cycle or between cycles so doubtful, that I wonder whether more truth will not in the end be wrung from interpretative studies of the crude data of the general type contained in [the *Study*], but more intensive, more scrupulously-worded and more expert. (Robertson, 1948a, pp. xvi–xvii)

III

With regard to the question of the cause, or causes, of the trade cycle, there were already many explanations extant in 1912 and Robertson was faced with no dearth of alternatives:

The causes of crises and depressions alleged before the various committees of Congress in the eighties amounted to some 180 in number, and included the issue of free railway passes and the withholding of the franchise from women. This list remained undefeated until M. Bergmann in 1895 was able to publish an exhaustive discussion in the German tongue of 230 separate opinions, arranged in eight categories. Indeed the problem of industrial fluctuation has exercised the minds of business men, economic writers and practical reformers of all schools throughout the past century: and within the last five years alone six weighty works, vaying in length from 280 to 742 pages have been published upon it in England, America and France. (Robertson, 1915, p. 1)

In the face of this *embarras de choix* how was yet another contribution to the debate to be justified? Robertson argued that, though it was clear that the importance of the subject was generally recognised, understanding was impaired because while each of the serious contributors could claim some justification for his own point of view, he had tended to promote it at the expense of the possible alternatives, with the result that:

there is as yet no single comprehensive explanation which may be said to hold the field. It is the author's conviction that the most important work which remains to be done lies in the direction of developing and synthesising the various and often conflicting opinions which have been already expressed. (Robertson, 1915, p. 2)

To comprehend the spectrum of available opinion was one thing but to arrive at a conclusion regarding their relative merits was another. Robertson's solution was to subject alternative theories to empirical testing, for he perceived that 'this problem more than any other in economics seems . . . to have suffered from the neglect of a sufficiently wide and precise study of fact' (p. 9). Consequently, and by means of resort principally to the *Economist* 'Annual Histories', he based his enquiry 'mainly on a study of the course of events, in the leading industrial countries, especially the United Kingdom, from about 1870 till the eve of the great war' (p. xviii).

The initial outcome of his research was submitted as a fellowship dissertation to Trinity College in 1913 but was rejected on the grounds that, as we noted in Chapter 7 above, he had completed only the first half of an exceptionally difficult task. That is, he had assembled a mass of facts, including histories of various products, and partial explanations (in itself a noteworthy achievement in so short a time) but had yet to render down his raw material into a positive thesis. It was the revised form of the dissertation, shorn of much 'consecutive industrial narrative' (p. 10) and arguing a theoretical position espoused by himself, that was published as the *Study*.

IV

In evaluating the significance of the *Study* for Robertson and Robertsonian economics, we shall approach the book afresh and attempt an appreciation based on the distinction we drew in the interpretation of the *Alice* books between the text itself and the 'frame materials' that complement it and provide a context of meaning (see above, Chapter 11). That is, we shall distinguish between the empirical investigation of the trade cycle that makes up the bulk of the *Study* and the literary references that provide the clue to Robertson's larger concerns.

On this new basis it will be possible to argue that whatever the conclusions with regard to the importance of Robertson's work in the development of trade-cycle theory, in this book he raised more fundamental issues. In raising these issues Robertson was to anticipate Keynes, with whose name they are now associated. Unlike Keynes, however, who saw only the symptoms and the problems to which they gave rise, Robertson gained an inkling into the nature of the cause itself. He caught at what must have seemed a very nebulous, elusive and indeed *outré* idea in economics at that time and resorted to the language of poets and philosophers as a means to convey his insight. The apparatus of thought by which economists could provide a more complete explanation was not to enter the professional literature for another seventy years.

V

The reaction of commentators and reviewers to the *Study* has been over-whelmingly favourable, in the sense that the work was seen to represent a personal triumph for Robertson, that it gave prominence to ideas that were unknown or neglected in Britain and that its conclusions were reached on the basis of an appeal to the facts. The verdict on the book's worth as an original or lasting contribution to trade cycle theory is more equivocal (see, for example, *The Times*, 28 January 1916, D7/1 RPTC; *Saturday Westminster Gazette*, 19 February 1916, D7/2 RPTC; *The Economist*, 11 March 1916, p. 510, D7/3; Hicks, 1942, p. 57; Hicks ed., 1966, p. 11; Hicks, 1981, p. 885; Hicks, 1982, p. 129; Ashton, 1951, pp. 298–302; Wilson, 1953, pp. 573–4; Wilson, 1980, pp. 1524–5; Robinson, 1963; Dennison, 1963, p. 42; Dennison, 1968, p. 530; Samuelson, 1963, pp. 522–3; Presley, 1978, Part I; Danes, 1979, ch. 1; Bridel, 1987, pp. 78–85; Bigg, 1990, pp. 120ff; Goodhart in Presley ed., 1992, pp. 21–9). Before beginning our own reading, some general con-clusions drawn from a review of these commentators may be dealt with here.

There is a widespread feeling that Robertson's emphasis on the importance of agriculture is misplaced, given that the sector was much shrunken in 1913 as compared to earlier periods and continued to decline thereafter; and given that economists have subsequently failed to find any systematic relation between agriculture and economic fluctuation. In the face of the general scepticism (Presley does argue Robertson's case for the period down to 1915), the amount of space devoted to agriculture in the *Study*, Robertson's *continued* support for the role of agriculture (see the *Lectures*, 1963, ch. 6) and his *continued* regard for the sunspot theory (see his plea for further work on the 'behaviour of the solar leopard' in the 1948 reprint of the *Study*, p. xi) seems little short of eccentric. As in the case of another, more famous, fellow of Trinity, Sir Isaac Newton, who for a decade spent his time as an alchemist, attempting to turn base metal into gold, posterity would argue that he ought to have known better. But Robertson, always happy to be in a 'minority of one', would refer his critics to the empirical evidence.

The role of agriculture in Robertson's theory does in fact change in line with the changing fortunes of another factor in his scheme, namely, the principle of acceleration – or repercussion, as it is referred to in 1915. From outright rejection to almost complete (qualified) acceptance in later work, is a develop-ment that runs contrary to the generally accepted pattern: that Robertson built on previous ideas and stayed loyal to ideas he had adopted. In fact, it is generally not noticed that Robertson used the generic term repercussion to refer also to what was later called (by Keynes) the multiplier (see *Study*, p. 125 and *Lectures*, p. 410). It is of great significance for what is to follow to understand that, while Robertson came to embrace the idea of the accelerator, which he evidently did not see as a threat to his position, he vigorously resisted the idea of the multiplier, which he evidently did see as a threat (see, for example, the 'New Introduction' to the *Study* (1948a, p. xii).

Of the writers reviewed, only Presley appreciates the extent of Robertson's change of view on the *accelerator* and even he could have pressed the point further without fear of misrepresentation, for in 1915 Robertson is dismissive, asserting that:

> The whole theory of repercussion, as expounded so glibly for instance by M. Lescure, appears to be engaged in making something out of nothing, and to rest upon a quicksand. (1915, p. 125)

Later in the book he speaks of discarding the 'shibboleth of "repercussion"' (1915, p. 164).

We should also notice something very significant about Robertson's understanding of the principle of repercussion. In the days before the Keynesian concepts of the marginal propensity to consume and to save, together with the principle of the multiplier that is based upon them and of the paradox of thrift to which they gave precision, Robertson believed that effects of repercussion were without limit:

> Does not the whole notion of the communication of prosperity from one industry to another *in an endless chain* imply an elementary confusion of thought? (1915, p. 125; emphasis added)

This is an understandable point of view for the time in which it was written, but later, when these ideas were at the heart of Keynes's *novum organum* (truly called), Robertson still failed to take cognisance of them and in this omission lay the intellectual basis for his dispute with Keynes.

It is Presley who also gives full weight to the position of agriculture, and as part of this he points out that, although in Robertson's later work agriculture is retained, its theoretical relationship with other variables is different. He notes that in *Lectures* there is no reference to the concept of effort elasticity of demand (in the usual case, total effort increases when the relative price of agricultural products falls) but instead Robertson applies at the macro level conclusions reached on the basis of observations made at the micro level.

Presumably, if we have regard to both sets of developments, that is, with respect to agriculture and to repercussion, we might argue that as Robertson came to accept the principle of repercussion, at least in its acceleration form, the need for the argument from relative marginal utilities *which was central to the 'Study'*, became less necessary and could be relinquished along with its manifestation as effort elasticity of demand.

VI

These changes all seem to point to one conclusion: that whatever the significance of the *Study* for Robertson and for the profession and for mankind at large, it does not seem to depend on the particular version of the theory of the trade cycle it contains: there must be something more. What was the message of Robertson's 'only real book', which was unique as the only large-scale work of empirical investigation that he undertook during his career (and at the start of it) if it was not simply another theory of the cycle? Why indeed did he embark on such a work which, for a man of his background, previous interests and aesthetic leanings, represented in its subject matter and method all that seemed most alien? It must have been something of deep concern, some question which he was determined to fathom.

We shall seek the answer in the emotional state that characterised Robertson's pre-war years and the world-view that sprang from it. The loss of faith and the disappearance of a sense of certainty had cut him adrift from his childhood moorings. The feelings he had revealed to Benson (above, Chapter 4), of hopelessness and purposelessness, cried out for relief in the discovery of some fixed points of existence. These, together with the acceptance of his sexuality and the prospect of a childless future, raised questions about the meaning and purpose of life itself (see Chapters 2 and 3 above).

Robertson's answer, which was worked out throughout his career had its origins in the *Study*, in which Robertson trawled the facts of industrial experience to arrive at conclusions concerning the question of how to maximise material welfare. This he saw as the best indicator of total human welfare (see Robertson, 1952, pp. 14–15; and 1963, pp. 16–17) through time. This in turn involved consideration of the larger question of present enjoyment in relation to prospective future prosperity. In this he was to give significance to the short period in a way that was different from other members of the Cambridge School, who merely sought to elaborate short-period adjustment mechanisms within the context of Marshall's long-period equilibrium.

Robertson's research, carried out in depth and at breakneck speed, enabled him to satisfy his desire 'to be useful' and to fulfil his requirement that if his chosen profession was not worth following for its own sake it should at least have a 'practical object' (1963a, p. 14), namely, to increase the sum of human welfare (see *Study*, p. 3). In the process he was able to show that the insights accorded him by his own condition could bring forth conclusions valid for mankind in general.

The rationale for all this is indicated by the biographical and literary clues we have examined. In a God-less universe, in which there is neither 'meaning' nor 'purpose', what is the sure basis for our attitude to a life which is not intended as preparation for eternal Bliss in Heaven but is unique and finite and ends in extinction? The answer, which follows from what was said above, seems to be current consumption. We must maximise current consumption and thereby maximise total welfare, or rather net welfare, as Robertson insisted.

Of course, the process of economic growth involves present sacrifice in return for benefits that can only be enjoyed in a future which may be beyond the life-time of those now living. Why should people give up present consumption, which is certain, for future consumption, which is at best uncertain? Why give up that which we have for the benefit of others we do not know?

Possibly the reason is bound up with the idea that those who expect to have descendants, who see themselves part of the ever-rolling stream of the generations, will perhaps see the future in a different light from those who expect to have 'no issue'. Why this should be the case was the mystery at which Robertson caught in his literary and philosophical references, his frame-materials.

In fact, in the *Study* the problem Robertson is seeking to solve has two aspects. He was, first, immediately concerned with more practical problems. If the universally desired growth process imposes costs in the present then: (a) for any given rate of growth, how is it possible to minimise necessary costs? and (b) is it desirable, even at minimum necessary costs, to sacrifice so much in the present for the promise of future prosperity? The first of these questions occupied the bulk of the text of the *Study* because Robertson concluded that the process of growth gives rise to fluctuations. That is, the trade cycle is the cost imposed on the present by the demands of the future.

The second issue is much larger and Robertson merely asks his reader to be aware of the problem, hinting that it is bound up with custom and unquestioned assumption, to which the contemporary cataclysm (the war) might administer a beneficial jolt.

The two problems are, in reality, closely related. The greater the blind enthusiasm for growth, the greater the chances of the conditions that produce severe, and excessive, fluctuations.

The published accounts of the *Study* have invariably been set within the confines of the first question and have treated the work as just another theory of the cycle: interesting, empirically based and new, at least in Britain, but nothing more. Those who have referred to the frame-materials, though not in those terms (Goodhart in Presley ed., 1992; and Goodhart and Presley, 1994), have made nothing systematic of them, not having seen them as the clue to the link between the cycle and the trend and the problem of intertemporal choice that lies at its centre.

15. The cycle and the trend

In what follows, we shall deal first with Robertson's theory of the cycle, as set out in the text of the *Study*; and then, in Chapter 16, place it in the context provided by the frame-materials, which relate the short-run cycle to the long-term trend.

I

The text of the *Study* is divided into two Parts or 'Books'. Part I, or Book I, deals with fluctuations in individual trades; and Part II, or Book II, with fluctuations in general trade. In both, Robertson's method is the same: namely, he introduces a proposition, discusses it and then relates it directly to the historical experience ('from about 1870 to the eve of the great war') of a range of 'trades'. For example, one of the 'phenomena of supply' associated with modern industry, which tends to result in over-investment taking place, is 'the length of time necessary to construct and prepare for use the requisite instruments of production', namely, 'the period of gestation' (1915, p. 13). The validity of the proposition is then examined against experience and practice in the following trades: coal, pig-iron, shipping, railways, cotton-spinning, coffee, copper, rubber; not forgetting the rigidities of transport supply and the building trade. Other 'phenomena of supply' and 'phenomena of demand' are dealt with in the same manner.

Robertson then applies his findings to the explanation of that 'alternation of general expansion and depression' referred to as the trade cycle (p. 121). In doing so he works, as became customary with him, from the particular to the general: from the micro to the macro or, more properly, the individual to the aggregate level. In fact, what Robertson is really saying is: given that we have identified factors that cause fluctuations in individual trades (in *any* individual trade), with all their peculiarities and idiosyncrasies, can these be used to explain the cycle in general industry (p. 121)? The explanation must not, of course, rely to any significant extent on the notion of 'repercussion' but must somehow retain consistency with the neo-classical concept of relative prices (exchange ratios or relative marginal utilities) that predominates at the microeconomic, individual industry level.

II

With respect first of all to the individual trades, Robertson begins by examining 'certain tendencies towards fluctuation which, granted an initial rise in the exchange value of the services rendered by any trade, are found to be inherent in the modern system of large scale competitive capitalistic industry' (p. 46), namely, those that encourage over-investment, leading to a downturn; and those that aggravate the ensuing depression.

The initial rise in exchange value could be due to changes in demand for the finished product but equally it could be due to a fall in costs of production – a supply-side change – as illustrated by the experience of a number of trades (pp. 47–65). And here Robertson singles out 'one form in particular of lowered costs which seems to be of considerable importance both in inducing immediate prosperity and in stimulating the over-investment which sows the seeds of future depression' (p. 66). This was invention, the emphasis upon which is generally regarded as Robertson's most original contribution, at least to English thought on the cycle.

From supply-side causes of changes in exchange value, Robertson moves on to consider changes on the demand side. He leaves until Part II questions of demand relationships as between consumptive and instrumental trades (p. 69) and concentrates on demand factors that operate more generally. Of these, we could simply mention the ones described as 'miscellaneous', which comprise changes of fashion, 'alternations of war and peace' and foreign tariffs (p. 72); and pass on to one that occupied a special place in Robertson's affections (and 'about one third in bulk' of the *Study*), namely, agriculture.

This influence, which he saw as being of 'more persistent and widespread importance than the others' (p. 75), continued to excite his interest in later years, not only because of a sneaking belief in the ultimate validity of the sun-spot theory, but also because of the strategic role agriculture played in his theory of the cycle. This is said not so much in respect of its effect on industry considered as a collection of individual trades, whether 'direct', 'normal' or 'psychological' effects on the instrumental and consumptive trades (pp. 75–120), but considered in relation to the fluctuations of general trade, dealt with in Book II.

III

Now, in seeking to explain the observed 'alternation of general expansion and contraction', it is necessary as a preliminary to be clear as to the entity to be explained. In the 'New Introduction' of January 1948 Robertson refers to 'the deliberate selection of *real national income* – or rather, what is now called gross national product, plus (or minus) any decrement (or increment) of stocks – rather than prices, profits or even employment' (Robertson, 1948a, p. ix) and cites Pigou's *Wealth and Welfare* (1912) as the inspiration for his choice. However, this formulation is intended, as he acknowledges, as a riposte to Keynesians, who claimed to have discovered the importance of output as a whole in the 1930s, and we shall turn instead to Robertson's treatment of the subject in the 'Preliminary Chapter' of the *Study* itself, which is more enlightening.

The clue to the nature of the variable in which fluctuations occur is to be found in Robertson's use of the terms 'industrial' and 'trade'. Industrial activity refers to the production of consumption and investment goods; it is contrasted with agricultural activity. Industrial activity is classified into trades, or groups of trades, and trade in general.

'Trade', of course, also connotes exchange, and whereas the proper measure of prosperity or depression for an individual trade is 'aggregate net receipts' (p. 3), the measure of general economic activity becomes the aggregate volume of exchanges or, more properly, the aggregate volume of consumption (p. 3). Even though in a growing economy this is not a straightforward idea – we need to include the utility of gross investment during the year, as well as that of finished goods (p. 5) – we have here the measure of economic success. Without further qualification for the time being, we may say that the end of all economic activity is consumption and that economic organisation should be such as will maximise the community's net utility (gross utility less disutility of input: see p. 200) derived from consumption.

IV

Production in the economy is of two kinds: consumption goods and capital goods. Capital goods are used in the production of consumption goods; and consumption goods constitute the real saving necessary for the construction of capital goods (pp. 171 n. 2, 236). Relative rates of production are regulated with reference to relative marginal utilities (exchange values). A rise in marginal utility will induce an increase in activity; a fall will induce a reduction. Estimates of the marginal utility of consumption goods are more likely to be accurate and stable than those for capital goods, which depend on estimates of future productivity (pp. 156–7).

The variation possible in the estimation of the marginal utility of capital goods is the key to understanding the cause and the nature of modern industrial fluctuation. In particular:

The most characteristic feature of a modern industrial boom is the utilisation of an abnormally large proportion both of the past accumulations and of the current production of consumable goods to elicit the production not of other consumable goods but of construction goods.   (p. 157)

There are two points to notice here. The first is that, as in this case, it is more important to explain the cause of the revival from depression than of the downturn from the boom. The reason for this is, as Robertson explained, 'each period of "expansion" contains as it were the seeds of its own dissolution' (p. 8). The second is that we should be clear as to what is being implied about the notion of *relative* marginal utility. There is, of course, no problem when considered as between individual trades but when applied to groups of trades or general trade, there must be something *relative to which* it can be rising or falling. In the above example, that something is a change in *expectations*. That is, the marginal utility of capital goods is revised (upwards) under the influence of (a) the psychological effects of an exceptionally good harvest; (b) the need to replace an unusually large amount of worn-out capital in leading sectors; (c) the application of some invention in leading sectors (p. 157).

Note here, incidentally, that Robertson in considering fluctuations in general trade, describes himself as 'breaking at some point arbitrarily into the magic circle of industrial change' (p. 121); and that the idea of 'arbitrarily' is picked up by Goodhart (in Presley ed., 1992, p. 24) and used somewhat reproachfully of Robertson's method. It is now clear *why* Robertson breaks into the cycle at the point of revival: namely, both because it is the most important point to explain and because it allows him to group together the three causes of revision of the marginal utility of capital goods – the revival being the only appropriate point at which to introduce (b), the need to replace a large amount of capital equipment.

In turn, and in anticipation of an investment boom, an increased demand for *consumption* goods will be expected and their marginal utility will be revised upwards. This will provide an inducement to manufacturers to increase output and to owners to release stocks they are holding.

Apart from expectations, the only other entity in relation to which the exchange value of the output of general industry can be rising or falling is the output of agriculture, the strategic importance of which in Robertson's scheme is now apparent. Despite the general scepticism surrounding the subject, Robertson explains the relationship between agriculture and industry and adduces evidence in support of its effect on the cycle (pp. 129–55).

V

Having eschewed the principle of repercussion (pp. 122–5), Robertson supplies the *incentive* for a change in behaviour on the part of producers and stockholders with his notion of increased productivity, in terms of satisfaction, of effort-input (p. 125). Such an increase in satisfaction can arise either through increased productivity due to a reduction in real costs (improved organisation and equipment) in the production of own output or, more likely, by the means described above, namely, a rise in the exchange value of the product due to an abundant harvest, or a rise in the expected value of marginal utility (pp. 126–9).

This notion is of particular interest and importance in the case of agriculture, where it is used to rebut the charge that a change in exchange values will merely redistribute income between the sectors, with no net increase in purchasing power. This charge fails to take into account the possibility of a rise in the productivity of effort of corn-consumers in terms of satisfaction; that is, that the effort-elasticity of demand is greater than unity. What this means is that a fall in the price of corn will lead to a greater than proportional demand for corn and that this demand will consist, at least in part, of an increased supply of industrial products, direct from increased production. Demand for *all* products has thus increased, because the extra effort expended on the acquisition of corn is not entirely at the expense of effort expended on the demand for other products (pp. 130–7).

As the economy moves from revival into boom, investment expands and consumption goods which constitute the real saving necessary to sustain the process of capital creation are sucked in increasing quantities into the 'vortex of exchange' (p. 240). Of course, during the expansion phase consumable goods are actually consumed but, on the logic of the Robinson Crusoe economy, the construction of capital goods precludes, to that extent, the production of consumables, so that there is a 'going without' in the present in order to provide for better times in the future.

Conversely in the depression, when consumption goods are relatively plentiful, there is again an argument in favour of their accumulation in readiness to sustain expansion in the coming revival. The more protracted the depression, the greater the denial of current in favour of future consumption.

This investment-saving relationship is at the core of the Robertson economic problem, which explains the cycle in terms of the trend: the occurrence of industrial fluctuation as a by-product of growth; it sees, in a sense, the one as an allegory of the other. Just as preparation for the capital growth of the expansion phase involves sacrifice which cannot be made good within the cycle, so in the long term, building for a better tomorrow involves (in Robertsonian terms) thrift which will not fructify in the life-time of the present generation.

VI

The problems of the cycle are readily explained on the basis of Robertson's empirical evidence and he is able to offer remedies that will minimise both cycle and loss. The problem of the trend is less easily explained and all Robertson can do is to hint at the forces at work and to place before the public the nature of the choices being made and the possibilities for change offered by the upheaval of war. The following passages explain in Robertson's own words the problem of the cycle and its relationship to the trend:

> the relapse in constructional industry is seen to be due to the existence or imminence of an over-production of instrumental as compared with consumable goods. Whether or not this over-production is indicated by an actual shortage of consumable goods which renders it impossible to maintain investment on the scale which has prevailed during the preceding years or months, and whether it is due to miscalculation or to the inevitable characteristics of modern large-scale production, its essential nature is the same, – *a failure to secure the best conceivable distribution through time of the community's consumption of consumable goods.* The aggregate satisfaction of the community over time is thereby diminished, and *the damage to that extent final and irremediable.* (p. 187; emphasis added)

The idea of an optimal distribution of consumption through time is an important one for Robertson, for he refers to it several times. In addition to the above he also relates it more explicitly to the events of the cycle: 'The fundamental meaning of over-investment is failure to attain the ideal distribution of the community's income of consumable goods through time' (p. 180). What this means is that:

> The check to investment [in a revival] arises from the recognition not necessarily that to maintain it upon the same or an increased scale would be physically impossible, but that it would involve a sacrifice of present enjoyment disproportionate to the result. Consumable goods may be abundant, but if it is known that with the close of the period of gestation they are about to become more abundant still, a wise community will devote them to eliciting the immediate production of other consumable rather than of constructional goods. (p. 180)

In each case, what is said about the cycle has implications for the longer term, as is seen by the following:

> the temptations to over-investment may involve a general rupture between the sacrifice involved in postponing consumption and the future satisfaction procured by means of that sacrifice. (p. 200)

Robertson uses the phrase again in the 'Conclusion' to the *Study*, where it assumes the form of a general principle of conduct, necessarily valid in both the short run and the long run:

> When fairly faced, the problem of the prevention of industrial fluctuation becomes nothing less formidable than the problem of maximising the community's aggregate of net satisfaction through time, – in other words of attaining the best distribution through time of its income of consumable goods which is practicable without undesirable restriction of the total of that income.   (pp. 241–2)

Though the two are in many ways different aspects of the same process, the remedies available for the moderation of the cycle are more tangible and more specific than any possible solution to the long-term question. In the former case, Robertson proposes measures that would both reduce what would now be referred to as 'shocks' that set off reactions in the system and ameliorate possible aggravations of the initial disturbance (p. 242). Thus any change would be beneficial which: (a) provides for inter-local and inter-temporal compensation in agriculture (to offset the significance of good and bad harvests); (b) reduces discontinuity in the process of investment, through devolution and decentralisation of industry; (c) minimises the possibility of miscalculation on the part of producers in both boom and depression (pp. 242–9); (d) removes obstacles that prevent the community from enjoying to the full in time of depression, the large income of consumable goods that over-investment in the boom has made available (pp. 249–53).

VII

But this last remedy for fluctuation begs the question, for consumption of consumable goods available restricts the accumulation that is required to sustain investment in the next revival, which by the same token is the investment upon which 'industrial progress depends' (p. 253). This produces a conundrum, the solution to which depends upon what Robertson calls 'more ultimate judgements' (p. 253). In particular, the community must come to a decision as to what is meant by the phrase 'most desirable distribution of . . . income through time' (p. 253). It is this question which raises the most fundamental issues regarding human existence and the values on which the 'more ultimate judgements' are to be made. In posing the stark alternatives Robertson concludes the book with one of his finest passages:

> Is the assumption valid upon which western civilisation seems to proceed, – that it is desirable so to manipulate one's income-stream that it shall flow in with an ever-rising tide? From some points of view the whole cycle of industrial change presents the appearance of a perpetual immolation of the present upon the altar of the future. During the boom sacrifices are made out of all proportion to the enjoyment over which they will ultimately give command: during the depression enjoyment is denied lest it debar the possibility of making fresh sacrifices. Out of the welter of industrial dislocation the great permanent riches of the future are generated. How

far are we bound to honour the undrawn bills of posterity, and to acquiesce in this never-closing hyperbola of intersecular exchange? (pp. 253–4)

The cycle is determined by the trend and is a necessary consequence of it. But what is the rationale for a desire for growth, given that we give up in our own lives 'material requisites of well-being' in order that they may shower in ever greater amounts upon those we do not know and shall never see?

For Robertson, who had already become aware of 'the harshness of human destiny' and of life itself as a briefly glowing splint in the howling blackness of everlasting night, the dilemma was particularly acute. And just as it was through *Alice* that Robertson rationalised his view of the reality of life and sought personally to come to terms with it, so it was, we shall find, through Heraclitus and Walt Whitman that he caught at the mystery of the link between present and future and its relationship to industrial fluctuation. It is to an investigation of these deeper influences that we turn in the following chapter.

16. Material cause and final cause

I

At first sight Heraclitus and Walt Whitman make strange bedfellows. The first was the Greek philosopher of the Classical period, Heraclitus of Ephesus, who flourished about 500 BC and who was known as 'the obscure' and the 'weeping philosopher' (in contrast to Democritus the 'laughing philosopher') on account of his melancholy views. The second was the nineteenth-century American poet whose work is chiefly remembered for its celebration of the vitality of a young country together with a barely concealed homoeroticism. Nevertheless, taken together they provide the context that gives new significance to Robertson's theory of the cycle.

II

The two ideas mainly associated with the philosophy of Heraclitus are that fire forms the material basis of the universe and that all things are in a state of flux. Under the influence of Plato, the latter has come to be interpreted as meaning that all things are constantly changing even though they appear to be stable (for example the hills, also the waters of a river into which we step). It is more probable, however, that Heraclitus intended the opposite: that behind the appearance of constant flux there is a reality of stability and order. It is, therefore, necessary to comprehend the *logos* ('reason'), the universal principle through which all things are interrelated. It is revealed, for example, in the relation that exists between opposites; and by a sort of law of conservation of matter, in which in rotation fire turns to ocean and earth and these turn back into fire.

But these views of Heraclitus are not mutually exclusive categories and, to go a step further, we might say that it is perfectly possible to be aware that beneath a surface stability, the enduring sameness of familiar things, all is change and decay; but that at a deeper level still the flux is governed by more permanent laws that determine the working of the whole universe. A useful example to bear in mind for what is to follow is to imagine that we are gazing upon a familiar landscape, knowing full well that even as we look the hills, lakes and rivers are changing in form and composition, even though imperceptibly slowly, but that the processes at work are readily comprehensible through study of the laws of physics and geography.

So much for physical processes, but what of the human element? It was an important part of Heraclitus' philosophy that men must learn to live in social harmony and that they failed to do so because they did not comprehend the *logos* but were instead guided by surface appearances.

The evidence suggests that Robertson, like the good classical scholar he was, understood Heraclitus in his various aspects. In the *Study*, although (a) he is mainly concerned to account for industrial fluctuation by way of both short-term and long-term economic causes, he is also (b) seeking to identify the deeper processes at work and is (c) gently suggesting that the familiar assumptions that governed economic life in the pre-war world may not be immutable (Preface, p. xix). The first of these represents the Heraclitan flux; the second, the *logos* or underlying principle; and the third, the conventions that governed western civilisation. We shall deal with them in turn.

First, Robertson refers to the Heraclitan flux in the quotation in Greek that appears on the title page of the *Study* and again in English in the Preface, where the alternative form of the name, Heracleitus, is used, possibly because it provides a more acceptable adjectival form (p. xx). It is clear from these references that the notion of the flux is being used to refer both to the industrial fluctuations associated with the idea of a trade cycle, and for the unplanned and unregulated atomism in economic organisation that under the influence of the individual urge, gives rise to them. In the Preface Robertson speaks of a 'thoughtless and anarchic industrial age' (p. xx) and again in the Preliminary Chapter, to the 'anarchic nature of modern industry' (p. 7). Robertson argues that in the absence of the 'conscious guidance of any single directing power, the astonishing fact is surely not that fluctuations should occur but that all things on the whole should work together so smoothly and steadily for good' (p. 7). The implication is that by understanding the forces at work we could do better and achieve a more ideal distribution of income through time.

This point is given its real significance by the wider sense in which 'flux' is being used, namely, as a metaphor for the world of change and decay in which time slips underneath the feet of those without the hope of Glory and for whom the possibility of (more) 'jam today' has a particular urgency.

To capture the idea of the impermanence of things Robertson invokes images of the sea. We saw earlier (Chapter 14, above) that use of the term 'fluctuation' in the title of the *Study* refers to the alternate rising and falling motion of the waves; while more wholesale change is conjured by his contrast, in the New Introduction of 1948, between the 'static and stable' world depicted (in his view) in Keynes's theory and his own premise for theorising, of being '*drenched* with the vision of eternal ebb and flow, relapse and recovery' (p. xvi; emphasis added).

It was, moreover, an image that endured. Robertson used it first in the text of the *Study*, in which he refers to the 'ebb of construction activity' (p. 61), and, more significantly, in the title of his lecture to the Liberal Summer School at Cambridge in 1923, published as *The Ebb and Flow of Unemployment* (1923). This paper is of particular importance for an understanding of Robertson's position and we shall meet it again below. We should note finally that Keynes was to invoke sea-images when in 1937 he employed allegory in an attempt to indicate to Robertson the reason for Robertson's inability to let go of his classical roots (see below, Chapter 25).

In the *Study* the notion of the existence of a state of flux is made explicit in the references to Heraclitus and given concrete economic form in the cycle of industrial fluctuation. But in its more general sense, which refers to the consciousness of time, decay and death in an amoral universe devoid both of purpose and meaning, there are links to our previous discussion based on the literary references in Robertson's work. Together they show that this was a factor that pervaded Robertson's outlook and shaped his approach to economics.

The first link, of course, is to Alice, who leaves behind her familiar middle-class Victorian world to dream of one that is chaotic, composed of discrete elements and events, and which refuses to obey the usual conventions of social intercourse, little realising that this is the 'reality' beneath the imposed artificiality of everyday life. The whole experience has a warm reassuring quality, however, because of the way Alice reacts in the face of indifference and hostility. As Donald Rackin wrote in his essay 'Love and death in Carroll's *Alices*':

> Essentially, the *Alices* stop time in their surface nonsense, presenting to the child in their readers and listeners an unthreatened and unthreatening vista of seemingly endless play, play (the Caucus Race or Tweedle brothers' battle) curiously, charmingly static and full of discrete counters within a safe, closed field. But for their adult audience they give something more; they also whisper some sad truths about *the world of flux beyond that pleasant field.* The walls of Caroll's nonsense are thus constantly, if surreptitiously, breached by Time and Death and conse-quently . . . by the love that springs from them both. So while Carroll's love-gift of the *Alices* helps the child Alice 'keep, through her riper years, the simple and loving heart of her childhood', another voice sings softly at the same time to other ears, to those for whom childhood's dreams might already be like a 'pilgrim's withered wreath of flowers / plucked in a far off land'.   (Rackin in Bloom ed., 1987, pp. 125–6; emphasis added)

The second link is with Shakespeare through Robertson's much praised and particularly affecting role as Justice Shallow in *Henry IV, Part 2*. In the exchanges between Shallow and Falstaff we have a contrast of views on the use of the past as a means of facing the future, when both have 'heard the chimes at midnight' and Shallow is revealed as an Alice figure, a 'second-childhood "Child of the pure unclouded brow"' (see above, Chapter 12).

In examining the themes explored in Shakespeare's plays, L.C. Knights has linked *Henry IV, Part 2* with the *Sonnets* as being concerned with the effect of time and change in men's lives. He explains the relationship between the two works as follows: '*Henry IV, Part II*, is markedly a transitional play. It looks back to the *Sonnets* and the earlier history plays, and it looks forward to the great tragedies.' With respect to the theme he writes:

> It is surely no accident that one of the first plays in which we recognise the great Shakespeare – the Second Part of *King Henry IV* – is a play of which the controlling theme is time and change. In that play and in the sonnets on time, we see clearly the beginning of the progress that culminates in *King Lear* and the great tragedies. (Knights, 1959, p. 45)

The response to the controlling forces of time and change in life, as portrayed in *Henry IV, Part 2* is given in the sonnets on time. Two hundred and fifty years before the Darwinian upheavals that produced the climate of thought in which the *Alice* books were written, they too point to love as the only certainty in the changing world:

> There is a keen and pervasive love of life . . . There is an equally keen, equally pervasive feeling for the stealthy and unimpeded undermining by time of what the heart holds most dear . . . And finally . . . there is a groping for some certitude to set over against *the perpetual flux of things*, an intimation that love 'stands hugely politic, that it nor grows with heat nor drowns with showers'. (Sonnet CXXIV, quoted in Knights, 1959, p. 50; emphasis added)

The idea of flux, therefore, is an important nodal point or junction through which several currents of Robertson's make-up flow; these are linked together and given a common element. There is, first, the important link between Robertson's literary references and the meaning of his economic writings. There is, second, the link between Robertson's temperament (Rackin – *Alice*) and his economics (the Heraclitan flux). There is, third, the link between life (Knights – Shakespeare and *Alice*) and his economics (Heraclitan flux and *logos*).

Of the last linkage we have not so far explored the element of *logos*, the underlying principle that links and explains apparently unrelated phenomena. It is the element that is in some ways the most important. For if the idea of flux describes the problem (industrial fluctuation in the narrow sense; the impermanence of life deprived of 'meaning' or 'purpose' in the broader sense), then it is the idea of *logos* that provides the key to the solution. What was the 'reason' at which Robertson hinted, that links industrial fluctuation (and, more broadly, economic change) with the larger mystery of life and death?

III

Robertson approached the second of the three aspects or levels of Heraclitan thought that we identified above, namely, the deeper processes at work beneath the short and long-term economic causes of industrial fluctuation, on the last page of the *Study*. It came in the form of the answer to the question he had raised on the previous page (p. 253) concerning the 'most desirable distribution of the community's income through time'. Robertson suggested that the choice between present consumption and future growth (the extent to which we should sacrifice present enjoyment in order to benefit those who are to follow) is a question of 'ethics, rather than economics' (p. 254). By reference to two quotations in Greek he reminds the reader that sacrifice is continuing to take place in

> an age which is apt to forget the [final cause – that for the sake of which] among the [manifestations of the material cause – the *sine qua non*, literally the without-which-not] and immolate ourselves, *if we must* with our eyes open and not as in a trance. (p. 254; English equivalent substituted for the Greek, emphasis added)

These ideas derive from Aristotle's analysis of causation in the *Physics* (II) and for Robertson must refer to the unifying principle underlying the Heraclitan flux. In terms of the *Study*, the 'final cause' is that which gives rise to behaviour that results in industrial fluctuation, which, in turn, constitutes the 'material cause' or necessary cost of the 'final cause' for the sake of which it was incurred.

As economics is a human activity, Robertson is searching for the drive or motivation that results in economic instability. In the absence of any economic theory at that time that could encompass the sense he had of what was going on, he turned to the realm of poetry, where ideas otherwise inarticulate often find their first shadowy adumbration.

We recall that the conclusion Robertson had derived from his empirical work was that fluctuation was a consequence of economic growth and was therefore the necessary cost of future prosperity: 'Out of the welter of industrial dislocation the great permanent riches of the future are generated.' But as the necessary cost of attaining these future riches must fall upon the living, to what extent is the present generation obligated to take part in the process? 'How far are we bound to honour the undrawn bills of posterity, and to acquiesce in this never-closing hyperbola of intersecular exchange?' (*Study* p. 254).

It is because choice is involved, of course, that the matter becomes one for ethical debate. For this reason Robertson feels justified in questioning the presumption that we must 'sacrifice ourselves as willing victims' to the customary imperative and to suggest that the wiser philosophy may be that we should live for the present. He leads us into the issues involved in making this choice with a quotation from Walt Whitman:

> Urge and urge and urge,
> Always the procreant urge of the world.
> [Walt Whitman, 'Song of Myself']

That the idea alluded to here was not a passing fancy, but an enduring conviction is shown by the fact that Robertson gave the quotation three times: on the title page of the *Study*, on the last page of the text and again, after an interval of thirty-three years, at the end of the New Introduction to the reprint of 1948. In economic terms the 'urge' is the push for growth but the 'vitality' (Robertson, 1948a, p. xvii) associated with it touches on deeper matters that constitute the 'final cause' (the reason or *logos*) for which fluctuation is endured. To discover what this is we must look more closely at Whitman, a poet in whose works many of the ideas discussed in this study are brought into juxtaposition. Indeed, Whitman provides the keystone of the arch of the argument we have been erecting in the foregoing chapters. The following are the points most relevant to our argument.

IV

The corpus of Whitman's poetical work is contained in *Leaves of Grass*, a title borne by no less than nine books between 1855 and 1892. In each successive edition, new poems were added, existing poems were revised and the relative position of poems changed. The last edition is definitive in that it was approved by Whitman before he died and thus represents his final views on the content of the poems and the order in which they should appear, the latter in Whitman's view being necessary for a proper understanding of the first.

It was Whitman's contention that his book was himself, as is shown by the lines he appended as epilogue to several editions of *Leaves of Grass*:

> Camerado, this is no book,
> Who touches this touches a man . . .

However, Geoffrey Dutton has cautioned us to see the finished book rather as 'a vast experiment in becoming' in which the 'self' breaks down into many different selves, just as the man himself *wore many different masks or personae* during his lifetime, each searching out its true relationship to, among other things, life and death, time, space and sex (Dutton, 1961, pp. 53, 56).

The most significant part of this experiment for present purposes is Whitman's poem, 'Song of Myself', which opens the sequence and which can be interpreted as a 'search for the achievement of a truly living identity' (Dutton, 1961, p. 65). It was from this poem that Robertson chose the lines quoted in the *Study*. These lines form part of a longer section in which are represented the themes that bear on an understanding of the place of the *Study* in the larger scheme of things:

> I have heard what the talkers were talking, the talk of the
>   beginning and the end,
> But I do not talk of the beginning or the end.
>
> There was never any more inception than there is now,
> Nor any more youth or age than there is now,
> And will never be any more perfection than there is now,
> Nor any more heaven or hell than there is now.
>
> Urge and urge and urge,
> Always the procreant urge of the world.
>
> Out of the dimness opposite equals advance, always
>   substance and increase, always sex,
> Always a knit of identity, always distinction, always a
>   breed of life.
>
> To elaborate is no avail, learn'd and unlearn'd feel that it is so.
>
> Sure as the most certain sure, plumb in the uprights, well
>   entretied, braced in the beams,
> Stout as a horse, affectionate, haughty, electrical,
> I and this mystery here we stand.
> (Whitman, 1965, pp. 30-1, lines 38-51)

The 'I' of this poem and of *Leaves of Grass* as a whole, has several aspects. Howard J. Waskow has detected a distinction between the real or ideal self and the actual self, 'the self in the actual pettiness of its particularity' (recall our portrayal of Robertson's life in these terms, see Chapters 1, 2 and 4, above). It is a distinction that is more overt in other poems and only hinted at here by the juxtaposition of 'this mystery' (see Waskow, 1966, pp. 158, 162, 163, 172). It is an idea that chimes with Dutton's notion of Whitman as successively wearing different masks or *personae* (see Dutton, 1961, pp. 25, 32, 49). The real self that lay beneath the impenetrable masks nursed a smouldering homosexual urge that was in real life sublimated in friendships with ferrymen, omnibus- and cab-drivers and, during the Civil War period, in hospital-visiting and wound-dressing (Dutton, 1961, pp. 13, 28, 10-11, 12, 30-7). In literature it was celebrated, most openly, in the 'Calumus' poems.

The 'I' of the poems can also be seen as 'generic', as Whitman celebrates himself as the ubiquitous representative man, exploring the web of relationships that link him to every part of creation. This is another aspect of the 'mystery' (Allen, 1975, p. 212). The links extend beyond death and the 'I' becomes, especially in 'Song of Myself', synonymous with the idea of the 'soul'. It is by the same token synonymous with 'mind', 'consciousness', 'spark of life', even 'God' (Allen, 1975, pp. 188–90). The soul outlives the body and expands or 'dilates' until it comprehends and becomes one with the whole of creation (Allen, 1975, pp. 196–8).

Whitman's 'soul-sight' has been identified by William James as:

> that divine clue and unseen thread which holds the whole congeries of things, all history and time and all events. however momentous, like a leashed dog in the hand of the hunter. (James in Allen, 1975, p. 194)

R.M. Bucke's rendering of 'soul-sight' as 'cosmic consciousness' makes explicit the idea of a consciousness of the cosmos, of the life and order of the universe (Bucke in Allen, 1975, p. 194).

This notion of cosmic unity in flux has been referred to as '*The Heraclitan obsession of Walt Whitman*' (see Allen, 1975, p. 213; also Waskow, 1966, pp. 23, 31; emphasis added). It is invoked in the third stanza of the extract quoted above:

> Out of the dimness opposite equals advance, always
>   substance and increase, always sex,
> Always a knit of identity, always distinction,
>   always a breed of life.

The link between Whitman and Heraclitus is strengthened in literary terms by Gerard Manley Hopkins, who feared the influence upon himself of the American poet (with whose mind he felt a unique affinity) and who wrote a poem entitled 'That Nature Is a Heraclitan Fire and of the Comfort of the Resurrection'. In this poem Hopkins describes the condition of man without the promise of the Resurrection (the hope of Glory) as brief, unique and utterly insignificant. The 'harshness of human destiny', consciousness of which was said to colour Robertson's outlook on life (see Butler, 1963, p. 42), is here bound up with the Heraclitan fire, 'nature's bonfire' which consumes the dead:

> . . . Million-fueled, nature's bonfire burns on.
> But quench her bonniest, dearest to her, her clearest-selved spark
> Man, how fast his firedint, his mark on mind, is gone!
> Both are in an unfathomable, all is in an enormous dark
> Drowned. O pity and indignation! Manshape, that shone
> Sheer off, disseveral, a star, death blots black out; nor mark
>   Is any of him at all so stark
> But vastness blurs and time beats level.
> (Hopkins, 1992, pp. 197-8, Poem 174)

In addition to the idea of cosmic unity in flux, William James's 'unseen thread which holds the whole congeries of things' also has an intertemporal dimension. James's mention of 'history and time and all events' draws attention to Whitman's notion of flux as progress in which all creation is an evolutionary journey. As Waskow puts it: 'Life is not undifferentiated flux, but a measured journey: "The earth neither lags nor hastens"' (Waskow, 1966, p. 31).

Three questions arise here:

1.   What is the thread that holds all together?
2.   What is the goal or destination of the evolutionary journey?
3.   What is the significance of Whitman's assertion that the journey is a measured one, the world neither lagging nor hasting?

We shall find that the answers are merely three facets of the same phenomenon, but it will be convenient to deal with them successively and to begin with the second: the question of the goal or destination of the evolutionary journey.

Although we shall argue below that Whitman was pre-eminently the poet of the present, he was very conscious of death as the end of earthly life and of the destruction of the body. To Whitman immortality came through the writings he would leave behind, in which he celebrated the gloriousness of life in all its manifestations. In addition, his notion of the soul that survives the body and dilates until it comprehends the whole cosmos is an expression of hope for salvation through 'inclusion'.

Inclusion here refers to the process that links two conceptions of Whitman's unity in flux: *the unity of All and the unity of One*. The process is of a kind in which the distinctions that exist between individual elements in the first are lost as individual elements merge in the organic fluidity of the second (Waskow, 1966, pp. 9, 10, 14, 18). It is in this sense that:

> The flux is not only 'process'; it is also 'progress' – it moves towards the One . . . rest, the permanence that comes from joining the One, can tempt one to desert the living flux.   (Waskow, 1966, pp. 40–1)

Note the parallels here with what has gone before. First. with Robertson's poem (in D9/3/3 RPTC) in which 'the earth shall yield us rest'; that is, rest from the flux. Second, with Robertson's poem 'Synthesis – a Mood' in which:

> The sundered members of the hyperbola
>   Are bended now towards a concentric round:
> *The shattered mirror of my life grows whole,*
>   The world's disordered beat serene and sound.
> (D9/3/24 RPTC; emphasis added)

This can now be seen as concerned with the struggle towards wholeness or oneness, occasioned by his consciousness of flaws and deficiencies in his make-up that led to the assumption of a succession of *personae* in which harmony and happiness might be achieved. Of Whitman, Geoffrey Dutton has written:

> [Whitman] was brought up in intimate contact with disease, despair and madness. If he struggles towards a whole and affirmative identity it is precisely because he knows what the alternatives are . . . In a group of several of his finest poems Whitman deals with the agonising doubts that accompany the effort to *make the broken identity whole.* (Dutton, 1961, pp. 74–5; emphasis added)

Disease and madness were not the problems for Robertson but despair and recurring psychological problems certainly were (see above, Chapter 4; and L/R 117, 134 KPKC) and the temptation would have been to follow Whitman's philosophy and *seek relief in the organic fluidity of the 'One'*. His dilemma, however, arose because of the countervailing pull of his *need for a reference back with its requirement to safeguard the discreteness of parts as a condition for the maintenance of nonsense-as-game.*

We also recall that the safe world of nonsense-as-game was threatened by the uniting power of *love*; that same love, on the other hand, that becomes the last resort in the face of the loss of Faith and the discovery of the cold, uncaring universe. For Whitman, who refused to confine himself within the precepts of orthodox religion, love is the 'unseen thread that holds the whole congeries of things' and, therefore, the subject of the first question we raised above. He celebrates the mystery of love in Section 5 of 'Song of Myself', certain that 'a kelson of the creation is love'. For Whitman, love becomes adhesiveness or the manly love of comrades. Comradeship 'provides for the living what immortality does for the dead – participation in the permanent spirit that lies behind the changing faces of things. *It is an alternative to the flux*' (Waskow, 1966, p. 41).

Traditionally, however, love is associated with marriage and procreation:

> Urge and urge and urge,
> Always the procreant urge of the world.

The 'opposite equals' advance, unite and reproduce their kind, in each case a similar yet distinct new member of the family and the race. The proximate incentive is sexual desire, and sex and matters sensual played a very important catalysing role in Whitman's verse. But what is the ultimate compulsion? What is the purpose?

This is the subject of the third question we raised above, concerning the significance of Whitman's assertion that the journey is a measured one: the world neither lags nor hastens. The implication is that there is progress, it is orderly and it takes place by way of an infinite number of small steps. In Whitman's view, 'Nature marches in procession, in sections, like the corps of an army'. Here we recall the *natura non facit saltum* (nature does not make leaps) which was a tenet of Alfred Marshall's approach to economics and is printed on the title-page of the *Principles*. With respect to Robertson, Presley has commented that the phrase could equally have been his motto (Presley, 1978, p. 67). For our own part we refer to the Preface of the *Study*, where Robertson invoked the idea in raising the possibility that the unusual circumstances of war would present the opportunity for a leap out of the measured grind of the flux:

> It may be that the old *Natura nihil facit per saltum* will be justified by our relapse into the Heracleitan flux. But it is at least possible that in industrial as in other matters we are in the presence of one of those definite mutations of the social life which it is within the collective power of man to fix and foster in accordance with his highest hopes.   (Robertson, 1915, p. xx)

It was also a basic hypothesis of the naturalist Charles Darwin and the foundation of his belief that evolutionary change always occurs gradually and slowly. In the course of his exposition of what was to become the theory of evolution, Darwin asks rhetorically:

> 'Natura non facit saltum'. . . Why, on the theory of Creation, should there be such variety and so little real novelty? Why should all the parts and organs of so many independent beings, each supposed to have been separately created for its proper place in nature, be so commonly linked together *by graduated steps*? Why should not Nature take a sudden leap from structure to structure? On the theory of natural selection, we can clearly understand why she should not; for natural selection acts only by taking advantage of slight successive variations; she can never take a great and sudden leap, but must advance by *short and sure, though slow steps*.   (Darwin, [1859] 1972, p. 180; emphasis added)

He also makes clear that the principle applies equally to tangible and intangible components of an organism: 'the canon in natural history of *natura non facit saltum* is applicable to instincts as well as to corporeal structure' (Darwin, [1859] 1972, p. 260).

Whitman came to know Darwin's work and found in it support for his own view of gradual evolution. However, Darwin's theory of natural selection depended on the occurrence of *fortuitous* (literally, by chance or accident) infinitesimal variations, which by conferring an advantage in the struggle for survival enabled a plant or animal to live long enough to reproduce. Whitman's conception of the forward march, by contrast, seems to hint at the idea of 'purpose' or 'intent':

... we are all onward, onward, speeding slowly, surely bettering,
Life, life an endless march, an endless army, ...
The world, the race, the soul – in space and time the universes,
All bound as is befitting each – *all surely going somewhere*
(Whitman, 1965, p. 220; emphasis added)

And for this reason it seems likely that the inspiration came not from Darwin direct but from Jean Baptiste Lamarck, an earlier evolutionist writer, who suggested that through time organisms adapt to their environment and transmit the characteristics so acquired to later generations. The idea that an intelligence was at work making choices implied the existence of a benevolent Creator and therefore of purpose in the universe.

V

However, it was Darwin who triumphed and it was Darwin's theory of natural selection, in conjunction with Mendelian genetics, that provided the basis for the modern theory of evolution. Two quotations from *The Origin of Species* will give the essence of Darwin's contribution. First, on the basis of the myriad observations he had made during his five-year, round-the-world voyage in HMS *Beagle*, Darwin concluded that:

> Owing to [the struggle for life] variations, if they be in any degree profitable to the individuals of a species, in their infinitely complex relations to other organic beings and to their physical conditions of life, will tend to the preservation of such individuals, and will generally be inherited by the offspring . . . I have called this principle, by which each slight variation, if useful, is preserved, by the term Natural Selection, in order to mark its relation to man's power of selection. But the expression often used by Mr Herbert Spencer of the Survival of the Fittest is more accurate, and is sometimes equally convenient.   (Darwin, [1859] 1972, p. 67)

Darwin discovered the principle that underpinned his theory of natural selection in the writings of the Reverend Thomas Robert Malthus (a man who, according to Keynes, was the first Cambridge economist and the discoverer of the principle of effective demand: see below, Chapter 26). In his *Essay on the Principle of Population* (1798), Malthus presented the mathematical argument that the growth of population would outstrip the means of subsistence and so result in a struggle for survival. Darwin realised that it was this struggle that gave unique importance to the random variations that conferred a competitive advantage on individual plants or animals:

> as more individuals are produced than can possibly survive, there must in every case be a struggle for existence, either one individual with another of the same species, or with the physical conditions of life. It is the doctrine of Malthus applied with

manifold force to the whole animal and vegetable kingdoms . . . Although some species may now be increasing in numbers, all cannot do so, for the world would not hold them.   (Darwin, [1859], 1972, pp. 68–9)

Darwin's principle of inherited characteristics was later confirmed by Gregor Mendel's experiments, which showed that the characteristics would not be lost through dilution.

VI

We can now begin to give some form to the something that lay behind Robertson's invocation of the idea of the 'final cause': the reason or *logos* that gave rise to economic growth and, therefore, to the trade cycle.

We have seen that, in the midst of the flux, the world of change and decay, there is a desire to reach the ultimate goal of the One: the organic wholeness which offers permanence or rest from the chaos of the flux. Unity in flux is achieved through love or, in the case of Whitman and by extension Robertson, adhesiveness or comradely love. The problem here for Robertson, with his need for a reference back, was that love was also the destroyer of the one-and-one-and-one of nonsense-as-game so that there must be perpetual conflict between the organic and the atomic, as much in his personal life as in his economics (see especially Chapter 22, below).

For most people, however, subject to no such restriction, the forward march of the generations is best captured by the notion of evolution. Darwin's theory was essentially neutral or 'meaningless' but supplied the mechanism and the element of gradualism. What is yet wanting is the element of purpose to link Darwin with Whitman's suggestion that all are 'surely going somewhere': that is, towards the One. Together with this sense of compulsion, however, we must also allow for the possibility of choice: the right to live for the present and not wholly for the future. We recall that Whitman was the poet of the present, choosing to celebrate *life* in all its manifestations.

These were the considerations which, we may surmise from the literary clues available, entered into the ethical dilemma to which Robertson pointed in the *Study*. Fluctuations (material cause) are the cost of growth and growth is explained (final cause) by 'the procreant urge of the world'. We are not, however, helpless slaves of the process and may choose to live more for the present.

To bring these various considerations together we shall introduce a more modern theory of evolution that claims descent from Darwin and Mendel but brings in the elements of blind compulsion tempered by choice. We shall argue on the 'as if' principle that this could be the something hinted at by Robertson. Robertson can have had no knowledge of it, and its validity in detail or otherwise is not material to the broader theme of this study. We shall employ it only in its popular, accessible form and comment that though controversial it does fit the bill.

In this modern theory of evolution, the stress is not on differential survival so much as on differential reproduction; that is, not on the death or survival of individuals but on their ability to outbreed their competitors. This gives rise to the notion of 'fitness', which is defined as the relative ability of an individual member of a species to pass on its genes to subsequent generations; that is, to increase the relative frequency of its genes in the gene pool. The twist, however, is that the motivating agent is the individual gene rather than the individual body, which becomes simply a gene-carrier, programmed to reproduce on behalf of the 'selfish gene'. This phrase and the ideas associated with it were popularised many years ago by Dr Richard Dawkins in his book *The Selfish Gene*:

> The argument of this book is that we, and all other animals, are machines created by our genes. Like successful Chicago gangsters, our genes have survived, in some cases for millions of years, in a highly competitive world. This entitles us to expect certain qualities in our genes. I shall argue that a predominant quality to be expected in a successful gene is ruthless selfishness.   (Dawkins, 1976, p. 2)

This proposition is expanded as follows:

> What is the selfish gene? It is not just one single physical bit of DNA. Just as in the primeval soup, it is *all* replicas of a particular bit of DNA, distributed throughout the world . . . a single selfish gene . . . is trying to get more numerous in the gene pool. Basically it does this by helping to program the bodies in which it finds itself to survive and to reproduce. But now we are emphasizing that 'it' is a distributed agency, existing in many different individuals at once. The key point . . . is that a gene might be able to assist *replicas* of itself which are sitting in other bodies. If so, this would appear as individual altruism but it would be brought about by gene selfishness.   (Dawkins, 1976, p. 95)

On this basis Dawkins sets out to explore the apparent contrasts of human behaviour: 'My purpose is to examine the biology of selfishness and altruism' (p. 1). The genes do not have it all their own way, however, for an important qualification to the main thesis is that gene-determined behaviour can be modified significantly by the influence of culture, that is, by *learned behaviour*. Both parts of the argument are relevant to an understanding of Robertson's views and Robertson's contribution as contained in the *Study*. For it can be used to explain *both*: (a) the 'urge and urge and urge' of people to reproduce their kind and to sacrifice present consumption in order to promote economic growth as a means of ensuring the greater welfare of those they will never see and, apparently, cannot possibly know; (b) why it might nevertheless be possible to effect 'one of those definite mutations of the social life' which would give rise to 'a less thoughtless and anarchic industrial age' if people could but see the Final Cause among the manifestations of Material Cause and then to 'immolate' themselves, if they must, with their 'eyes open and not as in a trance'.

With these words Robertson (1915, pp. xx, 254) indicated that the causes of the trade cycle arose from the time preferences (real choices) of human beings as well as the technical characteristics of capitalistic production. They also provided the starting point for his work on the management of the cycle, such that, as he later wrote, means might be found to 'limit the turbulence, without destroying the vitality, of the "urge and urge and urge, Always the procreant urge of the world"' (Robertson, 1948a, p. xvii).

This is not, of course, to argue that Robertson understood matters in the way in which we have explained them here, but such is the implication of the words he used and the references he made. Where mysteries too profound for *The Economist* 'Annual Histories' were involved, it was to ancient philosophical thought and to poetry that he naturally turned. He could never have surmised, however, that the questions he raised would one day be the subject of a new branch of economics that drew inspiration from and used the terminology of the theory of evolution. Two references to mark, as it were, the inauguration of the movement will suffice.

The first is to the *American Economic Review* of 1993, which published a group of papers on 'The Economics of Altruism' clearly inspired by the gene theory (*American Economic Review*, vol. 83, pt 1, 1993).

The second reference to which we draw attention is to a conference held at the London School of Economics in June 1993, as reported in *The Economist* at the end of that year (*The Economist*, 25 December 1993–7 January 1994, pp. 97–99). This conference drew together scholars from a number of disciplines (economics, biology, psychology, anthropology) to explore the common ground between economics and evolution and so bring to birth the new discipline of evolutionary economics. Some of the conclusions reached at the conference make clearer the relevance of the whole new development to the case of Robertson and the insights he provided. The following is the most significant:

> evolutionary biology – a theory in which the survival not of the individual but of its genes (in descendants and close relatives) became the criterion of fitness – so *economists have learnt to adjust their utility functions to include not just people's own consumption but also their children's . . . economists used to be puzzled by the way people continue saving right up to the ends of their lives. Now they recognise that 'utility' includes leaving something to your children.* (*The Economist*, 25 December 1993–7 January 1994, pp. 98–9; emphasis added)

On this basis, therefore, the reason that people choose to sacrifice consumption in the present, and thus on (neo-)classical assumptions help to promote economic growth, is that they are motivated to act in the interests of the gene-carriers they will never see. Individual people, of course, do not consciously choose to promote economic growth *per se*. Rather, they save in order to benefit their children and grandchildren. The saving thus accumulated will lead to investment and to economic growth, the growth of capacity output.

VII

It is 'as if' this were the process that Robertson sensed to be at work. It was a remarkable insight and one indeed previously overlooked by Robertson scholars. Nevertheless, it provides the coping stone to his empirically based theory of the cycle and reveals his achievement as being the more remarkable. That is, Robertson's perception of the importance of something we might now recognise as evolutionary economics to an understanding of the relationship between industrial fluctuation and economic growth transforms our assessment of his contribution.

17.   A plea for the present

I

If evolutionary theory, even as obliquely detected by Robertson, helps to explain the 'desire for economic growth' that in turn gives rise to the trade cycle, it can also explain Robertson's questioning of the trance-like acceptance of the 'perpetual immolation of the present upon the altar of the future'; the acquiescence in the 'never-closing hyperbola of intersecular exchange' (Robertson, 1915, p. 254).

This is because, as we noticed earlier, the gene theory that we are employing on the 'as if' principle specifically allows for the influence of learned behaviour so that we need not be the slaves of our genes. On this basis Robertson, in ignorance of the conclusions of evo-economics, is merely asking people to become conscious of the process in which they are engaging: first, because of the instability it creates in economic life (the cycle); but also, second, because the present is that which we know and over which we can exercise rational choice, whereas the future is an unknown quantity subject to the choices of others.

Robertson was peculiarly well placed to pose the question because of his detachment from the whole business. Childless and likely to remain so, without the hope of Heaven, regressive rather than progressive in outlook, his desire to be 'useful' would put his intellect at the service of the present. In the *Study* the emphasis is on the questioning of the process that gives rise to fluctuation. Later the emphasis shifts to the identification of means of achieving economic growth at minimum cost in terms of the cycle.

Again it was in Whitman that Robertson found the inspiration for his questioning of the status quo. For Whitman, though his whole life and work were in some ways a preparation for (the avoidance of) death, was intensely aware of life in the present. Indeed, it was as if, in seeking to celebrate life in all its myriad manifestations, he by the same token sought to affirm its unquenchability and, therefore, his own immortality as part of it. In the passage from 'Song of Myself', quoted above, Whitman wrote:

> I have heard what the talkers were talking, the talk of the
>   beginning and the end,
> But I do not talk of the beginning or the end.

But there was in this outlook a strong element of hope and of willing it to be so, for Whitman's joyous celebration of life revealed a determined optimism. Always progressive in outlook, a participant in the everlasting forward march of the world, Whitman was an Alice-figure *par excellence*. To Robertson, who shared his sexuality and his feeling of the need to be made whole, he would be inspiration, comfort and justification.

II

From the semi-detached standpoint of Whitman and Robertson, the lot of the majority of humanity would seem to be infinitely better served by concern for the present with all its pains, but also with all its loves, than the unknown future, however much its terrors might be rationalised away.

And this indeed is the message of the *Study*, in which a young economist analyses at great length the economic problems of the short run, brought about under the influence of the long run and with the emphasis now shifted to the former. The short run is now not to be seen as merely the phase of dynamic adjustment to long-run equilibrium *à la* Marshall but as a legitimate and important sphere of the economist's operations. This shift in emphasis is now indelibly associated with Keynes but it was Robertson who gave it first and it is for this reason as well as for his contribution to an understanding of the problems of managing the short period, that *in reality* Robertson was Keynes's 'parent in errancy'.

III

Keynes's own contribution to the shift in emphasis came in two stages: in his *The Economic Consequences of the Peace* (1919) and in *A Tract on Monetary Reform* (1923) (henceforth *ECP* and *Tract* respectively).

With respect to *ECP*, the oft-quoted passages, the eloquently expressed sentiments, take on a new meaning and significance when considered in the light of the foregoing argument. It will be recalled that Keynes drew a picture of a pre-1914 European civilisation in which security and prosperity were regarded as the norm and in which the expectation of change could only be in the direction of further improvement (see Keynes, 1919, pp. 9–10).

But what was regarded as natural and normal was in fact highly artificial: the product of special circumstances that the war swept away. These special circumstances concerned two aspects of economic life: (a) the feeding of a growing population; and (b) the growth of the capital stock. As regards the first, a growing European population, hard-working and enterprising, was either employed at home, producing manufactures on an unprecedented scale, or settled abroad as emigrants. To these were sent the manufactures from home, in exchange for 'unlimited' supplies of food and raw materials, the produce of the newly opened lands. As a consequence of these arrangements:

> That happy age lost sight of a view of the world which filled with deep-seated melancholy the founders of our Political Economy. Before the eighteenth century mankind entertained no false hopes. To lay the illusions which grew popular at that age's latter end, Malthus disclosed a Devil. For half a century all serious economical writings held that Devil in clear prospect. For the next half century he was chained up and out of sight. Now perhaps we have loosed him again. (Keynes, 1919, p. 8)

The Devil was loosed because Europe, with its economy wrecked, could no longer pay for the flow of food necessary to sustain its people. The main point of Keynes's case in *ECP* was that the problems created by the war were to be compounded by the terms of the 1919 Versailles Treaty, which would have the effect of further weakening Germany and, therefore, Europe.

The conditions necessary for economic growth seemed even more (literally) peculiar and hence more precarious and vulnerable:

> Europe was so organised socially and economically as to secure the maximum accumulation of capital. [Remarkably it] depended for its growth on a double bluff or deception. On the one hand the labouring classes accepted from ignorance or powerlessness, or were compelled, persuaded, or cajoled by custom, convention, authority, and the well-established order of Society into accepting, a situation in which they could call their own very little of the cake, that they and Nature and the capitalists were co-operating to produce. And on the other hand the capitalist classes were allowed to call the best part of the cake theirs and were theoretically free to consume it, on the tacit underlying condition that they consumed very little of it in practice. The duty of 'saving' became nine-tenths of virtue and the growth of the cake the object of true religion. There grew round the non-consumption of the cake all those instincts of puritanism which in other ages has withdrawn itself from the world and has neglected the arts of production as well as those of enjoyment. And so the cake increased; but to what end was not clearly contemplated. Individuals would be exhorted not so much to abstain as to defer, and to cultivate the pleasures of security and anticipation. Saving was for old age or for your children; but this was only in theory, – the virtue of the cake was that it was never to be consumed, neither by you nor by your children after you.   (Keynes, 1919, p. 18)

Or then again, perhaps this is not the whole story. Realising that a perceived process which is explained by analogy with a pointless baking of cakes will convince no one, Keynes qualifies his argument with the notion of society's deeper insight:

In the unconscious recesses of its being Society knew what it was about. The cake was really very small in proportion to the appetites of consumption, and no one, if it were shared all round, would be much the better off by the cutting of it. *Society was working not for the small pleasures of today but for the future security and improvement of the race, - in fact for 'progress'*. If only the cake were not cut but was allowed to grow in the geometrical proportion predicted by Malthus of population, but not less true of compound interest, perhaps a day might come when there would at last be enough to go round, and when posterity could enter into the enjoyment of *our* labours. In that day overwork, overcrowding, and underfeeding would come to an end, and men, secure of the comforts and necessities of the body, could proceed to the nobler exercises of their faculties. One geometrical ratio might cancel another, and the nineteenth century was able to forget the fertility of the species in a contemplation of the dizzy virtues of compound interest. (Keynes, 1919, p. 18; emphasis added)

It is indeed an ingenious argument, that society should allow the cake to grow in line with the population and so defeat the Malthusian Devil. What it presumably implies is that the growth of capital will increase productive capacity and so (to fit in with the other strand of Keynes's argument) provide the means to purchase increased amounts of foodstuffs abroad.

IV

There are, in fact, in Keynes's brilliant analysis, all the ingredients pursued in this study so far and necessary for a solution – *save that extra something sensed by Robertson*. Any collective wisdom embodied in the mores of society and giving rise to a particular attitude towards consumption and saving will derive from its *individual* members. It is, as we have seen, the 'procreant urge' that brings about both the growth in population and, in our example, the desire to provide for kin-selected descendants. This in turn results in the *self*-denial involved in current saving.

However, the war had produced a fundamental change, as Robertson had forecast it would. On Keynes's analysis this is because the principle of accumulation:

depended on unstable psychological conditions, which it may be impossible to recreate. It was not natural for a population, of whom so few enjoyed the comforts of life, to accumulate so hugely. *The war has disclosed the possibility of consumption to all and the vanity of abstinence to many.* Thus the bluff is discovered; the labouring classes may be no longer willing to forgo so largely, and the capitalist classes, no longer confident of the future, may seek to enjoy more fully their liberties of consumption so long as they last, and thus precipitate the hour of their confiscation. (Keynes, 1919, p. 19; emphasis added)

That is, the war that 'disclosed the possibility of consumption to all and the vanity of abstinence to many' had precipitated what Robertson had spoken of as 'one of those definite mutations of the social life'. The shared experience of war had changed attitudes (in our example, learned behaviour counteracting biologically determined behaviour). There was a new awareness of the importance and preciousness of life, in the aftermath of the Great Killing, and of the pleasures of the present over the promises of the future. In Keynes's terms, as much as in Robertson's, the war had torn off the blinkers of 'custom, convention, authority, and the well established order of Society' to expose to view new uncertainties but also the possibility of, and necessity for, new modes of thought and behaviour. In this sense the Great War was a major step in the process begun by Lyell, Chambers and Darwin. The instability of the pre-war situation remarked on by Keynes was not merely economic. The effects of the undermining of faith and belief had been disguised by 'custom, convention, authority' and so on, as expressed in the durability of great institutions. In other words, the form remained though the substance had ebbed away. The war shook the edifice as never before.

Thus the new concern for life and for the present (as manifested most spectacularly in the image of the 'Roaring Twenties') was induced by a glimpse of reality (mortality) beneath the veil of the familiar. But, of course, we have met this idea earlier in this study; however, before we recall it to mind it will be instructive to look first at someone else's interpretation.

V

In the course of his criticism of Keynesian economics, S. Herbert Frankel followed Schumpeter's suggestion that it is in *ECP* that we find 'the vision of things social and economic of which [the apparatus of the *General Theory*] is the technical complement' (Frankel, 1977, pp. 63–4). In exploring the meaning of *ECP* Frankel made reference to analysis by Berger and Luckman (1966) in which a distinction is made between the 'daylight side' of human life and the 'night side'. His view was that Keynes believed the war had exposed the 'night side' of Europe's culture and with it the 'unstable psychological conditions' (that is, the 'double bluff or deception') upon which economic growth depended (Frankel, 1977, pp. 63–8).

Frankel argued that, on Berger and Luckman's analysis, Keynes should have been able to put the effect of the war into perspective, contained his 'terror of the night side of Europe's culture' and shown a more robust faith in the resilience of European institutions (Frankel, 1977, p. 65):

> Just because the 'night side' has its own reality, often enough of a sinister kind, it is a constant threat to the taken-for-granted matter-of-fact, 'sane' reality of life in society. The thought keeps suggesting itself (the 'insane' thought *par excellence*)

that, perhaps, the bright reality of everyday life is but an illusion, to be swallowed up at any moment by the howling nightmares of the other, the night-side reality. Such thoughts of madness and terror are contained by ordering all conceivable realities within the same symbolic universe that encompasses the reality of everyday life – to wit, ordering them in such a way that the latter reality retains its paramount, definitive (if one wishes, its 'most real') quality. (Berger and Luckman, 1966, pp. 115–16)

In other words, by setting the 'marginal situations' in context, in relation to the 'reality of everyday life', we see how unthreatening they are and their hold over us is relaxed.

But, we interject, what if the 'night-side reality' is the 'definitive' true reality; and the 'reality of everyday life' just a comforting illusion? This is the possibility Frankel did not allow for. Such, however, was the vision of mid-Victorian society that we glimpsed beneath the surface of Lewis Carroll's 'nonsense' (recall the descriptions of Wonderland as madness and as a dream). There we found that Church and state and afternoon tea were just a reassuring but entirely artificial construct, the effect of which (not the whole purpose) was to protect us from the reality of life lived under sentence of death in a cold, uncaring and utterly 'meaningless' universe (see above, Chapter 11). If then for mid-Victorian society, we read Edwardian or early Windsorian England, we see that it was beneath this edifice that Lyell, Chambers and Darwin had set the charge and lit the train. It needed only the cataclysm of war to knock over the painted flats of traditional usage and authority and reveal the howling nightmare that lay behind. In such circumstances it is hardly surprising if, as Robertson surmised they would, people should choose (learned behaviour) to reappraise the real choices before them and re-order their time preferences.

VI

In economic terms, concern for the present life, the only life we have, makes us suspicious of the idea of the long run: the equilibrium in which, as Milton Friedman put it, 'all anticipations are realised' (Friedman, 1972, p. 925); and to emphasise the importance of the short run, in which things actually happen and in which we actually live. It was Robertson's achievement to have intuited this at a time when the 'unstable psychological conditions' that propped up European prosperity were hidden from view and the special economic relationships that kept the 'Malthusian Devil' safely chained up were unimpaired. It was left to Keynes four years later, in the aftermath of war and while still reeling from the shock of Versailles, to expose the artificiality and precariousness of the conditions upon which all Europe had relied and to prophesy the likely consequences of their removal. His theory of growth, however, dealt only with symptoms and failed to detect the 'final cause' that lay behind them.

What the experience of writing *ECP* did do, however, was to make him into a determined and optimistic fighter against the dark forces of time and ignorance that always threatened economic prosperity. Even so, it was a further four years and the best part of a decade after Robertson (exactly ten years if we reckon from 1913, the year in which the first version of the fellowship dissertation was ready) that Keynes made his name synonymous with the short period. He eschewed the cryptic, elliptical, allusive style in which Robertson dealt with profundities and staked his claim in the unmistakable, direct terms of the campaigning journalist:

> But this *long run* is a misleading guide to current affairs. *In the long run* we are all dead. Economists set themselves too easy, too useless a task if in tempestuous seasons they can only tell us that when the storm is long past the ocean is flat again. (Keynes, 1923, *CW* IV p. 65; emphasis in original)

VII

The outcome of all this is of the profoundest interest. Robertson had argued *before the war* that too much was being sacrificed in the short term as a means of providing for economic growth. On the basis of his real saving theory this meant that people might consider the possibility of consuming more now, or at least of saving in full realisation of what they were doing. Keynes, by contrast, was arguing *after the war* that the discovery of the bluff or deception would result in more consumption and, therefore, a diminished rate of growth.

Both, therefore, drew attention to the same phenomenon, on the basis of the classical assumptions they shared, but from different perspectives. *After* the war the perspectives were the same and Robertson shifted his ground, now seeing discovery of the possibility of consumption not only as a liberating influence but also as a restraint on economic performance. The ethical question remained and Robertson continued to believe that people should be aware of the real choices involved and not be duped into making sacrifices against their will, either: (a) as in the *Study* by the actions of industrialists, or (b) as in *BPPL* by the actions of bankers, whose funds could be used to *force* people to save. Throughout, Robertson's approach to management of the short period was informed by his desire to promote growth without undue sacrifice on the part of the present generation. The extracts in subsection VIII, below, indicate clearly: (a) that the foregoing interpretation of the message of the *Study* made on the basis of the 'frame-materials' is correct; (b) Robertson's awareness of consumption possibilities both as a constraint as well as a liberating agent; (c) that Robertson deprecated deceit in economic policy.

VIII

In his 1923 lecture published as *The Ebb and Flow of Unemployment*, Robertson sought to explain the difficulty of distinguishing between boom and slump in terms of 'desirable' and 'undesirable' respectively, by reference to a series of pairs of conflicting motives at work in industrial activity. One of these, the 'second great dilemma' was posed by the 'pair of rival sirens – Enjoyment and Thrift' (Robertson, 1923b, pp. 5–6). And here Robertson is referring to man's need to reconcile himself to the idea that, though the race lives on, the individual members of it must die. That is (and recalling our argument from *Alice*):

> the clash of interests between himself as an ephemeral being, passing away like a May-fly at the end of a summer's day, and himself as a trustee in some undefined, uncomfortable way for the future, for a great undying corporation in which he had only a life interest. (Robertson, 1923b, pp. 5–6)

In the light of what was said in the *Study* concerning 'sacrifices . . . made during the boom' (Robertson, 1915, p. 254), Robertson now characterises the boom in terms of the 'Thrift and Enjoyment' criterion, as:

> the Future's night out, a time when the leaders of industry are planning far ahead, when additions are being made daily to the capital equipment of industry, when houses are being built which will last hundreds of years, when ships are being ordered which will carry the world's trade for a generation, when dealers hoard their stocks upon their shelves. (Robertson, 1923b, p. 7)

Finally, and recalling what we said above about people being led by entrepreneurs into patterns of behaviour which they would not freely choose for themselves (Chapter 18, above), Robertson defines the boom in terms of another source of economic disharmony, namely 'the opposition between Man the Producer with an interest in scarcity, and Man the Consumer with an interest in abundance':

> [A trade boom] is a time when the Producer has the whip-hand, and the Consumer seeks the aid of the State through price-controls and Profiteering Acts, the hour of pride for those who make and sell, when, great though output may be, the exhilaration of business is founded in a scarcity of good things relating to the desire of men to use and possess them. (Robertson, 1923b, pp. 7–8)

In the light of these considerations the remedy for industrial fluctuation lies in a policy of stabilisation:

> The lesson to be learnt, then, is that, if we want to abolish the trade cycle, we must recognise the real conflicts of interests and impulses to which man is subject in his

business conduct, and seek to restrain him now from over-indulgence and now from starvation of those strands of his economic nature which give to western civilisation its character of restlessness and of progress. And it follows that our remedial thought and effort must be directed, not merely to providing stimulants for the depression, but to providing sedatives for the boom. The whole matter is summed up in one word, a word which has become increasingly fashionable in recent years, and which it seems to me that the Liberal Party in particular should adopt once and for all as the first plank in its social policy – the word Stabilisation. (Robertson, 1923b, p. 8)

But on Robertson's analysis the desire for growth would render fluctuation inescapable, and a dilemma arose which was to haunt Robertson's work throughout his career. More than thirty years later the conflict was reflected in the title of the lecture 'Stability and Progress' that he delivered to the International Economic Association in 1956 (see Robertson, 1963a, pp. 456–71). Robertson made the following points:

1. that countries should seek to form some idea of the rate at which they would wish national income to grow and, therefore, the proportion of current income that should be saved and invested in order to achieve the desired result (see p. 457);
2. 'there seems no reason to doubt the old view that an increase in the ratio of capital stock to output . . . has been not merely a symptom but a prime instrument of the enlargement of man's enjoyments and the lightening of his labours' (p. 461);
3. that it is unlikely that citizens will spontaneously provide the required amount of saving: that is, the amount required in addition to that done by governments and by industry (see pp. 463, 464);
4. in considering the reasons for this, Robertson argued that account must be taken of the disparity between the static population of automatons envisaged in economic theory; and the living and dying generations of real life:

> the Ramseyan equation [Ramsey, 1928] depends on the assumption that the economic operator whose utility function is involved realises that its income and its consumption are going continually to increase. *But the ordinary man is well aware* that on retirement his individual income is going to fall with a bump, and *that at death his individual consumption is going to cease*; and it seems to be *not only inevitable but reasonable that his savings policy, while influenced also by regard for his heirs, should partly be governed by that knowledge.* (pp. 458–9; emphasis added)

In other words, Robertson held true to the ideas formulated over forty years earlier but now, as we see, present consumption is not to be viewed as liberation from the 'Urge and urge and urge' but as the source of a brake on growth. Caught up in the practicalities of economic policy, Robertson realises all too clearly the effect on savings behaviour of the changed perception of mortality, as compared to the halcyon days before 1914. Nothing is more eloquent testimony to the depth of his insight obtained (unlike with Keynes) while all was still intact.

To form a balanced view of Robertson's thought and of his contribution it is, therefore, necessary to take account of his writings both before and after the war of 1914–18. Not to do so is to run the risk of forming a partial and misleading impression (as, for example, in the case of Skidelsky's account: see Skidelsky, 1992, p. 274).

IX

In the following chapters we shall see how Robertson formulated the theory for the management of the short period. It was an innovative approach, with the integration of investment, saving and money and with a subsequent restatement in terms of the rate of interest. Because of his temperament and outlook, however, this theory had to build on what had gone before, with the result that the innovations were essentially modifications to the existing, orthodox approach and carried forward the assumptions upon which it was founded. Keynes by contrast, unencumbered with emotional baggage, cheerfully overturned established relationships and changed the world.

PART IV

Robertson's Economics II: Development

18. *Banking Policy and the Price Level*

I

With the *Study* Robertson laid the foundations for all his subsequent work in the field of economic fluctuation. In brief, he had reached the following conclusions.

1. The trade cycle was a real, rather than a monetary or psychological phenomenon.
2. Industrial fluctuation was an inherent characteristic of the capitalistic mode of production.
3. Consequently, because economic growth involved capital formation, fluctuation was a necessary by-product of the growth process. Preparation for future prosperity, therefore, inevitably imposed irrecoverable losses of welfare on the present generation as access to consumption goods was denied, both in the process of capital formation during the boom and during the recession when consumption goods must be reserved for use in a possible upturn.
4. Because life was brief, unique and lived under sentence of death as extinction, consumption, the enjoyment of which was certain, was to be weighed in the balance with investment – the proceeds of which were uncertain.
5. An ethical dilemma therefore arose, as provision for the future competed with enjoyment of life in the present.
6. The corollary was that the exercise of choice involved the economics of learned behaviour, which in turn must be based on informed consideration of the costs and benefits involved.
7. In Robertson's terms it was a choice between duty and escape, a problem to be resolved in the usual way, by means of a compromise, with policy designed to limit the 'turbulence' created in the wake of economic growth, without destroying the 'vitality' that inspired it. That is, the cycle was to be reconciled with the trend.

The theory upon which a policy of management might be based had been worked out principally in terms of (on Danes's classification: see Danes, 1979) a co-operative non-monetary economy. However, Robertson had also found that where production was organised non-co-operatively, a 'genuine want of harmony' was revealed between the interests of the business and working classes (see Robertson, 1915, pp. 206–11), the effect of which was to increase the amplitude of the cycle. Similarly, Robertson had also found that where an economy was money-using, aggravation of the phenomena of both boom and depression occurred as compared to the non-monetary case, so that the amplitude of cycles was again increased (Robertson, 1915, pp. 217–28).

II

Robertson developed his theory of short-run management during the period of a decade and a half following his return to Cambridge in 1919. It was chiefly to this that he devoted the remainder of the creative, positive phase of his career. The work was carried out within the context of Cambridge School preoccupations with problems of short-run adjustment and with stabilisation policy (see Bridel, 1987; Bigg, 1990); and, for much of the time, in collaboration with Keynes. For present purposes, however, interest will centre on the way in which the elements of Robertson's theory (the key variables of saving, investment, money and the rate of interest) came to assume their characteristic relationship to each other. To understand this it is necessary to take into account the two sets of influences at work in the process of development: first, the theoretical objective that Robertson was seeking to achieve; and second, the constraints that operated on the means by which he sought to achieve that objective.

With respect to the first, Robertson's principal concerns were as follows.

1. To ensure that the economy delivered the amount of saving necessary to support the chosen rate of economic growth.
2. To ensure that growth was achieved at lowest possible cost in terms of lost consumption, which implied both that fluctuation was minimised and that saving was performed either voluntarily – or involuntarily only to the extent that it produced a social dividend.
3. To show that, though money was not of *fundamental* importance in economic life, in a modern economy its use played such a critical role in the saving process that stabilisation policy must centre on the activities of the principal producers of money – the banks.

With respect to the second, developments were constrained by Robertson's temperamentally determined need to retain a reference back. This in turn had two aspects. It implied the need to build on theoretical foundations laid by respected predecessors; this was the basis for what has come to be known as his evolutionary approach to economic theorising. It implied that economic relationships considered fundamental to classical economics, such as that saving determines investment and that the quantity of money *ceteris paribus* determines the price level, had to be incorporated into his analysis and thereafter regarded as sacrosanct.

It also meant that having once established the importance of the short period and devised a theory upon which it should be managed, Robertson was not prepared to move further away from orthodoxy. Though a strategy of compromise allowed for escape into present enjoyment, it also meant paying heed to the stern call of duty and Robertson never lost sight of the importance of economic growth: of the present always in relation to the future; of the cycle always in relation to the trend. The mutation of the social life produced by the war meant, in Robertson's (classical) terms, that the economist must be concerned with the provision of an adequate amount of savings to support economic growth. Consequently, he could never break away completely from the long run and commit himself wholeheartedly to the provision of 'jam today'. By the same token, the regressive element in his make-up meant that he was unable to repudiate past allegiances and overturn established theoretical relationships in the way that Keynes delighted to do.

In this way the key variables, savings, investment and money, assumed their characteristic configuration. By developing his theory additively, Robertson was able to retain the classical saving-determines-investment relationship. Upon this foundation, new relationships could be superimposed that both recognised the part played by the banks in financing investment and allowed for a quantity-theory-style adjustment to equilibrium via changes in the price level. When cast in interest-rate terms it became the familiar loanable-funds theory with which Robertson is popularly associated.

The new developments were revealed in a series of inter-war publications, principally in *Banking Policy and the Price Level* (1926), to which the first, 1922, edition of *Money* provided a necessary stepping-stone from the *Study*. The policy implications of *BPPL* were given greater precision in 'Theories of Banking Policy' (1928b); and Robertson provided a more popular account in a new edition of *Money* pubished in the same year. Then, in a series of two articles written in the light of Keynes's own attempt to provide a saving–investment theory of the cycle within the quantity theory tradition (Keynes, 1930, *CW* V), Robertson sought, first, to justify his own terminology of saving in 'Saving And Hoarding' (1933); and, second, to recast the analysis of *BPPL* in terms of the relationship between natural and market rates of interest, in 'Industrial Fluctuation and the Natural Rate of Interest' (1934).

III

Robertson, who was otherwise without issue, poured himself instead into the creation of a brood of published works which bore the imprint of their procreator and which lived on, like Whitman's poetry, to provide a kind of immortality.

His first-born 'child' (see 'New Introduction' in Robertson, 1948a, p. vii) was, of course, the *Study* and this remained his favourite, though as it was a war-baby he was to retain rather sensitive feelings regarding the circumstances of its birth. Indeed, he was later to charge himself, in mock reproach, with having failed to 'make amends' when peace returned and instead with having stolen its 'theoretical bones' for the benefit of a 'horrible little younger son' (Robertson, 1948a, p. vii).

This new arrival was *Banking Policy and the Price Level*. Though Robertson was later to refer to the work (Preface to the *Study*: Robertson, 1948a, p. vii) as 'this odd little book', there can be no question but that it was a planned addition to the family, conceived as a means of extending his views on fluctuation to the case of a growing monetary economy. As compared to the *Study*, the focus was necessarily narrower as Robertson was able simply to assume the broader philosophical context and to restate his conclusions on the real origins of the cycle from the former work. He could concentrate instead on 'a discussion of the relation between saving, credit creation and capital growth' and to use this analysis as the basis for making recommendations on the all-important questions of *banking policy* and the manipulation of the *price level* as a tool of economic management. That is, the essence of *BPPL*, we might notice at the outset, was the provision of a rationale for the use of monetary variation as a means of reconciling economic and ethical considerations in the provision of saving for the growth process.

We might also notice that the book's formidable reputation for being unreadable stemmed in part from inherent difficulties of exposition. In addition to the necessary complexity of an argument that stretched the quantity theory to accommodate saving and investment analysis, there were problems posed by Robertson's desire for precision of thought in relation to one of the book's key insights: that it took account of the distinction between: (a) the consequences of a decision to save by one individual taken separately; and (b) the consequences of the same action by all individuals taken together.

This distinction was also central to Keynes's new thinking in the early 1930s as he moved towards the *General Theory*. But whereas for Keynes adjustment to equilibrium came about through changes in real income, for Robertson adjustment remained a matter of changes in the price level. It is here that we find the basis for much of their subsequent disagreement.

To take account of this distinction in *BPPL*, Robertson invented his own terminology which, when sufficiently elaborated to encompass the variety of logically possible outcomes that he considers (a natural product of his taxonomic bent), produced what amounted to a private language. To others it could seem like affectation and it did nothing to help the dissemination of his ideas. It is true that in a later, expository lecture he did elect to 'eschew the use of certain strange and barbarous language for employing which elsewhere [he had] been severely taken to task' but this simplification was only, he noted, 'at the risk of blurring the clear edge of thought' ('TBP' in Hicks ed., 1966, p. 24).

Thus there was, given his premises, some technical justification for the text's apparent intractability; but against this consideration there must be set the constraints produced by the circumstances in which the book was written (see above, Chapter 8). In the face of Keynes's brow-beating, Robertson was determined to stake out his own ground and this precluded making concessions to the faint-hearted reader. Fully aware of what he was doing, Robertson tetchily defended himself in his introductory chapter:

> of economists alone it is apparently expected that their conclusions should be expressed in a form which can be understood without effort by the most general reader. I do not think this expectation is reasonable, and I have made no attempt to fulfil it. This is a difficult book.   (Robertson, 1926, p. 4)

He goes on to argue that if the book is difficult because it is concise (Keynes's criticism) it is also short and, therefore, quickly over.

We should also mention another factor which seems to have influenced the form and style of the book. Robertson had clearly taken to heart Pigou's strictures on the first version of his fellowship dissertation in 1913 in which he commended Marshall's dictum that the task of the academic author is to immerse himself in the material he has collected until the 'bones' of his own argument form in his mind and he can use the collected material as illustrations of it. In the *Study*, we recall, he had achieved a compromise position, but now with his new work there would be no holding back:

> The book may also offend in another respect – that it is highly abstract and theoretical. Occasionally, but not often, I have tried to bring out the relevance of an analytical argument by concrete illustration. The book is not intended to be a comprehensive treatise but a *theoretical skeleton*; and I want the *bare bones* to stand out strongly.   (Robertson, 1926, p. 5; emphasis added)

IV

Thus both because of the technical nature of the subject-matter and the spare, uncompromising style deliberately affected by the author, *BPPL* became known as the odd-man-out among Robertson's books, the one exception that belied his reputation as a literary economist. But its very inaccessibility, as we noted earlier (Chapters 1 and 8, above), served a purpose, in that it protected the theoretical heartland of Robertson's position and rendered it less vulnerable to assault. The private language of *BPPL* enclosed a private world in which important ideas and assumptions would maintain their accustomed positions and in which events would take place within proper bounds.

Consequently, just as the *Study* revealed Robertson's inspiration and motivation, so *BPPL* reveals the characteristic relationship between the principal elements, the key variables, of Robertsonian economics: saving, investment and the quantity of money. The significance of this will become clearer once we have examined the argument of the book in detail. Reference will be made as necessary to the work of other commentators. The following are of particular interest: Pigou (1926); Hawtrey (1926); Harrod (1927); Tappan (1928); Danes (1979); Bridel (1987); Bigg (1990); Laidler (1995); Costabile (1997).

V

What we shall attempt to make clear in what follows is the way in which the argument of the book supports and illuminates our main theme concerning the relationship between the economics and the man. To this end we shall need to determine: to what extent the argument of the book is developed additively; what pattern of relationship is imposed on the key variables; what importance is accorded to the role of money; what significance is to be attached to Robertson's choice of 'frictionless barter' as his standard case, defining the 'appropriate' degree of fluctuation.

We shall find that, in accordance with our previous argument, Robertson is attempting to take account of the changed conditions produced by the war. This means that the ethical question of individual choice, between present and future (*post mortem*) consumption, must now be balanced with the economic necessity of supplying the saving required for the growth process. This in turn has implications for the price level in a monetary economy and for the banks' responsibilities in influencing it. Throughout, the relationship between money, investment and saving is of great interest, for purposes of comparison with Keynes's new configuration put forward in the *General Theory*.

19. Managing the short period: real and monetary forces

I

A marked feature of Robertson's method of working was his aversion to rewriting his books as a means of taking account of criticism and of new developments in the subject. Even in the special case of his popular textbook *Money*, significant changes were incorporated in successive editions by adding new chapters and, where necessary, discarding redundant sections. Instead, each of his major theoretical works went on to find a new incarnation in which the core of the old was used as the basis for a substantially new work. Thus the *Study* itself appeared again only as a special reprint with a new introduction. Similarly, the argument of *BPPL* was in turn refined and developed in a series of journal articles. The book itself appeared in four editions substantially unchanged.

II

The first edition of *BPPL* appeared in January 1926 (which means that work on it was complete by 1925), and it was reprinted in August of the same year. By May 1932 a further printing had become necessary and duly appeared with alterations to only one page of the text and a rewritten (mathematical) Appendix to Chapter V, for Robertson explained that he was 'unready to undertake a thorough revision'. Such a one indeed was never undertaken and the book appeared again only once, as a Kelley reprint in 1949. This reproduced the 1932 edition unaltered, except for the correction of a few small misprints, but it was dignified by the addition of an informative Preface. This explained that Robertson's original object in writing the book was:

> first, to preserve and re-present some part of the analytical framework of my *Study of Industrial Fluctuation* (1915), which had fallen out of print and which I could not bring myself to attempt to re-write; and secondly, to interweave with the mainly 'non-monetary' argument of that work a discussion of the relation between saving, credit-creation and capital growth.   (Robertson, 1949b, p. vii)

Robertson's choice of the word 'interweave' to describe the means by which the transition from a barter economy to a monetary economy is taken account of is very revealing. It implied that the ideas and conclusions worked out in the *Study* remained valid and that the addition of money merely complicated the analysis. That is, fluctuations were still to be seen as a real phenomenon, an inevitable feature of the growth process, and price stabilisation was not always the correct policy to pursue.

Explicit confirmation that this was in fact the case was provided by Robertson himself. In 1949 he described the 'main theme' of *BPPL* to have been as follows:

> According to the enlightened orthodoxy then current [in the 1920s] in Anglo-Saxon countries, the objective of policy should be stability of industrial output, attained through stabilisation of the general price level, the latter being achieved through the operation of central banking. I found myself somewhat critical of this conclusion. (Robertson, 1949b, p. viii)

In 1926, Robertson's criticism of price stabilisation as the policy objective had been associated with criticism of the 'monetary' theory of the trade cycle, which, with the 'psychological' theory, made up the bulk of orthodox opinion ('the dominant schools of thought') on the causes of instability of industrial output (Robertson, 1926, pp. 2-3). Robertson, in 1926 as in 1915 (see Robertson, 1915, pp. 243-5), stood out against orthodoxy and, as in other areas, was prepared to advocate a view that was far in advance of its becoming fashionable in the economics profession: 'I hold that far more weight must be attached than it is now fashionable to attach to certain *real*, as opposed to monetary or psychological, causes of fluctuation' (Robertson, 1926, p. 1).

This view, we might add, also meant that in the management of the short period, monetary control could not be regarded as a 'panacea' but as merely 'one ingredient in a much more arduous and comprehensive programme' of what in *The Ebb and Flow of Unemployment* (1923), he had already referred to as 'Stabilisation' (Robertson, 1926, p. 4).

III

The structure of *BPPL* faithfully represented the 'additive' nature of Robertson's theorising. The order of chapters dealt in turn with: the 'real' causes of the cycle, which occurred as an inevitable, and to that extent desirable, consequence of economic growth (giving rise to 'appropriate' fluctuations); the way in which the introduction of money into the economy contributed to the occurrence of fluctuations in excess of those deemed 'appropriate'; the relationship between (bank) money, the price level and the different kinds of saving and investment in a monetary economy; the role of the banks in regulating the price level as a means of meeting both economic and ethical considerations in respect of the demands on the public's saving.

IV

The argument of *BPPL* proceeds as follows. It begins with the real elements – the 'bones' of the *Study* which, though they occupy only a small part of the book, clearly loom large in the argument. All page references are to the January 1926 edition unless otherwise stated.

What the theory seeks to explain is the quasi-rhythmical fluctuation in the volume of industrial production (defined as aggregate real income less agricultural output) movements in which are subject to independent influences (pp. 6–7). These fluctuations are explained by the reasons for which producers vary the scale of their output – now increasing it, now reducing it – over time. Here Robertson makes the distinction, important for his theory, between 'actual' changes in output, resulting in a new 'actual' scale or rate of output, and 'justifiable' changes in output, resulting in a new 'optimal', 'rational' or 'appropriate' scale or rate of output. With respect to the latter, however, there seems to be nothing sacrosanct about the particular use of 'justifiable' for *changes* and 'appropriate' for *scale or rate*, as Robertson uses 'appropriate' for changes as well (see pp. 18, 22, 34, 37, 38, 39).

In the simplest case, of a co-operative, non-monetary economy, producer groups may find a rational incentive to vary the scale of their output in the following: (a) a reduction in real operating costs either in particular industries due to specific inventions or generally as industry becomes more efficient in the later stages of the depression; (b) variations in the intensity of desire of any group for the products it purchases – and in particular the instruments of production – which give rise to variations in its own output with which to make payment; (c) a change – say, a fall – in the real cost of obtaining other products would give rise, where the effort elasticity of demand was greater than unity, to increased output of own product, for example, in the case of agricultural abundance due to the incidence of good harvests (pp. 8–18).

When the real analysis was extended to the non-co-operative case, and, therefore, closer to the real world, Robertson argued that the changes in output dictated by the self-interest of the employer would be 'considerably' greater than those dictated by the self-interest of the employee and 'somewhat' greater than those dictated by the self-interest of the co-operative group member (pp. 19–21). He also argued that it was the enlightened self-interest of the employer that should be seen as dictating the 'justifiable' changes in output and, therefore, the appropriate or 'optimum' rate of output of the community

(p. 22). This was both: (a) because the ultimate divergence of interest between employer and employee might not be as great as the immediate divergence (for, though employees may not choose to experience fluctuations, the economic growth of which those fluctuations are the by-product brings rising living-standards and greater rewards for posterity); (b) because, given the existing order of society, it is the employers who have control over the 'forces of technical progress' (pp. 21–3).

Robertson now had his 'standard case' but the conception of an appropriate or optimum scale of industrial output remained ambiguous. This was because modern industry's need to use 'very large, expensive and durable instruments of production' (p. 35) meant that: (a) the process of production became imperfectly divisible so that technical factors would dictate a larger expansion of industrial output than utility and cost would indicate; (b) a large part of the costs incurred in many trades would be 'crystallised' in durable instruments; (c) the costs of leaving many instruments, for example, blast-furnaces and mines, unused (their 'intractability') was such that the best rate of output would be higher than could otherwise be justified (pp. 35–7).

V

Having thus stretched the concept of 'rational' or 'appropriate' to allow for the technical constraints on modern industry, Robertson set out the reasons for which 'actual' fluctuations in industrial output would tend '*greatly*' (emphasis added) to exceed the 'rational' or 'appropriate' fluctuations (*sic*) (p. 34). He thought the main reason to be 'the stress of competition, aggravated by the length of time which is required to adjust production to a changed demand' (p. 37). That is, each firm, in ignorance of its rivals, would prepare to produce too large a share of increased output, resulting in over-production. This would in turn give rise to over-investment and the longer was the lag, the greater would be the opportunity for miscalculation and, therefore, over-investment in instrument goods (pp. 37–8).

Of greater interest, however, is Robertson's choice of 'remaining causes', for these turn out to be the fashionable trade-cycle theories of orthodoxy, now relegated to a subordinate role in Robertson's own ranking. It is a subordinate role because even though actual tend greatly to exceed justifiable fluctuations, the 'remaining causes' take second place to Robertson's 'main reason' for the discrepancy. They are of course: (a) psychological influences: the psychological interdependence of business – the herd instinct; and (b) monetary influences (pp. 38–9).

Nevertheless, Robertson does make clear that he does not regard them as other than of 'very great importance' (p. 38) and it is the case that monetary influences are given very much more attention than Robertson's designated 'main reason'. Indeed, they are the major preoccupation of *BPPL*, give rise to its 'main theme' (Robertson, 1949b, p. viii) and to its very title.

As to money's role as a 'remaining cause', Robertson argues that 'so far as the inducements to a producer to expand (or contract) output are clothed in the form of an increased (or diminished) stream of money demand, they are in many cases partly illusory' (p. 39). The reason for this is that responding to an increase (or decrease) in money demand may give a false impression because the rise (or fall) in the price level affects not only revenue but also costs so that 'actual' tend to exceed 'appropriate' changes in output.

VI

From this proposition we may derive the following conclusions, which are of immense importance for the shape of Robertson's argument in *BPPL*. The first is that in a money-using economy the causes of fluctuations will involve 'an initial disturbance of the general price level' (p. 34). The second is that monetary stimulus intended to bring about 'appropriate' changes in output could by the same token equally give rise to 'inappropriate' fluctuations. The third is that monetary policy should not, therefore, be governed by the 'enlightened orthodoxy then current in Anglo-Saxon countries' (Robertson, 1949b, p. viii), and seek to stabilise the price level as a means of stabilising industrial output. Rather, that because 'rational and justifiable fluctuations in output will occur' (p. 34), the aim should be to sanction price-level changes necessary to achieve appropriate changes in output and to seek to prevent those which would lead to inappropriate fluctuations in output (p. 39). Also, we should bear in mind for what is to come that, in seeking to prevent inappropriate fluctuations, monetary policy may have to deal with the consequences of the *two* sources of disturbance we have now identified: real and monetary. The fourth is that the conclusion that monetary policy should be more discriminating with respect to changes in the price level is reinforced by taking account of the fact that: 'production takes *time* [is roundabout – makes use of capital] and requires the aid of *saving*, and of the manner in which this fact is intertwined with our monetary system' (p. 34).

This last was the culmination of the argument in *BPPL*, the essence of the book's theoretical contribution. It was that which Robertson later concluded, 'chiefly attracted attention'. That is:

> the attempt in chs V and VI to elucidate – by means of a step-by-step analysis, some rather *outré* technical terms and some very primitive algebra – the inter-relation between credit-creation, capital-formation and 'abstinence' or, as I preferred to call it, 'lacking'.   (1949b, p. ix)

Before we turn to an examination of these chapters we need to go back and trace Robertson's introduction of money into the analysis. And in considering his treatment of money as a whole, we should bear in mind the circumstances in which the book was written and in particular what Keynes's contribution to it might have been. We have it from Robertson himself that Chapters V and VI were 'drastically rewritten at his [Keynes's] suggestion'. Also that given that Robertson had not preserved his original draft it was, in general, not possible to determine which of the ideas came from Robertson and which from Keynes, though in 1949 Robertson was able to credit Keynes with having contributed 'induced lacking' (1949a, p. x; 1926, pp. 5, 49 n. 1).

VII

There is, for the moment, one other question which is of great importance. It starts from the idea that Robertson first worked out how credit (bank) money operated – what it was that 'bankers were really up to' – and what the relationship was between money, the price level and (forced) saving, in writing *Money* (1922). Given that Keynes was the General Editor of the Cambridge Handbooks, was the allocation of this title to Robertson (who was not a monetary specialist) simply a matter of Keynes (who was the obvious choice for the task) being too busy at the time? Or might we rather attribute to Keynes the motive of deliberately choosing Robertson, as a means of training him for the role of collaborator? If Robertson had not been thus introduced to monetary analysis he would have been of far less use to Keynes. Given the difference in their temperaments, with Keynes as the dominant, entrepreneurial figure and with his undoubted shrewdness to spot such potential, and with Robertson as the protégé, this suggestion must remain a possibility.

In any case, however, whether or not Keynes was so motivated, the very fact that Robertson was landed with the job and thus began to think about credit creation and its relationship to saving set him by the same means on the road to *BPPL*. Were it not for this intervention, *BPPL* would not have been written, there would have been no loanable funds theory and therefore no controversy with Keynes – at least on matters now so familiar. What would Robertson have written in its place?

VIII

Robertson's fundamental view of the importance of money – a view that coloured all his subsequent analysis – is expressed in the paragraph with which he chose to begin the text of *Money* in 1922:

Money is not such a vital subject as is often supposed; nevertheless, it is an interesting and important branch of the study of economics. It is necessary for the economic student to try from the start to pierce the monetary veil in which most business transactions are shrouded, and to see what is happening in terms of real goods and services; indeed so far as possible he must try to penetrate further, and to see what is happening in terms of real sacrifices and satisfactions. But having done this he must return and examine the effects exercised upon the creation and distribution of real economic welfare by the twin facts that we do use the mechanism of money, and that we have learnt so imperfectly to control it. (Robertson, 1922, p. 1)

This was the opening formula he retained word for word in all subsequent editions.

That at least part of the justification for this view is to be found in Robertson's acceptance of orthodoxy, is indicated by his revealing remark in the Preface that:

[the book's] connection with its predecessor – Mr Henderson's Supply and Demand – is to be found in the emphasis laid on the theory of money as a special case of the general theory of value. Its bearing upon the remainder of the series is to be found in the conclusion to which the book leads up, that Money is after all a fundamentally unimportant subject, in the sense that neither the most revolutionary nor the 'soundest' monetary policy can be expected to provide a remedy for those strains and disharmonies whose roots lie deep in the present structure of industry, and perhaps in the very nature of man himself. (Robertson, 1922, p. vii)

Again, this was the judgement with which he prefaced later editions, except that for the phrase 'a fundamentally unimportant subject' he substituted 'a subject of secondary importance' (see *Money*, 1946 reprint, p. xii; *Money*, 1961 reprint, p. x). Although this change of wording indicated a softening of attitude, Robertson was still clear about the relative importance of the real and the monetary. It is a view reinforced by his retention of the idea of 'strains and disharmonies' having roots lying deep 'in the very nature of man himself'. This idea of the relationship between the nature of man and economics – in the form of the relationship between Robertson and his particular approach to economics – has, of course, provided our principal theme. The importance for this relationship of Robertson's attitude to money will be discussed below (Chapter 22).

IX

More immediately, in the light of the evidence of *Money*, it comes as no surprise to find that in *BPPL* it is real forces that are the prime movers and that monetary policy is to be directed towards the removal of the distortions and exaggerations that money-use undoubtedly produces.

Robertson began his discussion of the effects of the introduction of money with a statement confirming that:

> while the *results* of the causes of change [in the scale of industrial production] are correctly expressed by making the hypothesis of direct barter, the chain of motives brought into play by a monetary economy is different, and the results are reached in part by a different route.   (Robertson, 1926, p. 23; emphasis in original)

He illustrated the point by means of a worked example which was also intended to demonstrate the correctness of his view that a policy of price stabilisation was inefficacious (p. 27). This simple exercise accurately shadows Robertson's larger themes. We are to imagine an economy organised along co-operative lines (that is, Danes's co-operative monetary case), in which two goods are produced: wheat (representing agriculture) and iron (representing industry). A rise in wheat production reduces its relative price and for a given effort-elasticity of demand for wheat on the part of iron-producers stimulates an increase in iron production: this alters exchange ratios. Now, 'by what route and with what price accompaniments' will this result be reached in a monetary system?

The answer depends on the policy adopted by the monetary authorities (p. 24), which have power to inject money into the system by way of timeless loans to a conveniently existing class of wheat-merchants. The idea is that a stream of money is directed on to a commodity (like water from a hose) so that an impact price is established, followed by a reaction, if any, on its output. Which of a range of four possible monetary policies will be most effective, by way of incentive to increased iron production, for establishing the appropriate output (pp. 25–6)? The possibilities envisaged are as follows:

1. No change in the money stock, so that the incentive comes from the fall in the relative price of wheat (and the price level falls).

2. The money stock is raised to reflect the effort-elasticity of the iron group for wheat following the fall in the relative price of wheat. Though in money terms the unit price of wheat has now fallen, money receipts will rise due to the increased demand from iron-producers. Again the price level falls. In terms of Robertson's example: initial wheat output = 100 units; initial iron output = 100 units. In both cases unit price is £1, with a money stock of £100. Then wheat output rises to 150 units and consequently iron output rises to 120 units and the money stock is raised to £120 to equal this. Now: the iron-price of wheat is 4/5; and the wheat-price of iron is 5/4 . In money terms the unit price of wheat has fallen from £1 to 80p but sales have risen from 100 units to 150 units, so that money receipts rise from £100 to £120. The price level, as an arithmetic average of commodity prices falls from £1 to 90p.

3. The money stock is raised so as to preserve the ultimate stability of the price level as an arithmetic average.

4. In terms of the illustrative figures shown under (2), the money stock is raised from £100 to £150 in order to match the rise in output of wheat and so offset the fall in its price. With no fall in the price of wheat, there is no effort-elasticity of demand effect, as incentive to increase iron output. Such an incentive is, however, provided by the rise in the money value of iron output, from £100 to £150, and the rise in money receipts of iron producers.

Of the possible policy options, Robertson concluded that for the hypothetical cooperative case under consideration, it would not much matter which of them was chosen. However (2) has much to recommend it, being 'in a sense the most "natural" policy', in that it produces a money price of wheat that accurately reflects the new exchange ratio.

The incentive it provides, however, comes via lowered costs and for the economy type nearest to the real world, that is, *the non-co-operative monetary case*, it would be less effective than (4). This is because:

> a more direct and immediate stimulus to increased output is afforded by rising money receipts than by falling prices of the objects of expenditure. The employer is likely to pay more attention to rising money profits than to a lowered 'cost of living' for himself, or to the possibility of reducing money wages owing to the lowered cost of living of his workmen. (pp. 26–7)

Finally, on account neither of 'naturalness and theoretical attraction' nor of effectiveness, does Robertson recommend a policy 'aiming at ultimate stability of the general price level' (p. 27). He also found that these conclusions held good for a situation involving more than two commodities (pp. 27–9); and for the monetary interpretation of the case in which the incentive to increase output is provided by an alteration in the intensity of desire of any group for the products it purchases. The difference in this case, however, is that policy option 4 is less effective because it is the 'non-monetary' motive that influences employers, namely, the increased desirability of machines, rather than increased money receipts (pp. 29–33).

X

The message we are to take away from Robertson's five-finger exercise is, therefore, as hinted earlier, that:

> the moving causes of . . . fluctuations inevitably involve an initial disturbance of the

general price level and . . . a monetary policy designed to restore it to its original figure is neither the most natural response of the monetary system, nor the most effective in interpreting the underlying situation and establishing the results for which it calls.   (p. 34)

The full significance of this conclusion only becomes apparent when the analysis is extended to include saving and its relationship to investment. This, of course, was the subject of Chapters V and VI, the argument of which follows in the next chapter.

20.   Lacking and all that

I

Modern industrial production requires the use of capital and Robertson distinguished two principal kinds. The first was fixed capital: the 'fixed and durable instruments of production . . . [such as] factories, railways, machinery, and so forth' (Robertson, 1926, pp. 41–2). The second was circulating capital. Traditionally, this was the stock of consumable goods necessary to sustain those engaged in the more roundabout production processes. This is how Robertson saw it in the *Study* but, following the example of later writers (most immediately Henderson, 1921, pp. 124–5), he now acknowledged that it should properly be seen as consisting of goods in all stages of preparation from raw materials to finished article, together with fuels consumed. Despite this nod to new thinking, however, it is clear that Robertson remained wedded to the earlier idea (see Robertson, 1926, pp. 43, 93, 94, 97). This is possibly because of its association with the strict orthodoxy of the Robinson Crusoe economy, in which accumulated consumption goods constitute the saving that must be done before investment can be undertaken.

II

In Robertson's scheme the associated saving became 'the activity of providing capital', a significant phrase which he used twice within a few lines (p. 40). This involved the traditional idea of forgoing immediate enjoyment of consumption but was not adequately described by the terms customarily used to refer to it. That is 'the activity of providing capital' in a modern monetary economy was not properly represented by the term 'waiting', which carried the suggestion of 'voluntary postponement of benefits to be some day enjoyed'; nor by the older term 'abstinence' which 'while free from the suggestion of future benefit, imparts a flavour of moral struggle and merit' (p. 40). Instead, Robertson opted for the much more neutral phrase 'going without' as bearing the right shade of meaning but, typically, substituted his own term 'lacking', as being more convenient in use. This was to be Robertson's basic unit of descriptive currency, qualified and elaborated as his apparently endless taxonomy of cases required.

The benefit of Robertson's choice, given the working of the economy he envisaged, in which adjustment comes about through changes in the general price level, is indicated by his definition of lacking, whereby:

> A man is lacking if during a given period he consumes less than the value of his current economic output. This is not always the same thing . . . as spending on immediate consumption less than his legal money income during the period. (p. 41)

The opposite case is designated dis-lacking.

The point is that the amount of lacking done by individual transactors depends not only on their own actions but also on the actions of others. The intention to lack or not to lack, as the case may be, on the part of one, could be facilitated or frustrated by changes in the price level brought about by the behaviour of other transactors and by the banks. Where the outcome is an aggregate quantity of lacking insufficient to meet the demand, the banks will enter as a balancing factor. The banks might also be called upon as a matter of deliberate policy to offset the causes of excessive demand. The many possible outcomes are allowed for by Robertson's terminology.

We might begin with the fundamental distinction between lacking which is 'spontaneous' and lacking which is 'imposed' (pp. 47, 49).

III

Spontaneous lacking, Robertson explained, 'corresponds pretty well to what is ordinarily thought of as saving, and scarcely requires further definition' (p. 47). However, when a person 'saves' in the sense of refraining from expenditure on current consumption, he must decide what to do with the money proceeds. If having 'gone without' he then purchases an instrument or makes a loan to productive workers he is taking steps 'directly' to apply his lacking. Applied lacking can also be 'indirect', as when he provides the means for others to do the same thing. If, on the other hand, he merely adds the proceeds to his money holdings (performs new hoarding) his saving does not eventuate in capital creation and his lacking is *abortive*, in that, although his own consumption is diminished, that of others is, via a fall in the price level, thereby increased by the same amount (pp. 45–6).

Note here that in the case of applied lacking, Robertson is assuming that nothing is lost through the act of lacking so long as capital creation is set in train. In other words, in this instance prior saving is an efficacious means of promoting investment. This is so even though Robertson sees saving as a function of income which implies therefore a reduction in consumption.

Note here also that an integral part of Robertson's scheme is the idea that actions on the part of one member of the community will evoke an offsetting response on the part of others. The effects, however, will be mediated by changes in the price level (the quantity theory mechanism), not, as in Keynes's (1936) theory, through changes in income.

A third point is that Robertson seems to be arguing that lacking is abortive in that 'going without' on the part of one does not result in investment taking place. Is this because our putative investor doesn't know the ropes and thus is at a loss as to what to do; or is it that for whatever reason he or she simply wished to hold more money? In either case there is in principle scope for an outside agency (the banks) to exploit the situation for the public benefit. Before we examine this process it will be useful to look first at the other kind of lacking we introduced above: that which is 'imposed'.

IV

Imposed lacking is of two kinds: 'automatic' and 'induced'. Induced lacking is action taken by transactors to restore the real value of money balances reduced by a rise in the price level, by holding money off the market. It was introduced by Keynes and is ancestor to the Patinkin 'real balance effect'. It has been widely noticed by other commentators (see especially Laidler, 1995) and the only point of interest here is that it is stimulated by the same process that imposes automatic lacking (p. 49).

Automatic lacking begins with the idea of a daily stream of goods being purchased by a main daily stream of money. Action by some individuals to increase expenditure by reducing their money hoards or utilising newly created money will introduce an additional daily stream of money that will compete with the main daily stream and so deprive the rest of the population of part of their consumption. To the extent that consumption by this latter group is reduced below what was intended, they experience 'automatic stinting'; if below the value of their current output, automatic lacking also. In the opposite case, in which one section reduces its consumption by doing new hoarding, the pressure of money demand is reduced and the remainder experience 'automatic splashing' and 'automatic dis-lacking' respectively (pp. 47–8).

It will be useful also to note here the effect of all members of the community deciding to increase expenditure:

> If all members of the public simultaneously dishoarded to an appropriate extent, they might impose on one another Automatic Stinting which in each case exactly cancelled the intended Dis-lacking involved in the process of Spontaneous Dishoarding, so that on the balance neither Lacking nor Dis-lacking would be done

by anyone. Conversely if all members of the public increased their Hoarding to an appropriate extent, the real income of each might suffer no diminution; for the intended Lacking involved in his Spontaneous Hoarding might be exactly cancelled by the Automatic Splashing in which the Spontaneous Hoarding of his neighbours enabled him to indulge.   (pp. 48–9)

V

Lacking can also be distinguished by the kind of industrial capital with which it is associated. Fixed capital is provided for by long lacking and circulating capital is provided for by short lacking. Both long and short lacking can be spontaneous or imposed but in each case the proportions are different. The majority of long lacking is supplied directly by individuals and corporations whereas to a significant extent short lacking is supplied by way of the banks (p. 50). It will be convenient to discuss the provision of long lacking in the context of its relation with short lacking, and for the moment we examine the role of banks in the provision of short lacking.

VI

The notion that banks customarily facilitated the provision of lacking for circulating capital played a crucial part in Robertson's theory and, despite Hawtrey's denial of its empirical validity (Hawtrey, 1926), it continued to do so. This is because it is through this device that money enters the analysis: banks not only provide finance but create the money with which it is done. They are, therefore, the starting point for the quantity theory and the mode of adjustment via changes in the price level. Money is also an important cause of fluctuations being in excess of those deemed appropriate. It is, therefore, monetary (banking) policy that is charged with the task both of making sure that sufficient lacking is undertaken to meet the needs of investment and that at the same time changes in output are no greater than are justified, so that money is rendered 'neutral'.

Banks play their part in two ways (pp. 50ff). The first way is to enable savers to realise their intentions by transforming the spontaneous new hoarding of individuals into applied lacking. The second is by way of the infliction of imposed lacking. In the first case the stability of the price level is maintained and the ethical imperative, that transactors are allowed to exercise their free choice between present enjoyment and provision for the future, is being met. In the second case transactors are forced to forgo consumption in what is deemed to be the long-term social interest. Both cases raise important issues and we shall deal with them in turn.

VII

The first hinges on the notion of transformation. Where banking is of the primitive 'cloak-room' variety, the banks operate in effect as the agents of savers. Saved (metallic) money is deposited with the banks which then lend it to entrepreneurs. Entrepreneurs use it to pay wages to workers engaged to increase the stock of working capital. The expenditure of new wages inflicts no automatic lacking as there is no increase in competition for existing goods (the new output is not yet available), merely a transfer of spending-power (pp. 50–1).

Where, however, banking is of the modern kind, the process is more complicated. Now bankers create deposits and, therefore, increase the money stock by extending credit to entrepreneurs. The implications are profound because:

> By expending these loans businessmen procure practically the whole of that part of the expansion of Circulating Capital which they are not willing to provide by direct lacking. (p. 51)

At a stroke, we might say, investment has ceased to be saver-driven, or saver-constrained, for the Aladdin's cave opened by the banks gives entrepreneurs command over real resources to an extent that is limited only by their inclination and credit-worthiness. The question for Robertson, however, is whether what appears to be an instrument of compulsion is merely the same enabling process in a new guise. Once again his answer reveals the depth of his new insight and also the limitations imposed by the past:

> Since the expenditure of new money imposes Automatic Stinting on the rest of the public . . . it is tempting at first sight to suppose that under modern conditions a large part of the new Circulating Capital created during any given period of time is the product not of deliberate waiting; but of forced levies on the public. (p. 51)

On looking more deeply, however, Robertson puts his finger on a most important principle:

> On the other hand, since the additional loans give rise to additional money deposits in the hands first of the borrowers and then of those from whom they make purchases, it is almost equally tempting to suppose that the new Circulating Capital is the product of the New Hoarding of the owners of these deposits. (pp. 50–1)

This is the repercussive principle, to which Keynes was later to give utterance in the form of the 'multiplier'. People make *voluntary* decisions concerning increments of money deposits (increments of income for Keynes) created and brought to them as part of a process of which these individuals have no consciousness. For Robertson, however, constrained by the quantity theory mechanism, the answer must be sought in relative movements of the price level. Three cases are examined.

VII

(i)   The first begins with a situation we have already met. Some or all of the public decide to increase the size of their hoards. The reduced money-flow on to the market causes the price level to fall so that some (the remainder of the public) or all enjoy unexpectedly increased consumption. Therefore, though some or all are saving, in aggregate there is no lacking. However, if our modern banks make loans of appropriate amount, they can restore the price level and enable savers to achieve their aim. In Robertsonianese:

> the action of the bank [his example is of a single giant bank] imposes Automatic Stinting: considered in conjunction with the New Hoarding, it nips in the bud the Automatic Splashing which would otherwise occur as a by-product of the New Hoarding. The bank, therefore, while imposing Automatic Stinting is *not* imposing Automatic Lacking, but is in effect transforming Spontaneous New Hoarding into Applied Lacking *very much as a 'cloak room' bank does when it accepts cash from the public and lends it out to entrepreneurs.*   (pp. 53–4; emphasis added)

In other words, although modern banks have the power to make redundant the traditional role of the voluntary saver in financing investment, and, therefore, the orthodox saving–investment relationship, they are acting here in effect as agents, as in the case of cloakroom banking. However, by confining his insight within established procedures Robertson not only confirmed orthodox thinking about saving but reinforced it, by adapting it to modern conditions.

(ii)   Another case in which the banks are able to exercise their powers without apparent disturbance of the price level is that in which their action coincides with a general increase in individual productivity. By making loans to offset the resulting fall in the price level they can

> extract from the public an amount of Lacking – partly Automatic and partly Induced – equal to the increase which would have automatically taken place in the real value of the public's money stocks.   (p. 54)

(iii)   The third case also involves a rise in output but this time as a result not of an increase in individual productivity but of the 'absorption into employment of an increment of population' (p. 55). The new output will not become available until the end of the production period but in the meantime circulating capital will be increased. The effect on the price-level will depend on the hoarding behaviour of the new workers as they receive wages paid out of loans made by bankers.

In the first case we assume that they do no hoarding during the production period so that the required lacking has to be imposed on the public via a rise in the price level. Subsequently, however, they begin to hoard at the same rate as the old population and the reduced money demand would cause the price level to fall so that there would be a counterbalancing effect in the form of automatic and induced *dis*lacking on the part of the old population. The banks can take advantage of this situation *to return the provision of lacking to a voluntary basis* as quickly as possible. By making suitable loans to maintain the price level they would

> cancel the Automatic Dis-lacking of the old population with Automatic Stinting, prevent the occurrence of their induced Dis-lacking, and transform the Spontaneous New Hoarding of the new population into Applied Lacking available for crystallisation into a new increment of Circulating Capital. (p. 56)

If, conversely, new workers did hoard during the production period then, although strictly incapable of lacking because they have as yet no current economic output, the effect of their action would be to lessen the burden imposed on the old population and the price level would not need to rise so much. After the production period, however, no further increase in circulating capital could be provided for through the agency of the bank(s) except by way of imposed lacking and a concomitant further rise in the price level (pp. 56–7).

What these cases illustrating the process of transformation have in common is that the banking system takes advantage of specially favourable circumstances to ensure the delivery of short lacking by way of stabilising the price level. But what if, as Robertson puts it, 'there is no increase in individual productivity and no change in the attractiveness of Hoarding'? What in that case would be 'the rate at which, without disturbance to the price level, the creation of new 'Circulating Capital can be procured through the bank' (p. 57)?

The answer was given by an equilibrium condition which Robertson later refined into the much noticed 'four crucial fractions'. In *BPPL* it took a simpler form, useful for present purposes, which related the three principal magnitudes namely: (a) the period of production, D (time between when production set in train and delivery to consumer); (b) the period of circulation of money, K (the real hoarding of the public – the money stock – as a proportion of annual national income, giving an income velocity of circulation); (c) the proportion which circulating capital bears to annual output during a production period, n. Now, if $K = nD$, circulating capital can be expanded at a uniform rate while maintaining price-level stability. If, however, K is less than nD, either the growth of circulating capital must be restricted; or entrepreneurs must directly apply more lacking; or the price level must continuously rise.

Given that K and D are independently determined, the implication is that price stability is a matter of good fortune. Robertson's estimate was that England was not so favoured, because, whereas the value of the money stock was about half of annual income (that is, K was 6 months), the period of production D was not less than twelve months and the proportion n not less than three-quarters (p. 58 n.3).

In the long run, of course, it is possible that the need for a continuously rising price level in a growing economy would be alleviated by increases in individual productivity and more particularly by the adjustment of direct spontaneous short lacking to the growing demand for circulating capital. In the conditions of the cycle, however, with its short-term alternation of expansion and contraction, banking policy faces the conflicting objectives of maintaining price stability and of ensuring the provision of sufficient lacking (p. 59).

VIII

In considering the role of banks in the trade cycle, we have now reached the second of the two ways in which banks play their part in the provision of lacking, namely, by way of imposed lacking inflicted on the public. Such operations mean violating both the orthodox presumption in favour of price stability and Robertson's ethical presumption in favour of voluntary going without. The question is, therefore, whether there are circumstances in which that infliction of imposed lacking can be *justified*? The answer, of course, is given in the question, for:

> the fundamental feature of the upward swing of a trade cycle is a large and discontinuous increase in the demand for Short Lacking, occurring as the essential preliminary to an expansion of output 'justified' for one or more of the reasons set out [above].   (p. 21)

Given that other means of supply would be unable to respond sufficiently quickly, it is on the banks that the responsibility must fall to meet the demand. Consequently:

> it seems unreasonable to expect the banking-system *both* to ensure that appropriate additions are made to the quantity of Circulating Capital *and* to preserve absolute stability in the price level.   (p. 72; emphasis in original)

Perhaps so, but let us be clear what is being decided. Even though the changes in output are 'justified', they would *in the absence of modern (money-creating) banking* be limited by the availability of short lacking. The introduction of this slip-joint into the system, therefore, poses a dilemma which is resolved by a policy decision in favour of the social benefits of long-term growth – of which fluctuation is a necessary part – over the individual choice of transactors (see, for example, pp. 78–9).

Such a course is presumably made more acceptable by the changes wrought by the war, which disposed people more in favour of present consumption and therefore restricted voluntary saving. Nevertheless, plunder is the essence of the matter, as Robertson clearly understood when he referred to the phenomenon in his first post-war book:

> The community is in effect compelled, by the extra purchasing power put into the hands of the borrower, to share with him its current income of real things, and such hoards of real things as it may possess. Of course the additional loan will presumably justify itself by and by, by adding to the flow of real goods; and the shorter the period before the new goods are ready and the loan repaid, the less scope the money generated by the loan will have for running amok. But so long as it is outstanding, the loan is of the nature of a tax or compulsion to save imposed on the general community jointly by the borrower and the bank. (Robertson, 1922, p. 90)

IX

If it was in order for banks to connive at increases in the price level and the infliction of automatic lacking where fluctuations were deemed appropriate, Robertson was equally clear that they should seek to resist such effects in all other cases. The specific problem Robertson identified was that the rise in the price level necessary to satisfy *justified* demands would give rise to pressures that would force it higher and so inflict additional burdens on the public. That is, for a variety of reasons (see pp. 71–6) the justified rise in the price level would cause transactors to increase expenditure, increase borrowing from the banks or reduce the flow of goods to the market, so stimulating further increases in the price level.

When these monetary causes of aggravation are added to the inherent tendency in the real economy for industrial output to be expanded beyond the limits justified by the underlying conditions of utility and cost, we have brought together both real and monetary constituent elements of 'inappropriate' fluctuations.

It is to the banking system that Robertson assigns the task of preventing or checking 'these *secondary* phenomena of trade expansion' (p. 79). The banks' response should be to employ traditional weapons to provide disincentives, as follows: a rise in money rates of interest, which would discourage tendencies both to dishoard and to borrow more; sales of government securities to the public, which would, to the extent that they did not diminish hoards, divert expenditure into what Robertson referred to as 'unproductive' lacking; direct controls, such as rationing, on new money loans (pp. 76-8).

It is by the same token the duty of the banks to prevent an unjustifiable decline in the scale of industrial output and uneconomic falls in the price level. In this case, however, the task is likely to prove more difficult (pp. 80-1).

It is an important and indeed formidable role for the banks that apparently belies Robertson's view of monetary forces as being of only secondary importance. This impression is reinforced by the idea that should the banks fail to control the 'secondary phenomena' then an 'acute shortage of circulating capital' could arise due to the impossibility of extracting any more lacking from the public. In the face of such loss of control the only remedy would be the unpalatable and damaging one of taking extended action drastically to reduce demand (pp. 79-80).

Nevertheless, despite the serious consequences of mismanagement, money is a secondary power set to deal with 'secondary phenomena' and is thus distinguished from the primary forces that move the economy and which can be identified with the fluctuations which are necessary and therefore appropriate.

The culmination of Robertson's theoretical argument, in which the principles of management of the short period become more comprehensively visible, is contained in his final chapter, which discusses the relationship between short lacking and long lacking.

X

So far, we have been concerned with short lacking, which is required for all goods, both consumables and instruments, during the period of production. This lacking is released by the sale of finished goods and so becomes *available for re-embodiment* in the next batch. In the case of instruments, however, final sale requires the provision of long lacking for an indefinite period and at a rate equal to the increase in output, in each succeeding production period (p. 85). Long lacking differs from short lacking in that the bulk of it is presumed to be the outcome of voluntary decisions on the part of: private entrepreneurs, who expand their businesses by reinvesting their profits; directors of joint-stock companies who similarly expand by reinvesting their companies' profits; private citizens who purchase new issues of securities (p. 86). These decisions will be made on economic grounds and will take into account the benefits of acquiring instruments allowing for cost and likely return, as against the enjoyment of consumption or leisure and the relative advantages of hoarding (pp. 86–7).

However, long lacking is similar to short lacking in that voluntary (spontaneous) long lacking is unlikely to be sufficient fully to meet the rising demand (in this case from increased output of instruments). Therefore, it is again to the banks that businesses must look, to expand their lending and so extort the balance from the public. As in the case of short lacking, if the pressure reaches crisis proportions, the banks must act to reduce demand (pp. 88–91).

Nevertheless, in the main, 'the expansion of long lacking depends . . . on the initiative of investors' (p. 91). And because Robertson views long and short lacking as *complements*, such expansion gives rise to an increased demand for supplies of short lacking. That is, it is these 'investors', in Robertson's sense, who ultimately dictate the rate at which short lacking must be forthcoming: 'the pace is set by investors, with their increased offers of long lacking' (p. 92).

Inevitably too, they set the pace for the banks as the residuary providers of short lacking and it is in the maintenance of a proper balance between short and long lacking that the true extent of the managerial skill required of the banks is revealed.

Part of the problem is that instruments, unlike consumables, require the co-operation of short lacking not only while they are being constructed but also for their subsequent operation. This requires *inter alia* that the banks look both to the stage of the cycle reached and the nature of the trades with which they deal, as the following extracts indicate:

> Towards the end of a constructional boom . . . the pressure on the banking system is increased, and the rise in general prices aggravated, by the demands of the owners of numerous new instruments for Short Lacking to enable them to keep those instruments in effective operation. It is the business of the banking-system at such a time to make the best use of such supplies of Short Lacking as it is still able and willing to procure from the public, rationing those supplies intelligently as between those trades which both make and use instruments and those which use instruments to make consumable goods, and giving a decided preference to the latter.　(p. 92)

Similarly, at the opposite point of the cycle:

> During the whole of the first part of the depression the hands of the banking-system will be full in procuring Short Lacking to cooperate with the *existing* instruments of production. It is only at a later stage that it may be able usefully to crystallise large supplies of Short Lacking in the production of further instruments.　(pp. 92–3)

Robertson's argument on banking policy was cast in terms of the complementarity of short and long *lacking*, but its full significance only becomes apparent when it is recast in terms of *goods*: that is, of the fixed and circulating capital for which long and short lacking respectively provide.

XI

We have seen that Robertson's notion of fixed capital – machines, factories and so on – was straightforward and traditional but that he seemed to equivocate over the definition of circulating capital. That is, he claimed to espouse the new idea of a 'congeries of goods in all stages of their passage from the soil to the ultimate user or consumer' (p. 42); but at the same time he repeatedly stressed the importance of the older idea that circulating capital consisted of consumable goods (and that, therefore, short lacking involved a going without of such goods; see p. 43). Now, at a late stage in the argument Robertson again warned of the error involved in identifying a shortage of capital with a shortage of stocks of consumable goods (p. 93), before going on to argue that a lack of balance between the output of consumable goods and investment goods could well inhibit constructional expansion, both by increasing costs of production and subsequently of operation. Indeed, in the limit the outcome could be cataclysmic:

> There is . . . a limit to the extent to which entrepreneurs can transfer to themselves, for retransfer to their workmen, command over the community's consumable output without endangering a complete collapse of the monetary system and even of the social structure: but other things being equal, the greater at any time is the output of consumable as compared with constructional goods, the less is the danger of that limit being reached. (pp. 93–4)

This notion, of the essential complementarity in production of instrument goods and consumable goods, was another example of Robertson's thought being far in advance of his time. The implications of this insight were, of course, utterly lost among the constraints imposed by his classical inheritance but was independently rediscovered by Keynes in the early 1930s. Nevertheless, on Robertson's larger question, of the relationship between economic growth and the trade cycle – the very stuff of his whole enquiry – the policy role of the banks in promoting the general welfare becomes one of regulating the relative rates of output of consumable goods and investment goods:

> To a large extent . . . fluctuations in the desirability of acquiring instruments are the inevitable penalty of industrial progress: but they are also to a certain limited extent attributable to an avoidable lack of responsiveness in the flow of consumable goods required to cooperate with those instruments in the form of real wages. It is part of the duty of the banking-system to promote at each phase of the cycle such a balance between the different kinds of production as to minimise this source of instability

in the estimates made by the business world of the advantages of acquiring instruments. (p. 94)

When applied to schemes for the relief of industrial depression (that is, 'stabilisation' policies), the implication would be that there should be less concentration on 'public works' capital projects – which might easily be mistimed – and more emphasis on the encouragement of consumption-goods output, as a way of preparing for a possible constructional revival, when economically justified. It also meant that there was merit in the idea of state-managed buffer stocks of partly finished or finished goods which would be used to make good the 'shortage of capital' that could hold back recovery (pp. 94–103).

There are also implications for the policy of price stabilisation pursued by the great combinations of producers as a means of promoting stability of output. Robertson had opposed this policy in the *Study* and now offered the rationalisation that (say) failure to allow prices to rise in line with 'economically-justified' increases in demand for instruments would give rise to over-production and, therefore, a loss of balance between instrument goods and consumption goods production, with consequent aggravation of the ensuing depression (pp. 99–103). Note that it is in respect of this aspect of price stabilisation that (recalling the *Study*) a large portion of Robertson's heresy on the matter is to be found.

This concludes our exposition and critical review of the argument of *BPPL*. That it has been done at such length is a reflection of the book's importance, both for an understanding of the fundamentals of Robertsonian economics and more immediately as evidence in support of our principal theme: the relationship between the economics and the man. Before we turn to the arguments that establish the connection, however, we need to take one further step to complete our review of the 'economics' end of the relationship.

XII

Two years after the publication of *BPPL*, Robertson set out the essentials of the book in 'Theories of Banking Policy' ('TBP'), a lecture delivered at the LSE in February 1928 and published in *Economica* in the following June. This was clearly a scholarly work rather than simply a popularisation, but the effect was nevertheless to provide support for the position established in *BPPL* by way of unqualified reiteration of the theoretical argument. It thus reinforces the view that the position taken in *BPPL* was Robertson's definitive position at the end of his positive phase of development. Four points from 'TBP' are of interest here.

(i) First, the condition for equilibrium. This is now elaborated from the simple form K = nD met with earlier to take acount of: *a* the proportion of their assets (liabilities) that the banks devote to the provision of circulating capital; and *b* the proportion of existing circulating capital built up via bank loans rather than from spontaneous lacking.

Now, as proportions of a one-year time-period we have, for England and for the USA: D = 1, *a* = *b* = K = ¹/₂. Then, writing C as the amount of circulating capital, KR as the real value of aggregate bank deposits; and DR as the real income or output during a period of production, we obtain, when the industrial and banking systems are in equilibrium:

$$aKR = bC$$

and

$$C = {}^1\!/_2 DR$$

Substituting in and dropping R from both sides:

$$aK = {}^1\!/_2 bD$$

As the 'climax' of this part of his discussion (the building up of 'a rather elaborate scaffolding': Robertson, 1928, in Hicks ed., 1966, p. 24), Robertson reaches the following conclusion:

> Provided there is no change in the relative magnitudes *a* and *b*, or in those of the proportions K and D, a uniform rate of growth in population and output can be sustained without rupture of equilibrium. But to this end it is necessary that the banking system shall add to the supplies of bank money at the same rate. Once more, therefore, in the case of the normal processes of progress as in the case of an increase in the desire of the average member of the public to perform monetary saving, the creation of additional money by the banks is seen to be not merely blameless, but a positive duty.   ('TBP' in Hicks ed., 1966, pp. 31–2)

(ii) This elaboration of the condition for equilibrium provides the context for the second point, which concerns the implications for the banks of a situation in which the growth rate is not even. This could arise, for example, because of an acceleration in the industrial long-run growth rate; or even more significantly, because of the short-run movement of industry through the first phase of recovery from deep depression (the effect of the cycle). In either case the various factors of the equation are 'thrown out of gear' (p. 32) and it is in the technical reasons for this that the interest of this point lies.

First, under Robertson's scheme, a rise in output must be preceded by an increase in the amount of circulating capital, so that the proportion rises above the $C = \frac{1}{2}DR$ specified above. But second, and of the utmost importance for his dispute with Keynes, Robertson recognises quite explicitly that the new circulating capital must be provided '*before* the rate of output grows, and *a fortiori*, therefore, before the new real saving in monetary form which the new output facilitates is done' (p. 32). In other words, what we might *almost* call the *rate* of voluntary saving out of increased income only becomes available *after* investment has occurred and, therefore, cannot help in the business of making provision for it. On the other hand, Robertson deliberately leaves out of account any measures that the banks might adopt to increase what we might *almost* call the *propensity* to save: that is, the 'various expedients' they might employ 'to tempt the public into economy' (p. 32). This means that in this case there is no complication of the issue from the question of whether it is possible to increase investment by way of increasing saving at some prior date; and instead the whole weight of meeting the increased demand for circulating capital is thrown upon the money-creating powers of the banks, a rise in the price level and the imposition of what Robertson is now referring to as 'forced saving'. If we leave out of account these latter 'quantity theory' effects, we are left with the arresting idea that investment is financed by money balances, that increased investment produces increased output/real income and that this in turn gives rise to an increased rate of saving! Only the 'ancient ceremony' (as Robertson was later to describe it: 1963a, pp. 327, 346) of the Cambridge version of the quantity theory stands between Robertson and something very Keynesian. We shall return to this point below.

Robertson regarded the prior increase in circulating capital as a simple matter of 'physical necessity' but the role he gave to the banks in making provision for it was, he believed, based on practice and preference. In *BPPL*, the assumption that typically industry had recourse to the banks for loans to finance expansion was the means by which money entered the system and so provided the basis for the quantity theory mechanism of adjustment via changes in the price level. It was an assumption of crucial importance for his argument but was vulnerable to challenge on the grounds that it was empirically invalid (see Hawtrey, 1926). In 'TBP', however, Robertson reinforced his point by further arguing that over time the tendency to have recourse to the banks would strongly increase so that, in terms of the equations, b would grow. The effect of the two tendencies taken together would be to make bC 'considerably more than' aKR. The disequilibrium that this represents is what produces an increase in the price level and the imposition of forced saving on the public.

(iii) The third point concerns not the theoretical scaffolding but the *criteria* to be used for judging various principles of banking policy (namely, the gold standard, the principle of productive credit, price stabilisation). These criteria are of interest here because they embody the economic and ethical considerations worked out in the *Study* and modified for the post-war, monetary economy in *BPPL*, and can be seen as central to the Robertsonian creed. Robertson asked of each prospective policy three questions, namely:

> First, can it be relied upon not wantonly to extort forced savings from the public? Secondly, can it be relied upon efficiently to transmute all real saving offered to it by the public into industrial capital? Thirdly, is it likely to respond readily to the genuine requirements of industry for exceptional supplies of savings in exceptional circumstances?

In other words, can the banking principle in question be relied upon faithfully to put into effect the intentions of the public with respect to saving; but at the same time be sufficiently flexible to respond as necessary to meet the demands of the growth process (including the integral cycle) when the community's short-run saving plans must be overridden in the interests of long-run aggregate social welfare?

(iv) Robertson's own solution – the 'ideal banking policy' that he considered best met the criteria he had laid down, provides our fourth point. As a solution it is entirely predictable on the basis of his analysis as set out in *BPPL* and 'TBP' and reveals Robertson as less the radical figure he claimed to be in *BPPL* and more the pragmatist, willing to recommend necessary departures from an orthodoxy with which he was largely in agreement (as noted earlier, it is in respect of the price-stabilisation policies pursued by the large combines that much of his claim to being a heretic has validity). He concluded his examination of existing principles of banking policy with the suggestion that:

> the ideal banking policy might be one which was founded on the principle of price stabilisation as a norm, but which was ready to see the fruits of a prolonged and general increase in individual productivity shared in the form of lower prices, and perhaps to acquiesce in moderate price rises in order that advantage might be taken of discontinuous leaps in industrial technique.   (In Hicks ed., 1966, p. 42)

In concluding the article, Robertson took the opportunity to put the suggested policy measures into perspective. As he had done from the *Study* onward, Robertson pointed to the relationship between economic problems and the nature of man – of which relationship the theme of the present study is but a particular example – and argued that any thoroughgoing attempt to deal with the problem would have to begin with the transformation of man:

> it would be a policy that did not claim omnipotence, or feel competent of its ability to cure the evils of uncertainty except in alliance with a much more comprehensive

attempt to control and stabilise the desires and activities of the community than most monetary reformers – even, I think, most thoroughgoing Socialists – have yet visualised.   (p. 42)

With this review of the principal features of 'Theories of Banking Policy' we conclude our examination of Robertsonian economics during the positive, innovative phase of his career. Henceforward the mood would be reactive and the tone increasingly critical.

21. Robertsonian insights and Keynesian parallels

I

At this juncture it will be helpful to bring into focus the principal features of Robertson's system and to develop further some of the comments we have made along the way. The relationship of what is said to the main theme will be made clear if we again make reference to the set of questions posed earlier as an analytical framework (see end of Chapter 18). These questions can now be written in expanded form as follows:

1. To what extent is Robertson's theory developed additively?
2. What pattern of relationship is imposed on the key variables? This question in turn subsumes the following questions:
   (a) What is the nature of saving?
   (b) What is the relationship between saving and investment?
   (c) How is investment financed?
   (d) What is the nature of interest and what determines the rate of interest?
3. What importance is accorded to the role of money?
4. What significance is to be attached to Robertson's choice of 'frictionless barter' as his standard case, defining the appropriate degree of fluctuation (a choice he acknowledged, as in accordance with Cambridge practice, to Marjorie Tappan following criticism by Roy Harrod: see C3/1/2 RPTC)?

Though these questions are concerned with the economics, they nevertheless also evoke the man; for the economic concepts and relationships to which they refer faithfully reflect the underlying influence of temperament. The first three are answered in the present chapter; the fourth in the following chapter.

II

With respect to the first, we have seen that it was Robertson's practice to develop his theory additively, with new increments being added successively and no overt overturning of a previously established position. The process is exemplified by *BPPL*, in which the new monetary analysis is grafted on to a core of real theory taken from the *Study*. As part of the process Robertson successfully integrated savings and investment into his analysis without disturbance to his traditional quantity theory approach to money.

It is important to stress that there is nothing inherently reprehensible about this method. It is the basis of what has been described as Robertson's 'evolutionism' and the claim that, as compared to Keynes, Robertson was both consistent and constant: a safe pair of hands. It may, however, become reprehensible if new ideas and innovations are unreasonably constrained by old loyalties: if insights are stifled by tradition. It is on this basis that we argue that it is not so much that Robertson is an evolutionist as that he makes constrained advance. In other words, Robertson often produces ideas in advance of his time and in particular in advance of Keynes but is unable, because of his temperamentally determined need for a reference back, to follow them wheresoever they might lead.

III

It would be unfair and misleading to judge Robertson's theory as right or wrong by the degree of progress he had made towards the position established by Keynes in the *General Theory*. But it would be both valid and instructive if, as hinted above, it could be shown that in Robertson's thinking there were inklings later to be found fully developed in Keynesian economics but hopelessly lost in a theory moulded by the quantity theory and residual elements of Say's Law. That Robertson had conceived ideas later to be associated with Keynes will be demonstrated below after we have looked again at two of Robertson's main concerns in *BPPL*: to establish the nature of saving and to trace the relationship between money and saving–investment analysis.

With respect to the first of these, and eschewing the terminology of lacking as Robertson did in 'TBP', we can speak simply in terms of two kinds of saving: voluntary and forced (we ignore the complication of 'induced' behaviour; but see Laidler, 1995, p. 158 for an analysis of its true significance).

IV

The first thing to make clear is that in *BPPL* voluntary saving is, in conceptual terms, only a rump. That is, although it is credited with the bulk of the provision for fixed capital, there is no longer a theoretical reason why it need be retained. This is because *all* the necessary saving, and not just that required to meet excess demand, can be forced out of the public through the action of the banks. In the case of circulating capital, it is Robertson's own presumption that the banks will play the leading part.

However, this is not the end of the story. Having established the relative order of importance of forced and voluntary saving in conceptual terms, we can now point to theoretical objections to each as providers of capital.

Because of induced movements in the price level, voluntary savers can defeat their own attempts to 'go without'. For this reason Robertson puts particular emphasis on saving which is applied directly to investment, or is at least handed to those who will apply it directly – the principle is the same, rather than simply withheld from consumption. But let us try to imagine what voluntary direct saving really means.

What Robertson seems to have in mind is that, following a decision by a sizeable proportion of the population to save more in future, there will be a simple transfer from consumption expenditure to investment expenditure, without disturbance to the price level. The lag, inevitable in roundabout methods of production, between the giving up of the one and the inauguration of the other is simply disregarded (and with it, therefore, any possible effects from a fall in the price level).

Such a possible fall, as in the case of new hoarding, could, of course, be corrected by the banks, which are generally pursuing a policy of price stabilisation. But if prices are held constant this mechanism faces another threat. If following a decision to make more resources available for investment the population reduces expenditure on consumption, the flow of income will be reduced and with it the amount of saving out of that income. In other words, the attempt to save more is self-defeating, due to the paradox of thrift. The paradox of thrift (POT) is one form of the fallacy of composition (FOC), which is the belief that what is true for one is true for all: for example, that because one individual is able to choose to increase his saving this must, additively, mean that all individuals taken together can choose to do the same.

We have pointed out that Robertson used the idea of a distinction between the effects of action by one and the effects of action by all as a distinctive feature of his adjustment mechanism. But we have also pointed out that the distinction took effect through changes in the price level and, as we have now agreed, prices are being held constant. The only possible way in which this method can work is to imagine the community members drawn up in extended line facing the front and passing over *that which they have in hand* to would-be investors. Robertson, with his eyes fixed on the danger posed by a possible movement of the price level in frustrating savers' intentions, would lose sight of possible adjustment through changes in the circular flow of income – the mechanism of Keynes.

We should note that Robertson's concentration on the quantity-theory adjustment mechanism via the price level makes it less surprising that, though he recognised that increased investment would give rise to increased output/real income and that saving (consumption) was a lagged function of income, there was no recognition of the causal sequence that runs from investment to income and from income to saving. Such a link, of course, had to wait for Keynes's crucial distinction between the propensity to save (consume) and the rate of saving. This Robertson never saw. He was, moreover, bound to retain voluntary saving as a source of provision for investment for other reasons. It was his link with Say's Law, with traditional theory and with the notion of the individual's right to choose between present consumption and the welfare of descendants–secured through his own self-denial.

V

The provision of saving is no more certain when it is to be imposed on the public. Hawtrey (1926) criticised the forced-saving mechanism on four grounds:

1. that it depended upon appropriate movements in the price level and Robertson had not made proper allowance for the effects of changes in stocks of finished goods;
2. that it was not clear from whose incomes the saving was to be forced;
3. in Robertson's mathematical model forced saving plays an insignificant part and for all practical purposes could be excluded;
4. that the means by which the requisite change in the money supply was brought about would not operate because, contrary to Robertson, experience suggests that banks do not have the primary responsibility for meeting any increased demand for circulating capital.

These charges, if substantiated, would leave a very big hole in Robertson's monetary theory and so prevent the system from adjusting in the prescribed manner. More immediately they cast doubt on the conceptually more important route by which saving is provided for investment.

Finally, there is the question of whether the introduction of forced saving has any implications for the traditional saving-prior-investment sequence. On this count there is a difference of opinion between two commentators, with Bridel (1987) claiming that the sequence is maintained and Bigg (1990) arguing that forced saving introduced a fundamental change so that Robertson's composite theory, involving both voluntary and forced saving, becomes a half-way house between the classical and Keynesian positions.

Of the two, Bridel's case is the less convincing on two counts. First, because his treatment of saving-prior-investment accepts unquestioningly the efficacy of a thrift campaign as a means of providing for new circulating capital. Second, because he seems to confuse saving-prior-investment, with saving and investment prior to increased output (Bridel, 1987, p. 121).

Bigg's account seems nearer the mark once we understand precisely what it is that Robertson's innovation implies. We have already seen that in place of the orthodox position that investment must wait upon prior saving and that the only way to prepare for increased investment is to save more at some prior date, investors are freed both as to the source of the investible funds they require but, more important, as to the amount. However, what this implies is that Robertson has divided the process into its constituent parts, with the provision of the money balances to finance necessary purchases separated from the requisite 'going without' considered essential in orthodoxy. By doing this Robertson laid bare the essence of the process and reversed the *direction of causation* between investment and saving. As elsewhere, however, the insights are lost, both because Robertson feels bound to retain voluntary saving as the standard case, with bank-financed investment as a supplement only, and because the absence of a link between investment and saving via multiplier-induced changes in income meant that there could be no escape from the notion of 'going without'.

VI

The rate of interest formed no overt part of Robertson's main theoretical scheme – except in so far as it is referred to as a tool of banking policy. It is true that Bridel has argued that in Robertson's acceptance of the methods of Alfred Marshall and the Cambridge School he was by the same token taking for granted the operation of the rate of interest in equilibrating the capital market (Bridel, 1987, p. 115). As to this, the reply must be that there is no obvious role for the rate of interest in Robertson's analysis, which is centrally concerned with the relationship between saving and movements in the price level. Not until 1934, when he *recast* his theory in interest-rate terms as a means of replying to an initiative of Keynes's, did Robertson rewrite the distinction between voluntary saving and (bank-financed) forced saving as the distinction between the natural and market rates of interest.

Such was the basis of the interest rate theory with which he confronted Keynes. In this theory, the resources or 'loanable funds' available for investment were a composite, made up of the savings and the bank money familiar from our review of *BPPL*. It was thus possible for investment to be greater than saving *by definition*. Because the concept of 'loanable funds' was open to the same criticisms as we have directed against voluntary and forced saving as a means of preparing for increased investment, it is not surprising that Keynes found it an unsatisfactory compromise and dismissed the whole notion of modifying classical theory as likely to produce the 'worst muddles of all'. Further discussion of the whole matter can safely be left until Chapter 27.

VII

The absence of an overt role for the rate of interest in *BPPL* means that the version of the quantity theory to which Robertson owes allegiance at this stage is that which has been designated as working via the 'direct mechanism' (see Blaug, 1997, pp. 152ff.). In other words, a change in the supply of money will have its effect on the economy *directly* via expenditure in the commodity markets. It is to be contrasted with the 'indirect mechanism', in which changes in the quantity of money have their effect via changes in the rate of interest: a mode of adjustment not adopted by Robertson until 1934, in 'Industrial Fluctuation and the Natural Rate of Interest'.

Robertson's 'direct mechanism' works, as we have seen, via movements in the price level and changes in the real value of money balances. However, there are several general objections to the notion of a wealth effect, or real balance effect or Pigou Effect (as to the last incidentally, Samuelson remarked that to his surprise he had not been able to isolate it in all the Robertson pre-1940 literature; see Samuelson, 1963, p. 526). In Robertson's case they are threefold.

First, the very mode of operation via movements in the price level could be destabilising for the monetary and economic system as a whole. Curiously, Keynes, after his essay in price variability as the mode of adjustment in the *Treatise*, was to return in the *General Theory* to the orthodox preference for price stability as a characteristic of a stable economy. With his mode of adjustment via changes in real income Keynes had no need of price level adjustment and urged that money wages and the price level be stabilised as a means of maintaining confidence in the efficacy of a monetary-production economy. He further warned specifically of the dangers posed by a regime of frequently adjusting money prices (Keynes, 1936, p. 239; see also Fletcher, 1989a, pp. 155-7, Tobin, 1975).

Second, the principal empirically based criticism of the Pigou Effect was that it would be too small to have a significant effect on consumption. This was because price-level changes would affect debtors and creditors equivalently and, because the bulk of the money supply was of the 'inside', credit-money kind, the net effect would be small. This criticism is of particular relevance to Robertson's theory, in which the money supply is largely composed of bank money.

The final objection we have met already. It is that the requisite initial movement in the price level will not occur if either stocks bear the brunt of a change in demand (Hawtrey's criticism) or if there is a change in output. This last was the basis of the 'widow's cruse fallacy': a criticism directed against Keynes's *Treatise* on the grounds that although he was ostensibly concerned with fluctuation in the level of output (and employment), he was tacitly assuming that output was fixed so that profits used for expenditure would return to firms via changes in (higher) product prices (see Keynes, 1930, in *CW* V, p. 125; also Moggridge, 1993, pp. 187–9).

With respect to stocks, Robertson did not ignore them in *BPPL*. However, he treated them not as a potential threat to the price-adjustment mechanism but as a guide to banking policy. That is, by assuming a positive relationship between the size of stocks and the quantity of short lacking required to carry them, it is possible to infer the state of the short-term capital market by observing the behaviour of stocks at different stages of the cycle. This information would then form the basis for planning the loan policy of the banking system. For example, a diminution of stocks during the boom could indicate that the supply of short lacking was failing to match demand and so acting as a brake on stock-building. Conversely, if stocks increase during the first stage of depression the likelihood is that the demand for and supply of short lacking is being 'artificially sustained' (Robertson, 1926, p. 83). This presumably means that the process is being carried beyond what is justified by underlying factors of cost and utility and that a policy of restraint is, therefore, required (pp. 79, 82–3).

VIII

So far, the picture of Robertson as the innovative but fettered economist, forever touching on new ways of thinking but always held back by loyalty to his intellectual origins, has emerged intact. A similar ambivalence can be detected in his treatment of money, upon which he lavished most of his analytical attention in *BPPL* but which he ultimately believed should be considered as of 'secondary' importance (or even 'fundamentally unimportant'). The significance of this will not become apparent until we have dealt with the last question in our sequence (in Chapter 22, below).

For the moment we simply reiterate that it is clear from the analysis of

BPPL that money has real effects and is able both to reverse the classical saving-prior-investment causal sequence and to subvert the ethical consideration that the public should be free to choose between present and future consumption. It is also clear, however, that policy is to be directed towards ensuring that the system works as nearly as possible like a non-monetary competitive economy. This would imply that money would be rendered neutral so that only voluntary saving would occur and the classical causal sequence would be reinstated as the norm. However, allowance would also be made in exceptional circumstances for involuntary saving to be imposed on the public when justified in the long-term social interest.

IX

We are now in a position to bring together Robertson's 'Keynesian parallels'; that is, ideas grasped or glimpsed by Robertson and which were later to feature, within an entirely new framework, in the *General Theory*. A surprisingly large number of these was present in *BPPL* in 1926 but locked within the confines of the quantity theory and constrained by residual assumptions inspired by Say's Law. Though Robertson was not in any significant sense a precursor of Keynes – the central concept of effective demand and its attendant apparatus was entirely missing – he was, once again, in many respects in advance of his teacher. So much so that Keynes was later to acknowledge that much of his new way of thinking was already there 'in embryo' in Robertson's work (Keynes, *CW* XIV, p. 94). The following are the chief points to note.

(i)   There is clear recognition of the distinction between the effects of action by one and the effects of action by all: that what may be true for one individual taken singly may not be true for all individuals taken together. In Keynes's hands the fallacy of composition in the form of the paradox of thrift meant that an attempt on the part of all members of a population to emulate the prudent individual and increase their wealth through higher saving would result in falling incomes and a reduction in saving. It was *part* of the thinking that reversed the direction of causation between saving and investment.

In Robertson's hands it similarly resulted in all individuals taken together failing to 'go without' (to lack) as they had intended. The difference is that the effect is produced by a fall in the price level rather than via a fall in the flow of incomes. Consequently, the process is different from that of Keynes. The reason for this is that although the saving behaviour of one individual will be affected by the saving behaviour of others, this is only because the fall in expenditure by the *aggregate of individuals* brings down the price level and enhances the real value of money balances. There is no recognition of organicism in economics: of the essential two-sidedness of transactions, such that a fall in expenditure by one will result in a fall in income and, therefore, both consumption *and saving* on the part of others. It is in the former, Robertsonian, sense that we should interpret Pigou's comment that: 'what each one loses through his own action he gains through the action of other people' (Pigou, 1926, pp. 224–5).

(ii)   As a corollary of the above, both Robertson and Keynes gave investment the power to determine saving at a rate equal to the change in investment. The difference is that Robertson's investment-induced change in saving is only intended to be a supplement to saving initiated in the orthodox way by the decisions of savers. It is moreover *forced* out of the public by a rise in the price level. There was thus the possibility that (voluntary) saving and investment could initially be unequal. For Keynes, all saving is voluntary and generated by a rise in the level of incomes.

If we take into account Hawtrey's criticisms that: (a) Robertson accords the banks too important a position in the finance of investment and that other sources should be given greater weight; and (b) that for all practical purposes forced saving is insignificant and that Robertson could simplify his analysis by leaving it out of account and talking instead in terms of saving, the essential difference of Robertson's analysis from that of Keynes is brought into focus. That is, for Robertson, adherence to the quantity theory means that adjustment must come via the price level and, therefore, output must be fixed. The difference between this and Keynes's notion of an undifferentiated pool of liquidity to meet all demands for finance, on the one hand, and of saving generated out of a changing flow of real income, on the other, is complete.

(iii)   Nevertheless there is in Robertson's scheme the recognition that investment is financed by money balances (bank-loan, credit-money). This was an important aspect also of Keynes's new theory. The stumbling-block was that Robertson steadfastly maintained a belief in the need to 'go without' and in the role of saving (lacking) in somehow 'financing' investment. This gave rise to the concept of 'loanable funds' as a composite of saving and money.

(iv)   As a more particular aspect of the above, however, both Robertson and Keynes made use of the idea of the short-term finance of investment as being performed by a given fund, endlessly circulating between successive projects. In Robertson's case, however, the fund is the lacking required to provide the requisite circulating capital during each production period in a 'steady' community (that is, 'stationary or progressing at a uniform rate'):

While the identity of the goods in which Circulating Capital consists is constantly changing, the total outstanding supply of such Capital in a 'steady' community must itself be 'steady' . . . so that the total amount of Short Lacking required by the whole chain of trades involved is approximately steady . . . [and] Hence, in practice we find that congealed Short Lacking is continually being released by some entrepreneurs and absorbed by others. (*BPPL*, pp. 43-4)

For Keynes on the other hand, the revolving fund of finance for investment is purely monetary and he was later to castigate Robertson for confusing money with saving, as we shall see. He introduced the notion in 1939 as a supplement or 'coping-stone' to his theory of liquidity preference, as a means both of making allowance for the effects of Bertil Ohlin's distinction between *ex ante* and *ex post* and to provide

a bridge between my way of talking and the way of those [the loanable funds school] who discuss the supply of loans and credits etc. . . . to show that they are simply discussing one of the sources of demand for liquid funds arising out of an increase in activity. (Keynes, *CW* XXIX p. 282; see also *CW* XIV pp. 220, 230)

The idea was that entrepreneurs' need for finance at a time when investment was *ex ante* (planned) would give rise to an increased demand for money balances which would later be released for re-use by others when the investment became *ex post* (realised) and more permanent financial arrangements were in place. Keynes called this the 'finance motive' for demanding liquidity and he made it clear that, in keeping with the whole argument of the *General Theory*, the finance of investment had nothing to do with saving:

'finance' is essentially a revolving fund. It employs no savings. It is, for the community as a whole, only a book-keeping transaction. As soon as it is 'used' in the sense of being expended, the lack of liquidity is automatically made good and the readiness to become temporarily unliquid is available to be used over again. (Keynes, *CW* XIV p. 219)

(v)   It is also the case that for Robertson a rise in investment produces a rise in output (real income); and that consumption, and therefore saving, is a lagged function of income. Nevertheless, saving out of income fails to rise in line with investment, leaving Robertson's theory incomplete as compared to Keynes.

(iv)   What is missing here, of course, is the concept of the multiplier, based on the distinction between the marginal propensity to save (consume) and the rate of saving. This would ensure that income changed sufficiently to produce the requisite amount of saving, defined as that part of real income not devoted to consumption and thus leaving the 'finance' of investment as a purely monetary transaction.

Robertson did allude to the percussive principle, though not in terms of successive rounds of increments of income concerning which individuals make decisions to consume or save. Instead, given the quantity theory framework, he referred to successive receipts of money balances regarding which individuals make decisions to spend or hoard as we have seen.

(vii) Robertson embraces the very Keynesian idea of investment goods and consumable goods as complements rather than as substitutes in production. The impulse in Robertson's case, however, was his adherence to the earlier, Robinson Crusoe, conception of circulating capital as a stock of consumable goods demanded by the roundaboutness of production, rather than the operation of the multiplier in conditions of less than full employment.

X

The conclusion to be drawn from the above review is that the curious half-way house appearance of Robertson's theory derives from his practice of seeking to harmonise new insights and new departures with established 'truths'. The first was a product of his leaping intellect; the second the outcome of a temperamentally determined need for unbroken links with his origins. By 'links with his origins' we mean the need for a reference back to some secure past time or golden age, real or imagined, that has its parallel in the foundations of Robertsonian economics. It is to the establishment of this parallel that the last of the four questions posed at the beginning of this chapter alludes.

22. Economics and nonsense

I

In considering the question of the significance to be attached to Robertson's choice of 'frictionless barter' as his standard case, defining the appropriate degree of fluctuation, we have reached the crux of his argument and with it the culmination of our whole investigation. For here we have the link between Robertson and economics and literature and life.

II

The 'link between Robertson and economics and literature and life' is given by the parallel between: (a) the case of frictionless barter as the foundation of Robertsonian economics (see Robertson, 1926, p. 8; the exchange between Harrod, 1927, and Tappan, 1928; together with the comment of Robertson in C3/1/2 RPTC); (b) our interpretation of the significance of the *Alice* books, based on the Sewell conception of nonsense-as-game, as the inspiration for Robertson's philosophy of life (see above, Chapter 11). This parallel supplies the explanation for Robertson's choice of frictionless barter, as his standard case, for what Harrod described as 'aesthetic' reasons (see Harrod, 1927, p. 225; also Harrod to Robertson, 18 May 1926, quoted in Young, 1989, p. 26).

We begin with the idea that:

> The form of order that nonsense assumes is that of the game. Language is reorganised not according to the rules of prose or poetry but according to those of play, with the 'game as an enclosed whole with its own rigid laws which cannot be questioned within the game itself'. (Chapter 11, above)

By operating according to known rules and limiting the range of problems and possible outcomes the game is more certain than life and consequently confers upon the player a characteristic sense of freedom and security. In this way it 'can be seen as representing the distinction between risk and uncertainty' (see above, Chapter 11).

III

One of the most significant features that distinguishes nonsense from other forms is the nature of its construction: 'the relation between the whole and its parts'. Sewell was insistent that 'This universe . . . must never be more than the sum of its parts', and that 'The emphasis must always be on the parts rather than the whole.' Nonsense, that is, must go one-and-one-and-one: it must be additive. It follows, therefore, that:

> the maintenance of a universe of nonsense-as-game and the promise of freedom and safety (a haven from life's realities) that it provides, depends on the assurance that the whole can never be more than the sum of the parts.   (Chapter 11, above)

It further follows that any factor that causes the whole to be more than the sum of the parts constitutes a threat to nonsense-as-game and therefore to those who depend upon it for their sense of reassurance and well-being. Examples of such factors given by Sewell fall into two categories: unconscious states of mind and, of greater interest for present purposes, the engagement of the emotions. This latter occurs, for example, in the presence of beauty, which draws participants into 'some kind of union with the beautiful object', so weakening their games-player's sense of detachment. Beauty also causes the mind to perceive a whole that is more than 'a sum of ones'. That is, it sees *organism* rather than organisation.

IV

Similarly with love, which Sewell regards as the agent most destructive of nonsense, on account of its 'supremely unitive' quality, and which 'demands subjection of the whole individual – partly suppressing the logical intellect'. It will be recalled that in Sewell's scheme, love had been deliberately excluded from the *Alice* books as a way of creating the conditions for nonsense-as-game; but it had been allowed to enter into later Carroll books as C.L. Dodgson attempted to bring more of his troubled life within the safe, warm bounds of the game. Our own, preferred, interpretation was that the *Alice* texts possessed a dual character, being at the same time both a feast of Carroll's inimitable 'nonsense' entertainment and a horrifying post-Darwinian glimpse of the real nature of existence beneath the everyday 'normality' of Victorian society (recall Rackin in Phillips ed., 1972, pp. 391–416). We further argued that in successive productions the introductory and concluding 'frame-materials', which did so much to explain the nature of the texts by indicating the nature of Dodgson's own concerns and anxieties, became increasingly integrated with the nonsense texts.

V

On either Sewell's or the alternative reading the effect is the same: the qualities that are so prized in the 'pure' texts are lost as more and more features of the 'real world' invade the borders of the universe of nonsense-as-game. Interpreted in terms of economics, the equivalent of nonsense-as-game should now be clear. That which goes one-and-one-and-one and in which the whole is no more than the sum of the parts is what we now call microeconomics, in which aggregates are simple sums of individual outcomes. Microeconomics is so designated to distinguish it from macroeconomics, which is a separate system of economic analysis that deals specifically with economic wholes and in which an aggregate whole is in some sense different from the sum of the individual parts.

VI

Macroeconomics was Keynes's own creation, which he based on relationships discovered in the 1930s when moving forward from the *Treatise* (1930) to the *General Theory* (1936). It follows that the orthodoxy that preceded Keynesian economics – which we might, following Keynes's classification, designate Classical economics – was built on microeconomic foundations and proceeded on a one-and-one-and-one basis and dealt with aggregates that were no more than the sum of the parts. At the heart of this system lay 'frictionless barter' (see C3/1/2 RPTC). For Robertson, frictionless barter was the equivalent of nonsense-as-game and played the same role in his professional life as did *Alice* in his private life.

This is not, of course, to argue that Robertson's vision of Classical economics is in any way no-sense economics (any more than Lewis Carroll's 'nonsense' was no-sense prose) but that the system at its heart possessed the characteristics of game and of the world of *Alice*. Though it had referents in the real world – output, employment and so on – it was essentially a closed system which operated according to a set of known and accepted rules, in the safe embrace of which 'economising' could give rise to only a limited range of possible outcomes. This world is, therefore, more certain than the real world and consequently more reassuring for those who in some sense dwell there.

In particular, the dimension in which the system operates is that of equilibrium and of short-term tendencies towards and divergencies from that edenic fixed point of harmony. Time in the sense of the undirectional flow of existence, decay and death does not exist. Equilibrium is the antithesis of the nature of biography. Consequently, there can be no uncertainty, in the sense of situations in which there exists no scientific basis on which to calculate the probability of possible outcomes.

It follows that there is no room here for substantive money: that is, money which exists as an asset in its own right to be held as a hedge against an unknowable future. Instead, where money is used, it will be as a medium of exchange and a unit of account but not as a store of value. Money will be fundamentally unimportant and in the limit the 'monetary economy' will possess the characteristics of frictionless barter.

VII

We should recall that both Wonderland and Looking-Glass World are essentially moneyless. It is true that in *TLG* commerce is a feature in both the railway-carriage scene and in the episode of the Old Sheep Shop. However, in the first the notion of monetary value is ridiculed, and in the second, though money actually changes hands, the transaction is not completed by way of goods passing to the would-be purchaser. Instead the curious nature of the goods and the attitude of the shop-keeper both seem to emphasise that in this world the usual power of money to command assent is suspended.

This should not be surprising since, if nonsense must go one-and-one-and-one and if love the great unifier is, therefore, either deliberately excluded or naturally absent from the *Alice* books, it follows that money too must be either absent or shown to be fundamentally unimportant. For money, like love and beauty, has the power to bring together discrete elements both in the sense of creating meaningful aggregates and in promoting exchange. Only in situations in which the future can be accurately planned for do we dispense with the need for the information system, mode of exchange and means of combination that money supplies. *Because in this way money has the power to smooth our path it is by the same token the enemy of nonsense.*

As a corollary to the above, if we were to interpret the *Alice* books through the eyes of Austrian economics we should obtain a new and telling insight. In Austrian terms money is an institution, like the law, which through the trust it inspires promotes exchange, choice and economic and political freedom. Through the introduction of the institution of money, all participants become more *interdependent* but also, because the cash nexus has substituted for the human tie, each one becomes less dependent on the arbitrary power of any individual. Money is thus a uniquely liberating phenomenon. If money is excluded, this liberty is similarly banished; and this is precisely what happens in the *Alice* books, in which Alice is in a world of discrete *independent* entities and subjected to the coldness, rudeness and caprice of petty tyrants.

VIII

It should now be clear that there are (in the context we are considering) two alternative 'visions' of the economy: one which proceeds from an abstract economic 'model' which has at its back the world of frictionless barter; and another which takes as its premises the actual conditions under which people conduct their economic lives. We can avoid a fruitless discussion over the old question of whether a theory is testable by the realism of its assumptions if we argue as follows. First, that this difference of vision marks the distinction between Classical economics and Keynesian economics in general, and between Robertson's economics and Keynes's economics in particular – and that it is the differences *between* these views that is our especial area of concern. Second, a moment's reflection suggests that the chief difference lies in the theoretical treatment of money – in the first case it is unimportant and in the second case important – and that this again is the point of interest for the present argument.

The treatment of money thus provides a useful test of economic vision. Where money is merely a *numéraire* or accounting money, it indicates the presence of economic theory as nonsense-as-game, rooted in abstraction. By contrast, where money takes substantive, full-bodied form, it indicates the presence of uncertainty and a concern with the facts of human experience, in which life moves undirectionally from birth to death and in which biography is a branch of history.

In justification of a bias in favour of the latter vision in this study, we can demonstrate that it sits more easily with the main theme of the argument. Recall that Sewell's criteria for the existence of nonsense-as-game as safe refuge included the requirement that it should engage with and defeat chaos. That is, that preservation of the security afforded by nonsense-as-game depends on the maintenance of a one-and-one-and-one world by the exclusion of or defeat of the enemies of discreteness (Sewell, 1952, pp. 46, 53, 99). In economic terms, of course, this requires that money must be treated as being unimportant – and we are thus in an essentially classical microeconomic world.

If, however, we bear in mind the dual nature of the *Alice* texts, we can take a much more positive view of the relationship between order and disorder. That is, by reference to the maxims for life lived under sentence of death that we attributed to Alice, namely, that we must *inter alia* impose order and meaning on chaos (as well as be brave, keep smiling through our tears and find love – see above, Chapter 11), we could instead argue as follows. To seek to *escape* the world by way of taking refuge in nonsense-as-game is regressive and pessimistic; to seek to *change* the world by means of a policy based on theory appropriate to the world as we know it is progressive and optimistic. In this latter case the existence of uncertainty will mean that money is treated as being important. The theoretical positions delineated here and argued with reference to *Alice* are those held by our two main protagonists, Robertson and Keynes respectively. We shall deal with each case in turn: Robertson in the present chapter and Keynes in the next.

IX

Just as Robertson framed his economics texts with references to the source of his psychic security (the *Alice* quotations) so at the heart of his theoretical work lay the equivalent in terms of economics of the world of *Alice*: namely, the world of frictionless barter. In his successive major works Robertson carried forward this, the basis of Cambridge theorising (Robertson, 1915, p. 11; Robertson, 1926, p. 8; Tappan, 1928, p. 99; Robertson to Tappan *c*.1928 in C3/1/2 RPTC) as the sure foundation for his own work. But just as Lewis Carroll sought to bring more and more of his life within the protective confines of the world of nonsense-as-game, and by the same token destroyed the conditions necessary for the maintenance of his security, so Robertson, in attempting to modify classical theory in the interests of greater realism, found that his innovations threatened the integrity of his theoretical roots. There is, therefore, a parallel decline between the works of Carroll and Robertson with respect to the purity of the original vision. In Robertson's case the conflict between old certainties and new departures became apparent in the course of working out the theory of *BPPL*, and it was the way in which he resolved the conflict that made this his most important work and settled the way in which he would later respond to the challenge of the Keynesian Revolution.

X

The innovation that caused all the difficulties was, of course, the introduction of money and the role of the banks, which was intended to bridge the gap between frictionless barter and the real world. By introducing money additively Robertson sought to ensure that it would change nothing fundamental – that it would be seen to exacerbate rather than to be the cause of fluctuations. Nevertheless, given the role of the monetary system in the saving–investment process, money could be seen to have powerful effects.

These plainly did not accord with Robertson's notion of the relative importance of monetary influences in his theory. Consequently, his work on the short period suggested that policy should be directed to rendering money neutral, so as to make the economy approximate to the standard non-co-operative, non-monetary case in which fluctuations are at the justified or appropriate level. Of course, when money is neutral it is not important: it is not of substantive form and the theory consequently approximates to the one-and-one-and-one of nonsense-as-game.

In support of this line of argument we might recall that Robertson continued to refer to money as being unimportant, and in the 1948 edition of *Money*, in the new chapter (VIII) on the cycle, actually referred to money as mere 'counters' (Robertson, 1948b, p. 149), that is, money as *numéraire* or accounting money. Money, the enemy of nonsense, is kept firmly in its place.

But in thus seeking to maintain his sure foundations, his umbilical link with his intellectual origins, Robertson failed to exploit his insights into the real significance and importance of the short run. Because of his need to keep one foot in the timeless, long-run world of equilibrium, Robertson ultimately failed to reconcile the cycle and the trend.

XI

For all his penetration on the subject of the nature of human existence and the importance of the short run, Robertson failed for reasons already sufficiently rehearsed to achieve a concomitant revolution of theory. Only with the advent of Keynes is there a fundamental shift towards a theory of the economy based on premises appropriate to the realities of life. Though he came later than Robertson to a realisation of what was required, Keynes had less to lose by the overturning of established theoretical relationships. With his progressive approach to life, Keynes sought to engage with chaos and to impose upon it order and meaning. The achievement of this aim required a new economic vision and a new set of theoretical relationships: changes which must of necessity put him at odds with Robertson's chosen strategy of life.

PART V

Robertson, Keynes and the
Keynesian Revolution

23.　History versus equilibrium and the role of money

I

In 1939, in the midst of his dispute with Keynes, Robertson sought to distinguish his own theoretical antecedents from those of his adversary. In doing so, he obligingly confirmed the relevance of the argument of the previous chapter with the following explicit statement. Note both the recognition of there being two alternative 'visions' of the economy; and to which of them Robertson claimed to owe allegiance. The context, significantly as we shall see, is the question of the role of money in the theory of the rate of interest:

> In expounding any branch of economic theory, there are two courses open to us. We can start with a situation simplified to the greatest possible extent by abstraction and then gradually build up our theory by introducing successively the complications of real life. Or we can start by facing boldly all the complications of a momentary market situation, and then seek to discard the accidentals and distil the essentials. So it is with interest: we can begin by showing how it would emerge in a Crusoe economy, then introduce exchange, then money, or we can start with the actual world, with its (far from perfect) loan markets and its (far from orderly) monetary systems. (Robertson, 1939, in Hicks ed., 1966, pp. 150-1)

Despite Robertson's obvious exaggerations in describing what is meant by the notion of beginning from the characteristics of the real world, the correspondence with the distinction we made in the previous chapter is clear enough. What is really interesting, however, is the danger that Robertson sees as stemming from one of the two approaches to theory-making:

> The danger of this latter method is that the same motive which leads us to adopt it, namely, the desire to show ourselves at all costs 'in touch with real life', will tempt us to seek to produce an apparently simple result in circumstances in which simplicity involves the exaggeration of incidentals and the obscuring of fundamentals. (Robertson, 1939, in Hicks ed., 1966, p. 151)

But, of course, all depends upon where the 'fundamentals' are seen to reside. The danger of the alternative approach, which Robertson adopted, is two-fold. First, by reining in the power of money so as to make the theory of the real world conform to the characteristics of the other, abstract, world, Robertson was deceived as to (what Keynes would regard as) the true characteristics of the real world. Second, by being thus enabled to build theory additively, so that monetary factors would not disturb or usurp real relationships, he incorporated assumptions inappropriate for the real world. In particular he carried forward the classical, microeconomic view that the aggregate can be no more than the sum of the parts, with the result that the construction as complete contained a flaw that made it an insecure basis for policy-making.

Or, at least, it did on Keynes's view. While he recognised the value of Robertson's innovative attempts to sort out the relationships between saving, investment and money, he also claimed that Robertson's progress in the development of theory was hobbled by his unswerving devotion to Classical 'fundamentals'. And it was this view of Robertson's work – that it possessed the dual character of looking forward while always looking back – that provided the recurring theme of the Robertson–Keynes controversy. For it was what he considered to be the inappropriateness of Classical 'fundamentals', that is, the premises from which orthodoxy began, that provided the starting point for Keynes's attempt to develop a theory that would provide the basis for action to deal with real-world problems. In the *General Theory* (1936) he wrote:

> Our criticism of the accepted classical theory of economics has consisted not so much in finding logical flaws in its analysis as in pointing out that its tacit assumptions are seldom or never satisfied, with the result that it cannot solve the economic problems of the actual world. (Keynes, 1936, p. 378)

II

What the 'fundamentals' of Keynes's new economics were and how they differed from the classical premises adopted by Robertson can be explained in terms of the argument of the previous chapter. We do this by way of a series of quotations from the work of Joan Robinson, the Keynesian revolutionary who best understood the 'ambience' as well as the mechanics of the new order. In her essay 'What Has Become of the Keynesian Revolution?' (in M. Keynes ed., 1975) she succinctly stated the nature of Keynes's new vision and set out the implications for economic theory that flowed from it:

> Once we admit that an economy exists in time, that history goes one way, from the irrevocable past into the unknown future, the conception of equilibrium based on the mechanical analogy of a pendulum swinging to and fro in space becomes untenable. The whole of traditional economics needs to be thought out afresh. (p. 126)

Therefore, this means that: 'On the plane of theory, the revolution lay in the change from the conception of equilibrium to the conception of history' (p. 125). As a consequence of this:

> Keynes drew a sharp distinction between calculable risks and the uncertainty which arises from lack of reliable information. Since the future is essentially uncertain, strictly rational behaviour is impossible; a great part of economic life is conducted on the basis of accepted conventions. (p. 126; references in Keynes's works supporting this view are to be found in Keynes, 1936, ch. 12; Keynes, 1937, in *CW* XIV pp. 113-15)

In addition, and most important for present purposes:

> The existence of money is bound up with uncertainty for interest-earning assets would always be preferred to cash if there was no doubt about their future value. (p. 126)

This then provides the economic justification for money-holding 'outside a lunatic asylum' (Keynes, 1937, in *CW* XIV pp. 115-16); and raises the possibility that because there are circumstances in which money as an asset might be preferred to interest-bearing securities, changes in the demand for money could exercise an important influence on the level of economic activity.

We should notice that this effect is part of a wider phenomenon (see Fletcher, 1989a, ch. 1). In an uncertain economy the process of exchange between commodities – and especially intertemporal exchange – is facilitated by the existence of the institution of money in which the medium of exchange must by the same token also function as a store of value. Money promotes exchange by providing an information or communication system, which in the absence of the full information that would allow an 'ideal', optimum outcome under 'frictionless barter', gives the means by which independent agents might combine to seek the best outcome available. This, we should note, is the real meaning of the 'invisible hand'. Independent agents engage in self-interested voluntary exchange using the money asset to carry forward the value of the exchange between commodities and in so doing bring about the greatest satisfaction of the greatest number that is possible in the circumstances.

III

However, the idea that self-interested behaviour alone might not always bring the happiest results and that the above in fact constitutes only half the story is of the essence of Keynes's insight. The working out of this insight in terms of economic theory is what constitutes the Keynesian Revolution. It therefore plays the central part in what is to follow. At this juncture, however, it will help to restate the following propositions:

1. By locating the economy in time Keynes explicitly took account of uncertainty as an inescapable feature of economic life.
2. The existence of uncertainty means that in a social economy (that is, one consisting of more agents than Robinson Crusoe's) money will take substantive form and will be held as an asset alternative to commodities.
3. Conversely, the presence of substantive money betokens that this is an uncertainty economy which will have the following characteristics:
   (a) Production and consumption plans must be made on the basis of incomplete information so that economic activity will both be conducted on the basis of rules of thumb or convention (Keynes's 'pretty, polite techniques' – see Keynes 1937, in *CW* XIV p. 115) and will be subject to the effects of changes in expectations: that is, waves of optimism and pessimism.
   (b) Because money plays an integral (important) part in economic life, changes in the desire to hold it in preference to other, especially financial, assets under the influence of changing expectations will have important effects on the economy.

IV

The next step in the argument is to recognise that by locating the economy in time and allowing that 'history goes one way' Keynes was making economics relevant to the dimension of biography, the history of each of us that must come to an end. This would imply, therefore, a shift of emphasis away from the long run and towards the short run, in which events are acted out within the span of a human life. From the latter viewpoint economic success is bound up with present enjoyment ('jam today'), while building for a better tomorrow might mean sacrificing consumption in the interests of those we shall never see.

With respect to the link between the present and the future, we saw earlier (Chapter 16) that Robertson, using the means available to him, had drawn attention to the effects of the 'urge and urge and urge'; and that he had also, in effect, indicated the possibilities afforded by learned behaviour. We also saw how Keynes, galvanised by what he regarded as an unjust and foolhardy post-war settlement, had similarly sought to understand the human element involved in capital accumulation. His insights at that time were not so deep as Robertson's, and this was to remain the case. His intuition, however, unerringly led him to understand what was to be done and, in terms of theoretical development and in terms of optimism as to what might be achieved by action, Keynes went far beyond Robertson; his was the complete economics of learned behaviour.

In other words, we shall be arguing that the aim for Keynes, as it had been earlier for Robertson, was to modify the influence of primitive inducements in economic behaviour, with rational planned decision-making. In Keynes's case the inducements would be tamed and behaviour made subject to intelligent control and guided by the superior but disinterested wisdom of educated and enlightened public servants. The economic environment in which policy had to operate was characterised by uncertainty so that plans must be devised on the basis of theory that took account of the dark forces of time and ignorance. In all this, money would play a most important part.

V

Keynes's name had become indelibly linked with the short run from 1923, when he memorably reminded the world that '*In the long run* we are all dead'. But the book in which the phrase was used (*A Tract on Monetary Reform*) was concerned with the problems of short-run monetary management and not with deeper questions of human motivation. Similarly, in *ECP* Keynes had attributed the mainspring of economic growth to a vague notion of the collective subconscious of society. He never approached the intuitive grasp of what was to become evoeconomics, as Robertson had done. However, along the road to the *General Theory* he did attempt to put his finger on what might be the principal stimulant to economic endeavour; and to explore the economic relationship between the present and future generations. Because the answers he produced profoundly influenced his subsequent economic thinking, it will help if we examine the ideas briefly here.

They are contained in two publications: *The End of Laissez-Faire* (hereafter, *ELF*), a slim Hogarth Press production of 1926 which was based on two earlier lectures; and 'Economic Possibilities for Our Grandchildren' ('EPGC'), an essay of 1930 which had originated as a talk two years previously. If we could sum up the overall message that comes from the two of them taken together – a message that was duly incorporated into the *General Theory* – it is an optimistic one and one entirely appropriate to Keynes, the *Alice* figure.

Keynes argues that there is an economic 'promised land' in which material want is banished and which mankind should aim to reach. Human ingenuity and activity will supply the means. Practically, of the various extant systems of economic organisation, capitalism is the most successful and offers the best chance of economic advancement. It is, however, morally objectionable and offends against what should be regarded as an acceptable mode of behaviour. This is chiefly because of the nature of the principal motivation of those who do most to promote the increase of wealth, namely, the love of money. Nevertheless (*ELF*), by way of judicious modification and management, the benefits may be obtained with a much reduced appeal to the money motive. Alternatively ('EPGC'), on certain favourable assumptions the rate of capital accumulation over the ensuing century would be so great that the system would become redundant, and the money motive atrophy, as the majority of the population enters upon a new age of economic plenty with infinite leisure to cultivate more exalted pastimes.

In the *General Theory* this composite message was refined into the notion that the economic problem stemmed from a wholly artificial scarcity of capital and could be solved 'within one or two generations' by way, principally, of what Keynes described as 'a somewhat comprehensive socialisation of investment'. With the solution of the problem, not only would plenty reign but capitalism would have been purged of its most objectionable features. The money motive would be pursued for more reasonable rewards and, in particular, the class of passive interest-takers, the 'functionless investors' or '*rentiers*' who were kept in being by capital-scarcity, would disappear (see Keynes, 1936, pp. 374–8).

With respect to the question of the economic relations between the generations, on Keynesian terms investment and consumption can increase together in the short run, but when output becomes completely inelastic at full employment, a larger share for investment can only be accommodated by way of a lower propensity to consume. Therefore the question of the burden to be borne by the present generation so as to benefit a future generation belongs to *the long run*. This is because the speed with which the state of 'full investment', which will solve the economic problem for those who come after, will depend upon the extent to which those presently living would be prepared to restrict their own consumption (Keynes, 1936, pp. 220, 377). This point will be further dealt with below.

VI

Turning now to examine the arguments of the two publications in turn, the main points of interest for present purposes are as follows. If we recall the argument of Chapters 10 and 16, the most remarkable feature of *ELF* is the way in which Keynes makes use of Darwin's theory of evolution to explain the establishment of the doctrine of *laissez-faire*. It is, of course, a familiar idea in general but the interest lies in the comparison with the way in which we invoked natural selection, together with the gene theory, as a possible means of explaining the principal in-built motivation in human behaviour. Keynes does not detect the influence of an extra something that could be described by the gene theory (as will be confirmed when we turn to examine 'EPGC') but instead, as we hinted earlier, appealed to the money motive as the prime-mover in economic affairs. The full significance of this will become clear in the course of the argument below but for the moment we shall examine Keynes's ideas as they contain some features familiar from what has gone before.

Laissez-faire, the doctrine of non-intervention by government in economic life, became established in this country because it was supported by three contributory strands of thought:

> To the philosophical doctrine that government has no right to interfere (Bentham), and the divine miracle that it has no need to interfere (Paley), there is added a scientific proof that its interference is inexpedient. This is the third current of thought, just discoverable in Adam Smith. . . . (*ELF* in Keynes, *CW* IX p. 275)

It seemed also to be in accord with the facts of practical experience.

Adam Smith will play a larger part in the argument below, but William Paley, English theologian, we have met before (Chapter 10, above). The author of *Evidences of Christianity* (1794) and *Natural Theology, or Evidences of the Existence and Attributes of the Deity* (1802), he it was who argued that the nature of the earth, and all it contains, provides evidence of the truth of the biblical account of creation. It was against this sort of reasoning that Darwin had to fight – not least because it corresponded with his own earlier convictions – to get his theory of evolution accepted. Nevertheless, on Keynes's view, the triumph of evolutionism over creationism had the effect of strengthening the doctrine of free enterprise because, in Keynes's words, of Paley's 'idea of a divine harmony between private advantage and the public good' (*ELF* in Keynes, *CW* IX p. 274) which had helped to establish the doctrine of *laissez-faire* in the first place. Now, with the advent of Darwin, the idea was poised to become rooted in the national consciousness:

> By the time that the influence of Paley and his like was waning, the innovations of Darwin were shaking the foundations of belief. Nothing could seem more opposed than the old doctrine and the new – the doctrine which looked on the world as the work of the divine watchmaker and the doctrine which seemed to draw all things out of Chance, Chaos, and Old Time. But at this one point the new ideas bolstered up the old. The economists were teaching that wealth, commerce, and machinery were the children of free competition – that free competition built London. But the Darwinians could go one better than that – free competition had built man. The human eye was no longer the demonstration of design, miraculously contriving all things for the best; it was the supreme achievement of chance, operating under conditions of free competition and *laissez-faire*. The principle of the survival of the fittest could be regarded as a vast generalisation of the Ricardian economics. (*ELF* in Keynes, *CW* IX p. 276)

Thereafter, as Keynes argues:

> it was the political campaign for free trade, the influence of the so-called
> Manchester School and of the Benthamite Utilitarians, the utterances of secondary
> economic authorities, and the education stories of Miss Martineau and Mrs. Marcet,
> that fixed *laissez-faire* in the popular mind as the practical conclusion of orthodox
> political economy. . . .   (*ELF* in Keynes, *CW* IX pp. 279–80)

Of more immediate interest here, however, is the link with Darwin and
evolution, which so far has yielded a mechanism but no motive force. Keynes
supplied this by analogy. He argued first that the

> assumption . . . of conditions where unhindered natural selection leads to progress,
> is only one of the two provisional assumptions which taken as literal truth, have
> become the twin buttresses of *laissez-faire*. The other is the efficacy, and indeed the
> necessity, of the opportunity for unlimited private money-making as an *incentive* to
> maximum effort.   (p. 283)

And just in case the process appears rather tame Keynes makes clear what
natural selection combined with the money motive actually produces:

> It is a method of bringing the most successful profit makers to the top by a ruthless
> struggle for survival which selects the most efficient by the bankruptcy of the less
> efficient.   (p. 282–3)

With respect to the money motive he concluded:

> Thus one of the most powerful of human motives, namely, the love of money, is
> harnessed to the task of distributing economic resources in the way best calculated
> to increase wealth.   (p. 284)

And again:

> the essential characteristic of capitalism, namely the dependence upon an intense
> appeal to the money-making and money-loving instincts of individuals as the main
> motive force of the economic machine.   (p. 293)

VII

It was this motive, money-love, that Keynes substituted for what he took to be
the prime mover in natural selection (corresponding with one explanation
offered by Darwin himself), namely, sexual love (Keynes, 1926, in *CW* IX pp.
283–4, 293).

There are two points to note here. The first is that this was the role we attributed (Chapter 16, above) to the gene theory, the influence of which Robertson intuited though he could know nothing of its actual existence. It is clear that he detected something more than sexual love at work as he linked the 'procreant urge' with the notion of inter-generational sacrifice. The second is the simple fact that Keynes attributed to the money motive the role of stimulating economic activity and of promoting economic growth. This is what lay behind formal economic phenomena in explaining the expansion of a *laissez-faire* economy. In itself it would not, of course, be sufficient, but this is what, according to Keynes, will harness ability, aptitude, diligence and determination, to produce increased rewards.

It is not a surprising choice and might be seen to accord with common sense but it is remarkable for two reasons. The first is that it does confirm that money is to be considered as important and to play a central role in economic affairs. Keynes continued to hold this view though he detected both a positive and a negative side to the effect of the money motive. This leads on to the second reason, because one of Keynes's most significant innovations was to make money important in theory. And here lies an interesting double paradox: in classical (and Robertsonian) theory money was unimportant (a mere veil over the real economy which had at its back the world of frictionless barter); yet on a common-sense view it could be seen to move mountains. Keynes recognised this and, subsequently, his *General Theory* accorded to money much greater significance relative to real factors. At the same time, Keynes objected to the money motive on grounds of taste and wished to educate people (learned behaviour) to the acceptance of more modest and aesthetically less objectionable rewards.

Some of the areas of theory which would come to be transformed through greater awareness of the importance of money in Keynes's thought are indicated even at this early stage in the objections he registered to the 'fundamentals' or unreal assumptions underlying *laissez-faire*. Bearing in mind our discussion to date we find that Keynes touches on several familiar topics:

> The beauty and the simplicity of such a theory are so great that it is easy to forget that it follows not from the actual facts, but from an incomplete hypothesis introduced for the sake of simplicity. Apart from other objections to be mentioned later, the conclusion that individuals acting independently for their own advantage will produce the greatest aggregate of wealth, depends on a variety of *unreal assumptions* to the effect that the processes of production and consumption are *in no way organic*, that there exists a *sufficient foreknowledge* of conditions and requirements, and that there are adequate opportunities of obtaining this foreknowledge . . . Moreover, many of those who recognise that the simplified hypothesis does not accurately correspond to fact conclude nevertheless that it does represent what is 'natural' and therefore ideal. They regard the simplified hypothesis as health, and the further complications as disease. (Keynes, 1926, in *CW* IX p. 284; emphasis added)

Here we have the charge concerning inappropriate assumptions that in Keynes's view disqualified classical theory from dealing with the problems of the real world and which was to surface again in the *General Theory*. As components of this charge we can see that Keynes touched on three topics which have featured largely in our argument. First, failure to consider the possibility that the whole may not simply be the sum of the parts and the consequences for theory-making that it implies. Second, failure to take account of the fact that we do not live in a full information (frictionless barter) world. Later in the article Keynes referred to the 'greatest economic evils of our time' being the 'fruits of risk, uncertainty, and ignorance' (Keynes, 1926, in *CW* IX p. 291). Third, he criticised classical theorists for their method, or what we earlier referred to as 'vision'; that is, of beginning with an 'ideal' abstract model and then complicating it to simulate approximation to the real world, which suffers by comparison.

Finally with respect to *ELF*, the very title gives due notice that Keynes is going to ask the reader to think again about the possibility of a larger, justified role for the state in economic affairs. This role would be determined rationally by asking what things it was proper for government, of whatever form, to do and what things it was proper for government to leave alone (Keynes, 1926, in *CW* IX pp. 291–2).

Overall, unlike *ECP* which called for action in the aftermath of a wholly exceptional event, *ELF* questioned the accustomed assumptions on which ordinary economic affairs were conducted and pointed to a different and, what Keynes considered to be, superior way. Planning and management were clearly in the air.

VIII

If in *ELF* the call is for collective action to secure future prosperity, the call in 'EPGC' is for optimism, based on Keynes's prediction that the future will in fact take care of itself. He asks the reader to look beyond the cares of the present (1930) economic depression and to see it for what it is: a painful but necessary period of transition from one stage to another in the process of technical advance that has characterised the modern age.

The process that temporarily reduced the demand for labour and threw men out of work had in the longer term helped to raise living standards to previously unimaginable heights – despite a quadrupling of population over the relevant period. It had achieved this feat in tandem with an unprecedented accumulation of capital, which in turn stemmed from a fortuitous event in the sixteenth century (Drake's looting of Spanish gold) and the power of compound interest. On the basis of developments since, say, 1700 Keynes could confidently predict that the economic problem would effectively be solved – at least as regards absolute levels of necessity – within one hundred years. Thus, deprived of the problem that evolution had shaped him to solve, man would have to relearn his role and to move to the contemplation of ends, being no longer occupied with the means.

It is an interesting hypothesis. Keynes has combined elements from the arguments of *ECP* and *ELF* to arrive at the following summation. The evolution of man has been constrained by the need to solve the economic problem. The requisite striving is induced by way of appeal to the money motive. That is, avarice and usury will lead us to the promised land. Once there, however, learned behaviour will cause these objectionable features of capitalism to be replaced by the cultivation of 'the art of life itself' ('EPGC' in Keynes, *CW* IX p. 328).

Note here that, whereas in *ELF laissez-faire* was argued by *analogy* with the principle of natural selection, economics and evolution have now been made part of the same process. Sexual love has dropped out of account and economic necessity and the money motive supply the incentive to change. Clearly, survival has something to do with it but, given the mortality of man, there ought to be a leap in Keynes's thinking from this point to an understanding that survival is only through our descendants. But there is not: at this point Keynes goes beyond Robertson's notion of management of the short period as a means of maximising current enjoyment given the demands of the growth process, to argue that once we are in 'the lap of economic abundance' we should live wholly for the present! The economic problem it seems is solved for all time in *absolute* terms; and as for human need in *relative* terms, which Keynes recognises may be insatiable, he thinks of it only in the sense of a desire to be superior to one's fellow men. There is no suggestion that we may wish those who come after to be made *relatively* better off than ourselves. Evolution has come to an end, posterity is forgotten or (for the childless) does not exist, the process of capital accumulation which has improved the lot of each succeeding generation has ceased. Consequently:

> The accumulation of wealth is no longer of high social importance [neither, therefore, is the need for the incentive that drives it, so that] those walk most truly in the paths of virtue and sane wisdom who take least thought for the morrow. (Keynes, 1930, in *CW* IX pp. 329, 331)

What of the others? Keynes confirms the foregoing argument with the way in which he deals with the question of what is to be done about those still afflicted with the 'love of money'. Note that he makes clear that:

The love of money as a possession – as distinguished from the love of money as a means to the enjoyments and realities of life – will be recognised for what it is, a somewhat disgusting morbidity, one of those semi-criminal, semi-pathological propensities which one hands over with a shudder to the specialists in mental disease.   ('EPGC' in Keynes, *CW* IX p. 329)

Notice that the 'possession' of money is synonymous here with the accumulation of wealth (see Keynes, *CW* IX p. 329) and therefore must be synonymous at this stage of development of his thought with saving, as saving is the only way to accumulate wealth *in the sense that* the capital stock is growing and the community is becoming richer. Once economic abundance is attained and 'the accumulation of wealth is no longer of high social importance' (see above), money-love in this sense is to be condemned as an unhealthy obsession. Therefore, once we are living for the present age (the short run), saving is bad and spending ('money as a means to the enjoyments and realities of life') is good.

IX

In the *General Theory* Keynes sorted out the relationship between investment and saving. Now saving as a means to expansion only became meaningful at full employment, as the burden to be borne by the present generation as a means of improving the lot of a future generation. In the short run, spending was the means by which the economy might reach full employment, and this indeed was the concern of the whole of the main text.

But in the *General Theory* the lot of *any given* future generation is regarded in the same way as it is in 'EPGC': that is, that it would be improved willy-nilly by the outcome of a process by which the economic problem itself is solved. This would come about either through the agency of money-love ('EPGC') or through state action (*General Theory*). Either way, there is no appeal to the notion of a wish to benefit kin-selected descendants. In fact, in 'EPGC' Keynes seems expressly to disavow any such idea – and indeed to ridicule it:

Of course there will still be many people with intense, unsatisfied purposiveness who will blindly pursue wealth – unless they can find some plausible substitute. But the rest of us will no longer be under any obligation to applaud and encourage them. For we shall inquire more curiously than is safe today into the true character of this 'purposiveness' with which in varying degrees nature has endowed almost all of us. For purposiveness means that we are more concerned with the remote future results of our actions than with their own quality or their immediate effects on our own environment. The 'purposive' man is always trying to secure a spurious and delusive immortality for his acts by pushing his interest in them forward into time. He does not love his cat, but his cat's kittens; nor, in truth, the kittens, but only the kittens' kittens, and so on forward for ever to the end of catdom. For him jam is not jam unless it is a case of jam tomorrow and never jam today. Thus by pushing his jam always forward into the future, he strives to secure for his act of boiling it an immortality. ('EPGC' in Keynes, *CW* IX pp. 329-30)

X

The overall impression of Keynes that *ELF* and 'EPGC' together convey is one of optimism and of purposeful activity. In the long run things would come right but it would be at a time too far distant for the present generation to enjoy. In the short run they need not be passive victims of economic dislocation. The way forward was to identify the causes of the problem and then to overcome them by way, where appropriate, of collective action. These characteristics of Keynes's outlook found fullest expression in the *General Theory* but were given greater sharpness by an all-pervading sense of urgency. The promised land would still be reached but the process would have to be hurried along by state intervention. The short run becomes of overwhelming importance and the vast bulk of the book is devoted to an analysis of the working of a *laissez-faire* economy – again as the basis for state action to secure full employment.

Thus somewhat later in the day than Robertson but also more wholeheartedly, Keynes shifted the emphasis of economic theory and policy away from the long run and into the short run. Whereas Robertson, in the changed conditions of the world after 1914–18, had compromised and become more concerned to ensure that the new-found desire to maximise present enjoyment was not at the expense of adequate provision for future expansion, Keynes had moved irrevocably in the other direction.

XI

Keynes's uncompromising emphasis on the short run – on economics in the dimension of biography – was the counterpart of his attitude to both the long-run future and to the past. With respect to the first, he was childless and seemed not to detect the influence of the 'procreant urge'. With respect to the second, he was willing to learn from those economists who had gone before and to use their ideas to justify his own theories where appropriate; but he was not willing to be bound by them. In *ELF* he wrote:

A study of the history of opinion is a necessary preliminary to the emancipation of the mind. I do not know which makes a man more conservative – to know nothing but the present, or nothing but the past. (*ELF* in Keynes, *CW* IX p. 277)

In the years leading up to the publication of the *General Theory*, this view comprised two important elements. The first was the perception that received theory was unable to explain and to solve the current problem of unemployment of resources. The second was the willingness uninhibitedly to wreak such changes as might be necessary in established theoretical relationships between key variables. It was an attitude that placed Keynes firmly in the camp of the radical economists – the heretics and dissenters from orthodoxy – as he was proudly to acknowledge.

XII

We have now identified three main strands in Keynes's approach to economics: the first was his optimism, his confidence that all would come right or could be made to come right; the second was his faith in the efficacy of (collective) action as a means to achieve desirable goals; the third was his willingness to produce new theoretical constructions as necessary to serve as the handmaid of chosen policy – even where this meant overturning established relationships. With respects to the last, Danes (1979, ch. 4) has described Keynes as a 'revolutionary' in his approach to the development of economic doctrine in contrast to Robertson the 'evolutionary', and has used the distinction as the basis for an explanation of the conflict that arose between them. However, while this is useful as a first approximation, it smacks too much of simple choice among alternative methods or tactics to provide a full explanation. In the case of Robertson, of course, we have been at pains to show that there is more to it than this.

We should also note that there are other strands that go to make up Keynes's approach to economics than those to which we have given prominence. Moggridge, for example, one of Keynes's principal biographers, has drawn attention *inter alia* to the important parts played by intuition and by Keynes's belief in the power of rational argument. He has also pointed out that Keynes inherited the Cambridge tradition of regarding economics as a moral science: that is, one in which subjective factors – motives, judgements and values –played a full part (see Moggridge, 1993, ch. 2). These might usefully be borne in mind as we proceed, but for present purposes the most relevant points for consideration are those upon which Keynes is distinguished from Robertson, and here, as already indicated, it is the prevailing sense of optimism, the unremitting advocacy of plans and policies and the willingness to move theoretical heaven and earth to find the justification for them. This was Keynes the economist as *Alice* figure, progressive rather than regressive, who figuratively speaking kept smiling through good times and bad, who sought to impose order and meaning on chaos and meaninglessness and who, somewhat late in life, found love.

XIII

Superficially Keynes's life had much in common with that of Robertson (see Skidelsky, 1983, 1992; Moggridge, 1992). Both came from solid Victorian middle-class backgrounds, replete with intellectual stimulation and nurture; both had glittering careers as King's Scholars at Eton; both won open scholarships to Cambridge; both were elected to fellowships at Cambridge colleges; both became prominent economists.

The similarities made the differences all the more significant. Whereas Robertson's family were of the Established Church, Keynes's had a history of non-conformism and radicalism. At Eton, while Robertson was outstanding as a classicist, Keynes also shone at mathematics: his Cambridge scholarship was in mathematics and classics. At Cambridge, Robertson triumphed in the stiffly competitive environment of Trinity but ever wished himself elsewhere. Keynes, by contrast, felt sure that he must go to King's (which was, as we have seen, the object of Robertson's yearning) and duly flourished in its freer intellectual climate.

After graduation Robertson stayed on at Cambridge to write his fellowship dissertation and was then taken up by the war. Keynes, however, looked outside Cambridge and, unconstrained by international upheaval (he was seven years Robertson's senior and graduated in 1905), sat the Civil Service examination and wrote his fellowship dissertation while working in the India Office in London. This established a pattern, with Robertson, apart from his brief sojourn at the LSE and at the Treasury, wholly committed to academic life in Cambridge; and Keynes dividing his time – and his life – between Cambridge and London. Along with his teaching duties as a fellow of King's, Keynes was active in the financial world of the City of London and was ever on the heels of government in his quest to influence policy.

The pattern was repeated at the cultural level, with Robertson's artistic bent finding expression in his appearances on the Cambridge amateur stage; while Keynes, more worldly, was a member of Bloomsbury, an avant-garde group of intellectuals, writers and painters, based originally in Gordon Square in London but increasingly also in the summer months in Sussex. The core of the Bloomsbury Group was made up of Keynes's friends and near-contemporaries from Cambridge (including Lytton Strachey, Clive Bell and Leonard Woolf) together with the children of Sir Leslie Stephen, doyen of literary London, some of whom became linked by marriage to the Cambridge friends (Vanessa Bell and Virginia Woolf).

The essence of Bloomsbury lay in the artistic expression of unconventional ideas and beliefs and in unconventional modes of behaviour. Its inspiration and 'bible' was *Principia Ethica* (1903), a work by the Cambridge philosopher G.E. Moore, which sought to answer fundamental questions relating to the concepts of goodness and of the good life. Apart from the ideas themselves and the timing of their appearance, much of the tremendous impact the book achieved can be attributed to the personal qualities of the author, whose transparent honesty, endless quest for clarity of expression and meaning, and analytical scrupulousness inspired passionate devotion and loyalty among his pupils and followers. Aspects of the argument of *Principia Ethica* play a pivotal role in our present concerns and we shall meet the book again shortly.

The final and perhaps most significant difference between Robertson and Keynes was that Robertson never formed the lasting relationship that might have brought him the love and affection he craved. Keynes, by contrast, who in his earlier years had been promiscuously homosexual, met a Russian ballerina who became the love and delight of his life. They were married in 1925 when Keynes was forty-two.

XIV

Why Keynes was an *Alice* figure and why he was progressive rather than regressive in his outlook depend ultimately on factors too deep to identify. Proximately, however, all depends upon his attitude to life lived under sentence of death. Was death to be regarded as a purely negative event that renders endeavour and achievement futile, or as completion, a natural journey's end? For Robertson, all points to it being the first of these; but for Keynes, it was indubitably the latter. Though he had no belief in the existence of God (and in this was possibly more positively atheistic than Robertson) and therefore no 'Hope of Glory', an awareness that death was the end did not also mean that the value of life was in any way diminished. In this he was at one with the young Cambridge philosopher Frank Ramsey, as Rossana Bonadei has noticed (in Marzola and Silva, 1994, pp. 42–3, 54–5). Here Keynes's general outlook is seen to be epitomised in the following quotation from Ramsey's work which Keynes included in the 'Anthology' he appended to his obituary of his colleague at King's who had died at the age of twenty-six:

> My picture of the world is drawn in perspective and not like a model to scale. The foreground is occupied by human beings and the stars are as small as threepenny bits. I don't really believe in astronomy, except as a complicated description of part of the course of human and possibly animal sensation. I apply my perspective not merely to space but also to time. In time the world will cool and everything will die; but that is a long time off still and its present value at compound discount is almost

nothing. Nor is the present less valuable because the future will be blank. Humanity, which fills the foreground of my picture, I find interesting and on the whole admirable . . . You may find it depressing; I am sorry for you . . .   (Keynes, 1933, 1951 in Keynes, *CW* X p. 345)

In interpreting this passage in Keynesian terms, Bonadei uses language and employs another quotation strangely evocative of our earlier discussion of the Heraclitan element in Robertson's work:

What a man can do, he should do in a relatively short space of time, given that, as Keynes was fond of saying, 'in the long run we are all dead'; in this agreeing with Ramsey for whom 'the present is no less valuable because the future will be blank'. On the contrary, destiny and the present come together in a flux which is made and remade by the actions and decisions of those who have been able to live in the present without reservations. Doing good deeds means being proactive subjects in that 'flux', even while bearing in mind that every action takes its place in a world of probability and is acted out on a reality which has meanwhile changed and is no longer the context for that action.   (Bonadei in Marzola and Silva eds, 1994, pp. 54–5; see also p. 43)

As death is to be regarded as completion so life itself becomes the arena in which fulfilment is to be achieved, as is revealed in the following quotations from Skidelsky's major biography of Keynes. There is first the conviction that time is to be usefully filled with purposeful activity. Skidelsky comments: 'Maynard rushed through life with the clock ticking in his ear, yet rarely gave the impression of being hurried' (Skidelsky, 1983, p. 84); a sentiment that is graphically illustrated by the words with which Keynes abruptly terminated a letter to his father from Eton: 'In a minute and a quarter my light has to be put out and I have many things to do before then' (Skidelsky, 1983, p. 96).

Finally, free of thoughts of purposelessness and futility and of any fear of a Day of Judgement, Keynes found his inspiration in a philosophy that saw virtue in aesthetic experience and a life that could be lived for the present moment:

Keynes never needed a Jehovah because he had never experienced despair . . . his own religion of sweetness and light and optimism based on [G.E.] Moore's *Principia Ethica* had inoculated him and his Cambridge friends from that experience of a moral chaos which fuelled [T.S.] Eliot's quest for moral authority. (Skidelsky, 1992, p. 517)

Finally, Skidelsky puts his finger on the reason why the book was able to play this role (and so to be of significance for present purposes) by being part, as it were, of a process of seeking to come to terms with the loss of old certainties:

Moore's *Principia Ethica* was a product of a time, place and personality. In philosophic terms, it can be seen as a continuation of the enterprise of moral philosophy from the point where Sidgwick had left it, which was in a mess. It had inherited the problems which had given rise to Sidgwick's project, and tried, where Sidgwick felt he had failed, to overcome them – the problems of a Godless universe ushering in a 'cosmos of chaos', of the inadequacy of Hedonistic Utilitarianism, of the demand for a philosophy which would lighten the burden of conventional morality.   (Skidelsky, 1983, p. 134)

In providing a means of coming to terms with life in a Godless universe, meaningless and uncaring, and supplying a morality to replace outdated convention, *Principia Ethica* was a handbook for *Alice* figures and a philosophical guide for revolutionaries.

24. Keynes and the philosophy of revolution

I

The publication of *Principia Ethica* had a profound effect on Keynes and the book was to have a lasting influence on his life and work. Ultimately it inspired some of the theoretical innovations that led to the Keynesian Revolution. More immediately it stimulated Keynes to write his fellowship dissertation on a philosophical subject: probability. This work, eventually published as *A Treatise on Probability* (1921), was until recently treated by economists as an oddity, as something outside Keynes's main field of activity. In recent years, however, interest in Keynes's philosophical writings has blossomed and keen controversy has arisen as to the nature and extent of the relationship between Keynes's philosophy and his economics (see, for example, Skidelsky, 1983, ch. 6; 1992, ch. 3; Lawson and Pesaran, 1985; Carabelli, 1988; O'Donnell, 1989; Moggridge, 1992, chs 5, 6; Carabelli, 1992, 1994).

II

To an embryo *Alice* figure, Moore's book could not help but be appealing, providing as it did the justification for a life lived consciously and intensively for the present moment. Death, the afterlife and rewards in Heaven had no part to play in this new 'religion' that created, as Keynes said, 'a new heaven on a new earth'. Nevertheless, in Moore's treatment of the central ethical question concerning 'goodness', Keynes was troubled by what he saw as a potential conflict between 'being good' and 'doing good', in as much as Moore's concept of organic unities seemed to offer the possibility that an obligation could rest on an individual to be bad – for the sake of the good of the universe. The most apposite example would be that provided by the paradox implied by the notion of private vices–public benefits, as we shall see. In retrospect Keynes claimed to have been very selective about what he took from Moore: exalting the unworldly, 'religious' aspects and wilfully ignoring his moral teaching: that is, ethics in relation to conduct. Given that an *Alice* figure is by nature active, purposeful and creative (in the sense of building anew rather than accepting passively what is, and that the *General Theory* is the work of an *Alice* figure, it is obvious that important changes must have taken place during the intervening years. It is difficult to summarise a complex debate but the following generalisations could perhaps be justified.

First, there was the shift from espousal of the philosophy of passivity to advocacy of action. That is, under the influence of the extended process of writing *Probability* (the first version of the fellowship dissertation appeared in 1907; the book not until 1921) and of external events such as the war of 1914–18 and the Slump, Keynes eschewed the life of contemplation and became a campaigning reformer who sought to save the world on rational principles.

Second, Keynes changed his attitude toward rules of behaviour. From a position of outright repudiation of the obligation to obey general rules – to the extent that he claimed to be an 'immoralist': that is, to have the right to be his own judge in his own case – Keynes came to accept the value of conventional behaviour as a rule-of-thumb response to uncertainty.

Much of the controversy surrounding the question of Keynes's beliefs and how they changed has centred on 'My Early Beliefs' ('MEB'), a paper Keynes read to a meeting of the Memoir Club in September 1938 (reprinted in Keynes, *CW* X pp. 430–50). The paper is controversial because in it, Keynes, claiming to speak on behalf of himself *and* his contemporaries (some of whom were present at the meeting), sought to explain Moore's views as expressed in *Principia Ethica*; and to recapture the spirit in which the book was received and the influence it had on the outlook of those who first read it. We have introduced some of Keynes's views in the foregoing paragraphs.

III

For present purposes, what is of interest in 'MEB' is not whether Keynes was accurate in his interpretation of Moore's beliefs and doctrine, nor yet whether he had faithfully represented the reactions of his contemporaries. Rather, it lies in what Keynes thought he had taken from Moore, as recollected in the period of the *General Theory*. The following familiar passage from 'MEB' was intended by Keynes to epitomise the new religion:

> Nothing mattered except states of mind, our own and other people's of course, but chiefly our own. These states of mind were not associated with action or achievement or with consequences. They consisted in timeless, passionate states of contemplation and communion largely unattached to 'before' and 'after'. Their

value depended, in accordance with the principle of organic unity, on the state of affairs as a whole which could not be usefully analysed into parts. For example, the value of the state of mind of being in love did not depend merely on the nature of one's own emotions, but also on the worth of their object and on the reciprocity and nature of the object's emotions; but it did not depend, if I remember rightly, or did not depend much, on what happened, or how one felt about it, a year later, though I myself was always an advocate of a principle of organic unity through time, which still seems to me only sensible. The appropriate subjects of passionate contemplation and communion were a beloved person, beauty and truth, and one's prime objects in life were love, the creation and enjoyment of aesthetic experience and the pursuit of knowledge. Of these love came a long way first.   (Keynes, *CW* X pp. 436-7)

The first thing to notice is that 'states of mind' by their nature exist in the present and not in the remote future. For an economist this would imply that what is relevant is an economics that produces results in the short run, while we are still alive and able to enjoy them, rather than in the long run when we are all dead.

Second, there is also here an indication as to the means by which those results are to be obtained; a means, that is, that involves looking outside conventional ways of thinking. Twice in the passage Keynes makes reference to 'the principle of organic unity', which he understands to mean 'the state of affairs as a whole which could not be usefully analysed into parts'. In fact he refers to it four times in 'MEB' (see also *CW* X pp. 437, 441) and there are, in addition, indirect allusions on page 442 and in the quotation he includes from Moore on pages 443-4. The principle of organic unity, it might be concluded, loomed relatively large in what Keynes thought he had taken from Moore. Its significance will become apparent as we examine Moore's own understanding of the principle as set out in *Principia Ethica*.

IV

An indication of the importance of the principle of organic unity in Moore's scheme of thought is provided by the form in which he chose to introduce it. While it is part of Moore's general style of exposition to emphasise key words or even phrases by having them set in italics, in this case the scale of italicisation is unique. On two successive pages, first half a sentence and then a whole sentence of italics are devoted to a definition of the striking paradox that the value of a whole may be different from the sum of the values of the parts that compose it. Thus:

There is . . . a vast number of different things, each of which has intrinsic value; there are also very many which are positively bad; and there is a still larger class of things, which appear to be indifferent. But a thing belonging to any of these three classes may occur as part of a whole, which includes among its other parts other things belonging both to the same and to the other two classes; and these wholes, as such, may also have intrinsic value. The paradox, to which it is necessary to call attention, is that *the value of such a whole bears no regular proportion to the sum of the values of its parts.*   (Moore, 1903, p. 27)

And then:

> *The value of a whole must not be assumed to be the same as the sum of the values of its parts.*   (Moore, 1903, p. 28)

Having established his point, Moore provided reinforcement by way of repetition in similar terms but without italics (see, for example, pp. 29, 32, 36 (twice), 184).

In these instances, just as in the case of the passages quoted, the important word is 'sum': the value of the whole is different from the sum of the parts. In other words, the nature of a whole cannot be comprehended by way of the one-and-one-and-one of which it is composed; and Moore is clear that any attempt to assess the value of organic wholes by way of summing will give rise to the 'grossest errors' (p. 36). For present purposes we might say that if we choose to inhabit a world which by definition goes one-and-one-and-one, and that we approach a different world (the real world?) which does not conform to our chosen paradigm on the mistaken assumption that it does, then we may indeed commit the 'grossest errors' of which Moore warned.

That an organic whole was a concept based on a paradox that was not apparent to common-sense observation (and therefore must be introduced with such a flurry of italics) means that it is a new and literally unorthodox way of thinking; that is, one that involves looking outside conventional and usual ways of thought. It involves, therefore, the kind of relation that would be discovered by and acceptable to one whose outlook was progressive and indeed revolutionary; it would conversely not be acceptable to one whose outlook was regressive and fundamentally orthodox.

Moore is careful to point out that the 'peculiar relation between whole and part' that he was seeking to define had 'not hitherto been distinctly recognised or received a separate name'. He therefore 'appropriated' terms already in use among philosophers who claimed to have received inspiration from the work of Hegel. These were, as we now know, 'organic whole', 'organic unity', 'organic relation': all terms actually applied to wholes which possessed as a property the relation to which Moore sought to draw attention (Moore, 1903, pp. 29, 30).

V

Having established the nature of the organic relation, the next step is to look more closely at the wholes themselves. And here it is first necessary to notice that wholes as entities can possess intrinsic value: 'what is asserted to have intrinsic value is the existence of the whole' (p. 29; also pp. 26-7). Of greatest interest for us is the class of what Moore refers to as 'unmixed goods' (as against 'evils' and 'mixed goods').

These 'unmixed goods' which are themselves 'complex wholes' ('highly complex *organic unities*') and which exist in great number and variety, were the centrepiece of Keynes's recollection in 'MEB' of what he took to be important in Moore. They are to be regarded not only as in themselves 'by far the most valuable things we know or can imagine', but also as forming the object of all human endeavour 'and the sole criterion of social progress' (Moore, 1903, p. 189).

We have already seen that Keynes feared a possible conflict between 'being good' and 'doing good' and that it was to the former only – the religion of contemplation – that he gave admittance. In this, his recollection of 'states of mind' and of the things that produced them accurately caught Moore's conception. In Moore's words, these 'most valuable things' were 'certain states of consciousness which may be roughly described as the pleasures of human intercourse and the enjoyment of beautiful objects' (p. 188). And again:

> No one, probably, who has asked himself the question, has ever doubted that personal affection and the appreciation of what is beautiful in Art or Nature, are good in themselves; nor, if we consider strictly what things are worth having *purely for their own sakes*, does it appear probable that any one will think that anything else has *nearly* so great a value as the things which are included under these two heads. (pp. 188-9)

And on the same page: 'personal affections and aesthetic enjoyments include all the greatest, and *by far* the greatest, good we can imagine'.

Later we are reminded that:

> I began this survey of great unmixed goods, by dividing all the greatest goods we know into the two classes of aesthetic enjoyments, on the one hand, and the pleasures of human intercourse or of personal affection, on the other. (p. 203)

And finally, in summing up the argument of the chapter, Moore reaffirmed that: 'Unmixed goods may all be said to consist in the love of beautiful things or of good persons' (p. 224).

That the unmixed goods consist of 'certain states of consciousness' (Keynes's 'states of mind') serves to remind us that we must be aware of the objects of our love, whether persons or things and that it is not sufficient for them to be like Keats's musk rose, 'blowing in a green island far from all men's knowing'. And more relevant for present purposes is that this idea of engagement with the objects of love must not merely be cognitive but also emotional: that is, there must be both consciousness and feeling.

Now, 'love', 'beauty', 'emotion': these three we have met before, in our discussion of the enemies of nonsense-as-game; and, it will be recalled, the greatest of these was love: love being particularly potent as a destroyer of the discrete one-and-one-and-one nature of nonsense in the creation of the big 'One'. In *Principia Ethica*, the equivalent of the big 'One', an entity that does not correspond to the sum of the 'ones' that comprise it, is the organic whole. And the parallel is completely general as, apart from unmixed goods, Moore also delineated classes of mixed and unmixed evils and of mixed goods, each of them composed of 'highly complex organic wholes' which necessarily involve an emotional component (see Moore, 1903, pp. 207–22).

VI

The significance of all this for the present argument lies in the equivalence/ parallel between the big 'One' and the notion of an organic whole: in the relation between the whole and the parts; and what the parts in each case represent.

We recall that nonsense, which as game provides a refuge from the 'harshness of human destiny' for those of a regressive disposition, is composed of individual 'ones' which together are no more than the sum of the 'ones'. Nonsense-as-game and the refuge it offers is threatened by certain states of mind or consciousness induced by emotion (love) or the contemplation of beauty. These must be excluded if the refuge is to be preserved, for under the influence of these factors the essential, atomistic, nature of nonsense is lost and is replaced by the big 'One' which by definition possesses a value different from the sum of the 'ones'.

For Robertson a refuge was provided by the world of *Alice*, which being a nonsense world was also composed of 'ones'. The parallel in Robertson's professional life lay in the frictionless barter world of Marshallian microeconomics. Upon this rock Robertson built his church, with successive additions to the structure being made to follow the original ground-plan, leaving the foundations undisturbed. In particular, money was to be seen as unimportant and to be rendered neutral by policy.

Now the forces that threaten the world of nonsense are also component elements in the formation of organic wholes, which subsume the parts of which they are composed. For Keynes the idea of a whole the value of which was more than the sum of the parts was to have a profound influence on his philosophical work and more particularly also on his economics. It was Keynes's economic 'organic wholes' that were to pose a threat to Robertson's sense of security, as represented by the world of atomistic 'ones', sufficient to cause an open breach between them. The reason for this will be set out below but it can be stated briefly as follows.

Keynes's economics was economics set in history, which meant that it was necessary to take account of uncertainty (and thus to recognise the importance of money). Orthodox economics could no longer be sustained as it began from premises which did not take account of these factors. Under the influence of contemporary economic events Keynes sought to provide an explanation of unemployment within a traditional framework and incorporating innovations suggested by the work of Robertson and Wicksell. When this attempt ended in a logical impasse Keynes was forced to recast the theory in the form with which we are now familiar.

At the centre of the economics of uncertainty was the principle of effective demand based on expectations. At the centre of this again lay twin concepts that reversed causation in Classical economics and made income a determinate of expenditure. These concepts found their inspiration ultimately in the principle of organic unity, in the sense that the wholes they produced could not be obtained by summing the 'ones' to which they were applied. The first was the paradox of thrift, a variant of the fallacy of composition, which showed that it was not possible to increase investment and saving by saving more at some prior date. The second, the obverse of the first, was the multiplier, by which an increase in autonomous investment would cause income to rise to a level just sufficient to produce a quantity of saving equal to the new investment and so restore equilibrium.

These two concepts, the first, as it were, negatively and the second positively, showed that it is investment that gives rise to saving, rather than vice versa as argued by the Say's Law inspired Classical theory of the capital market. In doing so, they demonstrated that the economic system taken as a whole is more than the sum of its parts: that is, that the behaviour of the *macroeconomy* cannot be inferred from the outcomes of the behaviour of the individual elements (households and firms) that compose it. The premises of classical economics are overturned and with them the theoretical structures, no matter how elaborately contrived, erected upon the foundations they provided. The economic world of nonsense-as-game is subverted, as the traditional ordering of variables disappears and the refuge of security it offered is violated and laid waste. To those who, like Robertson, took this world as their professional and psychological starting-point, such a development could not but appear a dire threat which must at all events be resisted.

VII

The parallel we have drawn between the principle of organic unity and the devices Keynes employed to defeat Say's Law is based on arguments (derived from our main theme) that find support in the work of those who have examined the whole question of the relationship between Keynes's philosophy and Keynes's economics: the so called 'new Keynesian fundamentalists'. This group claim that links exist between Keynes's early philosophical writings and his later economics that establish him as a philosopher-economist. In seeking to show that in much of his work Keynes was constructively engaged with the problems of decision-making under uncertainty, the new fundamentalists disarmed much of the criticism levelled against the old Keynesian fundamentalists, whose insistence on the all-pervasive effects of uncertainty seemed in some eyes to offer little scope for any economic theorising.

The question that has principally preoccupied the new fundamentalists is whether there is continuity between Keynes's earliest philosophical views and his principal economics works, particularly the *General Theory*, or whether there was a radical shift after the publication of *Probability* in 1921. The accompanying debate has been surveyed by Gerrard (in Gerrard and Hillard eds, 1992, pp. 80–95).

VIII

For present purposes, this resolves itself into the issue of whether Keynes was an organicist or an atomist in his later thought. The majority of commentators have followed the organicist interpretation and in doing so accepted that Keynes changed his earlier view that induction (the method of *Probability*) and organicism cannot be made compatible.

The evidence usually adduced in support of or in opposition to the notion of Keynes's continued commitment to organicism now constitutes a canon of references. Purely philosophical writing is rare after *Probability*, so commentators must make what they can of what is extant. Different factions emphasise the importance of different texts or interpret the same texts in different ways.

One of the most celebrated references in the canon is to the passage from Keynes's memoir of F.Y. Edgeworth, which he included in the 'Lives of Economists' section of *Essays in Biography* (1933, *CW* X). It is one that has been variously interpreted but the actual wording would seem to bear out the majority view that it is clear evidence of Keynes's organicism:

> The atomic hypothesis which has worked so splendidly in physics breaks down in psychics. We are faced at every turn with the problems of organic unity, of

discreteness, of discontinuity – the whole is not equal to the sum of the parts, comparisons of quantity fail us, small changes produce large effects, the assumptions of a uniform and homogeneous continuum are not satisfied. (Keynes, *CW* X p. 262)

Carabelli, who is a leader among those who take the majority view, interprets the passage (though she slightly misquotes Keynes's words: see Carabelli, 1988, p. 153) to refer to:

The rejection of the 'atomic hypothesis' in the moral sciences and in psychology was to be the natural premise of the rejection of the individualistic approach which had dominated the end of the nineteenth century. . . . (Carabelli, 1988, p. 153)

The same point is taken up by Gerrard, who makes it more explicit and more apposite for present purposes. He draws the crucial distinction between that which is appropriate to the natural world and that which is appropriate to the world of man in society and so reveals the link with a main theme of this study (Gerrard in Gerrard and Hillard, 1992, pp. 86–7, 89).

This dual approach recalls our discussion of the world of *Alice* and of the ambiguity surrounding the meaning of the *Alice* texts, which, at different levels, provide both a delightful refuge of nonsense and at the same time a horrifying glimpse of a post-Darwin world, Godless and uncaring. As we pass 'through and through' and our perception of the meaning of the texts changes between levels – as for, example, with a 'trick' diagram like the Necker Cube, which can appear in turn both solid and hollow – we become aware of an important paradox. The paradox is that while the natural world is clearly atomistic, so that the atomic hypothesis is the appropriate means of analysis, it is also necessary that for Carroll's texts to work at the level of nonsense-as-game they too must be composed of 'ones'. Should love or any of the other agents of 'Oneness' enter, the refuge is destroyed and man must become an *Alice* figure, having to *create* meaning and order and to 'find love' as a means of maintaining psychic security.

The parallel for economics is, as we have already seen, that a theory of the economy that describes a purely abstract, full-information world of atomistic barter will appear to provide both a source of comfort and security in itself and a sure foundation for theory and policy in the real world. When confronted with the 'reality' of man in history, however, the need for society and its cement, the institution of money, as a means of organising for survival and progress in the face of uncertainty, will cause the old foundations to crumble. The theory of the monetary production economy overturns established relationships and imposes a new disposition of key variables. The trick as before is to see familiar, observed phenomena from a new perspective, so that the reality of the relationships between them is revealed. In this case the perspective glass is not love (emotion) or the contemplation of beauty but money and the role it plays in economic life.

IX

The particular relevance of Carabelli's work for the development of this line of argument can now be demonstrated, for she not only traces a direct link in Keynes's work between organic unity in philosophy and the fallacy of composition in economics, but also offers an explanation of the way in which money itself produces organicistic relationships. The following quotations illustrate the point. First, the implications of organicism (recall Moore, 1903, above) for a theory of the whole economy:

> For Keynes, a monetary macroeconomy is a system characterised by 'complexity', possessing attributes such as organic interdependence among variables, non-homogeneity through time and space, non-numerical measurability, physical heterogeneity, openness, incompleteness, indivisibility, secondary qualities, contingency and change.   (Carabelli, 1992, pp. 3–4)

In recognisable terms, this means:

> Complex magnitudes are indefinable in logical terms since the reduction of them to more simple terms is impossible. They cannot be reduced to simple terms without falling into logical fallacies and paradoxes. The fallacy of composition is well known to economists. The reduction of one theory into another . . . In economics the parallel is the theoretical reduction of macroeconomics into microeconomics. This reductionist strategy has involved the search for the micro-foundations of macroeconomics, the aggregation of microeconomics into macroeconomics and an emphasis on disaggregation.   (Carabelli, 1992, pp. 3–4; see also p. 21)

The attempt to establish the existence of the 'micro-foundations' of macro-economics is essentially a product of Classical thinking and can be seen as a way of trying to reinstate the certainties of equilibrium, atomistic, economics. By contrast, Carabelli makes explicit the importance of organicism and the fallacy of composition as an element in Keynes's revolutionary analysis:

> Keynes's attitude was strictly connected with his view of society as an organic unity. As a consequence of this attitude, a distinction between a logic relative to the individual, to his motivations and actions, and a logic relative to the collectivity as a whole had to be introduced. What was a private vice, might be a Mandevillian public virtue . . .

In particular:

> The substance of the doctrine of the 'fallacy of composition' played a crucial role in Keynes's theory of knowledge (in his concept of qualitative and organic probability) in his view on ethics. Its most known formulation was the so-called paradox of saving of *The General Theory*. For a single individual a means of accumulating was to abstain from consuming and allot his abstinence to saving. However, this attitude would have been foolish for the collectivity as a whole. (Carabelli, 1988, p. 213; see also pp. 143–4)

It is obviously the case that for any economist who disagreed with the notion of organicism in economics or, more pertinently, was constrained to disregard or fail to recognise its significance, the redisposition of variables by Keynes, together with the changes in the causal relationships between them, could not but seem at best illogical and at worst perverse and pointlessly novel. The relevance of this for the interpretation of Robertson's reaction to the Keynesian Revolution is clear enough.

X

We can move even closer to the point of the analogy we have drawn between alternative interpretations of the *Alice* texts and alternative approaches to economics by looking next at Carabelli's explanation of the relationship between organic interdependence and money, which she traces through a succession of Keynes's early and later writings. The essential link lies in the medium in which we find it most appropriate to express ideas (Carabelli, 1988, pp. 167–72).

Following Keynes, she points out that economic agents communicate through money, so that money rather than goods is the standard language. As a language, however, it is not to be thought of as being made up of mere signs which are 'neutral and transparent carriers of meaning'. Money is not, as Classical economics would have it, merely a neutral link between transactions in real things and real assets and does not therefore constitute a veil that can be lifted off the real world of goods. Instead, because 'money plays a part of its own' rather than being a mere referential sign (Keynes, *CW* XIII pp. 408–9; see also *General Theory*, chs 13–14), Keynes's language of money was more similar to ordinary language than to formal language. There is, therefore, a 'precious link' between this view of money and Keynes's notion of ordinary language as being the economist's peculiar tool of analysis (chosen as such despite his manifest proficiency in mathematics).

Therefore, because money is in common use in an economy and because moreover 'it plays a part of its own and affects motives and decisions', it is not merely a means to obtaining a desirable end but becomes an end of desire in itself. Money could consequently become a fetish. Keynes refers to Freud's explanation of money – love (see *CW* VI pp. 258–9; and *General Theory*, p. 374) and we recall our discussion of the phenomenon in the previous chapter. Here, however, money becomes a fetish as a consequence of man's inescapable condition. To possess money is a means of lulling 'disquietude' in the face of uncertainty: 'our desire to hold money as a store of wealth is a barometer of the degree of distrust of our own calculations and conventions concerning the future' (Keynes, *CW* XIV p. 116).

XI

In a later essay (in Gerrard and Hillard eds, 1992, pp. 3–31) Carabelli is more explicit about the relationship between money and organic interdependence – a continuing element in Keynes's thinking. The essential idea is that money and things cannot be isolated from each other. A change on the part of money will give rise to changes on the part of commodities: relative exchange values are disturbed so that the resulting money price changes are a complex outcome of the organic interplay between these influences. Because of the organic relationships involved, money can no longer be regarded as a mere *counter* that is neutral in its relations with commodities. Money, that is, has real effects.

Note further the implications of money being non-neutral as a unit of account (rather than as a medium of exchange), which arise because of its connection with the institution of central importance in the organisation of a monetary economy through time, the money contract. First, it is this that leads to Keynes's choice of the money wage as the standard of measurement in a monetary economy. Second, it invalidates the Classical, quantity-theory distinction between real and monetary levels. This is because there is no absolute and homogeneous unit in which to measure real aggregates (collections of goods and services, with particular problems relating to the measurement of capital through time). Therefore, quantitative macroeconomics is only possible if analysis is conducted in money terms, on the grounds that money is a homogeneous unit of quantity and therefore can be used to measure heterogeneous bundles. Keynes does not say why units of money are homogeneous, but Carabelli offers an explanation based on the parallel with language:

> We can advance the hypothesis that money is to economics the equivalent of ordinary language to society. Money is, by convention, the economic ordinary language . . . Therefore the intrinsic homogeneity of money stems, paradoxically, from its organic nature. Money, as ordinary language, works as a whole, not through its atomic components: this gives rise to complexity. Further, within the established convention, it allows intersubjective, societal and economic communication. (Carabelli, 1992, pp. 23–4)

It is of course immensely valuable for present purposes – given the importance of the argument from *Alice* – to have what we might regard as *sound technical reasons why money by its very nature gives rise to organic unity*. Money is the equivalent of love (or beauty) in its power to destroy the essential quality of atomism, whether of the Classical theory-behind-a-theory or of the refuge-world of nonsense-as-game. The next step is to consider the implications of this for the dispositions of the key variables and for the causal relationships that existed between them.

XII

If there is no reason to believe that the world is other than atomistic – composed of independent ones – then common sense would suggest that the whole will be no more than the sum of the parts and that aggregate outcomes can be adduced from the observation of individual behaviour. In this case the question of causality can hardly arise and the key variables assume their familiar dispositions as the foundations of Classical economics. Say's Law is upheld and economic success goes hand-in-hand with psychic security.

If, on the other hand, the significance of organic interdependence is perceived, the question of causality and of the dispositions of the key variables must be considered afresh. Immediately, old certainties are undermined and psychic security is threatened.

Money will, of course, play an important part in shaping the new order of things, once its true nature and role are perceived. If, on the one hand, money is to be, by convention, the ordinary language of economics – the common currency of economic relations; and on the other hand is, as Keynes insists, to play a part of its own and affect motives and decisions, then money will provide both the information system around which an undirected economy is organised and the motive force that drives it towards greater activity and greater rewards. That is, not only does money provide the system but also the incentive of increased rewards in the form of the means of universal command. Money-love brings rewards to isolated agents through the process of exchange and so draws them together into civil society. The many are thus made one, just as the atomic ones of Sewell's nonsense become one big 'One' under the influence of love and the perception of beauty.

The economic significance of this view is that the institution of money provides both a recognised means of exchange and, by greatly facilitating the process, actually encourages exchange and, therefore, the prosperity of society. The danger is, as we have seen, that in a state of uncertainty money must of necessity act as a store of wealth, as part of its function as a medium of exchange. Changes in the demand to hold money for asset purposes could as a consequence give rise to undesired consequences for output and employment.

XIII

There is, however, a previous question to be answered, with perhaps more fundamental implications. That question is not, how shall we dispose of saved income – whether in the form of money or financial assets – but how much of any new increment of income shall we save? For it is this question that is directly relevant to the role of money as a means of communication and agent of combination. What, we must ask, will be the effect on the system of a decision by one person to save more; and of all persons to save more? Will the outcome of the second follow directly from the outcome of the first – such that the level of aggregate saving is the sum of the saving done by each person taken separately? The answer will be different accordingly as the system is atomistic or organic. It was Keynes's major insight to see that the first situation exists only in the abstract – by assumption – and that in the actual world the two-sidedness of transactions will ensure that the system is organic.

Notice that this feature of economic relations is brought into prominence by recognition of the significance of the role of money. This is not only because money facilitates exchange by acting as the universal medium but also, as we have just seen because money is the unit of account that reacts organically with the relative exchange values of commodities to produce uniquely monetary values in a monetary economy.

Notice also that the point being made here is not simply one of exactness of measurement. Without money there would be no meaningful aggregates. Money is the non-neutral unit of account that allows the calculation of aggregates as *monetary* outcomes of the organic process. In a barter economy, aggregate wholes as measures of national income and so on cannot properly exist due to the lack of an absolute and homogeneous unit of quantity. Hence organic unity and its economic equivalent the fallacy of composition is essentially a feature of a monetary economy in Keynes's sense, not of one in which money is only a veil.

In a barter-type economy by contrast, that is, one in which money plays no significant part, there are only individual commodities linked by relative exchange values. The classical view (at least tacitly – though see the references to micro-foundations given by Tappan: together with the reply by Robertson in C/3/1/2 RPTC) would be that the system was atomic and that the whole would, therefore, be the sum of the parts. This conclusion would resolve questions of causation and disposition.

Economic success in this system is guaranteed at bottom by a simple formula which contains a hint of asymmetry. This arises in the following way. If, on the one hand, there is an extension of supply, by Say's Law the necessary extra demand with which to take it up automatically comes into being. If, on the other hand, there is a reduction in demand for a product due to a change in tastes or preferences, a change in exchange values will divert the now unallocated piece of demand elsewhere. In either case the level of demand is maintained and there can be no general oversupply.

XIV

It was Keynes's great insight, the essence of the Keynesian Revolution, to understand that the really significant point that relates to the role of money as means of communication and agent of combination concerns the pattern in which combination is achieved. Because the system is organic, economic success is no longer guaranteed by the outcome of a process in which the sum of individuals act in a self-interested way. The existence of organic relationships means that outcomes now depend upon the following two considerations: (a) what are known as *unintended consequences*; (b) whether self-interested behaviour involves *spending* or *saving*.

With respect to the notion of *unintended consequences*, we shall need to delve back further into the history of thought, and consideration is better deferred until we have looked more closely at the Keynesian Revolution as a whole. But with respect to (b), the point to be made is that Classical economics confused them – indeed, the idea that good comes indifferently from self-interested spending or saving is summed up in the familiar slogan that saving is spending – whereas Keynes distinguished clearly between them. Now spending was seen as expansionary and as creating wealth and, therefore, as A Good Thing; whereas saving was seen as contractionary and as destroying wealth and therefore as A Bad Thing. Keynes reached these conclusions, as we saw earlier, on the basis of both a negative argument (the paradox of thrift) and a positive argument (the multiplier relationship linking investment to saving via income) which were reverse and obverse expressions of the same organic relationship.

Early in 1932 Keynes suddenly realised that as the level of income increased, consumption would rise to claim only a fraction of the increase, leaving a residual to be devoted to saving. From this distinction between the marginal propensity to consume and the marginal propensity to save – and between the marginal propensity to save and the rate of saving – stemmed the laws governing expenditure and saving, which hitherto he had perceived only intuitively.

From this crucial insight flows all that is distinctive in Keynes's new economics. As a consequence it can be seen to have played a vital part in the events of the early 1930s that led up to the publication of the *General Theory*. It, therefore, also looms large in the controversy over the question of the sequence in which the elements of the new theory came into being. The whole matter will be discussed at length in Chapter 28 below.

XV

The next step is to give perspective to the preceding discussion, and to provide a context for what is to follow, with a summary account of the principal changes that constituted what we refer to as the Keynesian Revolution.

Before this, however, it will be helpful to reinforce and develop an idea touched on earlier: namely, that what Keynes achieved depended on his obtaining a new perspective that allowed him to see established and familiar phenomena in a different light, with the result that an alternative, revolutionary explanation could be offered of the manner in which those phenomena were brought into being. Such an idea is not, of course, without parallel in the development of human knowledge and Keynes's achievement is not unprecedented. We are reminded in particular of the complete reversal of outlook – given the evidence of common-sense observation – occasioned by Kepler's revelation that the earth was in orbit round the sun. The closer parallel, however, is with Darwin, whose scientific theory of evolution seemed to run contrary to the biblical account of the origins of the world and whose ideas have played an important part in the argument of the present study.

Like Darwin, Keynes saw what contemporaries saw and firmly believed and expounded orthodox explanations. Like Darwin, he was forced to battle for his insights against what amounted to the established religion in which he and his colleagues had all been brought up. And in the process of conceiving his new theory, Keynes too went on a voyage which proved to be more protracted than Darwin's circumnavigation in HMS *Beagle*. Keynes's voyage of preparation was the writing of *A Treatise on Money*, the completion of which, as with Darwin, led to a period of intense thought and of writing that produced the book which, in some respects, parallels Darwin's own.

The change in perspective involved in moving from old to new was, as suggested earlier, similar to that produced by those puzzle pictures that simultaneously present two entirely different images. Another parallel is with the interpretation of the Heraclitan flux: is it the case that all is change but appears unchanging; or that all is unchanging but appears to change? Perhaps most appropriate of all, given the argument from organic unity, is the Christmas game in which the object is to join the dots in a 3 × 3 pattern of nine, using only four lines and without taking the pencil from the paper and where the solution involves being prepared to think beyond the limits psychologically imposed by the pattern of dots.

In sum, therefore, on the above argument major advances in intellectual history take place when an enquirer places a new construction of meaning on a set of acts and relationships known to all but hitherto interpreted in an orthodox way that is constrained by vestiges of belief, convention, familiarity and common-sense. As a consequence, advance or the lack of it becomes a function of the struggle between mutaphobia and mutaphilia. Keynes, pragmatic, goal-orientated – an end-state liberal (see Clarke, 1993) – was unrestrainedly prepared to entertain such change as was necessary. Robertson, ambivalent, embraced elements of both and this led him in his professional work to attempt the sort of compromise that characterised his life in general. Hence his so-called evolutionism, with new departures constrained by the need for a reference back.

XVI

But what of motive for change? On the above view, advance is not a function of idle speculation but of pressing need to find the answer to a major question or solution to a current problem. Even Robertson began his career with a burning need to dig down to find the cause of things and so provide a rock-like foundation for his life and work. Thereafter, however, Robertson placed himself above the strife and took up his natural role of cloistered critic, ever ready to expose follies of thought or policy. The consequence was that his theory, worked out in the *Study* and elaborated in *BPPL*, never changed except in the form in which it was cast and the emphasis given to its different parts. With no pressing desire to bend the ear of policy-makers and with the need always to stand on his foundations, Robertson excluded the challenges that could lead to change. It is in this context that the impact of the *General Theory* on Robertson's world must be seen.

Keynes, by contrast, influenced by the post-war settlement at Versailles and the economic problems faced by Britain which culminated in the Great Depression and lacking any feeling of need to preserve 'ancient monuments', felt all the urgency proper to a campaigning political economist to get things right at whatever cost. The relevant elements of the revolution he produced can be stated as follows (see Fletcher, 1989a, chs 4, 6, 7, 9–15):

1. It was a revolution of principles, that is, of theory rather than of policy.
2. It was necessary because of the perceived conflict between orthodox economists' policy recommendations, for which there was a widespread consensus of support, and their theory.

3. The substance was contained in *The General Theory of Employment, Interest and Money* (1936):

(a) It was a 'general' theory in the sense that it applied to situations both of full employment and of underemployment equilibrium and, directly related to this, it was a complete theory in as much as it took account of the effects of both spending and of saving. This point will be taken up below.

(b) 'Employment' is now a function of the level of income and not the real wage; income is determined by the level of aggregate demand, consisting in Keynes's *laissez-faire* economy of consumption plus investment; investment is the more active component and is related to the consequent change in expenditure and income by the multiplier relationship; the real wage is determined as an outcome of the process and adjusts via short-run costs and the price level.

(c) Equilibrium in the system is at the 'point of effective demand' (POED), determined at the intersection of the aggregate demand and aggregate supply schedules; entrepreneurs seek to maximise profits by attempting to find the POED and employ labour on the basis of their predictions; fluctuations in employment, therefore, occur due to errors of prediction and execution and because the POED is itself shifting; in order to explain this central tenet of his approach Keynes distinguished between states of long- and short-period expectations and in the former examined the cases of shifting, stationary and static equilibrium.

(d) Effective demand replaces Say's Law as the central underlying principle governing the working of the economy.

(e) Interest is no longer determined by the classical forces of productivity and thrift and no longer works to balance flows of investment and saving in the capital market; instead, investment and saving are equilibrated by fluctuations in income and the equality of saving and investment becomes a condition of equilibrium income; this leaves interest to be determined in the money market; it becomes proximately a monetary phenomenon and equilibrates the supply and demand for money.

(f) The treatment of 'money' stems from Keynes's insistence that we cannot understand the working of a monetary economy by utilising the theory appropriate to a barter economy:

● Money is no longer a 'veil' which must be lifted so that we can examine the reality within.

● Money is now full-bodied and has an asset-demand, justified in both theory and practice; changes in the demand for money can influence economic activity.

- The money-using world of reality is an economy subject to uncertainty; uncertainty influences the state of economic activity through its effects on investment-planning and the demand for money.

(g) Interest and money are brought together in Keynes's speculative motive for holding money; through uncertainty as to the future course of the rate of interest, speculators move between holdings of money and financial assets, the variety of opinion determining the actual course of the market rate.

(h) It is no longer correct to think in terms of rigidities and imperfections as preventing the economy from reaching its hypothesised, natural full-employment equilibrium; rather, the economy moves in shifting equilibrium under the influence of changing long- and short-period expectations, with no one 'correct' level of income and employment to which it might gravitate.

XVII

As a vehicle for the promulgation of these ideas the *General Theory* has been adjudged less than perfect. Critics have thought the book untidy and badly organised, and the exposition of the argument it contains marred by obscurity, inconsistency and actual error. Various reasons have been put forward for this, but the seat of the problem would seem to be that the *General Theory* is very much a picture of Keynes's revolution in progress:

> The real problem with the *General Theory*, setting out as it did to overturn existing ideas, was that it had to face in two directions at once. It looked backwards to orthodoxy, to explain its inappropriateness for dealing with the real world and, at the same time, forwards, to construct a model of the new economics. In any revolution the process of transition from old to new will often appear to outsiders as confused, messy and inconclusive – but this, of course, is more a function of the transitional process itself than of the degree of clarity of the revolutionist's vision. (Fletcher, 1989a, p. 29)

In support of this idea we do, of course, have Keynes's own testimony that the composition of the book had been for its author 'a long struggle of escape . . . from habitual modes of thought and expression' (Keynes, 1936, in *CW* VII p. viii: bearing in mind that the 'habitual modes' from which Keynes struggled to escape were for Robertson sacrosanct foundations that must at all costs be preserved).

The notion of the *General Theory* as a book that looks backwards as well as forwards is also reflected in the organisation of the argument. The order in which the topics appear in the book is significant in that it reflects both (a) the relative importance of the targets at which Keynes directed his attack; and (b) the order in which Keynes put his theory together.

With respect to the first of these, the principal objective is to dispose of Say's Law and to install the principle of effective demand as the main organising concept. This cardinal point is accordingly dealt with (in Chapters 2 and 3) in the first of the six books that comprise the *General Theory*. The implication is that the target is not the quantity theory of money, as claimed from the Classical viewpoint by Friedman (1972, p. 919), who bases his case for 'counter-revolution' on just this argument. On the contrary, Keynes does not put the quantity theory firmly in its place until Chapter 21 (in Book V), although the seeds of doubt are sown at the end of Chapter 15 (in Book IV).

The backward–forwards feature is also discernible as a tactic in the detail of the argument. When dealing with the particularly sensitive topics of wages, saving and interest, Keynes first sets out and criticises what he takes to be the Classical position before going on to develop his own theory.

With respect to the second of the two points (the order in which Keynes put his theory together), the rate of interest is not introduced until *after* the chapters dealing with effective demand, expectations, the definitions of income, saving and investment, and much of the sequence devoted to the determinants of the components of aggregate demand. With these elements firmly in place, the intimate relationship between interest and money that is such a distinctive feature of the *General Theory* is explored in Chapters 13, 15 and 17 (in Book IV). To make the point quite clear, the rate of interest as a monetary phenomenon is introduced after the principle of effective demand and not before it.

The question of the order in which Keynes dealt with the rate of interest when building his own theory is a matter of considerable import, as we shall see. It is bound up with the question concerning the paradox of thrift as the key feature distinguishing Keynes's economics from that of Robertson. This will become clear as part of the process of tracing the advance of Keynes's thought between the *Treatise* 1930) and the *General Theory* (1936), as we make a Keynesian reply to Robertson's criticism of the Keynesian Revolution.

25. Terms of engagement

I

By the 'Robertson–Keynes controversy' we mean the differences of opinion between the two protagonists about saving, investment and the rate of interest (what they are and how they are related), that surrounded the publication of Keynes's two principal economics books, the *Treatise* and the *General Theory*. The written record of the differences is to be found in a number of journal articles, together with a much larger private correspondence conducted during the late 1920s and the 1930s (collected in Keynes, *CW* XIII, XIV, XXIX). The oral exchanges, the 'many a long talk, chasing the truth' to which Harrod makes respectful reference in his biography of Keynes (Harrod, 1951, p. 371) are, of course, altogether lost.

Sufficient evidence is extant, however, to indicate that quite apart from other possible sources of distress, such as the unfortunate misunderstandings that arose between Robertson and Keynes during the period of negotiations for the American loan, the effect of the academic controversy itself was to leave a dark and indelible stain on Robertson's life. The later editions of Robertson's textbook *Money* and, perhaps more disturbingly, his lectures delivered after Keynes's death (published in Robertson, 1963a), all contain explicit references that indicate just how deeply the matters at issue had touched him. And this conclusion holds true even after taking full account of the continuing irritant manifest in the form of Joan Robinson, Keynes's most combative and perspicacious supporter.

II

The reason why the controversy touched Robertson so deeply is, of course, the subject-matter of this study. We can distinguish two root causes. The first and minor cause was Robertson's determination to assert his independence in the face of Keynes's all-pervading and overweening influence that threatened to engulf him. This factor was first discernible in the style of Robertson's rewriting of *BPPL* following Keynes's bullying intervention.

The second and major root cause reinforced the first and loomed increasingly large as Keynes became, in Robertson's eyes, ever more radical as he proposed changes in economic theory that pointed to inherent weaknesses in the foundations of classical economics. To Robertson such changes posed a threat both to his professional and, more fundamentally, his personal security. He regarded them as quite simply inadmissible and set himself implacably to oppose them. Because Robertson's strategy for opposition mirrored his own method of economic theorising – that is, to give prominence to the parts at the expense of the whole – it provides a revealing guide to his own theoretical limitations and the temperamental constraints that imposed them. This last provides an answer to a question implicit in comments passed on the controversy by prominent commentators.

III

The question is: given that the controversy had such a searing effect on Robertson, was it all in some sense justified: was it worthwhile? The answers so far supplied by commentators would suggest that it was not and that what Robertson embarked upon was in fact a vast and expensive diversion that took him away from his own work – with consequent loss to the profession.

The first to suggest that disputing with Keynes was having deleterious consequences was Pigou. Writing to Keynes in 1938 he lamented that:

> Dennis has been spending years meticulously examining and criticising Mr Keynes on this and that, instead of getting on, as I think would be much better, with constructive work of his own.   (Keynes, *CW* XXIX p. 177)

Later, in 1953, Wilson was similarly to regret that:

> The defects of Keynes's theory of the rate of interest have engaged Professor Robertson's attention for many years – too much so, perhaps, because he has tended to neglect his own vastly important theory of the connection between economic progress and the trade cycle.   (Wilson, 1953, p. 556)

Wilson had been invited by the editors of the *Economic Journal* 'to attempt a survey of Professor Robertson's present views on effective demand and the trade cycle' but had found his task 'extremely difficult and perhaps impossible' on account of the fact that there existed

> no detailed positive statement of the position Professor Robertson would now adopt, and his additions [to work published much earlier] consist in the main of a criticism of Keynesian economics and a vindication of earlier views on these matters.   (Wilson, 1953, p. 553)

It is, therefore, in the rather negative role of provider of clues to Robertson's own views that Wilson regards the controversy:

> Their famous controversy could not, it is true, be avoided, even if we had some more detailed account of Professor Robertson's present views, but without the latter it must be given a more central position than might otherwise seem appropriate; for we must try to extract from his critical survey of Keynesian ideas some inferences about the extent to which the earlier Robertsonian theories might now be revised if their author were to set himself that task. (Wilson, 1953, p. 554)

Thin gruel indeed, especially as he refers to Hicks's famous demonstration of the logical equivalence of the loanable funds and liquidity preference theories (Hicks, 1939, pp. 153ff) 'to designate the controversy at least in part, a bogus one' (Wilson, 1953, p. 556).

For his own part, the context in which Hicks gave his demonstration was the conviction that in reading the *General Theory* he had been led back to a position on saving and investment very close to that occupied by Robertson. And it is in this context that he remarked that:

> Disputes about the meaning of saving and investment may appear to be arid, but they are in reality of immense importance, because they involve decisions about definitions which determine the whole course upon which theory will subsequently proceed. (Hicks, 1942, pp. 54, 55)

Forty years later, however, in seeking to clarify the state of mind in which he wrote the above, Hicks was more explicit in his views on the Robertson-Keynes controversy, which were very close to those of Pigou and Wilson:

> I felt myself to be temperamentally much closer to him than to the Keynesians, from whom he had separated himself so sharply after 1936, or a bit earlier. But my position was on the Keynes side of his. I regretted the feud, for such indeed it had become. I really wrote the review for him, to persuade him to turn away from the polemics which I had felt had become sterile, and to turn to more constructive work, on the basis of what I felt he had already achieved. (Hicks, 1982, p. 127)

The overall conclusion, therefore, is pessimistic: the dispute had served little useful purpose and had, moreover, kept Robertson from his own work; he had undertaken what in retrospect must be judged an ill-advised course of action.

IV

The question which must arise, however, and to which no one has so far given an adequate answer, is, why did he do it? Do we not need to look beyond Austin Robinson's idea of Robertson as the dutiful and suffering 'keeper of

Keynes's conscience' (see Robinson in M. Keynes ed., 1975, p. 13)? The answer should be clear enough: the Keynesian Revolution posed such a powerful challenge to Robertson, both professionally and personally, as to seem to threaten his very existence. Extraordinary lengths would, therefore, be justified in the battle to defeat it. Nothing else could explain the extent of the effect on Robertson, which was such that his dissent was left on record (in *LEP*, 1963) to his dying day.

In the event, Robertson had to swallow the bitter pill of watching the triumph of Keynesian economics and he died too early to witness its demise. He therefore took comfort in the findings of those who saw beneath what they believed to be the froth of Keynes's 'short-term' theorising, the still, permanent truths of Robertson's more orthodox position; and in pointing to those who, having embarked on Keynesian-style adventures, could be seen to have made a welcome return to the fold (as with Kalecki; see below, Chapter 28).

V

The course of the controversy has been faithfully traced in Professor Presley's *Robertsonian Economics* (Presley, 1978, Part II). This thorough piece of investigation yields us a double benefit. First, because Presley's study reveals an interpretation of *Keynes's* economics that is based on Robertson's own understanding of the nature of and relationship between the key variables. This has been subjected to close, critical scrutiny and reinterpretation in the present writer's *The Keynesian Revolution and its Critics* (Fletcher, 1989a). Second, and by the same token, Robertson's criticism of Keynes provides insights into his *own* thinking which acts as a very useful check on conclusions arrived at by alternative means in the present study.

In our own approach to the controversy we shall seek to interpret events in the light of our main theme. This interpretation is introduced in two parts or stages. The first is to notice that if we abstract from the detail of the controversy, one salient feature emerges which is of great interest for present purposes: the main focus of the debate was on the theory of the rate of interest. The writings of the principal commentators support this view, as we shall see. It is also implicit in the structure of the debate itself. This is despite the fact that, as we noticed earlier, Robertson's theory of fluctuation gave no explicit role to the rate of interest – beyond that of acting as a 'traditional' means for the banking sector to regulate borrowing and dishoarding. Not until 1934, two years before the publication of the *General Theory*, did Robertson *recast* his theory in interest-rate terms – and then as a response to Keynes's formulation in the *Treatise* and Hayek's in

Prices and Production (1931). The theory of interest he set out was never substantially to change and the 1934 version is compatible with the treatment in his published lectures (Robertson, 1963 chs IV–VI) as Presley has noticed (Presley, 1978, p. 134).

This was the 'loanable funds' theory of interest, of which Robertson was recognised to be the chief exponent. It was around loanable funds theory that opponents of Keynes came to rally after 1936 when rival camps of supporters took up positions in the liquidity preference versus loanable funds debate, which was destined to run and run. The course of this debate is not of consequence for present purposes, though the feature that provides the essential difference between the two theories, as argued in Fletcher (1989a, 1989b), will play a central role in the argument below.

The next stage is to notice that because Robertson recast his previous argument in interest rate terms, the new form retained the characteristics of the old. Thus real and monetary factors entered into the determination of the rate of interest in the same order of relative importance or precedence as they had into the theory of fluctuation. In both, real factors played the more fundamental role, while monetary factors, though they produced transitional real effects, were essentially subordinate. This means that, for Robertson, the 1934 exposition of his theory in interest rate terms was seen as a valid alternative expression of the same ideas as were contained in *BPPL* and which were similarly founded on sure classical foundations.

It followed that Robertson's 1926 distinction between real and monetary variables would carry over to the alternative interest-rate exposition. Thus the important natural rate, at which investment is equal to voluntary saving, must be determined by the real forces of productivity and thrift; while the market rate, which oscillates about the natural rate, must be determined by monetary forces (bank finance and dishoarding, giving rise to forced saving). In this way Robertson maintained in his interest theory the dispositions that had always marked his theorising and which formed the basis of his professional identity and personal psychic security.

It was for this reason that what he saw as Keynes's 'purely monetary' theory of interest posed such a threat to Robertson, overturning as it did the established order of precedence and denying the validity of inherited Classical foundations. Consequently, it is unsurprising that this aspect of Keynes's new economics should be seized upon as that which most obviously and blatantly violated the established order, by dropping the idea of the rate of interest as a real phenomenon and by making money predominant. Money, which should be unimportant – to maintain the one-and-one-and-one integrity of Classical theory – was now given an importance that Robertson attributed to its role in the determination of the rate of interest and which we attributed to the presence of uncertainty (see above, Chapter 22).

VI

The Keynesian theory of interest thus became the principal object of attack for Robertson and for the Robertsonians, who must choose to see the liquidity preference theory as taking precedence in Keynes's scheme – and indeed as having been developed first in chronological order.

As a corollary of this, Robertson's theory of interest, in which traditional Classical forces played the more fundamental role, had to be seen as the main object of Keynes's assault on neo-Classical and, therefore, Classical economics. By the same token, Keynes had to be seen to be determined to deny any influence of those same Classical forces on the rate of interest – as a means of releasing real forces for other employment. That is, with the rate of interest seen as a purely monetary phenomenon, real forces could be set to determine output and employment in a way that denied Say's Law and presented the opportunity and justification for state intervention in the economy in a most unClassical fashion.

In seeking to resolve the main issue identified in the above overview (the relative ordering of real and monetary variables), two questions will be seen to be of critical importance. The first concerns the essential difference between the liquidity preference and loanable funds theories, in which all hinges on Robertson's and Keynes's understanding of the nature of saving, the relationship between saving and investment and the finance of investment. The second concerns the nature of interest itself and specifically turns on alternative views about the relative order in which Keynes introduced the various elements of his new theory. That is, the question of whether the theory of interest was developed earlier or later than effective demand, saving, investment and the multiplier (dealt with below, Chapter 28). The two questions are of course intimately related.

There is abundant evidence to suggest that the rate of interest is widely regarded as central to the Robertson–Keynes controversy, also that the reason for this is not fully recognised. The most relevant contributions are: Presley (1978, pp. 181–2); Danes (1979, ch. 6); Cairncross (in Harcourt ed., 1985, p. 135); Bridel (1987, pp. 166ff); Goodhart (1989, p. 107); Moggridge (1992, pp. 592–3, 594, 596); Skidelsky (1992, pp. 590–3).

The message they convey is quite clear. Keynes's attack on classical economics was directed against the theory of interest based on the real forces of productivity and thrift (investment and saving). By developing a purely monetary theory of interest, that is, one in which, it is claimed, the interest rate is not affected by changes in investment and saving, these real forces could be employed elsewhere for the construction of Keynesian economics. This is the message, in various degrees of explicitness, of commentators sympathetic to Robertson. The deeper implications which flow from the reversal in importance of the ordering of real and monetary variables are not detected. They were, nevertheless, clear enough to Robertson, even if not articulated in so many words, as is evident from the way in which he dealt with the rate of interest in his own writings.

VII

Robertson's views on the rate of interest are dealt with in three parts: first, the pre-*General Theory* recasting of the analysis contained in *BPPL* in interest-rate terms; second, his comments published in the aftermath of the Keynesian upheaval; and third his definitive judgement, delivered after much cogitation and reflection which he left for posterity.

VIII

With respect to the first of these, Robertson's recasting was accomplished in two well-known articles that we have met before. In the first, 'Saving and Hoarding' (Robertson, 1933), which was concerned with definitions and intended as a preliminary to the second, there was a return to the use of 'certain strange and barbarous language' that he had eschewed in 'Theories of Banking Policy' (Robertson, 1928b, p. 24). Thus we are back in the private universe bounded by lacking and dislacking, stinting and splashing that he had created in *BPPL*. Here, now, intervals of time are measured in Robertsonian 'days', which govern the disposal of earned income.

This esoteric treatment is one sign that Robertson is, in the 1930s, restating and refining his own Robertsonian economics in the face of the possible danger of disorientation posed by new modes of expression. This interpretation is confirmed when we look at the second of the two-article series, 'Industrial Fluctuation and the Natural Rate of Interest' (Robertson, 1934), which was intended:

> to bring together (1) the concept of saving developed in the paper which precedes this, and (2) the attempts which have been made to analyse cyclical fluctuation in terms of a divergence between the 'natural' and the 'market' rates of interest. (Robertson, 1934, p. 64)

As a comment on this statement, Hicks, as editor of the volume in which the essay was reprinted, adds a footnote pointing out that the idea of analysing fluctuation by reference to natural and market rates of interest is 'the common (Wicksellian) element in Keynes's *Treatise on Money* (1930) and Hayek's

Prices and Production (1931)' (Hicks ed., 1966, p. 64 n. 2: see also Laidler, 1995).

Faced with the new terminology and the new mode of analysis, Robertson protects himself by entering the arena preceded by a warning of the dangers of losing one's bearings together with a reaffirmation of the validity of his own definitions. This takes the form of a characteristic quotation from *Alice*:

> 'This must be the wood,' she said thoughtfully to herself, 'where things have no names. I wonder what'll become of *my* name when I go in? I shouldn't like to lose it at all, because they'd have to give me another, and it would be almost certain to be an ugly one. But then the fun would be, trying to find the creature that had got my own name!'

The quotation, which stands at the head of the article, is from *Through the Looking Glass*. In the annotated edition Martin Gardner makes the following apposite comment:

> The wood in which things have no name is in fact the universe itself, as it is apart from symbol manipulating creatures who label portions of it because – as Alice earlier remarked with pragmatic wisdom – 'its useful to the people that name them'. The realisation that the world by itself contains no signs – that there is no connection whatever between things and their names except by way of a mind that finds the tags useful – is by no means a trivial philosophical insight. (Gardner, 1970, p. 227)

Giving names to objects is part of the process of creating meaning out of meaninglessness. For Robertson as for others, the creation of a private universe of meaning betokens identity and security.

When we turn to the substance of the article, we find that the analysis of fluctuation is carried out in terms of the relative movements of two rates of interest: a representative single 'actual' rate, the behaviour of which is governed by the action of the banks, and the equilibrium 'natural' rate.

In Figure 25.1, two curves represent, respectively, productivity and thrift: the first (D) as a declining function of the rate of interest ('the rate per atom of time at which industry could employ new lendings at various rates of interest'); and the second (S) an increasing function ('the rate of new available savings per atom of time' at various rates of interest. At the equilibrium rate of interest (r_0) new available savings are being absorbed by industry.

An expansionary 'shock' such as 'the discovery of the Diesel engine, South America or what not', shifts the demand schedule bodily to the right (D_1). At the initial rate of interest there is now an excess demand for funds which can be supplied in various ways. If the banks choose to supply it, then total lending will exceed new saving and the money supply will increase. If, however, the banks allow nature to take its course, the excess demand will draw the actual

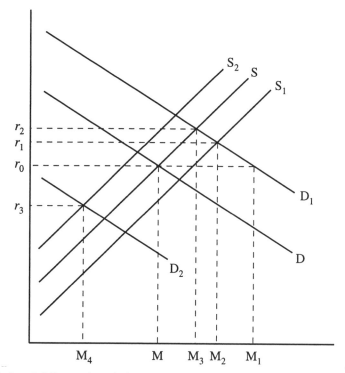

Industrial fluctuation: in interest-rate terms

rate upwards and this will have the effect of substituting newly mobilised past savings for bank lending. However, Robertson also notes that the rise in the money supply actively available will both raise income and cause a redistribution in favour of entrepreneurs that will increase saving. This in turn will shift the savings schedule to the right (S_1).

What happens after this is one of Robertson's particular interests. He sees the two 'real' schedules intersecting at what he terms a 'quasi-natural' rate (r_1), which would:

> equate industrial requirements and available new savings under the new conditions, towards which the actual rate is likely to rise, and which if it is reached will give *quasi-equilibrium*, with no *further* money-creation or mobilisation of past savings. (Robertson, 1934, p. 67)

The point about the quasi-equilibrium is that it is unstable, as forces are in motion that will undermine it.

We recall from our examination of the *Study* (the analysis carried over into *BPPL*) that the hubris of the Robertsonian boom leads to over-investment, crisis and depression. Two forces can be identified, which, in interest rate terms, will have the following effects. First, wages will rise, cutting back profits and reducing saving. The saving schedule will shift back, raising the quasi-natural rate (towards r_2) and dragging up the actual rate after it. Borrowings fall as the demand for instrument goods falls off. Second, the acute oversupply of instrument goods greatly reduces their marginal product and the investment demand schedule moves sharply to the left (D_2). As a consequence, incomes fall and are redistributed in favour of non-savers; there is also some 'distress borrowing' by firms and households. The savings schedule moves left. The quasi-natural rate has fallen to a low level (r_3) and so long as the actual rate remains above it there will be an excess supply of savings. In this situation bank loans will be curtailed and savings will be channelled into (immobilised in the form of) bank deposits.

Once the actual rate falls to the level of the quasi-natural rate, a new quasi-equilibrium will be established which is likely to be more durable than the old, due to the long life of capital (marginal productivity will remain low) and the resistance of wage-earners to further falls (movements in savings will progressively slow).

IX

This, in the new terms, is the course of the cycle that we traced in *BPPL*. The main point to notice for present purposes is that having taken the trouble to restate and to reaffirm his own categories and definitions in the preliminary (1933) article, they make no appearance in that of 1934. In other words, there is no mention of hoarding and dishoarding, lacking and dislacking – spontaneous and imposed – despite the fact that one or other of these devices will in their due seasons be brought into play. Similarly, we recall that when the cycle was analysed in *BPPL*, it was in these terms precisely and exclusively – despite the fact that, in the new terms, interest rates of various kinds must have been playing their part, though never featured.

How is this phenomenon to be explained? It is in fact further evidence in support of the idea that in 1934 Robertson was recasting his own theory, as set out in the *Study* and *BPPL*, in interest rate terms. That is, that he regarded the two modes of expression as equivalent and, therefore, as parallel. We may also argue that given that the later form was adopted in response to the work of others and that he made no attempt in 1934 to combine the two modes, it was because he preferred his own approach and thought the rate of interest as of little importance. This view in turn can be explained by the immensely important position occupied by the price level in Robertson's scheme. Movements of the price level gave rise to all that was characteristic in

Robertson's monetary economics. It was after all the quantity theory method of Classical economics. It enabled Robertson to combine his new insights with old certainties. By contrast, the new method led the way to new possibilities and to new uncertainties. It might lead to 'the wood where things have no names', in which case one might lose, along with one's name, one's identity and security.

In the event it led in Robertson's view to the thing that he feared most: the destruction of old certainties, as the rate of interest was raised to a position of command on the shoulders of money, itself newly ennobled as being of primary importance. In the *Treatise*, the book that had stimulated Robertson to restate his theory, that stage had not, of course, been reached. Instead, fluctuations occurred in response to changes in the price level relative to cost (giving incentive changes in windfall profits), which could be equivalently explained as the difference between investment and saving or in the divergence of the natural and market rates of interest (Keynes, *CW* V ch. 11). At this stage of his development, however, Keynes was dismissive of the Cambridge quantity equation – which he had employed in his earlier *Tract on Monetary Reform* (1923) – and the Fisher quantity equation (see *CW* V pp. 205–14).

It was the abandonment of these old forms and the move to the rate of interest that disturbed Robertson. In the process of arguing out the *Treatise* with Keynes, Robertson expressed his regret at the passing of what he considered to be a superior method:

> I know I shall never reconvert you to the old K and V method, but I can't refrain from suggesting how much stronger they make the *prima facie* case for public works. For on your and Kahn's s[short] p[period] method, all new money inevitably becomes completely inert in the end, and most of it pretty quickly. Hence your arguments can do nothing to allay the objections of those who urge that the budgets of *future years* will be burdened by the interest charges on the loan. But surely *prima facie* money once effectively introduced into circulation may be expected to stay there, and to circulate (thus affecting prices or employment as the case may be) with a velocity approximating to that of existing money, unless and until it is withdrawn by taxation, deflation, etc.   (Robertson to Keynes, 1 April 1933, in *CW* XXIX p. 17)

X

It was with the publication of the *General Theory* that Robertson's worst fears were realised. Why this was so can be gauged from the series of quotations given below. In brief, Robertson's view of what had occurred is as follows. Because of Keynes, the rate of interest had been raised to a position of great importance: it had become the linchpin of the whole theoretical system. Robertson believed this to be a false position because, in keeping with our argument so far, he saw the interest rate as relatively unimportant. Where it was proper for interest-rate terms to be employed, real and monetary factors should take their appropriate roles, as given by Classical theory suitably modified. Finally, and most significant of all, Keynes, having made the interest rate both a strategic variable and a monetary one, had cleverly routed monetary influence through a very narrow and easily blocked channel. By means of the 'liquidity trap' he was thus able to render monetary policy impotent and so let in fiscal policy, with a major role for the state.

The quotations below are taken from articles published between 1936 and the beginning of the 1950s. They are, with one exception, in chronological order. First, the rate of interest as linchpin of the system. In 'The Snake and the Worm', a paper read at the Tercentenary Conference of Harvard University in September 1936, Robertson pondered alternative explanations for the mass unemployment of the 1930s (was it simply the product of a phase of the cycle of particularly marked amplitude: 'the snake'; or was it caused by deeper tendencies inherent in capitalist economies: 'the worm'?) and the limits of action by the state. Robertson's view, as may be surmised, is that the current distress was part of the cycle, though complicated by a phase of structural change. This view, however, was expressed against the backdrop of the appearance of the *General Theory* only a few months previously (here dismissed as 'Mr Keynes's latest book') which Robertson saw as being dominated by the stagnation thesis. The point, for present purposes, is that stagnation is linked with a particular theory of the rate of interest:

> I must not attempt to carry the debate further, or I should have to make the parties fall at loggerheads over the nature of that central mystery of the economic scheme – a theme too intricate for the closing minutes of my half-hour, the theory of the rate of interest. But I have said enough, perhaps, to indicate what seems to be emerging, with increasing clearness, especially since the publication of my colleague Mr Keynes's latest book, as the true issue. It is not so much a conflict between different views of the most effective method of controlling cyclical fluctuation. It is rather a conflict of view between those who still believe that cyclical fluctuation is the worst enemy which controlled capitalism has yet to subdue, and those who think that they detect, lurking beneath the coils of the cyclical snake, a more insidious enemy still. This alleged enemy is a chronic and endemic tendency towards the stifling of enterprise, the leakage of thrift, and a consequent running-down of the whole system – a sort of worm seated at the very heart of the institutional and psychological bases of our society, and battening on the very growth of wealth which he strives unavailingly to prevent. Is he a real worm, or is he the figment of generous imaginations tortured by the tragedies of the worst and deepest slump of history? (Robertson, 1936, p. 92)

Robertson's own view was that the rate of interest should be kept firmly in its, undistinguished, place as he made clear in 'A Survey of Modern Monetary Controversy', read just over a year later:

if I have a personal heresy in these matters, it is that in recent years, alike in academic, financial and political circles, we have heard rather too much about that entity [the rate of interest] in connection with the processes of trade recovery and recession. (Robertson, 1937, p. 118)

In the same paper he summed up the issues raised in the controversy then in progress in the following words:

Thus the Blondinian, less sanguine than the Optimist about the power of the monetary authority to make the rate of interest what it pleases, is also less apprehensive than the Pessimist about the power of the hoarding instinct to oppose a chronic resistance to such a secular fall in the rate of interest as the forces of thrift and productivity may dictate. That is the nearest which I can get to putting in words of (approximately) one syllable the upshot of *all this pother about the rate of interest*. (Robertson, 1937, p. 123; emphasis added)

Also in the 1937 paper, Robertson raised the question of the determinants of the rate of interest and their relative importance:

How close and fruitful an approach to reality do we attain by considering the rate of interest as the resultant of two main forces – man's ingenuity in dealing productively with the forces of Nature on the one hand, and his reluctance to forgo the immediate consumption of the fruits of his efforts on the other? Of what order of magnitude is the difference made to the picture by taking account of two other factors – man's ability to control by means of specialised organs the supply of acceptable means of payment, and his readiness within limits to sacrifice income, whether present or future, in return for the advantages of avoiding trouble and of enjoying security against unforeseen contingencies? (Robertson, 1937, p. 119)

With respect to the last of these, Robertson makes clear that he is referring to liquidity preference (p. 120). His answer to the question, was always to stress the importance of the real as against the monetary, as the following extracts confirm.

First, in a lecture given at the London School of Economics in 1939, published as 'Mr Keynes and the Rate of Interest', Robertson hastened to reassure his sympathetic audience that his continued exchanges with Keynes had not produced a change of heart:

In the course of one of our brushes, Mr Keynes has suggested that I am a recent and reluctant convert to the view that the rate of interest is 'in some sense a monetary phenomenon'. This is, I am afraid, a misapprehension. (Robertson, 1939, p. 150)

Years later, in 1951, Robertson was still clear as to the relative importance of real and monetary factors. In a *festschrift* paper, 'Some Notes on the Theory of Interest', he confirmed his support for what would be termed the 'Classical' approach:

in the convenient sense of the word 'classical' in which it stands not for the work of the writers of a particular period but for an analysis conducted on the assumption that the monetary system operates in such wise as to interpret and not to distort the influence of real forces.   (Robertson, 1951, p. 203)

The essence of Robertson's approach, as is clear from this passage, from *BPPL* and from the argument to date, is always to favour theory grounded deep in real foundations. His criticism of Keynes was not only that monetary forces were exalted but that real forces were excluded. On this view, liquidity preference, in which expectations played a considerable part, was a vague and insubstantial basis for a variable with such an important role. These points are brought out in the following extract from the 1939 'Mr Keynes and the Rate of Interest', which contains an apposite reference to *Alice* (the Cheshire Cat in *AAW*):

> I have suggested that even from the momentary market point of view the Keynesian formulation tends to obscure unduly the parts played by Productivity and Thrift. Much more is this true when we pass to consider the trend of events over considerable stretches of time. I remain of opinion that from the long-period point of view the most important things to be said about the rate of interest are not things about 'liquidity preference' and the supply of money, but things about what Marshall calls productiveness and prospectiveness. In this connection the first thing to be said is that in one important respect Mr Keynes has understated his own case. While there are hints here and there of a broader treatment, in the main his plan is to set the rate of interest in a direct functional relation only with that part of the money stock which is held for what he calls 'speculative reasons', i.e. because it is expected that the rate of interest will subsequently rise. Thus the rate of interest is what it is because it is expected to become other than it is; if it is not expected to become other than it is, there is nothing left to tell us why it is what it is. The organ which secretes it has been amputated, and yet it somehow still exists – a grin without a cat . . . If we ask what ultimately governs the judgements of wealth-owners as to why the rate of interest should be different in the future from what it is today, we are surely led straight back to the fundamental phenomena of Productivity and Thrift.   (Robertson, 1939, pp. 173–5)

Notice here also the adumbration of what was destined to become a standard interpretation of the relationship between the loanable funds and liquidity preference approaches to interest theory: that the first dealt with the long run while the second explained short-run fluctuations only.

Finally, in a lecture delivered in 1948 and published as 'What Has Happened to the Rate of Interest?', Robertson made explicit reference to the commanding position to which the rate of interest had aspired in the Keynesian Revolution; and to its role via the liquidity trap in bringing hopes of economic prosperity low. This, we should note, ties in neatly with the first quotation we gave above, explaining as it does Robertson's view of the nature of the 'worm' that operates beneath the 'snake' of cyclical fluctuation:

In the nineteen-thirties, under the first impulse of Keynes's work, the rate of interest was elevated to a position of commanding theoretical importance. Roughly speaking, nothing was ever allowed to happen – money was not allowed to affect prices, wage-rates were not allowed to affect employment, I had almost added, the moon was not allowed to affect the tides – except through the rate of interest: it became, as never before, the keystone of the whole theoretical arch. But it also became the villain of the piece, and a very powerful villain. It was the dragon guarding the cave of 'liquidity preference' – of the ineradicable urge of capitalist society to run for cover and to play for safety; it became the rock against which the waves of social improvement beat in vain. (Robertson, 1949a, p. 188)

XI

When we move on to examine Robertson's published lectures containing the definitive statement of his views, we find that the picture traced out in the above paragraphs is faithfully reproduced. Robertson holds fast to his Classical foundations; real factors predominate; monetary forces change nothing fundamental.

With respect to the first of these, there are two points to notice. First, that among Robertson's many references to the work of others, three names predominate: Keynes, against whose theory his argument is almost wholly directed; Joan Robinson, in her role as continuing irritant; and Alfred Marshall. It is to Marshall's Classical theory that he appeals for support and reassurance. Second, Robertson deals with the rate of interest in the 'microeconomic' element of the *Lectures*, with three chapters in the section on the theory of distribution. Later he confirms that material dealt with in this section was 'mainly conducted on certain assumptions which, if you like, you can call "classical" or "semi-classical"' (Robertson, 1963a, p. 325).

About the second of these, therefore, we can say that the forces at work were also real. Robertson confirmed this, concluding that:

the history of the interest rate through time appears as the history of the results of a tussle, – a tussle between Fecundity and Invention on the one hand and Affluence and Thrift on the other. (Robertson, 1963a, p. 249)

He adds that later it will be necessary to take into account 'those monetary factors which in this discussion I have deliberately kept impounded'.

With respect to the third of these, however, when monetary phenomena are taken into account, the effect is, as we should expect, unspectacular. The context in which the rate of interest is introduced is itself of great interest for present purposes and we shall return to consider it later. For the moment, however, we notice that in the new surroundings, namely, the money ('macroeconomic') section of the *Lectures*, the question to be asked is:

Now that we are explicitly taking account of monetary phenomena, is there any need for us to revise the common-sense idea which we formed last term of what the rate of interest is - namely that it is the price of the use of investible funds, arrived at in the market, like other prices, as the result of the interaction of schedules of demand and supply? *I feel convinced that there is not.*   (Robertson, 1963a, p. 249; emphasis added; see also p. 391)

Though, of course, it was now necessary to modify the schedules to take account of net changes in hoards and new money creation to obtain the supply and demand for loanable funds; the distinction between real and monetary elements being reflected in a divergence between natural and market rates of interest.

XII

The line of argument which claims that Keynes developed liquidity preference theory as a means of denying the influence of the classical forces of productivity and thrift and of thus opening the way for the employment of real forces elsewhere has an important corollary. It is that if the contest between the liquidity preference and loanable funds theories could be resolved in favour of the latter, the former would fall and with it all the rest of Keynes's scheme. Thus the linchpin of the system would become its weakest link. This would explain why the debate proved to be so intense and so prolonged, with the attack on liquidity preference theory finding its most recent flowering in the form of the buffer-stock theory (see, for example, Goodhart, 1989; Goodhart and Presley, 1994; Mizen and Presley, 1994).

It is, however, a false belief, the basis of which is explained by the argument to date. In reality nothing else depends on liquidity preference theory, which was developed after, and not before, Keynes had worked out the relationship between investment and saving. This point was recognised by Clarke (1988, p. 264) who confirmed the findings of earlier work by Milgate (in Eatwell and Milgate, 1983, pp. 79–89; Milgate, 1982, pp. 111–122). There is also support, of a somewhat backhanded kind, from Blaug, who has argued that Keynes had to use the supply and demand for money for the determination of the rate of interest as there was nothing else left with which to determine it (Blaug, 1990, p. 21). We shall find that the question of the sequence in which Keynes developed his theory is of great significance.

26.   The glow-worm and the lighthouse

I

We have argued that Robertson's approach to interest theory was to make it a mirror-image of his analysis in *BPPL*, so that its foundations were grounded securely in Classical economics. The evidence is such that this claim could hardly be doubted. It would be reasonable to expect, therefore, that the Robertson–Keynes controversy over the rate of interest could contain clues to suggest that Robertson's formal theoretical position was shaped by the same temperamental factors as were at work behind the *Study* and *BPPL*. These factors were, in brief, that Robertson's outlook was regressive rather than progressive; and that the security afforded by a theory-behind-a-theory that functioned as nonsense-as-game would indicate a determination to emphasise the (discrete) parts at the expense of consideration of the whole. The key variables would keep their proper stations. The clues indeed are not hard to find, and we shall examine those provided by Robertson, by Keynes and by an outside commentator.

II

The first is provided by Robertson himself who, in the course of an exchange over terminology, suggested in a letter to Keynes that part of the difficulty in reaching agreement between them stemmed from the difference in their temperaments. Robertson makes a most revealing use of metaphor which indicates his view (accurate) of their respective theoretical approaches. Note also the reference to a difference in attitude towards predecessors:

> On the broader question of our respective attitudes to the work of our predecessors (and contemporaries of other schools), there *is* of course a difference of temperament, as there was between Marshall and Jevons. By way of varying your picturesque metaphors, may I suggest that I – managing to keep throughout in touch with all the elements of the problem in a dim and fumbling way – have been a sort of glow worm, whose feeble glimmer lands on all the objects in its neighbourhood: while you, with your far more powerful intellect, have been a lighthouse casting a far more penetrating, but sometimes fatally distorting, beam on one object after another in succession. (Robertson to Keynes, 1 January 1938, in *CW* XXIX p. 166)

Robertson's observation yields us two insights. The first follows directly from our main theme. Robertson in casting himself as the glow-worm whose feeble light lands more or less evenly on 'all the objects *in its neighbourhood*' means that he has grown up in the Classical tradition and intends that all variables be retained in their proper stations, convoy fashion. It is a passive, accepting-of-the-status-quo approach that finds comfort and reassurance in the contemplation of discrete objects in their accustomed place.

Keynes by contrast is the *Alice* figure, active and progressive, who does not seek the security of the familiar. Cast as the lighthouse, his powerful beam finds out dark, restful corners; throws concepts and variables into stark, merciless relief; and 'distorts' everything into new positions and new relationships. Keynes's lighthouse beam is an apt metaphor for the multiplier, as we shall see.

The second point is essentially the same as the first but is concerned with the approach to model-building at a more formal, philosophical level. Again the point turns on the distinction between active and passive, between the restless, questing approach and the accepting-of-what-is-discovered approach. It brings together in unlikely relationship searchlights and grapes and throws light on the method Robertson employed in the *Study*.

The story begins on the last page of the *Study*. Robertson makes reference to, but does not identify, 'the wisest of all English philosophers who counsels us to eat our grapes downwards' (Robertson, 1915, p. 254). There are two possible clues here. The first is that in his 'Essay on Man' Alexander Pope refers to the English philosopher Francis Bacon (1561–1626) as 'The wisest, brightest, meanest of mankind'. The second is that in his philosophical method, Bacon refers to sense experiences or perceptions as 'grapes, ripe and in season' which are to be 'gathered, patiently and industriously and from which, if pressed, the pure wine of knowledge will flow'. This last quotation is from Karl Popper's *Objective Knowledge* (1972) in which Bacon is cited as an exemplar of a particular scientific method and one with which Popper violently disagrees. This is what he dubs the 'bucket theory of science' in which:

> our knowledge, our experience, consists either of accumulated perceptions (naive empiricism) or else of assimilated, sorted and classified perceptions (a view held by Bacon and, in a more radical form, by Kant) . . . According to this view, then, our mind resembles a container – a kind of bucket – in which perceptions and knowledge accumulate.   (Popper, 1972, p. 341)

It is in this context that Bacon counsels us to gather our grapes of experience.

For Popper, this is far too passive an approach adequately to represent what he believes to be the 'actual process of acquiring experience, or the actual method used in research or discovery'. Rather:

In science it is *observation* rather than perception which plays the decisive part. But observation is a process in which we play an intensely *active* part. An observation is a perception, but one which is planned and prepared . . . An observation is always preceded by a particular interest, a question, or a problem – in short, by something theoretical.   (Popper, 1972, p. 342)

Thus for Popper, the theory, or hypothesis, precedes the observation, for it is in the formation of the hypothesis that we learn what kind of observations we should make:

This is the view that I have called the *'searchlight theory'* (in contradistinction to the *'bucket theory'*) . . . the aim of the scientist is not to discover absolute certainty, but to discover better and better theories (or to invent more and more powerful searchlights) . . . It is a principle which demands that we should dare to put forward bold hypotheses that open up, if possible, new domains of observations, rather than those careful generalisations from 'given' observations which have remained (ever since Bacon) the idols of all naive empiricists.   (Popper, 1972, pp. 346, 355, 361)

It would be too crude a generalisation to classify Robertson wholly with Bacon, and Keynes wholly with Popper; but on the strength of the argument to date it is clear into which camps they fall.

We recall that Robertson's fellowship dissertation was criticised by Pigou in its first version – and to a lesser extent in its second – for being too much dominated by the raw material which should have provided examples to support an overall theme. Though even Pigou's account of Marshall's ideal method spoke only of stewing on the raw material until the 'bones' of a theory emerged. There is not a 'bold hypothesis' in sight. Robertson's objective at that time was to sift the evidence of actual experience as a means of discovering the motor of economic life – and therefore of life itself. Having thus established his foundations with the *Study*, the rest was modification, refinement and reaction.

With Keynes, however, the case is somewhat different. The 'lighthouse' with its 'penetrating beam' is clearly of a kind with Popper's 'powerful searchlight'. Robertson admits, in a later section of the glow-worm–lighthouse letter, that 'This method of successive over-emphasis [as he dubs the effects of the lighthouse beam], is, I expect, very productive of knowledge and enlightenment in the end' (Robertson in Keynes, *CW* XXIX p. 167). In other words, Robertson's is simply a rather jaundiced view of what we now recognise to be the Popper method.

Other evidence also puts Keynes in the Popperian camp. Danes in his 1979 study of Robertson's work, depicts Keynes as possessing a revolutionary outlook and of habitually seeking to bring about revolutions in economics (Danes, 1979, ch. 4). This to a sympathetic observer might be construed as Keynes seeking to 'invent more and more powerful searchlights'.

Finally, we should note that it was indeed Keynes's own revolutionary approach that led him to criticise contemporaries for their inconsistency in advocating policies which could not possibly proceed from their theories. He spoke of:

> Post-war economists [whose] thought today is too much permeated . . . with facts of experience too obviously inconsistent with their former view [for] they have not drawn sufficiently far-reaching consequences; and have not revised their fundamental theory.   (Keynes, 1936, p. 20)

Clearly what was needed here was a little more bold hypothesising.

Overall, therefore, the evidence on philosophical method would seem to accord with our previous conclusions that on temperamental grounds Robertson's regressive outlook would incline more to find reassurance in established ideas and the non-disturbance of established relationships; whereas Keynes's progressive outlook eschews the familiar and does not hesitate to 'distort' established configurations with the aid of ever more powerful searchlights/bolder and bolder hypotheses.

III

Our second provider of clues as to the temperamental underpinnings of the formal theoretical position adopted by Robertson in his dispute with Keynes, is the outside commentator, J.R. Hicks. Hicks, in his 1942 review article of Robertson's *Essays in Monetary Theory*, unwittingly (intuitively?) hits on a simile that exactly captures the essence of the distinction between the respective approaches of Robertson and Keynes:

> For my own part, I rather regret the amount of criticism contained in these essays . . . Of all great economists, Mr Keynes is probably the most Impressionist; the *General Theory*, in particular, needs to be read at a distance, not worrying too much about details, but looking principally at the general effect. At least, that is how I have read it myself, and it seems that as a result I retain a higher opinion of it than Professor Robertson does. His own criticisms sometimes remind me of a man examining a Seurat with a microscope, and denouncing the ugly shapes of the individual dots.   (Hicks, 1942, p. 54)

There could not be a clearer depiction of Robertson's one-and-one-and-one approach of economic-theory-as-nonsense-as-game, as compared to Keynes's big 'One' in which, in Robertson's eyes, all seems jumbled and thrown into incomprehensible confusion. We recall that he actually told Keynes that 'a large part of your theoretical structure is still to me almost complete mumbo-jumbo' (Robertson to Keynes, 10 February 1935, in Keynes, *CW* XIII p. 506).

It is much to be regretted that, having hit on the Seurat-dots simile, Hicks was so ready to concede the point in the face of criticism by Coddington (see Hicks, 1982, p. 127 n. 2).

For our third provider of clues we turn again to Robertson himself, placed here because his contribution acts as a useful introduction to the hints and suggestions regarding the nature of Robertson's problems proffered by Keynes. Writing to Keynes in 1935, in the 'mumbo-jumbo' letter cited above Robertson acknowledged, as he had in the glow-worm–lighthouse letter, that there were on his own side obstacles to agreement that went beyond the purely economic. Though the remarks were probably intended to be fairly bland, the choice of words is, in the light of our previous argument, very revealing:

> You will probably conclude that this [inability to make sense of Keynes's theoretical structure] is due to ossification – or at least excessive conservatism – of mind.   (In Keynes, *CW* XXIX p. 167)

Though Robertson is often depicted as characterised by constancy of behaviour, as a safe pair of hands, in comparison with the supposed fickleness of Keynes, these remarks hint at something less positive. They betoken an extreme rigidity, an unbending conservatism, that springs from Robertson's need to cling to a secure past.

IV

Our final contributor of clues is Keynes, who with his famous intuition clearly sensed the all-important regressive element in Robertson's make-up. Keynes intimated both directly and via literary allusion that he believed that this problem had an inhibiting effect on Robertson's work and prevented agreement between them in the post-1936 controversy. Keynes was particularly acute in intuiting the tensions inherent in Robertson's attempt to reconcile old attachments with new departures in his thinking. In 1938 he wrote to Haberler:

> in recent times, I have never regarded Hawtrey, Robertson or Ohlin, for example, as classical economists. Indeed they have all been pioneers in the other line of approach; though Robertson (not the other two) seems constantly trying to make out that he does still hold the classical theory as well as one of the newer versions. (Keynes to Haberler, 3 April 1938, in *CW* XXIX p. 270)

That Keynes appreciated the problems of reconciliation that this juggling posed is shown by a letter to Robertson of 1936:

I see that you are saying that it all makes no difference, that Marshall related it all to a Royal Commission in an affirmative sigh, that it has been well known to Pigou for years past and is to be found in a footnote to *Industrial Fluctuations*, that Neisser's bunk comes to the same thing, and the like; though in truth, *you* are the only writer where much of it is to be found in embryo and to whom acknowledgements are due. But I would rather you said this, than that it was wrong! You are like a man searching for a formula by which he can agree without changing his mind. (Keynes to Robertson, 13 December 1936, in *CW* XIV p. 94)

Keynes intuited that the stumbling-block was emotional rather than intellectual; and in an article published in 1937, in which he reviewed the main points of departure initiated by the *General Theory*, he noted that:

My differences, such as they are, from Mr Robertson chiefly arise out of my conviction that both he and I differ more fundamentally from our predecessors than his *piety* will allow. (Keynes, *CW* XIV p. 109; emphasis added)

A clearer picture of what that 'piety' might mean was vouchsafed when commenting on a paper Robertson sent him in 1937. Note how Keynes, as usual, distinguishes between Robertson's intellectual strength and his emotional vulnerability:

It is a brilliant effort . . . But it is an extreme example of your chivalry towards the under-dog argument and your sentimental attachment to words which have once meant something to you! 'Even the muddiest river winds somewhere safe to sea' would be a good title. I feel, after reading it, that the strictly intellectual differences between us are probably very small indeed at bottom. But I am trying all the time to disentangle myself, whilst you are trying to keep entangled. You are, so to speak, bent on creeping back into your mother's womb; whilst I am shaking myself like a dog on dry land.

An interpretation of the significance of this passage was previously given in the present writer's *The Keynesian Revolution and its Critics* (Fletcher, 1989a, pp. 40ff), on which the following paragraphs lean heavily.

The literary quotation is plainly Keynes's adaptation of lines from A.C. Swinburne's 'The Garden of Proserpine' ('That even the weariest river / Winds somewhere safe to sea') and provides an oblique reference to Robertson's regressiveness – his urge to return to his beginnings. The meaning becomes unmistakable, however, when juxtaposed with the reference to Robertson being bent on creeping back into [his] mother's womb' (regressiveness to the point of 'nescience itself': recall the argument in 'Alice's evidence' above, Chapter 11), for one of the recurrent themes in Swinburne's poetry is the personification of the sea as mother-figure. But here danger lurks, because the sea can be both mother and lover 'whose embraces are at once more fatal and sexually keen than others' (Ian Fletcher, n.d. pp. 7,

23). Notice the regressive note struck in the following extract from 'The Triumph of Time':

> I will go back to the great sweet mother,
> Mother and lover of men the sea.
> I will go down to her, I and no other,
> Close with her, kiss her and mix her with me.

Keynes had identified the source of Robertson's difficulty; but what was his reaction to be? Being Keynes he would not allow matters to rest – especially when locked in a controversy whose outcome would mould the future shape of economic theory, determine the professional reputations of the protagonists and influence their personal relationship. The clue is given by a literary allusion Keynes had made the previous year in the *General Theory* when dismissing neo-Classical attempts to combine real and monetary variables in the theory of the rate of interest:

> But at this point we are in deep water. 'The wild duck has dived down to the bottom – as deep as she can get – and bitten fast hold of the weed and tangle and all the rubbish that is down there, and it would need an extraordinarily clever dog to dive after and fish her up again.' (Keynes, *CW* VII p. 183)

This paraphrase quotation, from Ibsen's play *The Wild Duck* contains the same symbolic elements as the Swinburne reference above: the sea – as a means of escape but also of destruction; 'tangle' as against 'keep entangled' and 'disentangle' (interestingly Robertson's term for saving released from capital projects is 'disentanglings'); the dog, which now has a reason for shaking itself on dry land.

The theme of the play is the choice between illusion and reality as a means of facing the human predicament. To illustrate this, Ibsen uses the legend that a wounded wild duck will dive down and drown herself by clinging to the bottom-weed rather than face the humiliation of capture by the hunter. But by a twist of the plot he allows the duck to be rescued from her chosen fate by the 'extraordinarily clever' dog and she now lives on in an attic as the symbol of a creature that is out of its element, but outwardly – and perhaps inwardly – content with its new life.

In using this parable in the *General Theory*, before the controversy with Robertson began in earnest, Keynes refers only generally to the members of the neo-Classical school whose attempt to graft on monetary influences to the Classical (saving and investment) theory of the rate of interest had fatally entrapped them in the weedy depths of the loanable funds approach. With the outbreak of hostilities with Robertson, however, Keynes becomes more specific and in the later Swinburne reference of December 1937 the identities of the wild duck and the clever dog are made explicit. Robertson, confronted with the implications of the Keynesian Revolution for his theoretical and, therefore, emotional integrity, seeks refuge in the comfort and security of his beginnings (womb–mother–sea–Classical economics); but Keynes, realising the destructive consequences for life and work of such a course, seeks to rescue him. How is he to do it? Can Robertson in fact be rescued?

This is the dilemma the play explores in relation to the central character, Hjalmar Ekdal, an incompetent professional photographer, who leads a narrow but comfortable life through the efforts of his family, who cover for his technical deficiencies. Two interpretations of the wild-duck symbolism when applied to Ekdal's situation are given in the play. First, that of the egregious Gregers Werle, which sees the creature in the attic as still the wild duck in the sea-deeps: capable of being rescued by a clever dog and consequently requiring only a 'sight of heaven and sea' to make it abandon its life of illusion and unreality. This interpretation implies that Ekdal can be shocked back into acceptance of the reality he requires for his fulfilment – by being confronted with the truth about his present position. Second, that of the wise Dr Relling, which sees the wild duck not as she *was* but as she *is*: damaged and in captivity but domesticated and content and from which state she does not wish to be, nor cannot be, rescued. This second interpretation, therefore, sees Ekdal as a willing and necessary prisoner of an illusory but comfortable existence – and one for whom exposure to reality would spell disaster.

The message is, therefore, that the notion of confronting individuals with 'reality' in their own and other people's interests is a dangerous one; and in the play the character advocating this policy is depicted as brash and naive, with no appreciation of human need and the reasons for which some people might choose 'an illusory but comfortable existence'. It is as though Falstaff (see above, Chapter 12) were to take Justice Shallow by the shoulders and shake him until he accepted that his memories of glory were nothing but a sham, that he had lived a life as shallow as his name and that he was on the brink of extinction. Realising that such a course would add nothing to the sum of human happiness, Falstaff keeps his peace and plays the old romancer at his own game.

Keynes never tried anything so brutal with Robertson but, as the Swinburne and Ibsen quotations show, he did make a more subtle attempt to convince him of his error. The quotations themselves indicate that this process had two stages. If we may argue by analogy with the general strategy that Keynes adopted to get the orthodox school to accept the argument of the *General Theory*, Keynes sought first (the Ibsen quotation) to confront Robertson with the 'truth' (challenging him directly on points at issue) so as to make him face 'reality' and so accept the new approach. As a strategy it was naive (owing much to enormous self-confidence and an absolute belief in the rightness of his case) and was no more successful with Robertson than it was with the orthodox-school economists. In this first stage, therefore, Keynes possibly accepts the Gregers Werle interpretation of the situation and casts himself as the extraordinarily clever dog able to effect a rescue.

In the second stage (the Swinburne quotation) he seems more inclined to accept Dr Relling's interpretation, as he senses that Robertson is constrained by deep-seated emotional forces (to which he alludes by his use of the mother–womb symbolism). But hand-in-hand with this insight goes his reference back to his former tactic (the dog shaking itself on dry land) because he sees Robertson as the key critic whom he must convince. As the controversy proceeded, therefore, Keynes's letters contain both argument over points of theory at issue together with hints at the true reason for Robertson's inability to reach agreement. The implicit assumption is that Robertson himself will sense that his theory is flawed but that he is prevented from abandoning it to follow Keynes – because of his need to maintain intact the link with the past. If Keynes believed this, he had an inkling of the truth; though, given the fundamental difference in their outlook it is unlikely that he would comprehend just how strong that need could be.

27.   'Incorrigible confusion'

I

Before turning to examine the issues of the Robertson–Keynes controversy it will be helpful as a preliminary to look again at Robertson's 'definitive' statement of his views on the rate of interest. This is because Robertson's treatment in *LEP* gives an unambiguously clear account of what it was that Robertson took issue with in Keynes's new theory and, therefore, provides a vital insight into his own thinking. Without this, much of the to-ing and fro-ing of the debate is incomprehensible.

We have already dealt at length with what is, in broad terms, the main threat posed to Robertson by Keynes's new hypothesis. This, we recall, turns on the relative rankings of real and monetary variables. Now, however, we look more closely at Robertson's objections to the theory itself. From this we shall see not only that they were based on a misunderstanding of Keynes's theory but also that his criticisms reveal a fundamental flaw in his argument. This flaw is the technical economic counterpart of Robertson's temperamental inhibitions. It is the point at which Robertson's desire to maintain at the core of his economics the theory-behind-a-theory equivalent of nonsense-as-game comes into contact with Keynes's new dispositions of the key variables. It is a kind of myopia, the effect of which is to prevent the one-and-one-and-one from becoming one big One. It is generally referred to as the fallacy of composition, in this case in the form of the paradox of thrift.

II

Turning back to *LEP* we recall that: Robertson dealt first with the rate of interest in the real, microeconomic context of distribution theory; that the introduction into the argument of the quantity of money involved no fundamental change in the view of interest he had established earlier; that the monetary influence on the rate of interest was to cause short-term deviations from a long-term norm governed by the real forces of productivity and thrift. What is of interest now is that the later stages of the treatment are dealt with in the chapter entitled 'The Stagnation Thesis'. That Robertson should choose to discuss monetary aspects of the rate of interest in this context is of great significance as it links up with the point made above, that the rate of interest is the 'worm' that operates below the coils of the trade-cycle 'snake'. Robertson explains that:

> What we have to do then is to look again at the stagnation thesis in its more distinctively monetary aspects. But we cannot do that effectively without bringing out again on parade the queer beast whom I have so far scarcely mentioned this term, though you have no doubt noticed him lurking in the background, - our old friend or enemy the rate of interest; so that it will be convenient for me at this point to spend a little time in bringing together some of what I have to say about the rate of interest in its monetary aspects. (Robertson, 1963a, pp. 375-6)

In other words, the connection is monetary; it is, as we learned earlier, concerned with Keynes's theory of liquidity preference.

The essence of the Robertson–Keynes controversy can be explained by reference to three key aspects of Robertson's discussion of the stagnation thesis. The first is that the stagnation thesis is defined as the doctrine that there is 'in a rich society . . . a deep-seated tendency for the desire to save to be continually outrunning the opportunities for profitable investment' (Robertson, 1963, p. 375). More specifically, it is concerned with 'the damaging effect, in a progressive economy, of an increase in the desire to save' (Robertson, 1963, p. 383).

Robertson provides, with a clarity that admits no possibility of misunderstanding, an account of his own view of the consequences of saving. This account in *LEP* is in fact a development of that in 'Mr Keynes and the Rate of Interest' (1939) in which Robertson had earlier explained the outcome of his personal decision to save rather than maintain his accustomed expenditure on clothing (in Hicks ed., 1966, pp. 167ff). There are two possibilities. If he saves and at the same time hoards the proceeds, money incomes and trade activity will decline. If, however, he purchases a security, the capital market will be eased and, 'subject to minor frictions', instrument-goods industry incomes will rise to maintain the general level of activity.

This is the view 'according to "classical" theory if you like to call it so' (Robertson, 1963, p. 384). The Keynesian challenge to 'this optimistic conclusion' is *according to Robertson* as follows. It takes effect, we should note, not at the saving stage but in the purchase of securities with the assumed proceeds. In Robertson's view, what happens is that the purchase of securities raises their price and, by the same token, lowers the rate of interest. The fall in the rate causes a movement out of bonds and into money-holding. Robertson's savings are shunted into inactive balances and the interest rate is checked at some new lower level. The level of economic activity falls.

Notice that in Robertson's version of Keynes's challenge to Classical theory, the problem is seen to lie in savings being lost into hoards – instead of ' being channelled into productive investment – and *not* in terms of the savings not coming into being. The analysis throughout is conducted in respect of *one person dealing with one trader*. There is no trace of an inkling anywhere of the distinction between the effects of action by one and the effects of action by all. There is no conception of the paradox of thrift (Robertson, 1963, pp. 383–6).

The second key aspect of Robertson's discussion concerns his understanding of 'liquidity preference', the phenomenon he sees as being responsible for the problem dealt with above: that is, that people will choose to hold money rather than bonds and so entrap savings.

The further point to notice under this head is that Robertson believes that the rate of interest is determined by the supply and demand for *speculative* balances *only* and that Keynes deliberately excludes active balances as a means of denying any influence on the rate of interest of the real forces of productivity and thrift (investment and saving in Keynes's theory). The effect of this misunderstanding on Robertson's part is to render liquidity preference as simply a theory governing speculative movements in the rate rather than a fully fledged theory of interest (Robertson, 1963, pp. 381–2).

Note, however, the ambivalence in Robertson's account. Though on the one hand he *must* see Keynes as confining 'liquidity preference' to speculative demands, as a means of excluding the real forces of productivity and thrift, when on the other hand he finds Keynes using the term to apply to the demand for money as a whole (as Keynes intended it should: see Keynes, 1936, pp. 168–174) he must see this as evidence of ambiguous thinking or of aberration. Here it becomes:

> the canker at the heart of the Keynesian theory of interest . . . [by which policy problems arise because] a magic phrase – liquidity preference – which had originally been chosen to denote one thing was quietly extended to cover also another thing with quite different economic implications. (Robertson, 1963, p. 380)

The third key aspect concerns the rate of interest at which proffered savings are swallowed or 'waylaid' into inactive balances. This effect had been referred to in 'Mr Keynes and the Rate of Interest' as 'this siding or trap' (Robertson, 1939, p. 168). In *LEP* it becomes 'this liquidity trap' (Robertson, 1963, p. 386), the enduring name for what has, quite wrongly, come to characterise Keynesian economics. And curiously, there is, again, a hint of doubt even in Robertson's own account. Whereas on the one hand Robertson has to believe that this is the basis of Keynes's objection to classical capital market theory (because he fails to understand the paradox of thrift and, therefore, that the savings will not come into existence); on the other hand he readily concedes that Keynes makes no such claim:

All the undertones of his book, with its emphasis on the ineffectiveness of thrift in promoting investment, lead one to suppose that he is treating the curve as being perfectly elastic . . . Yet in his book Keynes nowhere says that he is treating the curve as being infinitely elastic, and in one place (p. 207) definitely states the contrary; for he then says that while the limiting case where liquidity preference may become virtually absolute might become practically important in future, he knows of no example of it hitherto. All this makes it very difficult to be sure just what is being asserted. (Robertson, 1963, pp. 388-9)

In other words, Robertson doesn't understand Keynes's theory so attempts to make sense of it in terms of his own (Classical) way of thinking. At risk of labouring what is a most important point we finish this section with another quote:

The conclusion to which all this seems to lead is that the existence of the liquidity trap is much less likely than it has lately been fashionable to suppose to present a formidable long-run obstacle to the percolation of saved money through the capital markets into productive investment. (Robertson, 1963, p. 390)

III

It should be clear from the above sequence (the same sentiments can be traced throughout the *Lectures*: see especially Robertson, 1963, pp. 421-2, 441-2, 463) that behind the surface differences of formulation, discussion of the rate of interest involves much deeper issues. In fact, we shall find that the key to the Robertson–Keynes controversy lies in answering the Big Five questions we have met before. These concern: the nature of saving; the relationship between investment and saving; the finance of investment; the role of money; the nature of interest and the determination of the rate of interest. The first question is the most important as the answer to it will determine the answers to the rest. There is, therefore, the matter of sequence, of the order in which the various components of the theory were developed. This will be shown to be a major point of departure between Robertson and Keynes, in Chapter 28, below.

Behind the façade, therefore, lies the deeper issue of the relative influence of real and monetary forces. The Robertson–Keynes controversy should have been about the *way* in which investment and saving affected the rate of interest, not *whether* or not they did so. Given the constraints within which Robertson operated, however, it was inevitable that Keynes should be seen to have produced a purely monetary theory of interest. It was for this reason that the actual course of events ran as follows. The account presented here is a summary version of that traced out by Presley (1978, Part II, esp. chs 2, 11, 12) and critically reviewed in Fletcher (1989a, Part II, chs 4-10).

Robertson's allegations against Keynes (Robertson's version of events):

1. Keynes attempted to avoid the influence on the rate of interest of the Classical forces of productivity and thrift by the introduction of the multiplier: that is, the multiplier gave S = I via a change in income, not the rate of interest, which was now to be determined by the supply and demand for money.
2. The multiplier generated just the right amount of voluntary saving to finance investment without any resort to the idea of forced saving or disturbance of the rate of interest.
3. This was possible because Keynes failed to understand the distinction between *ex ante* and *ex post* and so could assume that the multiplier worked instantaneously.
4. This idea he confirmed by his notion that not only was saving equal to investment (S = I) but was equal by definition (S ≡ I).
5. In the real world the multiplier works subject to lags so that saving is delivered after the investment has taken place.
6. To avoid this charge Keynes introduced the finance motive: that is, the temporary demand for money for finance, while investment is still *ex ante* and until it becomes *ex post*.
7. In the face of Robertson's criticisms Keynes recants, as indicated by:
    a) His acceptance of Hicks's IS–LL (IS–LM) representation of his theory, which was made up of elements of both the liquidity preference and loanable funds theories but in which the loanable funds theory elements predominated. This shows that Keynes accepted the influence of productivity and thrift. For example, a shift upwards of the IS curve raises the rate of interest *ceteris paribus*, via the rise in income and excess demand for money. Therefore, the relationship is accepted but is *indirect* (via the change in income) rather than direct as in the Robertson case.
    b) With the introduction of the finance motive the relationship between investment and the rate of interest becomes direct, through the immediate effect on the demand for money.
8. Having had to introduce the finance motive under pressure from the loanable funds school, Keynes tries to protect himself:
    a) against the charge of forced saving, by assuming output perfectly elastic below full employment;
    b) against the charge of having acknowledged the influence of productivity and thrift, by use of the liquidity trap (so that the empirical validity of this becomes the criterion).
9. To counter the defence of Keynes, which has since become common, that the liquidity-preference theory explains short-run fluctuations while

leaving the Classical/loanable funds theory to explain the long-run movements of the rate of interest, Robertson pointed to Keynes's notion of the 'safe' or 'normal' rate to which dealers refer when forming their expectations. This, he claimed, must represent the long-run forces of 'productivity' and 'thrift'. Without this anchor the rate of interest in Keynes's theory cannot be explained: 'and yet it somehow still exists – a grin without a cat' (see Robertson, 1939, p. 174; also *AAW*, p. 91).

This in essentials was *Robertson's case against Keynes*. In the topics to which it gave prominence it can be seen to answer the question: how was Keynes able to subvert the Classical hierarchy of real and monetary forces by making the rate of interest a purely monetary phenomenon? Both the question and the answer to which it gave rise are a product of Robertson's own vision of economics and stem from his Classically based loanable funds theory; on Keynes's view they would thus carry forward the problems of Classical theory relating to saving, investment and the rate of interest.

The story goes as follows. In Robertson's world, we recall, investment is financed partly in the Classical manner from proffered savings and partly by the Robertsonian innovation of bank finance. The rise in the money supply pushes up prices and forces consumers to save. Investment would be fully financed and the requisite amount of 'going without' would occur, partly on a voluntary basis and partly through the coercive powers of forced saving.

Thus *from this standpoint* Keynes's new theory appeared both subversive of Classical hierarchies and actually impossible of operation. This is because, in his supposed attempt to isolate his purely monetary theory of interest from the influence of investment and saving and at the same time to release the interest rate from its traditional role of equilibrating the capital market, Keynes must be seen to introduce the multiplier apparatus. This worked instantaneously to generate just enough voluntary saving to finance investment. This process, note, employs no money and thus obviates the need for the Robertsonian innovation of bank finance and with it the whole notion of forced saving.

In Robertson's thinking, therefore, the multiplier posed a formidable threat: it denied Say's Law by wresting the initiative from saving and passing it decisively to investment; it upset the Classical ordering of real and monetary variables; and it shifted the key variables from their accustomed dispositions. Robertson was very conscious of this, and the importance of the multiplier is reflected in the part it plays in the debate. Having had to assume that the multiplier works instantaneously in order to make sense of it in terms of his own Classical mode of thought, Robertson's key argument is the revelation that in the real world the multiplier must work with a lag and so cannot perform the function that (he assumes) Keynes has assigned to it. Much of the rest of the debate, therefore, consists of Keynes's apparent attempts to make good the damage, by the introduction of an expedient (the finance motive); of Robertson's demonstration that this will lead back to classical conclusions; and of Keynes's desperate attempts to avoid them (perfectly elastic output below full employment and the liquidity trap).

Robertson's concern at the threat posed by the multiplier remained to the end and is duly recorded in *LEP* and in the final edition of *Money*. Part of his strategy was to attempt to make light of the whole matter by the use of suitably flippant language. Thus he was to describe the marginal propensity to save – a concept at the heart of the multiplier principle and one which he never succeeded in distinguishing from the rate of saving – as merely a 'potentially useful little brick' (*Money*, 1959, p. 178), and the multiplier itself as 'a magic carpet' (*Money*, 1959, p. 177). This was behaviour that drove even a loyal but painfully honest supporter like Professor T. Wilson to despairing expostulation:

> That the theory has its limitations is undeniable, but is it really nothing more than 'a little piece of algebra which serves in many expositions as a magic carpet to waft us from one platform to the next . . .' And is the Propensity to Consume nothing more than a 'potentially useful little brick'?   (Wilson, 1953, p. 563)

In 'Effective Demand and the Multiplier' Robertson descended from parody to outright contempt:

> Perhaps anything which happens can be expressed, with sufficient ingenuity, in terms of distortion of 'the marginal propensity to consume'. But when all this is said, it seems to be doubtful whether, for the analysis of a fluctuating world, the 'multiplier' constitutes much advance over more crudely monetary weapons of thought.   (In Hicks ed., 1966, p. 145)

Usually, however, Robertson's treatment of the multiplier can be described as gingerly feline and never more so than in the following quotation from the *Lectures*. Like an old maid observing an exhibit in the anatomy section of the waxworks, Robertson gazes at the multiplier with a mixture of horror and fascination: aware of the potential of what here lies neutered and impotent. Having laid stress on the temporal nature of the multiplier Robertson goes on to damn with faint praise:

> Now this seems to me, when thus expressed, to be quite a self-consistent little piece of apparatus, worth setting out, so to speak, under a glass case in order to get clear about its implications.   (Robertson, 1963, p. 420)

IV

That many of the criticisms were misconceived, in the sense that Robertson interpreted Keynes resolutely in terms of his own modified-Classical outlook, does not make them any the less real for Robertson, who was defending his very existence, professional and personal. The criticisms *were* nevertheless misconceived and deserve to be refuted in detail. This task was undertaken in the present writer's *The Keynesian Revolution and its Critics* (Fletcher, 1987, 1989a, chs 4–10; see also 1989b, 1996). The assessment of Robertson's case against Keynes, which occupies the remainder of this chapter, will deal specifically with issues which presently concern us. The assessment will, therefore, be in terms of the Big Five questions and will, in brief, show the following.

Keynes established, by reference to the paradox of thrift, that saving could not determine investment but was, rather, entirely a creature of investment. Investment was the more important component of aggregate demand and was at the centre of the principle of effective demand. The multiplier which it set in motion did not provide finance but acted to equilibrate changes in income brought about by changes in investment. Finance for investment was provided by money balances raised in the markets: no savings are involved (in contradistinction to Robertson's perception, in which no money was involved). The question of the finance of investment, therefore, becomes the touchstone of the distinction between the approaches of Robertson and Keynes and turns on the protagonists' respective treatment of money and saving.

V

In 1937, when commenting on his differences with Robertson, Keynes summed up the issues that he saw as preventing agreement between them as follows:

> It is Mr Robertson's incorrigible confusion between the revolving fund of money in circulation and the flow of new saving which causes all his difficulties. (Keynes, *CW* XIV, pp. 232–3)

Though Robertson remained 'incorrigible', the confusion itself was, on Keynes's view, symptomatic of orthodox thinking in general so that an important aspect of Keynes's own 'long struggle of escape . . . from habitual modes of thought and expression' (Keynes, 1936, p. viii) was to make clear the relative roles of money and saving:

> We have been all of us brought up . . . in deep confusion of mind between the demand and supply of money and the demand and supply of savings; and until we rid ourselves of it, we cannot think correctly.   (Keynes, 1939, p. 574)

The same point can be made by reference to the parties' understanding of the problem (supposedly) expressed in the 'Treasury View', for though they both rejected this argument against the efficacy of public works expenditures to relieve unemployment, they did so for very different reasons. These reasons stemmed in turn from a very different perception of the relationship between the key variables.

Robertson held to the orthodox belief that the Treasury View implied a shortage of saving. That is, public works by using scarce savings would pre-empt (crowd out in later parlance) private-sector investment. He rejected this view on the grounds that, though savings do indeed finance investment, in a depression people's saving intentions are frustrated, so that there is no corresponding increase in the stock of instrument goods (capital). In the *Study* he had dismissed Ralph Hawtrey's attack on the public expenditure proposals of the Minority Report of the Poor Law Commissioners in the following terms:

> Mr Hawtrey's attack . . . scarcely deserves formal refutation. He asserts that 'the Government by the very fact of borrowing for this expenditure is withdrawing from the investment market savings which would otherwise be applied to the creation of capital'. The whole point is that in times of depression savings are not otherwise so applied.   (Robertson, 1915, p. 253)

When he came to write the 'New Introduction' to the reprint of the *Study* in 1948, Robertson was tentatively to claim that these remarks constituted the 'first formal attack on what long afterwards came to be known as the "Treasury View"'. He also described how he had subsequently modified the 'real' analysis of the *Study* to allow for the effects of monetary influences, including the money-creating activities of banks and the desire of individuals to hold money:

> The endeavour to make plain to myself and others what bankers are really up to (*Money*, 1922, ch. IV), led me on to try to re-integrate the theory of money into that of the trade cycle; so that those common sense remarks about hoarding by farmers became transformed into the formal doctrine that under certain conditions the process of individual saving, so far from finding vent in the accumulation of useful stocks, may become completely abortive (*Banking Policy and the Price Level*, pp. 45–6, 96–7).   (Robertson, 1948a, p. xv)

Robertson's method of procedure, as exemplified by the above sequence of passages, of modifying Classical theory meant that the saving that financed investment was first real (a stock of consumable goods to provide subsistence during the period of construction of capital goods) and then real and monetary (with the addition of monetary influences – new bank money and hoards – which would facilitate or frustrate the intentions of savers). This is the basis of the 'incorrigible confusion' of Keynes's charge.

On Keynesian analysis the problem posed by the Treasury View is somewhat different. Because of the way in which his theory developed, Keynes was able to avoid the confusions of which he accused Robertson. For Keynes, saving was, on the anaysis of the *General Theory*, that part of *ex post* real income not devoted to consumption. At less than full employment the multiplier would produce a rise in real income just sufficient to accommodate the demands of both investors and consumers. The marginal propensity to consume would determine *by how much extra to the change in investment* real income would have to rise in order to meet both demands.

Saving was, therefore, a mere residual (Keynes, 1936, p. 64). As investment was taking place so, in effect, was saving of an exactly equivalent amount, since in the creation of real assets for investment purposes investment would be constituting that part of total realised real income that would not be devoted to consumption (see Fletcher, 1987, 1989a, p. 70; see also Chick 1987a, p. 26, in which she argues that Fletcher's interpretation of Keynesian saving was 'arguably also Keynes's').

Of course, as the multiplier worked itself out, successive rounds of expenditure out of received incomes would be diminished by the proportion of income not to be devoted to consumption. Concomitantly, savings in the form of money balances would accumulate until they equalled that part of real income not devoted to consumption, which in turn would be equal to the quantity of real income (physical assets) already devoted to investment.

Investment, however, could not be financed by the increase in savings to which it gave rise, since, when investment was *ex ante*, no saving had taken place; and when investment was *ex post*, savings only accumulated with a lag. Nor was it possible to increase the funds available to finance investment by increasing prior saving as this could only refer: (a) to a fall in the propensity to consume, which would have the effect of reducing the transactions demand for money as incomes fell; or (b) to a confusion with the attempt by individual transactors to become less liquid themselves so as to increase the liquidity of others: that is, to change their demand for money (Keynes, *CW* XIV, pp. 209, 216–17, 218–19, 220, 231–2).

Similarly, Keynes argued that as a means of restoring liquidity, saving is inferior to both investment and consumption, due to the effects of hoarding by wealth holders (Keynes, *CW* XIV, pp. 221, 222, 233; 1939, pp. 572–3). Instead, investment had to be financed by obtaining access to money balances at short and longer term in the money market and the capital market. As a consequence, if there is no accommodating increase in the money stock:

> the public can save *ex ante* and *ex post* and *ex* anything else until they are blue in the face, without alleviating the problem in the least – unless, indeed, the result of their efforts is to lower the scale of activity to what it was before.   (Keynes, *CW* XIV p. 222)

This means that the notion that Keynes had solved the problem posed by the Treasury View because the multiplier always generated just sufficient saving to finance investment is quite wrong. It provides, that is, a Classical answer to a Classical question. It is a notion that has cloaked the true extent of Keynes's radicalism and created confusion about the way in which the real and monetary elements of his theory are related. As we have seen, it led Robertson to claim that the multiplier must be supposed to work instantaneously (so as to deliver the requisite savings in time to finance the investment that produced them) and to make a mainstay of his attack on Keynes the argument that in the real world the multiplier works with a lag.

Moreover, the myth has persisted and can be found in the writings both of overtly monetarist commentators, such as Gilbert (1982, pp. 29, 78), who surveyed a wide range of opinion on Keynes, and, more surprisingly, of those more sympathetically disposed: see in particular Skidelsky (1992, pp. 452, 454n), whose major biography of Keynes explicitly subscribes to the Robertson position. By contrast we shall argue that the abandonment of this notion was a necessary aspect of Keynes's transition from old to new.

Instead, Keynes's version of the problem is that an increased demand for *money* due to the expansion of income raises the interest rate and so chokes the expansion off by deterring private sector investment. For Keynes:

> The increased demand for money resulting from an increase in activity has a backwash which tends to raise the rate of interest; and this is indeed a significant element in my theory of why booms carry within them the seeds of their own destruction.   (Keynes, *CW* XIV p. 110)

The implication of this is that:

> The investment market can become congested through shortage of cash. It can never become congested through shortage of saving. This is the most fundamental of my conclusions within this field.   (Keynes, *CW* XIV p. 222)

VI

The explanation for the different approaches of Robertson and Keynes to the question of the finance of investment can be seen to hinge on a single point: namely, whether or not they took account of the fallacy of composition in their analysis. We shall argue that the essence of Keynes's breakthrough in the early

1930s was to *see the significance* of the fallacy of composition for the construction of a theory of the whole economy whereas Robertson did not. Taking this into account had the effect of producing fundamentally different aggregate outcomes from those which would be forecast on the basis of a simple aggregation of individual outcomes. This in turn provides the true basis for the distinction between macroeconomics, the product of Keynes's new thinking, and microeconomics, the basis of classical (and Robertsonian) thinking. For example, if Robertson had been aware of the distinction he would not have taken exception to 'a prevalent tendency to suppose that the behaviour of "output as a whole" first attracted the attention of economists in the 1930s' (Robertson, 1948a, p. ix). We shall return to this point.

More specifically, the reason for this is that the fallacy of composition in the form of the paradox of thrift will determine the answer to the first and consequently most important of the Big Five questions: namely, that concerning the nature of saving. Once this is determined the answers to the rest will follow: the relationship between investment and saving; the finance of investment; the role of money; the nature of interest and the determination of the rate of interest. In the *General Theory* Keynes argued, with Robertson's loanable funds theory very clearly in mind, that:

> the old-fashioned view that saving always involves investment, though incomplete and misleading, is formally sounder than the new-fangled view that there can be saving without investment or investment without 'genuine' saving. The error lies in proceeding to the plausible inference that, when an individual saves, he will increase aggregate investment by an equal amount. It is true, that, when an individual saves he increases his own wealth. But the conclusion that he also increases aggregate wealth fails to allow for the possibility that an act of individual saving may react on someone else's savings and hence on someone else's wealth. (Keynes, 1936, pp. 83–4)

This conclusion can be explained as follows:

> The reconciliation of the identity between saving and investment with the apparent 'free-will' of the individual to save what he chooses irrespective of what he or others may be investing, essentially depends on savings being, like spending, a two-sided affair. For although the amount of his own saving is unlikely to have any significant influence on his own income, the reactions of the amount of his consumption on the incomes of others makes it impossible for all individuals simultaneously to save any given sums. Every such attempt to save more by reducing consumption will so affect incomes that the attempt necessarily defeats itself.

This outcome follows from 'the fact' that:

> there cannot be a buyer without a seller or a seller without a buyer. Though an individual whose transactions are small in relation to the market can safely neglect

the fact that demand is not a one-sided transaction, it makes nonsense to neglect it when we come to aggregate demand. This is the vital difference between the theory of the economic behaviour of the aggregate and the theory of the behaviour of the individual unit, in which we assume that changes in the individual's own demand do not affect his income.	(Keynes, 1936, pp. 84, 85)

From this insight everything else flowed.

The above extracts are taken from the main body of the text of the *General Theory*; but Keynes also provided 'frame-materials', in which he sought to explain the provenance of the ideas he was employing. In the second of the three chapters included in the 'Short Notes Suggested by the General Theory' (Book VI), Keynes made reference to a number of writers, including Major Douglas, Bernard Mandeville, T.R. Malthus, Silvio Gesell and J.A. Hobson, whom he numbered among:

the brave army of heretics . . . who, following their intuitions, have preferred to see the truth obscurely and imperfectly rather than to maintain error, reached indeed with clearness and consistency and by easy logic but on hypotheses inappropriate to the facts.	(Keynes, 1936, p. 371)

Note especially in this passage: that Keynes is enthusiastically allying himself with 'heretics' (with heterodoxy); that the heretics are seen as glimpsing the truth by way of their intuitions; and that the orthodoxy from which they have chosen to dissent is to be faulted in its premises, not its logical structure. In other words, Keynes has chosen historical antecedents made in his own image, and so the interest lies not so much in what the individual writers actually said but what it was that Keynes saw in their work.

Of the writers discussed by Keynes, the ideas of Douglas and of Gesell – and even Hobson, who was commended by Keynes for the stand he took against the orthodox belief in the unlimited benefit of thrift – are too far removed from present concerns to warrant further attention. Malthus will be dealt with below. Of Mandeville, however, there is more to be said, as his writings provide a unique insight into Keynes's own position.

VII

Bernard Mandeville (1670–1733) was a native of Rotterdam who studied medicine at Leyden but who married and settled in London. Here he practised as a doctor, specialising in the 'hypochondriack and hysterick passions', and published a treatise on the subject. In the early eighteenth century, however, he became notorious and the subject of bitter criticism for writings of a different sort. It was these writings that were to have an important influence on eighteenth-century and subsequent economic thought.

He had made his debut with translations of familiar fables from the French but in 1705 he published anonymously a sixpenny pamphlet in doggerel verse entitled *The Grumbling Hive, or, Knaves turn'd Honest*. This too was in the form of a fable – that is, a short moral tale with animals for characters – which sought to expose what he saw as one of the principal follies of mankind: namely, to commend for society behaviour which must result in poverty and misery; and to deprecate as antisocial, behaviour which was the source of prosperity, happiness and strength. The proceeding was scandalous because Mandeville's conclusions appeared to many as entirely subversive of conventional morality. This much is clear from the title of the work as reissued in 1714 (which consisted of the *Grumbling Hive* together with a series of prose remarks as *The Fable of the Bees; or, Private Vices. Public Benefits*). It was from later (1723 and 1724), greatly expanded versions of this book that Mandeville's public notoriety sprang. Jon Elster, in his *Logic and Society*, argues that Mandeville's

> importance for the history of the social sciences can hardly be exaggerated. If you want to find the origin of the notion of latent functions [a concept in sociology], go to Mandeville – not to Merton; for the concept of the invisible hand, go to Mandeville – not to Adam Smith. In his criticism of the fallacy of composition he is a pioneer again, as seen in the praise bestowed on him by Keynes. (Elster, 1978, p. 107)

This juxtaposition of the invisible hand and the fallacy of composition is of great interest for present purposes and we shall return to Elster's treatment below. There are, however, some preliminaries to deal with.

First, the suggestion that so upset churchmen and others: namely, that public benefits flow from private vices rather than from private virtues. For the moralist this means that what Mandeville summarised as 'Fraud, Luxury and Pride' (that is, apart from cheating and other crime, the more prevalent vices of pride, vanity, prodigality, avarice and lust) will contribute to the good of society; while honesty, frugality and self-denial will cause it to weaken and die. For the economist, however, it had a far more beneficial, even miraculous, message: namely, that individuals acting in an entirely self-interested (selfish) and unco-ordinated way could produce prosperity.

This brings us to our second point which is argued by Louis Dumont in his *From Mandeville to Marx: The Genesis and Triumph of Economic Ideology* (Dumont, 1977, chs 4, 5). This is that, just as the English philosopher John Locke had freed economics, as a 'mode of consideration of human phenomena', from the politics in which it was embedded, so Mandeville freed economics from morality of the conventional kind by giving it a morality of its own. By identifying economic prosperity with the public good and arguing that prosperity would be the outcome of each pursuing his or her own individual interest, 'selfishness' could be seen to work to mutual advantage. The link between the two was the working of the 'market' which reconciled and made harmonious individual interests. For Mandeville, the person in society is an individual, as in nature, and acts only for him- or herself; while society is just an objective mechanism that unites individual efforts and produces prosperity. Dumont sees Mandeville as instituting a very modern idea when he substituted the relationship between person and object (goods) in place of the relationship between person and person.

Finally and most importantly for what is to come, Mandeville's case is that it is by increasing expenditure on consumption that people both satisfy their own desires (self-gratification) and provide work for others. Consumption is the end of all things and in its satisfaction demand calls forth output (supply). Jobs and division of labour possibilities follow.

What lies at the heart of the above argument, of course, is Mandeville's recognition of the motive power of self interest ('vices'). Though this is crudely stated in the *Grumbling Hive*, Mandeville later cleverly shows how statesmen can use the interplay of vices to obtain the benefits while minimising the disbenefits. Though criminal activities are like dirt in the London Streets – a necessary accompaniment to prosperity – the pride/shame nexus provides a fulcrum of control. People are not naturally good but can be educated. Recalling our argument from Chapter 17 above, we can say that Mandeville recognised the possibility of learned behaviour.

Notice, however, that the motive power of self-interest would be of no avail without the beneficial ministrations of the co-ordinating mechanism. The two must go together, but it is in the relationship between them that the possibility of disagreement among economists exists. This is the basis of our distinction between the theoretical positions of Robertson and Keynes, and to see why this is so we return to Elster (1978).

In his chapter on the 'Contradictions of Society' Elster examines the logical possibilities which involve the free choice of actors and the sometimes unforeseen results of their actions. First, he defines the fallacy of composition simply as the inference that what is possible for any single individual must be possible for them all simultaneously (Elster, 1978, p. 99), a notion with which we are, from the argument of this and of previous chapters, thoroughly familiar. Of greater interest are two related concepts which mark a great divide in economic thought.

The first is the invisible hand, which Elster identifies with Mandeville's assertion that private vices give rise to public benefits. This, when self-interest is substituted for private vices, provides the central message of Adam Smith's the *Wealth of Nations* (1776). The invisible hand, therefore, is to be seen as a positive concept. Its negative opposite is the concept of 'counterfinality', which Elster defines as:

the unintended consequences that arise when each individual in a group acts upon an assumption about his relations to others that, when generalised, yields the contradiction in the consequent of the fallacy of composition, the antecedent of that fallacy being true. (Elster, 1978, p. 106)

Though they share a common ancestry, the invisible hand and counter-finality have very different implications and failure to distinguish between them can produce serious errors of theory. Just how profound are the differences of outlook involved can be gauged from the following:

Marx is sometimes said to have stood Hegel upon his head; more importantly, at least for our purpose, they both stood Adam Smith on his head. For Hegel and Marx history works itself out through the negative rather than the positive unintended consequences of human actions; through counterfinality rather than the invisible hand. (Elster, 1978, p. 108)

This being so, however, we are faced with an apparent paradox: if it is the case that Smith took the idea of the invisible hand from Mandeville, how is this to be reconciled with the fact that Mandeville was commended by Keynes for his recognition of the fallacy of composition?

First, there seems to be little doubt that Adam Smith took his inspiration from Mandeville. This was obviously Elster's position, and Dumont is even more emphatic:

It is widely admitted that the central theme of Adam Smith, the idea that self-love works for the common good, comes from Mandeville . . . the whole *Wealth* is an answer to the question: Mandeville was right as regards the place of self-love in economic phenomena . . . thus we are sent back from Adam Smith to Mandeville for the origin of the key assumption of the *Wealth of Nations*. (Dumont, 1977, p. 63)

It is equally clear that Mandeville comprehended both effects – indeed, this was the whole point of his assertion that public benefits flow from private vices (invisible hand) rather than from private virtues (counterfinality). Because society is an objective mechanism which reconciles the actions of independent agents, it will faithfully transmit the effects of changes of mood. Waves of optimism and pessimism will bring successive waves of spending and saving and hence prosperity and depression.

There is no doubt at all that this is the way that Keynes saw Mandeville's contribution. The coming together of men primarily for economic advantage produces society – in which all transactions necessarily have a dual character (see the extracts from the *General Theory* quoted above). This means that if expenditure rises, so must incomes; by contrast, if saving increases, expenditure must fall and so therefore, must incomes. Keynes denied that saving was the means to achieve national prosperity and quoted passages from

The Grumbling Hive and from the 'Remarks' which follow it, to support the contention (see Keynes, 1936, pp. 360–2; see also Kaye ed., 1924, pp. 32–3, 34, 197–8).

For the purposes of the present argument it will be appropriate to quote passages illustrative of both the positive effects of expenditure and of the negative effects of saving. Some of these were also quoted by Keynes, as indicated. The general principle that Mandeville is seeking to establish is, of course, the highly unorthodox and indeed outrageous one that private vices give rise to public benefits, as the following passage from *The Grumbling Hive* makes quite clear:

> . . . The Root of Evil, Avarice,
> That damn'd ill-natur'd baneful Vice,
> Was Slave to Prodigality,
> . . . That noble Sin; . . . whilst Luxury
> Employ'd a Million of the Poor,
> . . . And odious Pride a Million more:
> . . . Envy it self, and Vanity,
> Were Ministers of Industry;
> Their darling Folly, Fickleness,
> In Diet, Furniture and Dress,
> That strange ridic'lous Vice, was made
> The very Wheel that turn'd the Trade.
> (Mandeville, [1714, 1723] 1924, p. 25)

On the other hand the accepted private virtues give rise only to public dis-benefits, and in the following passage from 'Remark K', Mandeville completes the paradox by comparing the effects of prodigality with those of frugality:

> Frugality is like Honesty, a mean starving Virtue, that is only fit for small Societies of good peaceable Men, who are contented to be poor so they may be easy; but in a large stirring Nation you may have soon enough of it. Tis an idle dreaming Virtue that employs no Hands, and therefore very useless in a trading Country, where there are vast Numbers that one way or other must be all set to Work. Prodigality has a thousand Inventions to keep People from sitting still, that Frugality would never think of; and as this must consume a prodigious Wealth, so Avarice again knows innumerable Tricks to rake it together, which Frugality would scorn to make use of. (Mandeville, [1714, 1723] 1924, pp. 104–5)

More pithily, the conclusion to which Mandeville's argument leads is that 'all the Cardinal Virtues together won't so much as procure a tolerable Coat or a Porridge-Pot among them' (from 'Remark Q', in Mandeville, [1714, 1723] 1924, p. 184).

Mandeville's recognition of the essentially two-way nature of transactions is indicated by the following. First, passages from 'Remark L' deal with the case of international trade:

Buying is Bartering, and no Nation can buy Goods of others that has none of her own to purchase them with [the implication is that] . . . we know that we could not continue long to purchase the Goods of other Nations, if they would not take our Manufactures in payment for them. (Mandeville, [1714, 1723] 1924, p. 111)

Next a passage from 'Remark I' applies the principle to the mass of individuals within a country and shows how private vices conduce to the public good through being complementary. Here we find Avarice as 'a Slave to Prodigality':

Avarice, notwithstanding it is the occasion of so many Evils, is yet very necessary to the Society, to glean and gather what has been dropt and scatter'd by the contrary Vice. Was it not for Avarice, Spend thrifts would soon want Materials; and if none would lay up and get faster than they spend, very few could spend faster than they get. (Mandeville, [1714, 1723] 1924, p. 101)

Mandeville's challenge to the canons of conventional economic wisdom is set out in the following two passages. In the first, Mandeville's case is made in terms of Prodigality versus Frugality; in the second, in more familiar economic language. In both it is the contrast between the effects of spending and saving on the part of one family taken in isolation as against all families acting together:

It is a receiv'd Notion, that Luxury is as destructive to the Wealth of the whole Body Politic, as it is to that of every individual Person who is guilty of it, and that a National Frugality enriches a Country in the same manner as that which is less general increases the Estates of private Families. I confess, that tho' I have found Men of much better Understanding than my self of this Opinion, I cannot help dissenting from them in this Point. (Mandeville, [1714, 1723] 1924, pp. 108-9)

The second passage is one of those quoted by Keynes as illustrative of his point that saving is, contrary to established belief, destructive of national prosperity:

As this prudent Oeconomy, which some People call *Saving*, is in private Families the most certain Method to increase an Estate, so some imagine that whether a Country be barren or fruitful, the same Method, if generally pursued (which they think practicable) will have the same Effect upon a whole Nation, and that, for Example, the *English* might be much richer than they are, if they would be as frugal as some of their Neighbours. This, I think, is an Error. . . . (Mandeville, [1714, 1723] 1924, p. 182; also quoted in Keynes, 1936, p. 361)

Keynes also quotes a passage from the original fable, *The Grumbling Hive*, which argues that when the 'Knaves' have indeed 'turn'd Honest' and rejected private vices for accepted virtues, the effects are disastrous, with a fall in aggregate demand and consequent general over-supply (under-employment):

> Now mind the glorious Hive, and see
> How Honesty and Trade agree.
> The Shew is gone, it thins apace;
> And looks with quite another Face.
> For 'twas not only that They went,
> By whom vast Sums were Yearly spent;
> But Multitudes that liv'd on them,
> Were daily forc'd to do the same.
> In vain to other Trades they'd fly;
> All were o'er-stock'd accordingly.
> (Mandeville, [1714, 1723] 1924, p. 32;
> see also Keynes, 1936, p. 360, where
> the passage quoted is more extensive)

Finally, and given the issues with which he was concerned in the 1930s, Keynes took the opportunity to enter a plea for active schemes of improvement by including a passage from 'Remark Q', which argues in favour of intervention by the state and conveniently includes the line: 'let a Government's first care be to promote as great a variety of Manufactures, Arts, and Handicrafts, as Human Wit can invent' (Mandeville, [1714, 1723] 1924, pp. 197-8; Keynes, 1936, p. 361). Could an aesthetically inclined reformer of the twentieth century have asked for better historical underpinnings?

Keynes explicitly compared the insight displayed by Mandeville the heretic with the orthodox view of saving held by Adam Smith:

> Compare Adam Smith, the forerunner of the classical school, who wrote, 'What is prudence in the conduct of every private family can scarce be folly in that of a great Kingdom' – probably with reference to the above passage from Mandeville. (Keynes, 1936, p. 361)

To reinforce Keynes's point we can turn to the index of the *Wealth of Nations*, where we find the following entry:

> *Parsimony* is the immediate cause of the increase of capitals, 337. Promotes industry, 337-8. Frugal men, public benefactors, 340 . . . (Smith, [1776] 1976, p. 1059)

All redolent of a draughty manse and fingerless mittens. But the question arises as to how it was possible for Smith to have taken up the idea of the invisible hand, but to have failed to follow Mandeville with respect to the other side of his theory, which is concerned with counterfinality. In other words, why did he not accept the obvious implication of Mandeville's argument, which is that, *if prosperity is to be our goal, self-interested behaviour is not enough*. There must be self-interested *expenditure*: self-interested frugality, or parsimony, will land society in poverty.

The plain fact is that Smith had very little to say about saving as such in the *Wealth of Nations* and it may have been that he thought that common sense (see the extract from the *Wealth of Nations* quoted by Keynes, above) and consistency would suggest that *all* forms of self-interested behaviour would promote prosperity. Mandeville, that is, had simply gone a paradox too far.

However, despite its slender theoretical basis, saving plays a very important role in Smith's thesis and it can be argued that:

> the most definitely and 'revolutionary' contribution of the *Wealth of Nations* was surely that relating to economic growth and the theory of employment, interest and money, with its extreme emphasis on the beneficence of individual saving and on the smoothness with which this was implemented in capital accumulation. (Hutchison, 1978, p. 24)

More particularly, and in keeping with his overall philosophy:

> Smith's point is not simply the importance of accumulation: *but how - within the simple system of natural liberty - individual frugality and initiative in free markets will be fully and smoothly implemented and converted into capital accumulation and the economic progress of society, without any intervention of government.* It is the 'simple system' which enables the frugal or parsimonious man, concerned simply to 'better his own condition', to be a public benefactor. (Hutchison, 1978, p. 15; emphasis in original)

In other words, there may have been another factor at work in persuading Smith to adopt his position on saving, which is that it leaves provision for economic progress and the benefit of society entirely at the initiative of the individual working through the classical capital market. This leaves virtually no macroeconomic role for the state (see Hutchison, 1978, pp. 15, 24-5).

Finally, we might add that Smith may have thought that he had already stuck his neck out far enough in going against his teacher at Glasgow, Francis Hutcheson, by substituting egoism as the motive force in society for Hutcheson's altruism ('sympathy' or 'benevolence'). Smith's best-known line was, of course:

> It is not from the benevolence of the butcher, the brewer, or the baker that we expect our dinner, but from their regard to their own interest. (Smith, [1776] 1976, pp. 26-7)

It is interesting to note that a more recent advocate of free markets, F.A. Hayek, has also chosen to see only the positive side of Mandeville's thesis. He has seen Mandeville's real contribution to be the solution of the ancient conundrum based on the distinction between institutions which are *natural* and those which are the work of man: that is, *artificial* or designed. According to Hayek, Mandeville has clearly seen that institutions which are the work of man are also without conscious design from inception, having grown spontaneously as the product of many hands over many generations. By contrast, he refers dismissively to Keynes's interest in Mandeville and resolutely ignores any idea of saving as a destructive activity and of the paradox of thrift (Hayek, 1978, ch. 15).

VIII

Now we can see more clearly the implications of the theoretical positions adopted by Robertson and Keynes respectively. For Keynes as for Mandeville, self-interested behaviour is only valuable in promoting prosperity if it is self-interested *expenditure*. By the same token it became a characteristic of Keynesian economics to argue that saving was destructive of economic health, as was made clear in a sixpenny pamphlet by G.D.H. Cole, *Saving and Spending; or The Economics of 'Economy'* (n.d.) which had a title page slogan, or maxim, adapted from a famous line in William Wordsworth's sonnet 'The World is Too Much With Us' as: 'Saving, not spending, we lay waste our powers' (Cole, n.d., p. 1). Keynes, therefore, comprehended the dual nature of Mandeville's thesis and fully exploited both aspects for the making of the *General Theory*. On this basis Keynes's truly revolutionary breakthrough was to make precise the effects of (investment) spending and of saving, in the form of the multiplier and the paradox of thrift, in his concepts of the marginal propensities to consume and to save. This, as we shall see, came as early as the spring of 1932.

Robertson, on the other hand, followed Smith and thus got only half a theory instead of the 'general' (spending *and* saving) theory of Keynes. We recall that Dennison wrote that Robertson, as a tyro economist, took as his exemplars Smith and Marshall: the one the 'forerunner of the classical school' as Keynes designated him; and the other the father of Cambridge economics. Also, that it was to the *Wealth of Nations* and the *Principles* that he constantly turned for inspiration and sustenance:

> Throughout his life, he constantly refreshed his memory of these two works . . . and throughout his later work the influence of these two majestic works was of major importance.　(Dennison, 1992b, p. 17)

On this bedrock as we have seen, Robertson built his own theory and, in view of our comments on Smith, we might raise again a point made in Chapters 18 and 19 above: that is, how revolutionary and how dangerous was Robertson's treatment of the banking system, which was given the power to circumvent private initiative in the finance of investment through voluntary saving; and how important it was, therefore, for Robertson to retain individual saving as the norm and to argue for the role of bank finance as essentially supplementary. Hence also his advocacy of price stability as a norm of policy, with departures from this to be treated as exceptional. The possibilities for misunderstanding on Robertson's part when faced with Keynes's 'whole' theory from the viewpoint of his own 'half-theory' should now be painfully clear.

28. A question of sequence

I

The importance of the fallacy of composition in the form of the paradox of thrift for Keynes's new economics was made clear in simple language many years ago by Joan Robinson (1937, chs I–V). And here again we might notice that Robertson's comments on this book reveal his incomprehension of the processes at work (see, for example, Robertson, 1948b, p. 174; 1963a, p. 352).

Keynesian textbooks (see, for example, Dillard, 1954, ch. 4; Boulding, 1966, vol. II, ch. 6) also gave prominence to the paradox of thrift as an important *Keynesian* phenomenon, but then with the hegemony of neo-Classical 'bastard-Keynesian' economics the idea dropped out of sight because of its redundancy in an obstacles-to-adjustment-to-full-employment view of Keynes. In more recent times, however, there has been a welcome resurgence of interest.

Several contributions have drawn attention to the importance of the fallacy as an element in Keynes's thinking (see, for example, Steindl, 1985; Harcourt and O'Shaughnessy, 1985; Carabelli, 1988; O'Donnell, 1989; Harcourt, 1994). In Fletcher (1987, 1989a), it played the key role in the discussion of the Robertson–Keynes controversy. Clarke (1988, pp. 230, 269–72) carefully chronicled instances of Keynes's appeal to the phenomenon and argued that it became 'the unifying conception' in the evolution of his new line of thought and 'informed all his thinking by the end of 1932'. Two major biographies of Keynes differ markedly in their treatment of the topic, with Skidelsky (1992) according it more attention than Moggridge (1992, pp. 499, 541, 553), who questions its significance as a new element in Keynes's moves forward towards the *General Theory*.

II

The essence of Keynes's theorising stemmed directly from this insight, because it became necessary to arrange the key variables into an order consistent with it. A sequence of theory-building was imposed in which as Keynes solved one problem he was forced in turn to solve others, so that his theory emerged in logical order, based on a clear vision of first principles. The significance of this is obvious in the context of the Robertsonian belief that Keynes adopted liquidity preference theory as a means of opening the way for the redisposition of real forces. It is thus at this point that the issue of the paradox of thrift and the issue of the ordering of real and monetary variables are brought into conjunction in the question of the sequence in which Keynes's theory developed. Goodhart's explicit assertion of the Robertsonian position was that:

> with interest rates thus separately determined by liquidity preference the way was open for the establishment of the general level of incomes and output as the variable that would equilibrate planned investment and saving via multipliers, accelerators and all that collection of quantitative adjustment mechanisms. . . . (Goodhart, 1989, p. 107)

In reply the present writer argued that:

> The evidence clearly shows that Keynes, beginning from the income-consumption relation, first determined that saving is wholly the creature of investment and that it is not possible – due to the 'paradox of thrift' – to increase the rate of investment by saving more at some prior date; also, that given the relation between investment, income and saving, there could be no rate of interest at which, in equilibrium, saving would not be equal to investment. This . . . left Keynes without a theory of the rate of interest.
> The solution, which, he tells us, came to him appreciably later, began with the everyday, schoolbook definition of interest itself and gave the rate of interest as the liquidity premium on money ruling in the market. (Fletcher, 1989b, p. 131)

The evidence on which this alternative view is based has emerged from the debate over the nature and timing of the transition in Keynes's thought between the *Treatise* (1930) and the *General Theory* (1936), though subsequent developments have rendered its confident conclusions less unequivocal in detail. Contributors to the debate have provided a variety of criteria for identifying and dating the various points of departure (Clarke, 1988; Dimand, 1988, 1994; Moggridge, 1992, 1993; Skidelsky, 1992; Meade, 1993; Patinkin, 1993, 1994). But if we apply the criterion of recognition of the fallacy of composition, we are directed to Clarke's account of events. Clarke uses Keynes's letter to Harrod of August 1936 (Keynes, *CW* XIV p. 85), in conjunction with other available evidence, to date Keynes's 'moments of transition' giving 'four distinct chronological stages' (Clarke, 1988, pp. 229–230, 256–282).

1. By May 1932   The consumption–income relation (the fundamental psychological law)

2. Summer 1932   Effective demand–supply and demand for output as a whole

3. October 1932   The rate of interest as an expression of liquidity
                     preference

4. Last of all   The marginal efficiency of capital

On this evidence, therefore, Keynes's interest-rate theory succeeds rather than precedes the innovations regarding the relationship between investment, saving and fluctuations in real income.

In qualification, however, we should mention Moggridge's reservations regarding the timing schedule adopted by Clarke. Moggridge finds that the evidence favours 1933 rather than 1932 as the year of inception of the *General Theory* and, more seriously, throws some doubt on the strict acceptance of Keynes's account of the sequence of development (Moggridge, 1992, pp. 562–4). Moggridge argues that:

> In assessing how far [Keynes] had got at any moment, however, I believe that we must go further than mere 'disjointed flashes' ['of illumination' – as on Clarke's criterion] and seek out the evidence that, even if Keynes had not fully specified the route to his destination, he was reasonably certain that his 'flash' was not a 'mirage'. (Moggridge, 1992, p. 559; 1993, p. 97)

As a benchmark he adopts Patinkin's criterion of 'the development of the theory of effective demand, most notably the equilibrating role of changes in income implicit in the multiplier' (Moggridge, 1992, p. 559; see also pp. 561, 562). On this basis he concludes that at the time that Keynes had 'developed a clear notion of liquidity preference' in the autumn of 1932, 'it is not apparent that the penny had dropped sufficiently clearly for Keynes that he could be considered to have successfully found a route for his intuition' (p. 562). Also, by giving more weight than Clarke to the later of two lots of additions to Keynes's biographical essay on Malthus and to various policy pronouncements made by Keynes in the first quarter of the following year, Moggridge considers that 'the basic output-adjustment framework of the *General Theory* was in place . . . by early 1933 *at the latest*' (p. 564; emphasis in original).

In addition he plays down the importance of the fallacy of composition as an innovatory element in the process, on the grounds that:

> the notion . . . had been in Keynes's thought since his undergraduate contact with [G.E.] Moore and can thus hardly be 'new' to the *General Theory*, although Keynes may have recognised the greater significance of organicism in economics as he got older. (Moggridge, 1992, p. 564)

Nevertheless there are, especially for present purposes, sound reasons for adhering to the Keynes–Clarke version of events.

The first is that Keynes provided not one but three separate accounts of the sequence of development of his ideas. Apart from the letter to Harrod referred to above, he had previously written to A.P. Lerner in similar vein (see Keynes, *CW* XXIX pp. 214–16) and later provided confirmation in a published article (Keynes, *CW* XIV pp. 109–23, esp. pp. 119–23), which strongly suggests that we have a true indication of the way in which the process presented itself to Keynes's mind. Why should he dissemble? Surely not in anticipation of this kind of charge?

In addition he provided further confirmation of the, for present purposes, crucial sequence in which the investment–saving relationship was established prior to his interest theory. In 'Alternative Theories of the Rate of Interest' (Keynes, 1937, *CW* XIV, p. 212), Keynes confirmed that:

> the initial novelty lies in my maintaining that it is not the rate of interest, but the level of incomes which ensures equality between saving and investment. The arguments which lead up to this initial conclusion are independent of my subsequent theory of the rate of interest, and in fact I reached it before I had reached the latter theory. But the result of it was to leave the rate of interest in the air.

In other words, whatever the date at which an acceptably recognisable theory of effective demand can be discerned, Keynes is clear that his interest theory came later than his theory of investment and saving. In the Harrod letter, the rate of interest theory came 'appreciably later' (Keynes, *CW* XIV p. 85).

Second, it would be wrong to reject the fallacy of composition as the crucial addition to the mixture, on two grounds. First and more generally, it is important to recognise that part of Keynes's achievement was to see familiar ideas in a new light and to breathe life into lifeless forms. From this new perspective saving lost its initiatory role and was forced instead to shadow investment; while the bearishness function, which had been available since the *Treatise*, was only seen in its proper light, in the form of the liquidity preference function, once the investment–saving relationship was sorted out and it was necessary to rethink the theory of the rate of interest.

To illustrate this point we might note that retention of a significant part for the fallacy of composition helps to answer a query raised by Robertson as he surveyed the components of Keynes's new theory and searched vainly for the novelty they contained:

> Both over the *Treatise* and this book I have gone through real intellectual torment trying to make up my mind whether, as you often seem to claim, there is some new piece on the board or rather a rearrangement, which seems to you superior, of existing pieces. (Robertson to Keynes, 29 December 1936, in Keynes, *CW* XIV p. 95)

Despite the fundamental changes in the relationship between the key variables that had occurred between the *Treatise* and the *General Theory*, Robertson can find nothing new and thus failed to see the significance of the fallacy of composition, which is both a new piece on the board and, in addition, produces a new arrangement of pieces.

Also, and more particularly, recognition of the significance of the fallacy of composition directs attention to the critical breakthrough phase that initiated the development of the theory of effective demand. Clarke puts much greater weight on this phase than Moggridge, who emphasises the *completion* of the process – at least in fundamentals – as indicated by evidence that for Keynes 'the penny had dropped sufficiently clearly' or 'the penny had firmly dropped' (Moggridge, 1992 pp. 562, 564). By the same token, Clarke is concerned with *cause* – moments of transition relating to expenditure; whereas Moggridge is concerned with *effect* – as is indicated by his adoption of Patinkin's criterion of 'the equilibrating role of changes in income implicit in the multiplier' (Moggridge, 1992, pp. 559, 561, 562).

III

The opening phase was crucial, note, because once investment was set to determine saving the die was cast and it only required time and experiment for the rest to fall into place. It is on this ground that it is possible to argue that, whatever the doubts concerning the date by which the penny had dropped, the changes from which all else flowed preceded Keynes's new interest theory by several months. The significance of this initial phase in allowing Keynes to move forward on firm foundations from first principles can be explained as follows. The starting point is the Harris Foundation lectures on 'An Economic Analysis of Unemployment' that Keynes delivered in Chicago in *June 1931*.

The 'secret' that Keynes vouchsafed to his audience, 'the clue to the scientific explanation of booms and slumps', 'the clue to the whole business' was cast in the purely *Treatise* terms of changes in the profitability of business as indicated by the *inequality* of investment and saving (Keynes, *CW* XIII p. 353-4). Keynes went on to explain why this represented an important advance on previous theory:

> In the past it has been usual to believe that there was some preordained harmony by which saving and investment were necessarily equal. If we entrusted our savings to a bank, it used to be said, the bank will of course make use of them, and they will duly find their way into industry and investment. But unfortunately this is not so, I venture to say with certainty that this is not so. And it is out of the disequilibriums of savings and investment, and out of nothing else, that the fluctuations of profits, of output, and of employment are generated.   (Keynes, *CW* XIII p. 355)

In other words, because in orthodox thinking saving determined investment, saving and investment were necessarily identically equal; whereas on Keynes's analysis, which owed much to discussions with Robertson, they were defined to be unequal except in equilibrium. Thus an excess of investment over saving betokened expansion (via the incentive of windfall profits); and an excess of saving over investment betokened contraction (via the disincentive of windfall losses).

However, the basis on which saving and investment were held to be unequal depended on what came to be regarded as a rather eccentric definition of savings, and in August Richard Kahn was reproaching him for criticising Robertson, who had merely adopted 'a perfectly simple-minded and natural definition of saving – receipts minus expenditure' (Keynes, *CW* XIII p. 238). Keynes was subsequently to redefine income and saving to include windfalls and so embrace the 'simple-minded' idea that saving and investment were once again necessarily equal.

Nevertheless, the *Treatise* episode must be regarded as a preliminary to and precondition for the big move forward in 1932 – in as much as it drew attention to the dangers inherent in the classical assumption of the 'pre-ordained harmony' between saving and investment. As Keynes explained to Robertson in March 1932:

> The old 'common-sense' view not only held that savings and investment are necessarily equal . . . but inferred from this that therefore one need not bother . . . The mistake of the 'common-sense' view lay not in the belief (using words as it chose to use them) that an increase of savings S¹ [new definition] necessarily means an increase in the value of investment. The mistake lay in supposing that a decreased expenditure on consumption leads (*cet par*) to an increase of S¹. This is why it was wrong to infer that there was no need to bother.   (Keynes, *CW* XIII pp. 278–9)

Keynes could now see that although saving and investment were, once again, equal by definition, the direction of causation was reversed and the link between a reduction in consumption and a rise in saving (investment) was broken. Instead:

> S¹ always and necessarily accommodates itself to I. Whether I consists in housing schemes or in war finance, there need be nothing to hold us back, because I always drags S¹ along with it at an equal pace. S¹ is not the voluntary result of virtuous decisions. In fact S¹ is no longer the dog, which common sense believes it to be, but the tail. (Keynes, *CW* XIII p. 276)

Such a view was clearly in accord with Keynes's awareness of the implications of the fallacy of composition.

IV

In his University lectures in the Easter Term (that is, from April to June) 1932, entitled 'The Pure Theory of Money', Keynes set out the fundamental relationships that govern Keynesian economics:

> whenever there is a change in income, there will be a change in expenditure the same in direction but less in amount . . . [also] the volume of output and the volume of investment go up and down together; or in more familiar language, the volume of employment directly depends on the amount of investment. (Keynes, *CW* XXIX p. 39)

It is easy to see why this insight should have assumed the position of 'vast importance' in Keynes's own thinking that he accorded it in his letter to Harrod of 30 August 1936 (Keynes, *CW* XIV p. 85). Realisation that a portion of income would remain unspent as income rose because of a deficiency of consumption demand left the onus on investment to fill the gap. But coupled with his conclusions that investment was the 'dog' that wagged the 'tail' saving and that investment determined output, Keynes had struck a mortal blow at Say's Law, sustained as it was by the 'common-sense' view that any income not devoted to consumption would automatically be translated into the alternative form of expenditure, investment, at an unchanged level of income. But, in addition, Keynes's new conception was formed in terms of changes in output and, because $Y \equiv C + I$, the relationship between investment and output was a proportional relationship. Clarke (1988, p. 261) has drawn attention to the demonstration by Rymes (1989, ch. 2) that Keynes's exposition in the Easter Term lectures 1932 was 'premised on the multiplier'.

We should also note that viewed in the light of Keynes's recognition of the fallacy of composition and the spending–expansion/saving–contraction dichotomy, Keynes's insight into the consumption–income relation means that the multiplier becomes a retarder, limiter and stabiliser, explaining why a change in expenditure will have finite rather than infinite effects. This, note, puts the Patinkin–Moggridge criterion of 'the equilibrating role of changes in income implicit in the multiplier' in its true light: as that which completes the process in the theory of effective demand.

V

Keynes's course was now set, and by the time he wrote to Hawtrey on 1 June 1932 it is clear that, though there was still much to be resolved, the new way of thinking was firmly in place:

As I mentioned to you, I am working it out all over again . . . I now put less fundamental reliance on my conception of savings and substitute for it the conception of expenditure. Also generally speaking I do not have to deal with absolute amounts of expenditure, but with increments and decrements of expenditure. This is, so to speak, the inverse of saving, since saving is the excess of income or earnings over expenditure; but since there are two senses in which income can be used, it is much preferable to use a term about which everyone agrees. The whole thing comes out just as conveniently in terms of expenditure. (Keynes, *CW* XIII p. 172)

By establishing that expenditure determines income, that investment is the key component of aggregate expenditure and that we must think in terms of increments and decrements of expenditure, Keynes had set the stage for the appearance of the theory of effective demand. It is likely that this second stage of the Keynes–Clarke account of events was reached during the summer of 1932, given that the third stage, the theory of interest (which came 'appreciably later'), can with certainty be dated to October of that year. This is the position taken by Clarke, who argues that Keynes gave his 'first consistent exposition' of the theory of effective demand (the theory of the demand and supply for output as a whole) in his Michaelmas Term lectures (Lecture Two, 17 October) now retitled 'The Monetary Theory of Production' (Clarke, 1988, p. 265; Rymes, 1989, pp. 47ff). We should note that Keynes linked the theory explicitly with the fallacy of composition. Two weeks later (Lecture Four, 31 October) came the notion of interest as the measure of liquidity preference (the order of topics of the lectures, as in the *General Theory* (see above, Chapter 26), perhaps reflecting the logic of development of the ideas in Keynes's thought). There can, therefore, be no grounds for arguing that Keynes adopted his interest theory as a preliminary 'for the establishment of . . . [his own idiosyncratic?] collection of quantitative adjustment mechanisms' (Goodhart, 1989, p. 107).

VI

The suggestion that Robertson failed, for whatever reason, to take account in his work of the fallacy of composition, in the form of the paradox of thrift, is a contentious one and has been met with emphatic denials. Nevertheless, that is the conclusion to which the evidence unmistakably leads us.

In the first place, there is in Robertson's work a wealth of references to the relationship between investment and saving that enable us to quote chapter and verse in support of the claim. This much is clear from our examination of the relevant sections of the *Study*, *BPPL*, *LEP* and the selection of essays in Hicks ed. (1966). In the second place, students of Robertsonian economics have drawn attention to this deficiency in Robertson's work and in doing so have elicited vehement denials from those supporters unable to accept such a possibility.

The published contributions to the debate have so far been few but it will be useful to record them so as to establish precedence. The first acknowledgement was in John Presley's *Robertsonian Economics* (1978), which deals fully with Robertson's treatment of saving, investment, money and the rate of interest. It is a strongly sympathetic treatment and argues for the acceptance of Robertson's approach and the rejection of Keynes's. In a comparison of Robertson's and Keynes's treatment of the relationship between investment, saving and the rate of interest Presley comments:

> The encouragement of thrift is no longer a virtue but a vice in a depressed economy; an increase in the propensity to save out of total income . . . reduces the value of the multiplier, yielding less output from a given level of investment, and more unemployment. It does not bring a lowering of the rate of interest and a subsequent encouragement to invest. [Footnote] If disposable income falls, consumption will decline . . . It also yields less total saving since disposable income is reduced. DHR [Robertson] did not comprehend this fact (see *Lectures on Economic Principles* p. 387), failing to appreciate the paradox of thrift. (Presley, 1978, p. 182 and n. 18)

This was Presley's only reference to the point, but we should note that the context in which he makes it reinforces our argument concerning the critically important position it holds: determining the nature of saving, the relationship between saving and investment, the nature of the finance of investment and having implications for the determination of the rate of interest.

These points were fully brought out in Fletcher, *The Keynesian Revolution and its Critics* (Fletcher, 1987, 1989a, chs 4–10), a book intended to 'explain and justify the Keynesian Revolution and to defend Keynes against his principal critics' (text from jacket). Robertson is identified as 'Keynes's most important critic' (1987, p. xxi) but his case is held to fail because of a weakness in his argument which 'stems from his attempt to develop and adapt classical economics, a policy which causes him to incorporate untenable ideas relating to saving in his analysis'.

It is argued that Robertson incorporated these ideas because he

> failed to understand the nature of saving and the 'paradox of thrift' and [that] the implications of this failure ran through the strata of his argument like a geological fault. Once the error was recognised, the loanable – funds theory, the whole intricate apparatus of reconciliation between old orthodoxy and new insights would be revealed as invalid. (1987, p. 45)

The argument that led to this conclusion drew a contrast between Robertson's evolutionary approach, of building on classical ideas; and Keynes's revolutionary approach, in which classical logic is stood on its head and repudiated. Possible reasons for Robertson's inability to let go of classical modes of thought, based on some literary clues intuited by Keynes, are suggested (see above, Chapter 26). It is a conclusion that is also reached on the basis of the logic of Robertson's theory. But the main piece of evidence that is brought forward is Robertson's criticism of Keynes's new theory, which is held to provide a clear guide to Robertson's own thinking. Note is taken of Presley's explicit recognition of Robertson's failure to understand the paradox of thrift, though it is pointed out that 'the recognition is tucked away in a footnote with scarcely an inkling of its significance' (1987, p. 45) .

We should also mention here Fletcher (1989b), 'Keynes, Money and Monetarism: a Note', which comments upon Goodhart's (1989) claim that Robertson's loanable funds theory of the rate of interest and his approach to the specification of the demand for money were superior to the Keynesian equivalents. This 'Note' drew attention for the first time to the significance for this question of the *sequence* of development in Keynes's thought in moving forward from the *Treatise* (1930) to the *General Theory* (1936). As we have seen, this involved a new perception of the relationship between income and expenditure, based on an awareness of the fallacy of composition in the first stage of reform and, therefore, a new understanding of the nature of saving and of its relationship to investment. It was this sequence that enabled Keynes to apportion such roles to real and monetary variables as enabled him to avoid the confusion into which he claimed Robertson had, by following a different path (that is, not recognising the significance of the paradox of thrift), so completely fallen.

Finally, the basis of the present argument was set out in Fletcher (1996), *Robertson, Keynes and the Keynesian Revolution*.

The validity of Fletcher's arguments of 1987 was denied in a review by Bleaney (Bleaney, 1987, pp. 1036-7). He found the idea that Robertson's difficulty was that he failed to understand the paradox of thrift as a result of which he continued to accept the notion that saving determines investment, 'unconvincing' (p. 1036). Bleaney also stated that he 'cannot believe' that Robertson was guilty of the error of failing 'to distinguish between the act of saving and the provision of finance for investment'.

The claims were also denied by Goodhart in his Robertson Centenary Lecture at Trinity College, Cambridge, who accused Fletcher of seizing upon a 'single invalid footnote' in Presley's book (namely, Presley, 1978, p. 182 n. 18). Goodhart's defence of Robertson depends, first, on a reference to Robertson as critic of the Treasury View (a point we dealt with earlier; and second, on the argument that Robertson 'assumed a different ordering of events' and that '*within his own framework of assumptions*, DHR's logic [is] impeccable' (Goodhart in Presley ed., 1990, p. 19; emphasis added). This defence, even if it were valid on its own terms, does not answer the point at all.

VII

But even on its own terms there is a problem, long apparent to students of Robertsonian economics and which was alluded to by Goodhart himself. The problem relates to a logical inconsistency in Robertson's price–output adjustment mechanism. It was a problem similar in kind to that which dogged Keynes in the *Treatise* and which, following its identification as the widow's cruse fallacy, led him to recast his theory in terms of quantity adjustment. The recasting involved Keynes in the overturning of long-established relationships such as Robertson was never to contemplate, with the consequence that his adjustment mechanism retained a serious flaw. The following comments were in each case made by scholars sympathetic to Robertson.

The first is by Wilson (1953, p. 566), who confessed to feeling not entirely convinced by Robertson's protestations of 'bewilderment' over the Keynesian claim to have discovered the monetary theory of production (that is, of variable national output) when his own position was so equivocal. In commenting on Robertson's explanation that although

> the formal analysis . . . is carried out on the simplifying assumption that the production and sale of commodities remains unchanged . . . the ultimate concern . . . was with changes in *output*.   (Robertson, 1949b, pp. xii–xiii)

Wilson concludes: 'This is all very difficult, and perhaps we, in turn, may express some bewilderment.'

Hicks (1982, p. 129) pointed out that in the 1920s both Robertson and Keynes were concerned with 'fluctuations not only of output and employment, but also of prices' and that:

> They had also shared a view of price-formation, inherited from Marshall, according to which all markets were what I would now call flexprice markets. Price responded immediately (or almost immediately as matters) to fluctuations in demand and supply. This had indeed made it quite hard to see how output and employment *could* fluctuate, when prices were so flexible – a point which in his early books caused Robertson quite a lot of trouble.

The same Hicksian terminology had also been employed in another contribution by Wilson (1980, p. 1533) who, in arguing that Robertson 'was assuming a *flexprice* model in the product market', related this to his failure to take account of the possible influence of changes in inventories of finished goods. We have, of course, already met this criticism. We saw that in 1926

R.G. Hawtrey recognised both the central part played by changes in the price level as a means of adjustment in Robertson's model and the dependence of this mechanism for its operation on Robertson's failure to take account of the effects of changes in stocks of finished goods. For Hawtrey, this omission undermined the credibility of Robertson's argument.

It was, moreover, to remain a bone of contention between them. This much is clear from the Hawtrey–Robertson correspondence in the Hawtrey Papers at Churchill College, Cambridge. This correspondence, which in retrospect could be seen to fall into two phases or 'episodes' (see Robertson to Hawtrey, 1 March 1960, HPCC), followed an exchange in the journals (Hawtrey, Robertson, *Economic Journal*, 1933, vol. 43, pp. 699–712) and dealt with Hawtrey's criticisms of several related aspects of Robertson's theoretical apparatus.

Hawtrey attacked, for example, the notion of the Robertsonian 'day' and the associated lag as artificial concepts (Hawtrey to Robertson, 27 October 1933, 1 November 1933, 4 November 1933; June 1937, HPCC). He also voiced his doubts *inter alia* on historical grounds about the ability of invention to play the part in the course of the trade cycle that Robertson claimed for it. It is, however, Hawtrey's continued insistence that Robertson had failed to recognise, or had wilfully ignored, the role of stocks that is of particular interest here.

Robertson had previously met the charge with what can only be described as obfuscation or evasion, choosing to view Hawtrey's concern with stocks as an obtrusive obsession or 'King Charles's Head' (see Charles Dickens, *David Copperfield*) and as 'too lacking in generality to be intellectually satisfying' (October 1933, HPCC). For his part Hawtrey claimed that, in this as in other matters, his case could be supported ultimately by an appeal to the facts of actual experience (Hawtrey to Robertson, 27 October 1933, 1 November 1933, 4th November 1933, October 1934, HPCC). In October 1933 he wrote:

> My objection ('King Charles's Head') is that, when you assume that there is no change in stocks of commodities, and therefore that the retail price level is adjusted instantaneously to every change in demand, you are departing from the facts. My own analysis does not in any way preclude this hypothesis; I only disregard it because it is not true.
>
> How can you say that my own solution is on this account 'lacking in generality'? It is the making of an assumption, not the avoidance of it, that limits generality . . . In real life the accumulation of unsold stocks comes first, then follows the reduction of output, and last of all comes the fall in prices. It is, I think, rare for this sequence of events to be departed from.   (Hawtrey to Robertson, 27 October 1933, HPCC)

Goodhart, in his Centenary Lecture (in Presley ed., 1992, p. 20) also recognised that Robertson's was a two-stage process with a change in demand influencing only prices in stage one and hence giving rise to the Robertsonian mechanism of adjustment (including forced saving) which led on to a change in output in stage two. Goodhart conceded that:

> the weakness of DHR's position is that he fails to appreciate sufficiently that initially shifts in demand will be met by fluctuations in inventories at given prices, rather than by price changes . . . he himself can, I believe, be criticised for not giving enough weight to the critical role of inventory adjustment, for example as argued by Hawtrey and Harrod, in causing fluctuations in nominal expenditures to impinge initially on real output rather than on prices. Even when directly attacked on this point, Dennis tended to duck the issue.

Also, we might note that, even if Robertson had successfully established the case for his price-adjustment mechanism, subsequent work has indicated that price and wage flexibility is a less efficacious means of promoting full employment than the stable wage–price regime advocated by Keynes (see Tobin, 1975, pp. 195–202).

In any case, finally, Keynes viewed wage–price stability as a fundamental condition for the existence of a monetary economy and would have viewed Robertson's notion of a continually adjusting price level with horror (see Keynes, 1936, pp. 237–9; also Fletcher, 1989a, ch. 12).

There is no doubt whatsoever that Robertson continued to hold to the view that saving determines investment and that he was, therefore, unaware of the logical weakness at the heart of his approach. He gave an explicit statement of his belief in 1954 and repeated it in identical terms in his lectures as published in 1963, the year of his death (see Robertson, 1954 in Hicks ed., 1966, p. 244; and Robertson, 1963a, pp. 421–2). Here in his 'Thoughts on Meeting Some Important Persons' (the 'Thoughts', we recall, being his own ideas which had been taken up and made popular by others), Robertson meditated on the curious anomaly of one who had been hailed by Joan Robinson as both precursor and true heir of Keynes, who had now, it seemed, returned to the paths of orthodox righteousness by espousing the notion that saving governs investment. The conjunction of Robertson with Kalecki constitutes a strange meeting indeed. He wrote:

> The increase in saving may itself generate an increase in capital outlay . . . high-brow opinion, you know, is like a hunted hare; if you stand long enough in the same place, or nearly the same place, it is apt to come round to you in a circle. Mr Kalecki, than whose no brow is higher . . . offers the following thought: 'A reasonable interpretation of the inter-relation between the level of income and investment decisions should be based I think, on the fact that with the high level of income there is correlated a high level of savings, and that the stream of new savings stimulates investment because it makes it possible to undertake investment without increasing indebtedness.' The wheel has come full circle. If you want to be really up to date you can now say that it is not so much investment which governs savings as savings which governs investment. But you had better be careful to give

Mr Kalecki as your authority, otherwise you may be suspected of vulgar schoolboy error. (Robertson, 1963, pp. 421–2)

Whatever the implications of this statement for the claim that Kalecki anticipated Keynes, its implications for Robertson as principal critic of the Keynesian Revolution are, on the arguments presented above, clear enough.

29. Afterwards: a postscript

In 1936 Keynes published the book that was to inaugurate the Keynesian Revolution. *The General Theory* challenged economists to accept new assumptions about the way the economy worked and to stand established relationships on their heads.

As the principal opponent of the new thinking at Cambridge, Robertson bore the brunt of the attacks on cherished beliefs and sacrosanct assumptions. Inevitably there was friction, but the element of bitterness that seems to have crept in arose from a clash of personalities between Robertson and his colleague Joan Robinson – and Robertson gave as good as he got.

The release which came at the end of 1938, when Robertson was finally persuaded to accept a proffered chair at the London School of Economics, did not last long. Within a year Britain was at war with Germany and Robertson's sojourn among like-minded colleagues gave place to a subordinate position in the Treasury. Here he was treated less seriously than a former Reader in the University of Cambridge and Professor at the LSE might have expected. He was employed on rather low-grade work calculating the balances of payments with Britain's non-sterling area trading partners, though after the USA entered the war this was supplanted by Lend-Lease business and planning for post-war schemes of international co-operation.

From 1943 he worked also in Washington, again in a subordinate capacity, until Keynes was persuaded to include him in the British Delegation to the Bretton Woods Conference of 1944. Here again there seems to have been hesitancy in entrusting Robertson with a leading role, but once the leap of faith was made he was to earn Keynes's highest praise. All seemed set fair for a healing of the wounds left by the upheavals in Cambridge, only for them to be torn open again by a misunderstanding over a negotiating point that led to Keynes's searing rebuff. This dismal outcome set the tone for the next two decades as Robertson returned to Cambridge as Professor of Political Economy in 1944. Though Keynes died not long after, in 1946, his influence lived on through his disciples, and the battles Robertson fought with them in the Faculty over teaching arrangements and new appointments continued to shadow his declining years.

There was at least the consolation afforded by the many public honours he received in recognition of his achievements, not least the fellowship of Eton

College in 1948, which gave him particular pleasure, and the honorary degrees awarded by universities at home and abroad.

There were also, however, irksome public duties to perform, including service on the Royal Commission on Equal Pay (1944–6) and membership of the Cohen Council on Prices, Productivity and Incomes (dubbed 'The Three Wise men', 1957–8). He was also called upon to give evidence to expert inquiries, including the Committee on the Rating of Site Values (1948) and the Canadian Royal Commission on Banking and Finance (1962).

Robertson exercised his right to delay retirement until the age of sixty-seven and continued working almost to the end. He became ill shortly after returning from Canada in 1962 and entered the Evelyn Nursing Home, Cambridge, where he died of heart failure, with emphysema in the lungs, on 21 April 1963. The funeral was held at the Cambridge Crematorium three days later, on the 24 April.

At a memorial service held in Trinity College Chapel on 25 May 1963, colleagues and friends gathered to pay tribute to one who had for so many years been a loved and respected senior member of the College. They gave thanks for

> his life of service to [the] College, to the University, and to the nation, for his wit and wisdom, and for the simple and unfailing goodness of his heart . . . (G11/7 RPTC)

They also recognised the characteristic element in his make-up that had always acted as the final arbiter in determining behaviour and which has featured so prominently in the present study: his sense of duty. The congregation sang Paul Gerhardt's hymn, in the translation by the poet Robert Bridges, which begins with the line:

> The duteous day now closeth . . .

It was a fitting valediction for an economist who, whatever his personal desires, always felt the need 'to be useful'.

Bibliography

MANUSCRIPT COLLECTIONS CONSULTED

Trinity College, Cambridge: Robertson Papers	RPTC
King's College, Cambridge: Keynes Papers	KPKC
Rylands Papers	RPKC
Magdalene College, Cambridge: A.C. Benson: Diaries	BDMC
Churchill College, Cambridge: Hawtrey Papers	HPCC

INFORMATION AND DOCUMENTS

Institutions

BBC Written Archives Centre
(Mr James Codd)

Cambridgeshire County Record Office
(Ms Sue Neville, Archivist)   CCRO

Eton College: Eton College Collections
(Mrs P. Hatfield, College Archivist)

Imperial War Museum: Department of Printed Books
(Mrs Sarah Patterson)

Jesus College, Cambridge
(Dr E.F. Mills, College Archivist)

King's College, Cambridge: Modern Archive Centre
(Ms Jacqueline Cox, Modern Archivist; Dr Peter Jones, Fellow and Librarian)

Liverpool Daily Post and Echo Ltd
(Mr Colin Hunt, Head of Library Services)   LDPE

Liverpool Record Office
(Ms Gina Kehoe)   LRO

Magdalene College, Cambridge: Pepys Library
(Dr R. Luckett, Pepys Librarian)

Marshall Library, Cambridge University
(Ms Alex Saunders, Archivist)

Trinity College, Cambridge:
  Wren Library
  (Mr Jonathan Smith, Manuscript Cataloguer)
  Chapel
  (Mrs Selene Webb, Chapel Secretary)

University Library, Cambridge
(Mr David J. Hall, Deputy Librarian; Kathleen Cann, Department of Manuscripts and University Archives)

Whittlesford Society, Whittlesford, Cambridgeshire
(Mr Ian L. Wright and Mr Tony Carter)

Individuals

Professor H.J. Blumenthal (late of the University of Liverpool)

Mr Nicholas Byam Shaw (Chairman, Macmillan Limited)

Dr J.R.G. Bradfield CBE (Trinity College, Cambridge, and Chairman, New Towns Commission)

Dr G.C. Harcourt AO (Emeritus Reader in the History of Economic Theory, University of Cambridge and Emeritus Fellow, Jesus College, Cambridge)

Professor Robin Marris (late of the University of Cambridge)

Professor J.R. Presley (University of Loughborough)

Dr George Rylands CH (late of King's College, Cambridge)

Professor David Vines (Balliol College, Oxford)

STANDARD SOURCES

Who's Who, 1963

Who Was Who, 1961–1970

BOOKS, INCLUDING PUBLISHED PRIMARY SOURCES, ARTICLES AND DISSERTATIONS

Alexander, Peter (ed.) 1951, *William Shakespeare: The Complete Works*, The Players Edition, London and Glasgow: Collins.

Allen, Gay Wilson 1975, *The New Walt Whitman Handbook*, New York: New York University Press.

Amadeo, Edward J. 1989, *Keynes's Principle of Effective Demand*, Aldershot, UK: Edward Elgar.

Anyadike-Danes: *see* Danes.

Ashton, T.S. 1951, 'Industrial Fluctuation' *Economica*, August, pp. 298–302.

Auden, W.H. 1966, *Collected Shorter Poems 1927-1957*, London: Faber & Faber.

Backhouse, Roger 1985, *A History of Modern Economic Analysis*, Oxford: Basil Blackwell.

Bakewell, Michael 1996, *Lewis Carroll: A Biography*, London: William Heinemann.

Basileon (originally *Basileona*), a magazine of King's College, Cambridge, issues no. 13 ('Being the Sixth Book of King's'), June 1911; no. 15 ('Being the Eighth Book of King's'), June 1913, Cambridge: King's College.

Batey, Mavis 1980, *Alice's Adventures in Oxford*, London: Pitkin Pictorials.

Beale, Tony 1973, 'C.L. Dodgson: Mathematician', pp. 26–33 in Crutch, Denis (ed.) *Mr Dodgson*, London: Lewis Carroll Society. Reprinted pp. 294–302 in Gray, Donald (ed.) 1992, *Alice in Wonderland*, New York: W.W. Norton.

Becke, A.F. 1936, *Order of Battle of Divisions. Part 2A: The Territorial Force Mounted Divisions and the lst-Line Territorial Force Divisions (42-56)*, London: HMSO.

Bell, John (ed.) 1985, *Wilfred Owen: Selected Letters*, Oxford: Oxford University Press.

Bell, Quentin 1968, *Bloomsbury*, London: Weidenfeld & Nicolson.

Berger, Peter L. and Luckman, Thomas 1966, *The Social Construction of Reality: A Treatise in the Sociology of Knowledge*, New York: Doubleday.

Bigg, R.J. 1990, *Cambridge and the Monetary Theory of Production: The Collapse of Marshallian Macro-economics*, Basingstoke and London: Macmillan.

Blaug, M. 1986, *Great Economists before Keynes: An Introduction to the Lives and Works of One Hundred Great Economists of the Past*, Brighton, Sussex: Wheatsheaf Books.

Blaug, M. 1990, *John Maynard Keynes: Life, Ideas, Legacy*, Basingstoke and London: Macmillan Press and Institute of Economic Affairs.

Blaug, M. 1997, *Economic Theory in Retrospect*, Cambridge: Cambridge University Press

Bleaney, M. 1987, Review of *The Keynesian Revolution and its Critics: Issues of Theory and Policy for the Monetary Production Economy*, by Gordon A. Fletcher, Basingstoke: Macmillan, 1987, in *Economic Journal*, vol. 97, December, pp. 1036-7.

Bloom, Harold (ed.) 1987, *Modern Critical Views: Lewis Carroll*, New York: Chelsea House Publishers.

Boianovsky, Mauro and Presley, John R., 1998, 'Dennis Robertson and the Natural Rate of Unemployment Hypothesis', *Economic Research Paper 98/11*, Department of Economics, Loughborough University.

Boulding, K.E. 1955, Economic Analysis, 3rd edn., New York: Harper & Brothers.

Boulding, K.E. 1966 *Economic Analysis*. Vol II: *Macroeconomics*, 4th edn, New York: Harper & Row.

Braithwaite, R.B. 1932, 'Lewis Carroll as Logician', *Mathematical Gazette*, vol. XVI, pp. 174-8.

Bridel, P. 1987, *Cambridge Monetary Thought: The Development of Saving-Investment Analysis from Marshall to Keynes*, Basingstoke and London: Macmillan.

Brittan, S. 1977, 'Can Democracy Manage an Economy?' in Skidelsky, R. (ed.) *The End of the Keynesian Era*, London and Basingstoke: Macmillan.

Butler, George 1894, *The Public Schools Atlas of Modern Geography*, London: Longmans, Green.

Butler, J.R.M. 1963, 'Sir Dennis Robertson, CMG, MC, FBA', in *Trinity College Cambridge: Annual Record 1962-1963*, pp. 40-2, Cambridge: Trinity College.

Cairncross, Alec 1993, *Austin Robinson: The Life of an Economic Adviser*, Basingstoke and London: Macmillan.

Carabelli, A. 1988, *On Keynes's Method*, Basingstoke and London: Macmillan.

Carabelli, A. 1992, 'Organic Interdependence and Keynes's Choice of Units in the *General Theory*', in Gerrard, Bill and Hillard, John (eds) *The Philosophy and Economics of J.M. Keynes*, Aldershot, UK: Edward Elgar.

Carabelli, A. 1994, 'The Methodology of the Critique of Classical Theory: Keynes on Organic Interdependence', in Marzola, A. and Silva, F. (eds) *John Maynard Keynes: Language and Method*, Aldershot, UK: Edward Elgar.

Card, Tim 1994, *Eton Renewed: A History from 1860 to the Present Day*, London: John Murray.

Carroll, Lewis, 1865, *Alice's Adventures in Wonderland*; 1872, *Through the*

Looking-Glass, in Gardner Martin (ed.), 1970, *The Annotated Alice*, London: Penguin.

Carroll, Lewis 1886, *Alice's Adventures Under Ground*, facsimile edn, London: Macmillan. New edn ed. with Introduction by Russell Ash and Foreword by Mary Jean St Clair 1985, London: Pavilion Books, in association with British Library.

Carver, Michael 1978, *Harding of Petherington: Field Marshall*, London: Weidenfeld & Nicolson.

Chick, Victoria 1987a, Review of Fletcher, G.A. 1987, *The Keynesian Revolution and Its Critics: Issues of Theory and Policy for the Monetary Production Economy*, Basingstoke and London: Macmillan, p. 26 in *The Times Higher Education Supplement*, 15 May.

Chick, Victoria 1987b, 'Finance and Saving', vol. 2, pp. 336-7 in Eatwell, J., Milgate, M. and Newman, P. (eds), *The New Palgrave: A Dictionary of Economics*, London: Macmillan.

Clark, Anne 1979, *Lewis Carroll: A Biography*, London: Dent.

Clark, Colin 1977, 'Memoir', *Encounter*, June.

Clarke, P. 1988, *The Keynesian Revolution in the Making 1924-1936*, Oxford: Clarendon Press.

Clarke, P. 1993, 'Discussion' of Peacock, (Sir) Alan 1993, 'Keynes and the Role of the State', pp. 33-6 in Crabtree, Derek and Thirlwall, A.P. (eds), *Keynes and the Role of the State*, Basingstoke and London: Macmillan Press.

Coddington, Alan 1983, *Keynesian Economics: The Search for First Principles*, London: George Allen & Unwin.

Cole, G.D.H. n.d., *Saving and Spending; or, The Economics of 'Economy'*, London: New Statesman and Nation.

Costabile, Lilia 1997, 'Robertson and the Post-Keynesian Approach to Growth and Cycles', in Arestis, P., Palma, G. and Sawyer, M. (eds), *Capital Controversy, Post-Keynesian Economics and the History of Economics: Essays in Honour of Geoff Harcourt*, vol. I, London: Routledge.

Coveney, Peter 1967, 'Escape', pp. 240-9 in *The Image of Childhood*, revised edn, London. Reprinted in Gray, Donald (ed.) 1992, *Alice in Wonderland*, New York: W.W. Norton.

Cradock, Percy (ed.) 1953, *Recollections of the Cambridge Union, 1815-1939*, Cambridge: Bowes.

Danes, M.J. Anyadike- 1985, 'Dennis Robertson and Keynes's *General Theory*', in Harcourt, G.C. (ed.), *Keynes and his Contemporaries*, Basingstoke and London: Macmillan.

Danes, M.J. Anyadike- 1987, 'Robertson, Dennis 1890-1963', vol. 4, pp. 208-10 in Eatwell, J., Milgate, M. and Newman, P. (eds), *The New Palgrave: A Dictionary of Economics*, London: Macmillan.

Danes, M.K. 1979, *Dennis Robertson and the Construction of Aggregative Theory*, University of London: Ph.D. Thesis.

Darwin, Charles [1859] 1972, *The Origin of Species*, new edn, London: Everyman.

Dawkins, Richard 1976, *The Selfish Gene*, Oxford: Oxford University Press.

Deacon, Richard 1985, *The Cambridge Apostles: A History of Cambridge University's Elite Intellectual Secret Society*, London: Robert Royce.

De Marchi, N. 1987, 'Paradoxes and Anomalies', vol. 4, pp. 796-9 in Eatwell, J., Milgate, M. and Newman, P. (eds), *The New Palgrave: A Dictionary of Economics*, London: Macmillan.

Dennison, S.R. 1963, 'Notes on Dennis Robertson as an Economist', pp. 42-44 in *Trinity College Cambridge: Annual Record 1962-1963*, Cambridge: Trinity College.

Dennison, S.R. 1968, 'Robertson, Dennis Holme', in Sills, David L. (ed.) *International Encyclopedia of the Social Sciences*, vol. 13, pp. 529-33, New York: The Macmillan Company; The Free Press.

Dennison, S.R. 1992a, 'Bibliography of the Writings of Sir D.H. Robertson', Appendix II in Dennison, S.R. and Presley, J.R. (eds), *Robertson on Economic Policy*, Basingstoke and London: Macmillan.

Dennison, S.R. 1992b, 'Biography', ch. 2 in Dennison, S.R. and Presley, J.R. (eds), *Robertson on Economic Policy*, Basingstoke and London: Macmillan.

Dennison, S.R. 1992c, 'Preface' in Presley, J.R. (ed.), *Essays on Robertsonian Economics*, Basingstoke and London: Macmillan.

Dennison, S.R. and Presley, J.R. (eds) 1992, *Robertson on Economic Policy*, Basingstoke and London: Macmillan.

Dillard, Dudley 1954, *The Economics of John Maynard Keynes*, London: Crosby Lockwood.

Dimand, R.W. 1988, *The Origins of the Keynesian Revolution: The Development of Keynes's Theory of Output and Employment*, Aldershot, UK: Edward Elgar.

Dimand, R.W. 1994, 'Mr Meade's Relation, Kahn's Multiplier and the Chronology of the *General Theory*' in *Economic Journal*, vol. 104, September, pp. 1139-42.

Dodgson, C.L.: see Carroll, Lewis.

Dumont, Louis 1977, *From Mandeville to Marx: The Genesis and Triumph of Economic Ideology*, Chicago: University of Chicago Press.

Dutton, Geoffrey 1961, *Walt Whitman*, Edinburgh and London: Oliver & Boyd.

Eatwell, J. and Milgate, M. (eds) 1983, *Keynes's Economics and the Theory of Value and Distribution*, London: Duckworth.

Elster, Jon 1978, *Logic and Society: Contradictions and Possible Worlds*, New York: John Wiley.

Elton, G.R. 1967, *The Practice of History*, London: Methuen.

Eshag, E. 1963, *From Marshall to Keynes: An Essay on the Monetary Theory of the Cambridge School*, Oxford: Basil Blackwell.

'Evo-economics: Biology Meets the Dismal Science', *The Economist*, 25 December 1993-7 January 1994, pp. 97-9.

Fellner, W. 1952, 'The Robertsonian Evolution', *American Economic Review*, vol. 42, no. 3, pp. 265-282. Reprinted as ch. 7 in Presley, J.R (ed.), *Essays on Robertsonian Economics*, Basingstoke: Macmillan.

Fletcher, G.A. 1987, *The Keynesian Revolution and its Critics: Issues of Theory and Policy for the Monetary Production Economy*, Basingstoke and London: Macmillan

Fletcher, G.A. 1989a, *The Keynesian Revolution and its Critics: Issues of Theory and Policy for the Monetary Production Economy*, 2nd edn, Basingstoke and London: Macmillan.

Fletcher, G.A. 1989b, 'Keynes and Monetarism: a Note', in Hill, R. (ed.), *Keynes, Money and Monetarism*, Basingstoke and London: Macmillan.

Fletcher, G.A. 1996, *Robertson, Keynes and the Keynesian Revolution*, Liverpool Research Papers in Economics, Finance and Accounting no. 9605, Liverpool: University of Liverpool.

Fletcher, Ian n.d., *Swinburne*, Writers and their Work no. 228, London: Longman, for British Council.

Frankel, S. Herbert 1977, *Money: Two Philosophies. The Conflict of Trust and Authority*, Oxford: Basil Blackwell.

Friedman, M. 1972, 'Comments on the Critics', *Journal of Political Economy*, vol. 80, pp. 906-50.

Gardner, Martin (ed.) 1970, *The Annotated Alice: Alices's Adventures in Wonderland and Through the Looking Glass by Lewis Carroll*, London: Penguin Books.

Gardner, Martin (ed.) 1974, *The Annotated Snark: The Full Text of Lewis Carroll's Great Nonsense Epic 'The Hunting of the Snark'*, London: Penguin.

Gerrard, B. and Hillard, J. (eds) 1992, *The Philosophy and Economics of J.M. Keynes*, Aldershot, UK: Edward Elgar.

Gilbert, J.C. 1982, *Keynes's Impact on Monetary Economics*, London: Butterworth Scientific.

Gittings, Robert 1978, *The Nature of Biography*, London: Heinemann.

Goodhart, C.A.E. 1989, 'Keynes and Monetarism', in Hill, Roger (ed.), *Keynes, Money and Monetarism: The Eighth Keynes Seminar held at the University of Kent at Canterbury*, Basingstoke and London: Macmillan.

Goodhart, C.A.E. 1990, 'Dennis Robertson and the Real Business Cycle: a Centenary Lecture', Financial Markets Group Discussion Paper 92.

Reprinted as ch. 2 in Presley, J.R. (ed.) 1992, *Essays on Robertsonian Economics*, Basingstoke and London: Macmillan.

Goodhart, C.A.E. and Presley, J.R. 1994, 'Real Business Cycle Theory: a Restatement of Robertsonian Economics?', *Economic Notes*, vol. 23, no. 2, pp. 275–91, Siena: Monte dei Paschi di Siena.

Gordon, Jan B. 1971, 'The Alice Books and the Metaphors of Victorian Childhood', Vanguard Press. Reprinted pp. 93–113 in Phillips, Robert (ed.) 1972, *Aspects of Alice*, London: Gollancz.

Gray, Donald J. (ed.) 1992, *Lewis Carroll: Alice in Wonderland*, 2 edn, Norton Critical Editions, New York: W.W. Norton.

Greenacre, Phyllis 1955, 'The Character of Dodgson Revealed in the Writings of Carroll', in *Swift and Carroll*, International Universities Press. Reprinted pp. 316–31 in Phillips, Robert (ed.) 1972, *Aspects of Alice*, London: Gollancz.

Guiliano, Edward 1982, 'Lewis Carroll, Laughter and Despair, and *The Hunting of the Snark*', in *Lewis Carroll: A Celebration*, Clarkson N. Potter. Reprinted pp. 103–10 in Bloom, Harold (ed.) 1987, *Modern Critical Views: Lewis Carroll*, New York: Chelsea House Publishers.

Haberler, Gottfried 1946, *Prosperity and Depression: A Theoretical Analysis of Cyclical Movements*, 3rd edn, New York: United Nations.

Hahn, F.H. 1990, 'John Hicks the Theorist', *Economic Journal*, vol. 100, June, pp. 539–49.

Hansen, Alvin H. and Clemence, Richard V. (eds) 1953, *Readings in Business Cycles and National Income*, London: George Allen & Unwin.

Harcourt, G.C. (ed.) 1985, *Keynes and his Contemporaries: The Sixth and Centennial Keynes Seminar held at the University of Kent at Canterbury, 1983*, Basingstoke and London: Macmillan.

Harcourt, G.C. 1992, 'Marshall's *Principles* as Seen at Cambridge Through the Eyes of Gerald Shove, Dennis Robertson and Joan Robinson', in Sardoni, Claudio (ed.), *On Political Economists and Modern Political Economy: Selected Essays of G.C. Harcourt*, London: Routledge.

Harcourt, G.C. 1994, 'John Maynard Keynes', in Mason, R. (ed.), *Cambridge Minds*, Cambridge: Cambridge University Press.

Harcourt, G.C. and O'Shaughnessy, T.J. 1985, 'Keynes's Unemployment Equilibrium: Some Insights from Joan Robinson, Piero Sraffa and Richard Kahn', in Harcourt, G.C. (ed.), *Keynes and his Contemporaries*, Basingstoke and London: Macmillan.

Harrod, R.F. 1927, 'Mr Robertson's Views on Banking Policy', *Economica*, June, pp. 224–30.

Harrod, R.F. 1951, *The Life of John Maynard Keynes*, London: Macmillan.

Harth, Phillip (ed.) 1970, *The Fable of the Bees: Bernard Mandeville*, ed. with an introduction, London: Pelican Books.

Hawtrey, R.G. 1926, 'Mr Robertson on Banking Policy', *Economic Journal*, vol. 36, September, pp. 417–33.

Hawtrey, R.G. 1932, *The Art of Central Banking*, London: Longmans.

Hayek, F.A. 1978, *New Studies in Philosophy, Politics, Economics and the History of Ideas*, London: Routledge & Kegan Paul.

Heath, Peter 1974, *The Philosopher's Alice*, New York: St Martin's Press. Part reprinted pp. 45–52 in Bloom, Harold (ed.) 1987, *Modern Critical Views: Lewis Carroll*, New York: Chelsea House Publishers.

Heath, Stephen 1994, 'I.A. Richards, F.R. Leavis and Cambridge English', ch. 2 in Mason, Richard (ed.), *Cambridge Minds*, Cambridge: Cambridge University Press.

Henderson, (Sir) Hubert 1921, *Supply and Demand*, rev. edn, Cambridge Economic Handbooks I, London: Nisbet.

Henkle, Roger 1980, 'Comedy from Inside', pp. 201–11 in *Comedy and Culture: England 1820–1900*, Princeton, N.J.: Princeton University Press. Reprinted in Gray, Donald (ed.) 1992, *Alice in Wonderland*, New York: W.W. Norton.

Hession, Charles H. 1984, *John Maynard Keynes: A Personal Biography of the Man Who Revolutionised Capitalism and the Way We Live*, London: Collier Macmillan.

Hibberd, Dominic 1992, *Wilfred Owen: The Last Year 1917-1918*, London: Constable.

Hicks, J.R. 1942, 'The Monetary Theory of D.H. Robertson', *Economica*, N.S. vol. 14, February, pp. 53–7.

Hicks, J.R. 1965, 'Dennis Holme Robertson 1890–1963', *Proceedings of the British Academy*, vol. 50. Reprinted as 'A Memoir: Dennis Holme Robertson 1890–1963' in Hicks, J.R. (ed.) 1966, *Sir Dennis Robertson: Essays in Money and Interest*, London: Fontana.

Hicks, J.R. (ed.) 1966, *Sir Dennis Robertson: Essays in Money and Interest*, London: Fontana Library.

Hicks, J.R. 1981, 'Robertson, Sir Dennis Holme (1890–1963), Economist', pp. 885–6 in Williams, E.T. and Palmer, Helen K. (eds), *The Dictionary of National Biography, 1961-70*, London: Oxford University Press.

Hicks, J.R. 1982, *Money, Interest and Wages*, Oxford: Basil Blackwell.

Hill, P. and Keynes, R. (eds) 1989, *Lydia and Maynard: Letters between Lydia Lopokova and John Maynard Keynes*, London: André Deutsch.

Hopkins, Gerard Manley 1992, *The Poetical Works*, Mackenzie, Norman H. (ed.), reprinted with corrections, Oxford: Clarendon Press.

Housman, A.E. 1896, *A Shropshire Lad*, London: Kegan Paul. Illustrated edition with wood engravings by Agnes Miller Parker, 1940, London: George G. Harrap.

Howarth, T.E.B. 1978, *Cambridge Between Two Wars*, London: Collins.

Howson, Susan 1993, Review of Dennison, S.R. and Presley, J.R. (eds) 1992, *Robertson on Economic Policy*, Basingstoke and London: Macmillan; Presley, J.R. (ed.) 1992, *Essays on Robertsonian Economics*, Basingstoke and London: Macmillan, *Economic Journal*, vol. 103, July, pp. 1082-4.

Hudson, Derek 1976, *Lewis Carroll: An Illustrated Biography*, London: Constable.

Humphreys, A.R. (ed.) 1966, *The Second Part of King Henry IV*, Arden Edition of the Works of William Shakespeare, London: Methuen.

Hutchison, T.W. 1978, *On Revolutions and Progress in Economic Knowledge*, Cambridge: Cambridge University Press.

Johnson, E. and Johnson, H.G. 1978, *The Shadow of Keynes: Understanding Keynes, Cambridge and Keynesian Economics*, Oxford: Basil Blackwell.

Johnson, H.G. 1971, *Macroeconomics and Monetary Theory*, London: Gray Mills Publishing.

Kahn, Richard 1984, *The Making of Keynes' General Theory*, Cambridge: Cambridge University Press.

Keynes, J.M. (1971-89) *The Collected Writings of John Maynard Keynes*, Sir Austin Robinson and D.E. Moggridge (eds), London: Macmillan, for the Royal Economic Society (referred to in text as Keynes, *CW* I-XXX).
Volumes consulted:

II   *The Economic Consequences of the Peace* (1919) 1971.

IV   *A Tract on Monetary Reform* (1923) 1971.

V   *A Treatise on Money, I: The Pure Theory of Money* (1930) 1971.

VI   *A Treatise on Money II: The Applied Theory of Money* (1930) 1971.

VII   *The General Theory of Employment, Interest and Money* (1936) 1973.

VIII   *A Treatise on Probability* (1921) 1973.

IX   *Essays in Persuasion* (1931) 1972.

X   *Essays in Biography* (1933) 1972.

XIII   *The General Theory and After: Part I, Preparation*, 1973.

XIV   *The General Theory and After: Part II, Defence and Development*, 1973.

XXIX *The General Theory and After: A Supplement to Vols XIII and XIV*, 1979.

XXX   *Index and Bibliography*, 1989.

Keynes, J.M. 1919, *The Economic Consequences of the Peace*, London: Macmillan.

Keynes, J.M. 1924, 'Alfred Marshall, 1842-1924', *Economic Journal*, vol. 24, September. Reprinted in Pigou, A.C. (ed.) 1925, *Memorials of Alfred Marshall*, London: Macmillan. Reprinted in Keynes, *CW X*.

Keynes, J.M. 1926, *The End of Laissez-faire*, London: Hogarth Press.

Keynes, J.M. 1931, *Essays in Persuasion*, London: Macmillan.

Keynes, J.M. 1933, *The Means to Prosperity*, London: Macmillan.

Keynes, J.M. 1936, *The General Theory of Employment, Interest and Money*, London: Macmillan.

Keynes, J.M. 1937a 'The General Theory of Employment', *Quarterly Journal of Economics*, vol. 51, February, pp. 209–23. Reprinted pp. 109–23 in Keynes, *CW* XIV.

Keynes, J.M. 1937b, 'Alternative Theories of the Rate of Interest', *Economic Journal*, vol. 47, June, pp. 241–52. Reprinted pp. 201–15 in Keynes, *CW* XIV.

Keynes, J.M. 1939, 'The Process of Capital Formation', *Economic Journal*, vol. 49, September. Reprinted pp. 278–85 in Keynes, *CW* XIV.

Keynes, J.M. 1949, *Two Memoirs: Dr Melchior, A Defeated Enemy* and *My Early Beliefs*, introd. David Garnett, London: Rupert Hart-Davis.

Keynes, M. (ed.) 1975, *Essays on John Maynard Keynes*, Cambridge: Cambridge University Press.

Knight, Frank H. 1921, *Risk, Uncertainty and Profit*, Boston and New York: Houghton Mifflin. Reprinted as no. 16 in Scarce Tracts in Economic and Political Science, 1933, London: London School of Economics and Political Science.

Knights, L.C. 1959, *Some Shakespearean Themes*, London: Chatto & Windus.

Laidler, David 1995, 'Robertson in the 1920s', *European Journal of the History of Economic Thought*, vol. 2, no. 1, pp. 151–74.

Lawson, A. and Pesaran, H. (eds) 1985, *Keynes's Economics: Methodological Issues*, London: Croom Helm.

Lee, (Sir) Frank 1963, 'One Wise Man', *The Economist*, vol. 207, April, p. 312.

Lehmann, John 1978, *Thrown to the Woolfs*, London: Weidenfeld & Nicolson.

London Gazette 1917, 14 August; 4th Supplement 16 August, p. 8381, London: His Majesty's Stationery Office.

Maas, Henry (ed.) 1971, *The Letters of A.E. Housman*, London: Rupert Hart-Davis.

Mandeville, Bernard [1714, 1723] 1924, *The Fable of the Bees, or, Private Vices, Public Benefits*, ed. F.B. Kaye, with a commentary, critical, historical and explanatory, 2 vols, Oxford: Oxford University Press. Liberty Classics edition, 1988, Indianapolis: Liberty Press.

Marshall, Alfred 1890, *Principles of Economics: An Introductory Volume*, London: Macmillan.

Marshall, Alfred 1930, *Principles of Economics: An Introductory Volume*, 8th edn, 1920 reprinted, London: Macmillan.

Marzola, A. and Silva, F. (eds) 1994, *John Maynard Keynes: Language and Method*, Aldershot, UK: Edward Elgar.

Mason, Richard (ed.) 1994, *Cambridge Minds*, Cambridge: Cambridge University Press.

Meade, J. 1993, 'The Relation of Mr Meade's Relation to Kahn's Multiplier', *The Economic Journal*, **103**, May, pp. 664–5.

Meade, J.E. 1975, 'The Keynesian Revolution', ch. 10 in Keynes, Milo (ed.), *Essays on John Maynard Keynes*, Cambridge: Cambridge University Press.

Melchiori, Giorgio 1989, *The Second Part of King Henry IV*, New Cambridge Shakespeare, Cambridge: Cambridge University Press.

Milgate, Murray 1982, *Capital and Employment: A Study of Keynes's Economics*, London: Academic Press.

Mizen, P. and Presley, J.R. 1994, 'Buffer Stock Ideas in the Monetary Economics of Keynes and Robertson', *History of Political Economy*, vol. 26, no. 2, pp. 193–202.

Mizen, P., Moggridge D. and Presley, J. 1997, 'The Papers of Dennis Robertson: the Discovery of Unexpected Riches', *History of Political Economy*, vol. 29, no. 4, pp. 573–92.

Moggridge, D.E. (ed.) 1974, *Keynes: Aspects of the Man and his Work: The First Keynes Seminar held at the University of Kent at Canterbury 1972*, London and Basingstoke: Macmillan Press.

Moggridge, D.E. 1992, *Maynard Keynes: An Economist's Biography*, London: Routledge.

Moggridge, D. 1993, *Keynes*, 3rd edn, Basingstoke and London: Macmillan.

Moore, G.E. 1903, *Principia Ethica*, Cambridge: Cambridge University Press.

Motion, A. 1998, 'Back to the Front', a review of Wilson, Jean Moorcroft, 1998, *Siegfried Sassoon: The Making of a War Poet*, London: Duckworth, in *The Times*, 21 May.

Newsome, D. 1980, *On the Edge of Paradise: A.C. Benson; the Diarist*, London: John Murray.

O'Donnell, R.M. 1989, *Keynes, Philosophy, Economics and Politics: The Philosophical Foundations of Keynes's Thought and their Influence on his Economics and Politics*, Basingstoke and London: Macmillan.

Ollard, Richard 1982, *An English Education: A Perspective of Eton*, London: Collins.

Onions, C.T. (ed.) 1964, *The Shorter Oxford English Dictionary: On Historical Principles*, 3rd edn rev. with addenda, Oxford: Clarendon Press.

Page, Norman 1983, *A.E. Housman: A Critical Biography*, London: Macmillan; New York: Schocken Books.

Patinkin, D. 1976, *Keynes's Monetary Thought: A Study of its Development*, Durham, N.C.: Duke University Press.

Patinkin, D. 1993, 'On the Chronology of the General Theory', *Economic Journal*, vol. 103, May, pp. 647–63.

Patinkin, D. 1994, 'Mr Meade's Relation, Kahn's Multiplier and the Chronology of the General Theory: Reply', in *Economic Journal*, vol. 104, September, pp. 1143-6.

Patinkin, D. and Leith, J. Clark (eds) 1977, *Keynes, Cambridge and the General Theory*, London: Macmillan.

Phillips, Robert (ed.) 1972, *Aspects of Alice*, London: Gollancz.

Pigou, A.C. 1912, *Wealth and Welfare*, London: Macmillan.

Pigou, A.C. (ed.) 1925, *Memorials of Alfred Marshall*, London: Macmillan.

Pigou, A.C. 1926, 'A Contribution to the Theory of Credit', *The Economic Journal*, **36**, June, pp. 215-27.

Pigou, A.C. and Robertson, Dennis H. (eds) 1931, *Economic Essays and Addresses*, London: P.S. King.

Polhemus, Robert 1980, 'The Comedy of Regression' and 'Play, Nonsense and Games: Comic Diversion', in *Comic Faith: The Great Tradition from Austin to Joyce*, Chicago: Chicago University Press. Reprinted in Gray, Donald (ed.) 1992, *Alice in Wonderland*, 2nd edn, New York: W.W. Norton.

Popper, Karl R. 1972, *Objective Knowledge: An Evolutionary Approach*, Oxford: Clarendon Press.

Presley, J.R. 1978, *Robertsonian Economics: An Examination of the Work of Sir D.H. Robertson on Industrial Fluctuation*, London: Macmillan.

Presley, J.R. 1981, 'D.H. Robertson 1890-1963', in O'Brien, D.P. and Presley, J.R. (eds), *Pioneers of Modern Economics in Britain*, London: Macmillan.

Presley, J.R. 1992, 'Robertson and Keynes: Three Phases of Collaboration', in Presley J.R. (ed.), *Essays on Robertsonian Economics*, Basingstoke and London: Macmillan.

Presley, J.R. (ed.) 1992, *Essays on Robertsonian Economics*, Basingstoke and London: Macmillan.

Proctor, Dennis (ed.) 1973, *The Autobiography of G. Lowes-Dickinson*, London: Duckworth.

Quiller-Couch, (Sir) Arthur (ed.) 1939, *The Oxford Book of English Verse 1250-1918*, new edn reprinted, New York: Oxford Universty Press.

Rackin, Donald 1966, 'Alice's Journey to the End of Night', PMLA, vol. 81. Reprinted pp. 391-416 in Phillips, Robert (ed.) 1972, *Aspects of Alice*, London: Gollancz.

Rackin, Donald 1982a, 'Love and Death in Carroll's Alices', *English Language Notes*, vol. 20, no. 2. Reprinted pp. 111-27 in Bloom, Harold (ed.) 1987, *Modern Critical Views: Lewis Carroll*, New York: Chelsea House Publishers.

Rackin, Donald 1982b, 'Blessed Rage: Lewis Carroll and the Modern Quest for Order', pp. 15-23 in Guiliano, Edward (ed.) *Lewis Carroll: A*

Celebration, New York: Clarkson Potter. Reprinted in Gray, Donald (ed.) 1992, *Alice in Wonderland*, New York: W.W. Norton.

Ramsey, Frank 1928, 'A Mathematical Theory of Saving', *Economic Journal*, vol. 38, December, pp. 543–59.

Redgrave, Corin 1995, *Michael Redgrave: My Father*, London: Richard Cohen.

Robbins, (Lord) Lionel 1970, *The Evolution of Modern Economic Theory and Other Papers on the History of Economic Thought*, London: Macmillan.

Robbins, (Lord) Lionel 1971, *Autobiography of an Economist*, London: Macmillan.

Robertson, A. (ed.) 1904, *Arachnia*, London: Macmillan.

Robertson, D.H. 1914, 'Some Material for a Study of Trade Fluctuations', *Journal of the Royal Statistical Society*, January, pp. 159–73. See also copy of notes for eponymous lecture, 16 December 1913, in D4/1 RPTC.

Robertson, D.H. 1915, *A Study of Industrial Fluctuation: An Enquiry into the Character and Causes of the So-called Cyclical Movements of Trade*, London: P.S. King.

Robertson, D.H. 1922, *Money*, Cambridge Economic Handbooks II, London: Nisbet.

Robertson, D.H. 1923a, *The Control of Industry*, Cambridge Economic Handbooks IV, reprinted 1924, London: Nisbet.

Robertson, D.H. 1923b, *The Ebb and Flow of Unemployment*, The New Way Series, no. 6, London: Daily News.

Robertson, D.H. 1926, *Banking Policy and the Price Level: An Essay in the Theory of the Trade Cycle*, London: P.S. King.

Robertson, D.H. 1928a, *Money*, Cambridge Economic Handbooks II, rev. edn, reprinted 1937, with new Preface, reprinted 1946, London: Nisbet.

Robertson, D.H. 1928b, 'Theories of Banking Policy', *Economica*, vol. VIII, June, pp. 131–46. Reprinted pp. 23–42 in Hicks, J.R. (ed.) 1966, *Essays in Money and Interest*, London: Fontana Library.

Robertson, D.H. 1931, *Economic Fragments*, London: P.S. King.

Robertson, D.H. 1933, 'Saving and Hoarding', *Economic Journal*, vol. 43, September, pp. 399–413. Reprinted pp. 46–63 in Hicks, J.R. (ed.) 1966, *Essays in Money and Interest*, London: Fontana Library.

Robertson, D.H. 1934, 'Industrial Fluctuation and the Natural Rate of Interest', *Economic Journal*, vol. 44, December, pp. 650–6. Reprinted pp. 64–74 in Hicks, J.R. (ed.) 1966, *Essays in Money and Interest*, London: Fontana Library.

Robertson, D.H. 1936, 'The Snake and the Worm', Harvard Tercentenary Conference Paper. Reprinted pp. 85–94 in Hicks, J.R. (ed.) 1966, *Essays in Money and Interest*, London: Fontana Library.

Robertson, D.H. 1937, 'A Survey of Modern Monetary Controversy', a paper read before the Manchester Statistical Society, November. Reprinted pp. 105–24 in Hicks, J.R. (ed.) 1966, *Essays in Money and Interest*, London: Fontana Library.

Robertson, D.H. 1939, 'Mr Keynes and the Rate of Interest', Lectures at the London School of Economics, Summer Term. Reprinted pp. 150–87 in Hicks, J.R. (ed.) 1966, *Essays in Money and Interest*, London: Fontana Library.

Robertson, D.H. 1940, *Essays in Monetary Theory*, London: P.S. King.

Robertson, D.H. 1948a, *A Study of Industrial Fluctuation: An Enquiry into the Character and Causes of the So-called Cyclical Movements of Trade*, reprinted with a new introduction as no. 8 in the Series of Reprints of Scarce Works on Political Economy, London: London School of Economics and Political Science.

Robertson, D.H. 1948b, *Money*, Cambridge Economic Handbooks II, rev. edn with additional chapters, reset 1959, reprinted 1961, London: James Nisbet.

Robertson, D.H. 1949a, 'What Has Happened to the Rate of Interest?', *Three Banks Review*, March. Reprinted pp. 187–202 in Hicks, J.R. (ed.) 1966, *Essays in Money and Interest*, London: Fontana Library.

Robertson, D.H. 1949b, *Banking Policy and the Price Level: An Essay in the Theory of the Trade Cycle*. Reprinted with a new preface, New York: Augustus M. Kelley.

Robertson, D.H. 1951, 'Some Notes on the Theory of Interest', in *Money, Trade and Economic Growth: Essays in Honour of John Henry Williams*, New York: Macmillan. Reprinted pp. 202–22 in Hicks, J.R. (ed.) 1966, *Essays in Money and Interest*, London: Fontana Library.

Robertson, D.H. 1952, *Utility and All That*, London: Staples.

Robertson, D.H. 1953, 'Thoughts on Meeting some Important Persons', seminar talks in USA, April. Reprinted pp. 234–44 in Hicks, J.R. (ed.) 1966, *Essays in Money and Interest*, London: Fontana Library.

Robertson, D.H. 1954, *Britain in the World Economy: The Page-Barbour Lectures at the University of Virginia*, London: George Allen & Unwin.

Robertson, D.H. 1955, *Wages: The Stamp Memorial Lecture Delivered Before the University of London on 9 November 1954*, rev. edn, London: Athlone Press.

Robertson, D.H. 1956, *Economic Commentaries*, London: Staples Press.

Robertson, D.H. 1963a, *Lectures on Economic Principles,* London: Fontana Library.

Robertson, D.H. 1963b, Review of *Lectures on Economic Principles*, London: Fontana Library. Anonymous review in *The Economist*, 6 June, p. 936.

Robertson, D.H. and Pigou, A.C. 1931, *Economic Essays and Addresses*, London: P.S. King.

Robinson, E.A.G. 1947, 'John Maynard Keynes 1883–1946', *Economic Journal*, vol. 57, March, pp. 1–68.

Robinson, E.A.G. 1963, 'Sir Dennis Robertson CMG', *The Times*, 22 April, p. 22a.

Robinson, E.A.G. 1992, 'My Apprenticeship as an Economist', in Szenberg, Michael (ed.), *Eminent Economists: Their Life Philosophies*, Cambridge: Cambridge University Press.

Robinson, Joan 1937, *An Introduction to the Theory of Employment*, London: Macmillan.

Robinson, Joan 1975, 'What Has Become of the Keynesian Revolution?', in Keynes, Milo (ed.), *Essays on John Maynard Keynes*, Cambridge: Cambridge University Press.

Rosenberg, N. 1987, 'Mandeville, Bernard (1670–1733)', in vol. 3, pp. 297–8 of Eatwell, J., Milgate, M. and Newman, P. (eds), *The New Palgrave: A Dictionary of Economics*, London: Macmillan.

Rymes, Thomas K. (ed.) 1989, *Keynes's Lectures 1932–35: Notes of a Representative Student*, Basingstoke: Macmillan.

Samuelson, P.A. 1963, 'D.H. Robertson (1890–1963)', *Quarterly Journal of Economics*, vol. LXXVII, no. 4, pp. 517–36.

Samuelson, P. *et al.* 1993, 'The Economics of Altruism' [a symposium], *American Economic Review*, vol. LXXXIII, pt. 1, Papers and Proceedings, pp. 143–61.

Sardoni, Claudio (ed.) 1992, *On Political Economists and Modern Political Economy: Selected Essays of G.C. Harcourt*, London: Routledge.

Sewell, Elizabeth 1952, *The Field of Nonsense*, London: Chatto & Windus.

Shackle, G.L.S. 1967, *The Years of High Theory: Invention and Tradition in Economic Thought 1926–1939*, Cambridge: Cambridge University Press.

Shelston, Alan 1977, *Biography*, London: Methuen.

Shimmin, Hugh ('A Local Artist') 1866, *Pen and Ink Sketches of Liverpool Town Councillors*, Liverpool.

Skidelsky, R. 1983, *John Maynard Keynes*, Vol. I: *Hopes Betrayed, 1883–1920*, London: Macmillan.

Skidelsky, R. 1992, *John Maynard Keynes*, Vol. II: *The Economist as Saviour, 1920–1937*, London: Macmillan.

Smith, Adam (1776), *An Enquiry into the Nature and Causes of the Wealth of Nations*, reprinted in Todd, W.B. (ed.) 1976, *The Works and Correspondence of Adam Smith*, Glasgow Edition, Oxford: Oxford University Press. Liberty Classics Edition, 1988; Indianapolis: Liberty Press.

Stallworthy, Jon 1974, *Wilfred Owen: A Biography*, London: Oxford University Press and Chatto & Windus.

Stallworthy, Jon (ed.) 1990, *The Poems of Wilfred Owen*, London: Chatto & Windus.

Steindl, J. 1985, 'J.M. Keynes: Society and the Economist', in Vicarelli, F. (ed.), *Keynes's Relevance Today*, Basingstoke and London: Macmillan.

Strachey, Lytton 1918, *Eminent Victorians*, London: Chatto & Windus. Illustrated edn, with a foreword by Frances Partridge, 1988, London: Bloomsbury.

Tanner, J.R. (ed.) 1917, *Historical Register of the University of Cambridge to the Year 1910*; Supplements: *1911-1920* (1922), *1921-1930* (1932), Cambridge: Cambridge University Press.

Tappan, M. 1928, 'Mr Robertson's Views on Banking Policy: a Reply to Mr Harrod', in *Economica*, (N.S.) vol. 8, March, pp. 95–109.

Thomas, Imogen 1987, *Haileybury 1806-1987*, Haileybury: Haileybury Society.

Tobin, J. 1975, 'Keynesian Models of Recession and Depression', *American Economic Review*, vol. 65, pp. 195–202.

Traversi, Derek 1957, *Shakespeare, from Richard II to Henry V*, London: Hollis & Carter.

Vaizey, (Lord) John 1977a, 'My Cambridge', in Hayman, Ronald (ed.), *My Cambridge*, London: Robson Books.

Vaizey, (Lord) John 1977b, 'Keynes and Cambridge', in Skidelsky, R. (ed.), *The End of the Keynesian Era*, London: Macmillan.

Waskow, Howard J. 1966, *Whitman: Explorations in Form*, Chicago: Chicago University Press.

Whitman, Walt 1965, Blodgett, Harold H. and Bradley, Sculley (eds), *Leaves of Grass*, Comprehensive Reader's Edition, New York: New York University Press.

Wilkinson, L.P. 1980, *A Century of King's 1873-1972*, Cambridge: King's College.

Wilkinson, L.P. 1981, *Kingsmen of a Century 1873-1972*, Cambridge: King's College.

Wilson, T. 1953, 'Professor Robertson on Effective Demand and the Trade Cycle', *Economic Journal*, vol. 63, September, pp. 553–78. Reprinted as ch. 6 in Presley, J.R. (ed.) 1992, *Essays on Robertsonian Economics*, Basingstoke and London: Macmillan.

Wilson, T. 1980, 'Robertson, Money and Monetarism', *Journal of Economic Literature*, vol. XVIII, December, pp. 1522–38. Reprinted as ch. 3 in Presley, J.R. (ed.) 1992, *Essays on Robertsonian Economics*, Basingstoke and London: Macmillan.

Wilson. T. 1985 'Comment' on Anyadike-Danes, 'Dennis Robertson and Keynes's General Theory', in Harcourt, G.C. (ed.), *Keynes and his Contemporaries*, Basingstoke and London: Macmillan.

Young, Warren 1989, *Harrod and his Trade Cycle Group: The Origins and Development of the Growth Research Programme*, London: Macmillan.

Index